T0360526

Introduction to
MICROFINANCE

Introduction to
MICROFINANCE

Todd A. Watkins

Lehigh University, USA

World Scientific

NEW JERSEY · LONDON · SINGAPORE · BEIJING · SHANGHAI · HONG KONG · TAIPEI · CHENNAI · TOKYO

Published by

World Scientific Publishing Co. Pte. Ltd.
5 Toh Tuck Link, Singapore 596224
USA office: 27 Warren Street, Suite 401-402, Hackensack, NJ 07601
UK office: 57 Shelton Street, Covent Garden, London WC2H 9HE

Library of Congress Cataloging-in-Publication Data
Names: Watkins, Todd A., author.
Title: Introduction to microfinance / Todd A. Watkins (Lehigh University, USA).
Description: New Jersey : World Scientific, [2018] | Includes bibliographical references and index.
Identifiers: LCCN 2017051524| ISBN 9789813140738 (hardcover) |
    ISBN 9789813143005 (softcover)
Subjects: LCSH: Microfinance.
Classification: LCC HG178.3 .W38 2018 | DDC 332--dc23
LC record available at https://lccn.loc.gov/2017051524

British Library Cataloguing-in-Publication Data
A catalogue record for this book is available from the British Library.

For any available supplementary material, please visit
http://www.worldscientific.com/worldscibooks/10.1142/10054#t=suppl

Desk Editor: Jiang Yulin

Typeset by Stallion Press
Email: enquiries@stallionpress.com

Printed in Singapore

LIST OF CO-AUTHORS

Todd A. Watkins, Ph.D.
Lehigh University

with

Nicole Bohrer

Anais Concepcion

Andrea Lavin

Michael Lefkoe

Samuel Korab

Puja Parekh

Danielle Schaeffer

Colin Sloand

Michael Roth

Muhongayire Sheilla Rukundo

and

Jonathan Abbey
Patrick Adduci
Vinicius Aguiar
Nicholas Alakel
Samuel Anderson
Stephanie Andrica
Kelver Arellano
Jose Arias
Kathryn Auletta
Sai Lu Mon Aung
Joshua Azarchi
Greg Baglione
Cristina Baquerizo
Jonathan Baram
Kevin Basek
Kara Beck
Jaclyn Bedford
Nicole Behany
Stephanie Behrens
Ian Bernaiche
Yazata Bhote

Rebecca Bliss
Ryan Bobbit
John Bogorowski
Victoria Bonsall
Alexandra Boyle
Dabney Brice
Stephen Brodeur
Douglas Brown
Stephen Buryk
Sean Camperson
Xiqian Chen
Hazel Cheng
Priya Chokshi
Cassandra Christman
Nicholas Cicione
Allyson Coff
Amalia Cote
Sarah Crump
Brian Czornyj
Hubert Dagbo
Nicholas Davis

Mark Degenhart
Veronica Demkin-Dick
Liyala Dickens
Justin Dinardo
Racquel Doherty
Nan Dong
Connor Donovan
Jonathan Dubin
Griffith Dudley
Alexandra Duprey
Alexandra Ferhring
Alvaro Fernandez
Houda Ferradji
Rose Ferris
Kevin Fitzpatrick
Matthew Forrest
Nicholas Fraboni
Ariel Frazier-Freeman
Spencer Freund
Derek Freyberg
Jourdan Friedman

Simona Galant
Kendall Garden
Kaytlin Gill
Ariel Glassberg
Sydney Glenn
Lauren Goewey
Matthew Goor
Frederick Graves
Aaron Gray
Sarah Gregori
Andrew Griffith
Olivia Handerek
Carter Hartmann
Amalia Hatalis
Maria Hatalis
Gwendolyn Hauck
Matthew Heaney
Lisa Hecht
W. Samuel Henderson
Jeff Herrigel
Klay Heston
Caitlin Higgins
Victoria Horvath
Daniel Ibanez
Daniel Jones
Sean Joy
Mudassir Mehboob Kadri
Nowell Kahle
Marissa Karl
Harrison Katz
Timothy Kempton
Mina Khan
Jason Kim
Yu-Yen Lee
Ryan Lefever
Courtney Lenzo
Mark Levande
Jeffrey Liebman
Jialin Lu
Joseph Lucia
Peter Lysiak
Ehsanul Mahmud
Michael Martinez
Salvatore Mauro
Colin Mcleod
Ji Mei
Neil Merchant
Stacey Middlebrook
Aaron Monieson
Devin Monroe
Savannah Monser-Kernosh
Melissa Montalvo

Tim Mooradd
Ellen Moroney
Marie Murray
Alexa Naas
Tomer Nahumi
Sarah Nearhood
Manh Nguyen
Sebastian Nicewicz
Drew Nielsen
Natsumi Nishio
Cortlandt Okafor
Kyle Pahowka
Mario Paredes
Greyson Parrelli
Jaykishan Patel
Rich Paul
Katherine Pauley
Jeffrey Pazdro
Max Perricone
Shae Petroff
Sang Phan
Cindy Phuong
Michael Pluta
Matthew Poillon
Andra Portnoy
Cal Portnoy
Robert Powell
Ashley Pritchard
Ami Probandt
William Queen
Aleah Quigley
Ajay Raju
Catherine Revercomb
Brittany Richard-Persaud
Matthew Richards
Jonathan Ripa
Jessica Rivera-Rincon
Michael Roach
Joel Robinson
Jorge Rodriguez-Shaw
Alexi Rodriquez
Sean Rose
Jared Rubin
Jessica Rubin
Dorothy Ruderman
Samantha Russell
Daniel Ryan
Kathleen Ryan
Emily Sagalow
Steven Sanczyk
Andrew Sandor
Angel Santamarina

Patrick Scanlan
Ellen Schaaf
Rachael Schiffris
Eric Sciorilli
David Seduski
Edwin Seipp
Timothy Shanahan
Andrew Shang
Andrew Sherry
Nathan Shores
Jose Sierra
Aaron Siev
David Silfen
Daniel Slesinski
Philip Snyder
Christopher Spagna
Brendan Spillane
Ian Stanford
Tyler Stauffer
Lauren Sternick
Robert Storer
Jakub Stosik
Kelsie Strobel
Blair Sullivan
Daniel Sursock
Adam Svetec
Christopher Tadeu
Mengfei Tang
Martina Tibell
Melissa Tickle
Erin Tormey
Rebecca Trofa
Jackson Tu
Mariangelica Vargas Nufio
Daniel Vari
Erick Walker
Asher Wallen-Friedman
Tyler Walton
Shen Wang
Yizhou Wang
May Weiser
Jennifer Weldon
Qiwei Wen
Gail Whiffen
Trina Whiteside
Mark Whitmeyer
Jeffrey Wieand
Kendall Wilkins
Yiming Xu
Wendy Yan
Mengni Yao

CONTENTS

LIST OF FIGURES

LIST OF TABLES

LIST OF BOXES

Chapter

AN INTRODUCTION TO MICROFINANCE

"Where once the poor were commonly seen as passive victims, microfinance recognizes that poor people are remarkable reservoirs of energy and knowledge. And while the lack of financial services is a sign of poverty, today it is also understood as an untapped opportunity to create markets, bring people in from the margins and give them the tools with which to help themselves."

— Kofi Annan, Nobel Peace Prize winner and former Secretary General of the U.N.

Figure 1.1.   A field officer of Amret Microfinance disbursing funds in Siem Reap, Cambodia

The inequality of wealth distribution across the globe is no secret. One out of every three people in the world live on less than $3.10 per day. Nearly one in 10 lives in extreme poverty, which according to the World Bank is an income of less than $1.90 per day.[1] The global distribution of poverty is uneven as well, with more than 75% of those living in extreme poverty living in South Asia or Sub-Saharan Africa. This sobering fact has driven various organizations such as the United Nations, World Bank, and many non-governmental organizations, or NGOs, to initiate programs targeted at reducing poverty. Microfinance is just one of many innovative tools in the global effort to shrink the wealth gap.

A common misconception is that microfinance is synonymous with microcredit: loans—small ones. While it is true that microfinance has its origins in microcredit, as we will see throughout this book, it is now much more. Microfinance today involves a wide array of services for the poor and low-income people, from savings accounts to mobile money, insurance and many other services, both financial and non-financial such as healthcare and education.

1.1 Microfinance Begins

We begin our exploration where the microfinance industry started, with very small loans. In 1973 an antipoverty organization in Brazil called Accion noticed a high prevalence of small, informal enterprises that often needed funds to expand their business. Accion's staff members in the city of Recife, Brazil wondered: If these small business owners could borrow funds at commercial interest rates, could they start to lift themselves out of poverty? It was in this context that the first microfinance loan was granted.[2]

Within a few years, other institutions and individuals across the globe were also beginning to experiment with microcredit and with other microfinance services. The Bangladesh Rural Advancement Committee (BRAC), a non-profit organization in Bangladesh, was also an early microlender. In 1976, similarly in Bangladesh, in the village of Jobra, economist Muhammad Yunus observed that if the poor were given access to credit they could pull themselves out of poverty. His first loan, a total of $27 to a group of villagers, was an early experiment in group lending. By 1983 he had established the Grameen

Bank, one of the most prominent microfinance institutions today with one of the strongest socially driven missions. Around the same time, the Indonesian state-owned bank, Bank Rakyat Indonesia (BRI), also began to experiment with not only microloans but also microsavings.

Accion, BRAC, BRI, and Grameen Bank soon discovered something remarkable: the poor could save money, and they could borrow money and reliably repay with interest. What set these pioneering organizations apart from earlier efforts at banking for the poor is that they all found ways to expand to serve very large numbers of the poor without subsidies. They treated financial services for the poor like a business that could sustain itself, and in some cases even turn a profit. All of these organizations continue to lend to the poor today. Their initial successes proved that the poor often have the skills and drive to enhance their incomes and the well-being of their families if they have access to finance or ways to save. The idea that the poor can lift themselves out of poverty is at the heart of microfinance.

The success of the early pioneers also demonstrated that microfinance can be a sustainable, business-minded intervention in efforts to reduce global poverty. The early experiments inspired the creation of new microfinance institutions (MFIs), organizations that offer financial services to the poor. Initially, many MFIs financed their operations through donors and grants, and many today still rely on charitable contributions. However, in the decades since the 1970s, hundreds of MFIs have matured to become fully commercial enterprises that by charging interest and service fees cover their costs and earn profits. MFIs that can fully cover their operational costs (and therefore do not need donations) are called **self-sufficient** or sustainable, suggesting that if run properly they can serve the poor in perpetuity.

Since Accion's experiment in Recife, microfinance has grown from the obscure efforts of a few philanthropic institutions into an industry that reaches more than 200 million clients through the branches of many thousands of institutions.[3] Microfinance has matured from funding exclusively micro business loans to providing savings, insurance, mortgages, mobile banking, healthcare, and education. The public has become increasingly aware of the industry, in part due to the success of Yunus, who received the Nobel Peace Prize in 2006. More recently, in 2009 American President Barack Obama awarded him the Medal of Freedom, the highest American civilian honor.

Despite microfinance's long history, impressive growth, and Nobel nod, many Westerners still do not know what microfinance is. However, visit a poor village or slum in Brazil, and seemingly everyone can tell you what microfinance is. Visit Peru, one of the most saturated and competitive microfinance markets, and discover the personal stories almost anyone can tell of how microfinance has touched their lives, or the lives of someone they know—both the good and the bad. But for those of us further removed from day-to-day microfinance, the questions remain: What is microfinance? What are its methods? Does it work? What are its prospects and challenges? This book tackles those questions and more.

Section in Bulletpoint

- One-third of the world's population lives on less than $3.10 per day.
- Microfinance began in the 1970s in Brazil, Bangladesh, and Indonesia.
- Microfinance can be a sustainable poverty alleviation tool that covers its own costs while empowering the poor by giving them the financial tools to lift themselves out of poverty.
- More than 200 million clients now use microfinance services offered by many thousands of institutions worldwide.

Discussion Questions

1. According to World Bank statistics (easy to find online), is the fraction of people living on incomes below $3.10 per day rising or falling globally? What regions have experienced the biggest changes?

2. Think of some other methods, beyond microfinance, to alleviate poverty. Which are self-sustainable, i.e. covering their own costs, and which are not? Discuss why an institution that aims to alleviate poverty may invest in non-sustainable methods.

3. Do you think microfinance alone is enough to alleviate poverty? Why or why not?

4. Try to list all of the financial services you currently use; things like savings accounts, credit cards, and ATM withdrawals. Many people in

developed countries use more than 20 such services, so you probably use more than you initially realize. Now imagine living without these financial services. How important do you think financial services are to your way of life? If your income increases, does your need for financial services increase or decrease? In what way?

1.2 Microfinance Defined

Simply stated, **microfinance** refers to the offering of financial services to poor and low-income people. Traditionally, the poor have been considered "high risk" and have not been well served by institutions like banks, mutual funds, and credit card companies. A central goal of microfinance is poverty alleviation, by building, as Robert Christen of the Gates Foundation and his colleagues put it, "a world in which as many poor and near-poor households as possible have permanent access to an appropriate range of high quality financial services, including not just credit but also savings, insurance, and fund transfers."[4]

As we will see in Chapter 2, just like you, people living in poverty need access to financial services to help them provide for their families, save for big expenses like weddings, funerals or school fees, smooth out fluctuations in income streams, run their businesses, build assets, and manage risk. As we will explore in Chapter 3, the traditional banking and finance sector has until recently largely not served the poor, denying them access to savings accounts, insurance products, or credit to finance their small business enterprises. The poor are often turned away because they do not have a preexisting financial history, cannot afford traditionally high fees for banking services, have limited or no assets that might serve as collateral to secure loans, have no credit record or documentation of employment, and sometimes cannot read or write to fill out the paperwork for bank accounts or loans.

Can the Poor Really Use Financial Services?

Many poor people without access to financial services can immediately benefit from the availability of savings, insurance and credit. Even though the poor do not have much money, they still need and regularly use financial services. In fact, the poor across the globe have long developed informal financial services to meet this demand. Some practices date back to ancient civilizations, such as storing wealth in the form of cash crops or livestock, stashing currency or valuable objects within the home, and borrowing from close-knit communities and family. The first record of money lending dates back 3,000 years to the ancient Sumerian city of Uruk, south of modern-day Baghdad, Iraq. Other historical financial services include insurance-like cooperative burial clubs in Ancient Greece and Ancient Rome that covered funeral costs for deceased members or others in their families. The first recorded loan agreement that included interest dates back to 172 B.C. in Egypt. In short, money-oriented services aimed at the poor are certainly not second-millennia fads; even William Shakespeare in the 16th century featured a persecuted moneylender, Shylock, in *The Merchant of Venice*.

Fortunately, informal financial services have come a long way since ancient times. As we will see in Chapter 4, the poor also participate in savings and credit cooperatives in which groups of community members create their own informal village banks. Often such informal cooperatives even write charters and hold their members accountable to the rules of the union. Members usually contribute a small amount of funds regularly as savings. Members can then borrow from the large cumulative fund, which they must pay back. Rotating savings clubs, found in nearly every culture worldwide, work similarly. Participants save a small amount periodically, often weekly. Members take turns taking the weekly pot of saved currency. Similarly, tens of thousands of collaborative, informal so-called "friendly societies" emerged in the United Kingdom in the 19th century to provide credit, savings and insurance services to millions of poor and working class people. In the developing world today, collectors still walk through villages taking and protecting people's savings for a small fee in exchange for this informal service.

Still, these informal savings and lending methods are risky because their informality means that they offer no legal protection to the participants. For example, what is to stop a credit cooperative member from not paying back a loan? Or participants with an early turn in the rotating savings clubs from taking the whole pot when it is their turn and then refusing to contribute their fair share to others later in the rotation? Cash crops used to store wealth can spoil, livestock can die, currency in the mattress can get stolen, and moneylenders can charge very high fees if borrowers have no other options in times of need.

The poor need access to safe savings methods—ideally, methods that earn interest and have limited fees. People sometimes need loans, hopefully with interest rates that are reasonable, not so high that they force borrowers to be indebted to lenders forever. The poor also need access to more than just savings and credit. For example, the poor can have large families entirely dependent on income from one provider in a dangerous job or on crops that big storms can wipe out. As a result, they need life insurance or crop insurance. Another common financial service in demand is remittances, which are money transfers from family members or friends working in cities or abroad in more developed nations back to those living in rural areas. In short, the poor need access to a full range of financial products. Microfinance was born from this demand.

Box 1.1. Faces
Felix Loyola's Story as Told to Jose Arias

Felix Loyola was born a campesino—a fieldworker. Since he began working at the age of nine, Felix grew up believing he was stuck in a place he thought he would never leave. He harvested agave cacti for tequila, bananas, guavas, and, his favorite, mangoes. He earned less than $1 a day and was living a life of hungry days and cold, sleepless nights. When he married his wife, Luciana, he realized his situation needed to change. He dreamed of having children who could read and write, would go to college, and live a better life than he had. Growing up among the freshest ingredients Mexico had to offer, he and his wife decided they wanted to open a restaurant. Unfortunately, Felix did not have any capital to begin with. In 1998 Compartamos Banco was developing a lending group in a town nearby called Miacatlan. Felix heard that a bank was giving out small loans to people who had no assets. He and his wife traveled to Miacatlan, and were selected as key members of this group. In October of 1998, Felix took out his first loan of $95 with an annual interest rate of 25%. He quickly allocated the newfound capital to buying a large griddle and chickens in order to make his "tacos famosos." Today, Felix owns a modest restaurant

(Continued)

Box 1.1. (*Continued*)

outside of Miacatlan, and both his children are attending a local private school.

Felix Loyola's story is a true account of one man's experience with microfinance as he himself told it to Jose Arias in January of 2009. Jose was, at the time, a sophomore enrolled in an introductory microfinance course at Lehigh University as well as an active member of the university's microfinance club and co-contributor to this text. Being of Mexican descent with relatives still living in Mexico, Jose decided to call his grandfather and ask if he knew anything about microfinance or knew of anyone who borrowed from a microfinance institution. His grandfather responded enthusiastically, divulging his own knowledge of microfinance before mentioning Felix's name. He gave Jose Felix's number and Jose called Felix to interview him over the phone for his own personal story.

Source: Jose Arias, personal communication.

Microcredit: The Roots of Microfinance

Services offered by **microfinance institutions (MFIs)** now range from loans, savings, and insurance to money banking, healthcare, and well beyond. Yet **microcredit**, the offering of small, uncollateralized loans, is where microfinance has its roots and is the topic of Chapter 5. The prefix "micro" comes from the fact that the loans (or savings, for microsavings) tend to be very small. In developed countries like the U.S. and in Europe, a smallish loan for a business may mean $10,000, but in the developing world, $100—100 times less—may be enough to start an informal microenterprise or to escape from perpetual reliance on local moneylenders who charge high fees. A hundred dollars in savings can mean the difference in whether or not a family can send children to school, or maybe even whether the kids can eat for a month if mom or dad falls too sick to work.

Most microcredit agreements, like most loans outside of family or close friends, come with interest. At first, the notion of charging interest to a person who earns only a dollar a day may seem inhumane. As we explore in Chapters 8 and 9, many advocates for the poor argue that microcredit with high interest can do more harm than good, trapping clients in endless cycles of debt they cannot repay. On the other hand, proponents of the industry point out that by charging interest, MFIs can operate without huge subsidization or dependency on donor funds.

Self-sufficient MFIs charge fees and interest rates that allow them to cover their costs and stay in business. Unfortunately, administrative and processing costs are typically much higher than at traditional commercial banks. It is much more time consuming and expensive to lend 5,000 small $200 transactions than to lend out just one commercial business loan worth the same $1 million. That is because processing and administrative costs are not directly dependent on the size of the loan. It costs essentially the same to process a $100 loan as a $1000 one. Suppose a transaction costs the bank $25 either way. The interest rate would need to be 25% just to break even on the $100 loan but only 2.5% for the $1000 loan. Furthermore, because the poor often live in hard-to-reach rural places and cannot readily trek into a city branch, MFI staff may need to travel to the borrowers, adding costs in terms of fuel and hourly wages.

According to the Consultative Group to Assist the Poor (CGAP), an independent policy and research center that focuses on the spread of financial services to the poor, globally the average annual interest rate charged by an MFI in 2011 was 27%.[5] Although an interest rate of 27% sounds high compared to loans like mortgages in developed countries, it is comparable to many credit card rates. Moreover, it is far below what informal moneylenders typically charge, annual percentage rates that often run in the hundreds, and in some places, thousands of percent. Of course, just because the poor have few alternatives, MFIs aiming to help them presumably should not try to extract the highest possible fees. Unfortunately, some MFIs do charge high rates—70% or 90% annual interest are unusual but not unheard of—to cover inefficient operations or generate higher than normal profits for investors. Nevertheless, the majority of MFIs stay true to their social mission and strive to keep charges to their clients down by improving efficiency, achieving economies of scale and, increasingly, through innovation. Indeed, one recent analysis concluded that inflation-adjusted interest rates (including fees etc.) in 2009 were about 20% in South Asia and 30–35% throughout the rest of the world; and four-fifths of microcredit clients paid 35% a year or less.[6]

Beyond covering costs, charging fees and interest also allows MFIs to generate more funds with which to expand their outreach and services to even greater numbers of the poor. Today, hundreds of millions of clients willingly use MFIs and are willing to pay, suggesting they get value from the services. Given how broad and complex the microfinance industry has become, both sides of this debate are undoubtedly true. Some low-income clients thrive, while others struggle. Some MFIs' methods can do harm; other MFIs deeply improve lives. We explore these contradictions and the evidence on both sides throughout the book.

Group Lending

A key innovation in the success of microcredit is the practice of **group lending** (explored in detail in Chapter 5), forms of which are sometimes called solidarity groups or village banking. Not all microfinance loans are done in groups—individual loans are increasingly common—but the practice still dominates the industry in various regions. The group lending innovation came in response to obstacles financial institutions face when serving the poor. Recall that commercial banks often do not lend to the poor because they lack sufficient financial history and collateral, and also because accounts are small and tend to have high transactions costs per account. Well, MFIs face these same obstacles. For example, how are MFIs to distinguish between people who are good and bad credit risks without some sort of previous records? Without collateral how can they protect themselves against late payments (called delinquency) or failure to repay the loan (called defaulting)?

Group lending is one approach to combating all three problems: insufficient client information, lack of collateral, and high operating costs per transaction. The MFI lends funds to a group of people, often about five or six, though the groups can grow quite large to even 20 or 30 individuals. The total amount loaned to the group is the account figure on the MFI's books, all disbursed and repaid at the same time. Thus, by pooling several clients into one loan agreement, MFIs keep their costs per client in check.

It also helps the MFIs feel more comfortable about potential risks, because the groups self-select. Community members know each other well and have information the MFI lacks about potential clients. Potential clients will only want to enter agreements with others they believe to be reliable, because if they misjudge their peers then the group as a whole is liable for any financial delinquency on the part of any of the group's participants. In other words, if Sonja fails to make her payments this month, the rest of the group must chip in to meet Sonja's payment obligation. In this way the group behaves as collateral. As for Sonja, she would eventually have to pay back her group or face the consequences, which range from a bruised reputation in her community (with consequences in the future should she need community support) to exclusion from lending groups in the future.

Box 1.2. In Your Backyard
Microfinance in Arkansas

Microfinance's potential to help alleviate poverty might work in wealthy countries as well as poor countries. However, developed countries have different hurdles to overcome in regard to poverty. For example, critics point out that in many developing countries self-employment is commonplace and accounts for the majority of microfinance clients, while in the U.S. the self-employed make up less than 10% of the workforce. Furthermore, most new small businesses in the U.S. fail within a few years, bringing into question their ability to repay loans. So too, there is already a wide array of financial services available in the U.S. Can microfinance add anything?

It was not until the 1980s that the U.S. began to really look at microfinance as a means of poverty reduction. In 1985, then-Governor Bill Clinton approached Muhammad Yunus, founder of the Grameen Bank, and asked him to implement a microfinance program in Arkansas. However, before a program could be designed and launched, Yunus wanted to discover for himself what American poverty looked like and see if there was any truth in the critics' concerns.

In February 1986 Yunus met with some of the poorest residents in Arkansas and asked them what they would do with a bank loan.

(Continued)

Box 1.2. (*Continued*)

Slowly, poor Arkansans began to describe to Yunus their business ideas, and their entrepreneurial spirit gave him hope that a microcredit program could be implemented in the U.S. In Pine Bluff, Arkansas, the Good Faith Fund was piloted. The program showed promise, and so the model was repeated across the country, in places like South Dakota, Oklahoma, and Chicago, reaching urban, suburban, and rural American communities alike.

However, microfinance has never quite caught on in the U.S. or other high-income economies as much as in developing countries, though it is certainly growing. Part of the reason microfinance is slow to catch on in rich countries stems from differences between the needs of the poor in developed and developing countries, such as the scale of funding needs. Accion, one of the largest MFIs currently operating in the U.S., says its average microloan granted in the U.S. is about $10,000, with a range to $50,000, or in some cases even $1 million. Compare this to the average $500 loan of Accion's affiliate Compartamos Banco in Mexico. Furthermore, while the poor in the U.S. are often refused loans for the same reasons as are the poor in developing countries—lack of financial history and insufficient collateral—group lending does not seem to work in the U.S. as it does in developing countries. A partial explanation may be that American culture is more individualistic, though an alternative theory lies in the fact that American microcredit borrowers graduate from MFIs to commercial banks faster and more frequently than their developing nation counterparts. This, coupled with competition from other financial service options—e.g. local credit unions, payday lenders, credit card companies, and government small business assistance programs—reduces the potential for economies of scale. As a result, funding needs and operational costs for microfinance institutions in the U.S. are higher per client than in most developing countries.

Still, both Grameen America and the Accion U.S. Network have active programs, each with tens of thousands of clients in the U.S.,

(*Continued*)

suggesting microfinance can work in the developed world. However, it must do so under excellent management; even then large-scale growth remains elusive.

In practice, the repayment rates of microcredit borrowers, both in groups and as individuals, have been remarkably high, above 95% for well-managed MFIs and even near 99% for some. Those sorts of results have helped the industry grow by creating faith within the industry that the social collateral of groups is an effective substitute for client information and collateral. In turn, lenders and investors have become more willing to provide loans to the poor. The poor have turned out to be a low-risk investment.

Furthermore, it may be that the flexibility and incentives for repeat loans may be more important than social pressure. In many MFIs, if a borrower or a group successfully repays, each subsequent loan can be larger than the last, called progressive lending—a system that creates incentives for repayment. Individual loans are steadily rising as a fraction of microcredit. More than a quarter of 1,080 leading MFIs in a 2009 survey were primarily individual lenders.[7] Even the pioneer Grameen Bank has dropped group joint-liability lending altogether, although it retains group meetings. Nevertheless, group lending remains a principal method for thousands of MFIs worldwide, particularly those aiming at providing financial access to the poorest clients.

Savings and Beyond

We have already seen that the poor have various informal methods of saving on their own, such as storing cash or livestock, but these methods carry risks—and in the case of livestock, expenses too. As we discuss in more detail in Chapter 2, the poor must save, even more than most. Otherwise, their income could not cover traditional large costs, such as weddings and funerals, school fees for their children, or investment opportunities like acquiring a dairy cow to sell milk. Many poor also often suffer significant unpredictable day-to-day fluctuations in income and might go without any income for days or weeks. Savings tools that allow them to store money

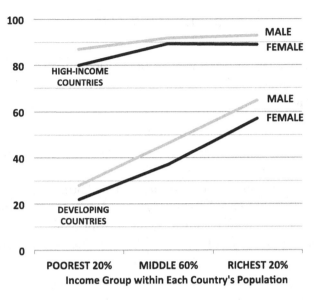

Figure 1.2. Adults worldwide with an account at a formal financial institution (%)

Source: Demirgüç-Kunt and Klapper (2012).

from good income days can help them smooth out their purchases of food and other basic consumption to get through the irregular ups and downs. Furthermore, just like you, the poor need savings in case of emergencies, such as illness or natural disasters.

By offering savings accounts, banks provide a safe, secure, and formal way to build funds. Yet the commercial banking sector is often hard to access physically and financially. Branches may not be located conveniently within a rural village and banks often have minimum deposit requirements. As a result, according to a worldwide survey by the World Bank and Gallup, more than three of every four of the poorest people in developing economies lack any sort of formal account, savings or otherwise, at any financial institution (see Figure 1.2). The poor lack access to savings accounts that allow for tiny, frequent deposits, are physically accessible, and easy to withdraw funds from when needed. Encouragingly, innovative MFIs like BRI have found ways to provide accessible savings accounts that are also financially viable from an institutional perspective. Note, however, that most governments try to protect people and their savings from dishonest operators. So, not just any institution can take deposits, only licensed and regulated formal banks can. For this reason, in recent years a substantial number of MFIs are changing from being NGOs (which lack legal status to take deposits) to being formally licensed banks, as we explore further in Chapter 8.

Box 1.3. In the Field
BRI Mobilizes Savings

Bank Rakyat Indonesia is one of the pioneers of savings mobilization. It was one of the first MFIs to realize that the poor not only could save but also need to save. All of its clients have deposit accounts, while not all are borrowers.

Table 1.1. Bank Rakyat Indonesia

Began commercial microfinance	1984
Location	Indonesia
Clients (Dec. 2015)	43 million microsaving customers; 7.9 million borrowers
Women as % of borrowers	60%
Self-sufficiency ratio*	135%
Legal status	Commercial bank, stock traded

Note: * Self-sufficiency ratio is a measure of whether an MFI is covering its expenses. If the ratio (financial revenue/financial expenses + operating expenses) is below 100%, the MFI needs subsidies to operate.

BRI by 2015 had grown to 43 million microsavings client accounts and boasted a microsavings deposit portfolio of $14 billion. Its own borrowers' savings have become the bank's primary source of funding, allowing it to become completely self-sufficient and independent of all governmental or private donor funds. BRI has taken microsavings to the next level by also providing more than 22,000 ATMs—including some mobile ones on boats to reach remote areas—and more than 10,000 accessible branches throughout the many islands that make up Indonesia.

(Continued)

Box 1.3. (*Continued*)

Figure 1.3.   Owner of a *tambal ban*, tire repair business, in Gorontalo, Indonesia

Note: Millions of Indonesians like him use local BRI branches for their savings. *Source*: © Neil Liddle, 2008[†].

The importance of this self-sufficiency became clear during the deep Asian financial crisis in the late 1990s. Bank customers throughout much of Asia lost faith in their banking systems, causing many banks to collapse. In Indonesia alone 82 other banks failed and 13 more were taken over by the government. Yet BRI survived. The microsavings business saved the bank because during the crisis BRI's millions of savers kept their trust and funds in BRI's local branches.

Source: Bank Rakyat Indonesia, Annual Report 2015.
[†]Licensed under Creative Commons Attribution 2.0: https://creativecommons.org/licenses/by/2.0/legalcode.

Increasingly, MFIs are doing even more than providing financial services. Today, it is common to see institutions provide services such as free business training, empowerment workshops, and healthcare. This is because MFIs have found that poverty is more than just a financial problem. Poverty can also mean inadequate housing conditions, lack of healthcare, and lack of education. For these reasons, microfinance cannot exist in a vacuum. It is but one tool, a financial tool, in poverty reduction. There is still much work to be done by charitable and government organizations alike around the globe.

Section in Bulletpoint

- Microfinance provides financial services of all sorts to the poor and low-income people around the globe.
- The poor are often excluded from the formal financial sector because traditional banks consider them too risky and costly.
- Thus, the poor often resort to informal methods of saving and borrowing that leave them legally unprotected in the event of fraud or disaster.
- Microcredit, one part of microfinance, involves small loans to the poor and low-income people.
- Microcredit began with loans to groups that share liability for repayment of all group members' loans, a key innovation that helped the industry grow.
- Beyond microcredit, microfinance now includes a full suite of services including savings, insurance, healthcare and education, among many others.
- Some microfinance institutions are limited in the services they can offer based on their legal status. For example, in many countries, only banks can take savings deposits.
- Microcredit interest rates tend to be higher than traditional commercial rates because of higher operating cost ratios.

Discussion Questions

1. Why are the poor often excluded from the formal financial sector? Can you think of any other reasons not discussed in the chapter?

2. What are some innovations of microfinance that address the challenges of serving the poor?

3. Why do microfinance institutions charge interest on microloans? Why are the interest rates so high?

4. How does group lending help MFIs manage the loans they give out? Briefly discuss advantages and disadvantages of this method.

1.3 Microfinance as an Industry

How Big Is Microfinance and Who Uses It?

The microfinance industry has certainly come a long way since the 1970s. The dawn of microfinance was the work of only a handful of institutions, namely Accion, Grameen Bank, BRI, FINCA, ASA, and BRAC. Today, there are probably more than 10,000. By 2012 there were more than 3,700 MFIs reporting data to the Microcredit Summit Campaign, which tracks industry data and promotes industry goals and policy. However, thousands of additional smaller institutions do not report data, so exact numbers are unavailable. Part of the complexity stems from the fact that MFIs can take on many forms: some are commercial banks, while others are nonbank financial institutions; some are government-owned, and others are NGOs. Many MFIs are part of organizations like NGOs or churches that primarily deal in other charitable activities or implement microfinance in a manner different from the standard, so they are difficult to define or count. Still, even without exact numbers, the growth of the industry is impressive. It went from a handful of organizations to many thousands. The early pioneers showed the world that microfinance could work and sustainably achieve large scale; and the industry boomed.

Data on the number of people using microfinance also provide a picture of rapid growth. According to Microcredit Summit Campaign estimates (Figure 1.4), at the end of 1997 there were 13 million clients of MFIs. That grew 16-fold by the end of 2013 to 211 million clients worldwide, of which 114 million were the very poorest, those living on less than $1.90/day.[8] Other estimates vary, but all are similar in rough magnitude.

Of these hundreds of millions of microfinance clients, an estimated 75% are women.[9] As we explore later in Chapter 7 on gender issues in microfinance, a common mission of many MFIs is to enhance the lives of women, particularly in regard to healthcare and empowerment. Indeed, some MFIs—including Bharat Financial Inclusion Ltd. (BFIL), the largest MFI in India—cater exclusively to women. Every one of BFIL's more than 6 million clients is female. Note that BFIL (formerly called SKS) played a central role in the overall industry downturn in 2011, seen in Figure 1.4. That first-ever decline was largely related to turmoil in the large microfinance sector in India.

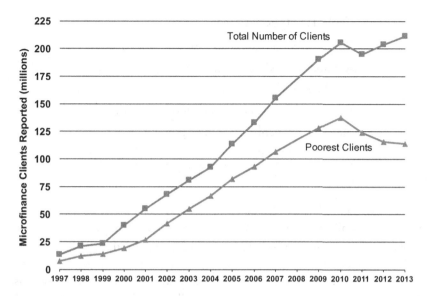

Figure 1.4.   Growth in microfinance clients, 1997–2013

Data source: Microcredit Summit Campaign (2016).

Who Provides Microfinance?

The microfinance industry has become multilayered and fairly complex in industry structure. The industry is growing rapidly, has hundreds of millions of clients, and manages hundreds of billions of dollars in assets, loans and savings deposits. The many industry players continue to experiment with what works across all facets of the sector. Part of that experimentation is in the types of legal entities that MFIs can be. MFIs can serve a variety of niches and come in a variety of different legal structures, including those listed in Table 1.2.

These different legal statuses come with varying levels of freedom and regulation. A majority of MFIs are NGOs, often small and dependent on donors. NGOs are typically nonprofit organizations, community groups, church-affiliated programs, and so on that are not regulated by a government banking authority. Banking regulations aim to protect citizens who save their money in banks from losing those funds, such as through bank failures or fraudulent activities. Nearly all countries require banks that want to take deposits to become regulated, i.e. to have official banking licenses, which are given only to banks with solid financial strength, good record keeping systems, controls against theft and fraud, and other safeguards, all of which

Table 1.2. Types of MFIs

Non-governmental organizations (NGOs)
Member-owned cooperatives
Nonbank financial institutions
Rural banks and agricultural development banks
State-owned banks, including postal banks
Commercial banks

can be costly to implement and maintain. Because becoming a regulated bank can be cost prohibitive, most NGOs elect not to. As a result, they cannot take deposits and are limited in how they can spend their funding.

Member-owned cooperatives take many forms, such as credit unions, village banks, or self-help groups, but generally provide services only to their members; regulations on cooperatives vary widely by country. Nonbank financial institutions are similar to banks but are classified under a different type of license. A government banking agency also typically supervises them. They usually have lower requirements in terms of how much capital they must have, and are limited in what types of services they can offer. Whether they can take deposits or not depends on the country. Some countries like Peru and Ghana have created special regulations targeted specifically at microfinance operations, allowing them to behave differently than traditional banks. Rural banks and agricultural development banks are regulated banks that operate in nonurban areas and focus mainly on the agricultural sector. Most were started as government-owned banks or private banks with heavy government subsidization. Purely state-owned banks are similar to the banks most of us normally think of, but are owned by the government. Commercial banks are the supervised for-profit banks with which most of us are generally familiar.

Adding to the complexity, any one of these types of organizations may deal primarily with something other than microfinance and only provide microfinance services as a peripheral to their main operations. For example, an NGO called World Relief focuses on providing health education and services, child development support, agriculture and food security, and disaster response, in addition to microfinance.[10] Giant corporations, such as Wal-Mart, also dabble in microfinance internationally by creating operating

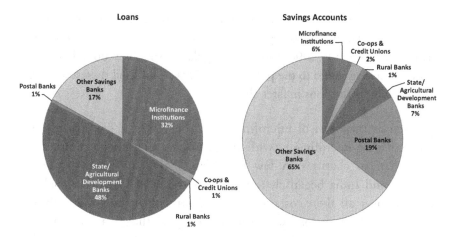

Figure 1.5. Share of savings accounts and active loans in alternative financial institutions

Data Source: Roodman (2012).

divisions that deal primarily with microfinance. In fact, a very large percent of microsavings accounts and active microloans comes from organizations that do not primarily engage in microfinance (Figure 1.5). Institutions that focus strictly on the provision of microfinance services make up minorities of both savings accounts (6%) and active loans (32%).

Commercialization: Does It Undermine Social Missions?

Increasingly, some NGOs and nonbank financial intermediaries have been transforming themselves into regulated banks. This allows them not only to meet their clients' demand for savings, but also to access savings deposits as a low-cost source of funding, and also to make investments in other types of activities that only regulated banks may do.

Most MFIs that have so far transformed into regulated commercial banks had their roots as an NGO, rural bank, or state-owned bank. For example, the very first MFI to transform was a non-profit NGO in Bolivia called Prodem, which in 1992 became the BancoSol, a for-profit regulated bank. Similarly, BRI in Indonesia and Compartamos Banco in Mexico both become for-profit companies with shareholders buying and selling ownership shares in the companies on stock markets. BRI had been a state-owned bank since 1946 until the Indonesian government sold some shares to the public in 2003. Compartamos Banco began in 1990 as an NGO, became a non-bank financial institution in 2000, and then a regulated bank in 2006, followed by its owners selling shares to the public in 2007. We profile all these and many other leading institutions in later chapters.

Even at the birth of microfinance in the 1970s, a few institutions were managing microfinance with an approach more akin to commercial banks than to charities. A few pioneering MFIs in Indonesia, Latin America, and India began charging interest rates on loans that enabled them to cover all their costs while maintaining their borrowers' ability to repay. While these institutions proved early on that financial viability without charitable subsidies was possible for MFIs, it was not until the 1990s that commercialization truly gained significant momentum. It is useful to understand the primary benefits from commercialization for the individual borrowers, MFIs, and the industry as a whole. As detailed in Chapter 8, these benefits include the lowering of interest rates through competition and lower costs from scale efficiencies and increased access to traditional capital markets, competitive incentives for more innovative financial products, and, importantly, greater long-term institutional sustainability.[11]

However, as institutions commercialize they become more and more responsible to their investors, who can put additional pressure on MFIs to generate profits. An argument often raised against the commercialization of microfinance is that a profit-seeking organization might lose its focus on serving the poor. Additionally, regulated institutions are required to have boards of directors that meet certain qualifications to guide the institution's governance. A new board may have directors with goals that differ from the NGO's founding vision. From this argument stems a vigorous debate in microfinance regarding **mission drift**: i.e. how commercialization might shift the goals and focus of an institution from generating returns for society (often called the social bottom line) to generating returns for shareholders (called the financial bottom line).

By adding shareholders to the equation, a commercial MFI now has two responsibilities: creating profits for its investors and providing superior products and services to improve the lives of its clients. This combination of commercial and social missions is often called the **double bottom line**. Unfortunately, even though the poorest of the poor may have the most immediate need for financial services, they are rarely the most profitable customers. Thus, an MFI that is increasingly concerned about profitability may tend to move away from the very poorest and serve clients that will earn them a higher return. So even though commercialization can potentially increase the numbers of clients reached, reduce costs to those clients, and create incentives for financial products better tailored to their needs, does it actually ensure outreach to the "right" clients? Or does it merely mean that a commercial MFI will increase its client base and asset portfolio by serving higher-income clients, thus actually decreasing poverty alleviation among those who need it the most?

There is currently no clear-cut answer, only the knowledge that socially driven NGOs still have an important role to play in the industry. Because NGOs have no pressure to generate a profit, they can more readily target the poorest of the poor. On the other hand, they have less capital with which to reach them and expand their services and have a harder time achieving economies of scale to reduce costs for clients.

Outreach

We have learned that something like 200 million clients are being served by microfinance institutions. But how poor are they? The answer to that question is concerned with what is called **depth of outreach**, or going **down-market**, which in financial industry jargon means serving poorer communities. For alleviating poverty, we might hope to see microfinance coverage emphasize areas with greater levels of poverty. Focusing on the correlation between the presence of microfinance and levels of poverty will help us better see the depth of outreach, not just the scale.

As you can see in Figure 1.6, many severely poor parts of Sub-Saharan Africa have limited microfinance coverage (lighter) while severely poor regions of Asia have strong (darker) microfinance coverage. It is curious as to why Asia is better served than Africa. Population density is one central factor; it is more cost effective for MFIs to serve many people when they live close together. Bangladesh has more than 1000 people per square kilometer, 50 times denser than Zambia at fewer than 20. Yet Peru has perhaps the most

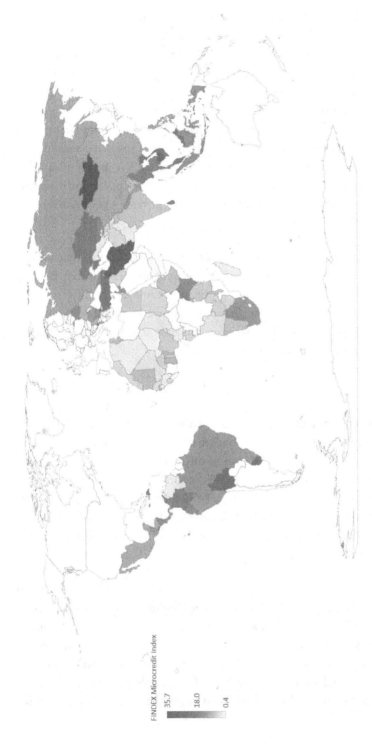

Figure 1.6.   Global FINDEX Index of Microcredit Market Penetration

Note: Darker = Greater penetration as share of potential market.
Source: World Bank, Global Findex Database, 2014.

advanced microfinance sector in the world despite a population density very close to Zambia's.

Other key factors are government policies and economic and political stability. Historically, Asian governments have a better record when it comes to economic development, growth and political and regulatory stability. By contrast, various African nations regularly suffer political and economic upheavals, which make it difficult for MFIs to invest and serve the poor due to hostile regulatory environments, unpredictable economic swings, and sometimes high rates of domestic migration that displaces clients. In optimal environments, MFIs can set up branches and introduce various financial services to a settled client population, invest for the long haul without risk of the broader economy collapsing and with little difficulty from a regulatory perspective.

Key Players and Intermediaries

Microfinance Institutions and Networks

By reading this chapter you have already become somewhat familiar with the names of a few key players in the microfinance industry. Certainly, the major early microfinance innovators are still instrumental within the industry. In addition, within the past two decades, new MFIs have begun to emerge as leaders. Table 1.3 lists the top MFIs in each region according to number of borrowers.

MFIs can grow to be quite large, or in the case of South Asian MFIs, enormous. Among regions, Europe and Central Asia (ECA) has fewer borrowers, largely because the potential markets there for microcredit are simply relatively small. For example, Mongolia's Khan Bank captures one-third of Mongolia's entire estimated potential market for microcredit services.[12] On the other hand, despite BRAC's 4.9 million borrowers, it only serves well fewer than one in 10 potential clients.

Hence, when looking at an MFI's impact it is important to consider both the scale and depth of its outreach, just as we must examine the scale and depth of the industry's outreach as a whole. Both a large gross number

Table 1.3. Largest MFIs in each region by number of borrowers, 2015

Region	MFI	Country	Number of borrowers
East Asia and Pacific	BRI	Indonesia	7,850,000
	ASA Philippines	Philippines	1,073,580
	Card NGO	Philippines	816,619
Europe and Central Asia	UniBank	Azerbaijan	447,918
	Khan Bank	Mongolia	358,914
	CREDO	Georgia	196,947
Latin America and Caribbean	Compartamos Banco	Mexico	2,861,721
	CrediAmigo	Brazil	2,030,821
	AgroAmigo	Brazil	1,097,759
Middle East and North Africa	Al Amana	Morocco	328,361
	ABA	Egypt	283,979
	Enda	Tunisia	270,563
Sub-Saharan Africa	Capitec Bank	South Africa	3,684,000
	African Bank	South Africa	1,500,000
	LAPO	Nigeria	800,6111
South Asia	Grameen Bank	Bangladesh	8,806,779
	Bandhan	India	6,717,331
	ASA	Bangladesh	5,362,966
	BFIL (formerly SKS)	India	5,325,244
	BRAC	Bangladesh	4,923,936

Note: Clients as of 2015, except Capitec 2/2016, UniBank and LAPO 12/2014; and African Bank Ltd. as reorganized 4/2016. For consistency, the table does not include the Vietnam Bank for Social Policies or the Postal Savings Bank of China, large but essentially government-run subsidized banks.

Sources: Microfinance Information Exchange, www.mixmarket.org; Bank Rakyat Indonesia, Annual Report 2015; Capitec Annual Report 2016; Grameen Bank Monthly Report 12/31/2015.

of borrowers and a large share of the potential market, known as **market penetration**, are beneficial to helping alleviate poverty. A large number of clients indicates that many people have access to financial services. However, market penetration is still important because it means that a greater share of

Table 1.4. Largest MFIs worldwide by number of depositors, 2015

MFI	Country	Number of depositors
BRI	Indonesia	43,000,000
Grameen Bank	Bangladesh	8,806,779
Equity Bank	Kenya	8,780,150
ASA	Bangladesh	6,313,359
BRAC	Bangladesh	5,799,933
Banco Caja Social	Colombia	5,292,794
Tameer Microfinance Bank	Pakistan	4,958,736
Capitec Bank	South Africa	3,300,000
Khan Bank	Mongolia	2,364,853
Caja Popular Mexicana	Mexico	2,010,829

Sources: Microfinance Information Exchange, www.mixmarket.org; Bank Rakyat Indonesia, Annual Report 2015; Capitec Annual Report 2016; Grameen Bank Monthly Report 12/31/2015.

the community, no matter how small, is potentially better off. A stronger, financially empowered community as a whole can have greater externalities that help alleviate poverty. Community members are consequently able to help each other more effectively.

Remember, the figures in Table 1.3 only represent the number of people who have received credit from the listed MFI. Many of these MFIs also provide savings, thus they serve even more clients than these numbers reveal. Table 1.4 ranks the top 10 MFIs in terms of number of depositors.

BRI is clearly a very large outlier, serving nearly five times as many depositors any other microfinance deposit taker in the world. Overall, most of microfinance's depositors are found in Asia. Note overall that six of the 10 depositor-leading MFIs in Table 1.4 (including four of the top five) also appear in Table 1.3 as leaders in terms of scale of credit.

While many MFIs operate independently, some are part of larger collaborative structures. **Network groups** usually involve a central umbrella organization that assists a group of collaborating but separately managed member MFIs. Several of the very first MFIs have also become networks, such as Accion and FINCA. Think of network groups as a club of MFIs that usually have something in common such as region of operation or ideology. For example, Accion is a large network group with 35-member MFIs, such as Compartamos Banco in Mexico, MiBanco in Peru, and Akiba in Tanzania. Accion members are in 21 countries, predominantly in Latin America but also in Africa, Asia and even five in the U.S.[13] Accion provides start-up and management aid to member MFIs, while simultaneously making concerted efforts at sharing best practices, promoting effective policies, supporting microfinance-related research and development, and offering technological services.

MFI Funders and Service Providers

In addition to MFIs and networks that directly provide financial services, a supporting layer of the industry involves the more than 100 investment institutions that raise funds specifically for MFIs. Among the best known are Oikocredit, and private investment groups like Triodos Microfinance Fund, Symbiotics, and BlueOrchard, which invest directly in MFIs by buying equity ownership shares or investing in debt securities. These **microfinance investment vehicles** attract large investors to long-term, potentially return-generating securities that fund MFIs and other socially minded companies.

Not all such funders are as exclusive nor do all funds generate a return. For example Kiva.org allows internet users to fund microfinance directly through minimum investments of just $25. Kiva works with MFIs on the ground that transfer your loaned funds to borrowers of your choice. The borrowers then makes repayments back to the MFIs, and in turn the repayments are credited to your Kiva account but without interest. The idea behind having the principal loaned amount paid back to the lender is simple: a majority of Kiva lenders use the money again to keep loaning to more people. MicroGraam.com in India works similarly, allowing internet users in India to fund clients of small non-profit NGOs doing microfinance in India. The minimum MicroGraam loan online is remarkably small, 100 rupees, less than $2. MicroGraam even offers its investors the option of getting some interest. In 2014 MicroGraam and Kiva teamed up to open MicroGraam's partner NGOs to non-Indian investors through Kiva. Of course, there are also plenty of organizations that accept good old-fashioned donations.

Service providers are a little harder to define. They are organizations that provide a service within the microfinance industry to MFIs or for the broader public interest in microfinance. Many undertake academic research on microfinance or initiate related development programs. Some, such as Omtrix in Costa Rica and Mecene Investment in South Africa, manage funds for MFIs. Others, like Mifos.org or Craft Silicon, provide technical services, such as banking software and database management computer systems, or enable MFIs and their clients to use ATM networks, credit cards, and mobile phone banking. Many network groups also provide services to member organizations, particularly when it comes to advocacy and policy. Another group includes the private rating agencies such as MicroRate and Planet Rating that evaluate the financial performance and social impact of individual MFIs. These offer investment-rating reports on specific MFIs for investors much like Standard & Poor's does for stock market investors. Many of these reports are available on another service provider, the Microfinance Information Exchange (MIX), a leading source of detailed data on the industry. You will notice many of the tables and graphs in this book rely on MIX data.

Box 1.4. In the Field
Accion—The Business of Fighting Poverty

Accion International has been innovating microfinance for more than 40 years, longer than any other organization. As a network, Accion has helped build and strengthen some of the most successful microfinance institutions in the world. Among their partner MFIs are BancoSol in Bolivia, Compartamos Banco in Mexico, Banco Solidario in Ecuador, and Bancompartir in Colombia to name a few. The network tends to focus on Latin America and the Caribbean, although Accion also has operations in Africa, Asia, and the U.S. It serves the microfinance community as a whole by providing services that build and expand other MFIs, advocating for improved policies, undertaking research and development, and providing technical services. Through its think-tank, the Center for Financial Inclusion, it works towards full, global financial inclusion with an emphasis on quality of services, dignity, transparency, affordability, and MFI sophistication.

(Continued)

Box 1.4. (*Continued*)

Table 1.5. Accion International

Began microfinance operations	1973
Locations	Latin America, Asia, Africa, and U.S.
Clients (2015)	6 million borrowers; 4.8 million savers
Women as % of clients	75%
Self-sufficiency ratio	Varies across 35-member institutions
Legal status	Non-profit

Figure 1.7. Microfinance client microentrepreneur and her grocery near Accra's Tudu market, in Ghana, where Pan-African Savings and Loans serves about 78,000 clients like her

Note: Pan-African Savings and Loans is a partnership of Accion and EcoBank, West Africa's top independent regional bank.

From 2004 to 2015, Accion and its partners disbursed more than $70 billion in microloans to more than 19 million clients. Three of four of the network's clients are women and it boasts a worldwide repayment rate of 97%.

Source: Accion International, www.accion.org.

The CGAP and the Microcredit Summit Campaign are two other very well-known service providers. The Microcredit Summit Campaign organizes large meetings of microfinance leaders to talk about industry trends, goals, and issues, and to identify and share best practices. They also advocate women's issues and healthcare and publish a widely read annual report on the current state of the microfinance industry. That industry growth graph you saw earlier, Figure 1.4, uses data from that report. CGAP is a consortium jointly funded by more than 30 public and private development organizations, including the World Bank, the U.S. Agency for International Development, the United Nations Development Program, the European Investment Bank, and the Gates Foundation. CGAP offers advisory and technical services, training, research and analysis, and fosters development of industry standards, performance metrics and impact assessment. CGAP also often suggests potential innovative products, financing methods, management techniques, and ways to use new technologies.

Without service providers, microfinance institutions would confront greater obstacles both individually and industry-wide. Individual MFIs would face financing and expansion problems and have a harder time keeping up with new ideas, best practice management techniques and the latest technologies. On the industry level, service providers help set standards, propose and lobby for policies, and facilitate communication throughout the industry.

Section in Bulletpoint

- Microfinance has grown tremendously over the last few decades to more than 10,000 MFIs serving more than 200 million people, but access to microfinance is highly variable across countries.
- The largest MFIs each serves millions of clients.
- MFIs can take on different legal forms; those forms can limit the types of funding the MFIs can accept. Because of this, some NGOs go on to apply for banking licenses.
- External funds for MFIs come both from investors, such as specialized microfinance investment vehicles looking for a return on their funds and from conventional charitable donations.

(*Continued*)

- The double bottom line means MFIs must balance financial returns and sustainability with social goals in poverty alleviation.
- Asia and Latin America are the largest microfinance markets.
- The industry is supported by a layer of service providers that provide advice on best practices, ratings for investors, technology, fund management, advocacy, industry standards, and research.

Discussion Questions

1. Suppose an MFI is currently an NGO but is considering becoming a regulated bank. What are some pros and cons? In particular, how would the change affect the services they could offer, their funding source options, and their institutional governance?

2. What factors might help contribute to an MFI's ability to increase its scale? What about for an MFI that wants to improve its depth of outreach?

3. What reasons can you think of that might help explain why there are some places where there is severe poverty yet no or little microfinance?

4. If you were to run a microfinance institution, what key issues and tensions do you think would arise as you decide how to balance the double bottom line of financial performance and social mission to help the poorest? Is one more important? What could you do to try and meet both goals?

Chapter Summary

Poverty continues to affect billions of lives across the globe. Microfinance is but one tool of many that strives to alleviate poverty. Specifically, microfinance serves the demand the poor have for financial services. The poor have been traditionally excluded from formal financial services, but through innovative financial products, such as group lending, microfinance institutions have been able to address the challenges in lending to the poor while delivering products—microcredit, microsavings, insurance, and more—that can help clients lift themselves and their families out of poverty.

With the help of network organizations, microfinance investment vehicles, donors, and technical support providers, microfinance institutions attempt to reach the underserved and to include them as fully as possible in financial systems around the world. This effort has grown from a handful of organizations serving a few clients to many thousands of microfinance institutions reaching hundreds of millions of low-income people across the globe.

The following chapters will take a closer look at poverty, microfinance, the industry, the impact of microfinance on the poor, and the key players that make microfinance possible.

Key Terms

depth of outreach
A gauge of how poor microfinance clients are relative to others in a given service region and the degree to which financial services are available to the very poorest.

down-market
Related to depth of outreach, MFIs that serve very low-income clients are said to go down-market; also true for other financial industries.

double bottom line
The dual goals of ensuring financial sustainability while also focusing on social goals in poverty alleviation.

group lending
Providing loans jointly to groups of people. A key innovation that helped foster the rapid growth microfinance; remains a dominant practice in the industry.

market penetration
Refers to the share of a potential market served; for MFIs, often measured as a percentage of potential clients or of potential value of loans or deposits.

microcredit
Also called microloans; small-value loans, often given without the need for collateral.

microfinance
The provision of financial services to underserved populations. Financial services offered to the poor include different forms of financing, varying from credit and savings to insurance and pension funds.

microfinance institution (MFI)
An entity that provides financial services to the poor. MFIs vary in form from NGOs to non-banking financial institutions to regulated e-banks.

microfinance investment vehicles
Investment groups that invest in MFIs; often pool private equity shares or debt securities for socially minded investors and companies.

mission drift
Refers to when an MFI shifts from helping the poor to a focus on financial returns.

network groups
Large, collaborative umbrella organizations that assist individual member MFIs in reaching their social and financial goals through financial, technical, and managerial assistance.

self-sufficient
An institution that covers its own cost and therefore does not require subsidies or donations.

service providers
Organizations that provide a service, such as academic research, fund management, and rating agencies, within the microfinance industry to MFIs and/or the public interest. They usually serve to promote microfinance policy and advocacy.

Notes:

[1] Cruz et al (2015).
[2] See www.accion.org/content/1970s-microlending-begins
[3] Microcredit Summit Campaign (2016).
[4] Christen, Rosenberg, and Jayadeva (2004).
[5] Rosenberg et al (2013).
[6] Roodman (2012).
[7] Microfinance Information Exchange (2009).
[8] Microcredit Summit Campaign (2016).
[9] Microcredit Summit Campaign (2016).
[10] See www.worldrelief.org/about
[11] Robinson (2001).
[12] Microfinance Information Exchange (2010).
[13] Accion International (2015).

DAILY FINANCIAL LIVES
OF THE POOR

"If it's hard to imagine how you would survive on a dollar or two a day, it's even harder to imagine how you would prosper....How do you make sure there is something to eat and drink every day, and not just on days you earn?...How do you deal with emergencies?...In short, how do you manage your money if there is so little of it?"

— **Daryl Collins et al,** *Portfolios of the Poor*

Figure 2.1.   The poor in this local market in Calla Jahuira, Peru—and everywhere—use a remarkably complex array of financial tools in their everyday lives to navigate the ups and downs of their incomes

This chapter seeks to explore the concept of poverty and shed light on the daily lives and challenges of the world's poor. By the end, you should be able to answer the following questions: How do the poor manage their income and expenses? What does poverty mean? What are overall patterns of poverty around the world? And why is it so hard to escape poverty?

To get a sense of the daily lives of the poor, we begin with a true story about the day-to-day financial activities of a family living in a slum of Dhaka, Bangladesh. They live on an irregular and uncertain stream of income that averages 78 cents per family member per day. Even with such little income, they use at least 13 different kinds of financial instruments to help them manage their household finances.

The chapter then expands on those financial tools and why and how the poor use them. We then broaden the discussion further and discuss the concept and meaning of poverty itself, how it is measured, and its global scope and distribution.

This chapter thus provides a basic understanding of the patterns of poverty generally and of the surprisingly complex financial activities of the poor, background necessary in understanding the broader context of development and the emergence of the microfinance industry. Additionally, by focusing primarily on the financial needs of the poor, this chapter helps us understand where the demand arises for the financial and social services that microfinance institutions (MFIs) provide, setting the stage for our discussion throughout the rest of the book about microfinance and its role in poverty alleviation.

2.1 The Portfolios of the Poor

One Poor Family's Financial Story

What is it like to live on a dollar or two a day, a few hundred dollars in a whole year? That is the norm for billions of people around the world. But for those of us fortunate enough not to have to live on so little, it is hard to imagine everyday life. Those daily realities are hard to comprehend even for the poverty professionals at places like the World Bank who measure overall statistics along the lines we discuss in this chapter's second section, such as national poverty rates or income levels.

To help all of us better grasp those daily financial challenges, poverty researchers from New York University, Oxford and several other places tracked details, penny by penny financial diaries, of how 250 families in villages and slums of Bangladesh, India and South Africa managed their money over the course of a year.[1] Remarkably, without exception, every single one of those 250 households across two continents—including the very poorest—had savings of some sort. All had debt of some kind too. Indeed, none used fewer than four different kinds of financial instruments, and many used 10 or more, which led the researchers to name their book about these financial diaries *Portfolios of the Poor*.

That Warren Buffet and other rich people have financial portfolios is no surprise. But how can it be that the poor use so many financial services too? To find out, we start the chapter looking at one of these families and their financial diaries.

Meet Khadeja and Hamid

The *Portfolios* research team introduces Khadeja and Hamid like this: "The couple married in a poor coastal village of Bangladesh where there was very little work for a poorly educated and unskilled young man like Hamid. Soon after their first child was born they gave up rural life and moved, as so many hundreds of thousands had done before them, to the capital city, Dhaka, where they settled in a slum.… Home was one of a strip of small rooms with cement block walls and a tin roof, built by their landlord on illegally occupied land, with a toilet and kitchen space shared by the eight families that lived there."[2]

This family of three lived on about $70 a month, on average—about 78 cents each per day. Of that, $15 monthly paid the rent if they could, though it wasn't always on time. The rest went mostly for food and fuel for cooking. But the income didn't come steadily; the average masks unpredictable ups and downs. Most of their income came from Hamid's occasional work and depended on whether he worked on a particular day. He bounced back and forth between periods of unemployment, serving as a backup rickshaw driver picking up the occasional passenger, or doing odd jobs in construction. Khadeja, too, sometimes contributed income doing sewing, while managing their home and raising their child.

Figure 2.2.   Cycle-rickshaw drivers in Dhaka, Bangladesh, earn unsteady and unpredictable incomes day by day

To those of us in rich countries, 78 cents per person daily seems a meager income. Yet the unfortunate reality is that this family is not especially poor by worldwide standards. Their income puts them above well more than a billion other people. Khadeja and Hamid are poor, but not the poorest of the poor.

How then can this "unremarkable poor household," in the words of the *Portfolios* authors, possibly use a wide portfolio of financial tools? Like what? And for what?

One way to picture Khadeja and Hamid's financial situation is akin to a business balance sheet. At any slice of time, the family had "assets" such as cash in their pockets, savings and so on, but also "liabilities" like back rent they owed and loans they had taken out.

Ignoring (for now) non-money items, Table 2.1 is what their family balance sheet looked like in November 2000. Each line represents a financial tool, either formal or informal. That particular month they were simultaneously using 13 different ones.

Table 2.1. Hamid and Khadeja's closing balance sheet, November 2000

Financial assets	$174.80	Financial liabilities	$223.34
Cash in hand	2.00	Back rent owed	10.00
Home savings	2.00	Shopkeeper credit	16.00
Private loans owed to them	40.00	Savings held for others	20.00
Remittances to the home village	>30.00	Wage advance	10.00
Savings with a moneyguard	8.00	Private interest-free loan	14.00
Microfinance savings account	16.80	Microfinance loan account	153.34
Life insurance	76.00		
		Financial net worth	−$48.54

Source: Collins et al (2009).

On the positive asset side, Hamid always kept $2 in his pocket to use as needed while on the road; the couple kept a similar amount stashed away at home in the likely case day-to-day income did not cover minor expenses, and they had sent ("remittances") about $30 to his parents for safe-keeping back in their home village. Another relative owed them $40. Hamid also had asked his employer to keep ("moneyguard") $8 he planned to send back home. Note these first five financial tools are all informal but nevertheless quite real ways to store assets. In addition, two formal assets included a life insurance policy they owned and a savings account with a local MFI.

When we look at what they owed others, at first it seems curious that many of their liabilities are similar to their assets. Despite giving one family member a loan, they had borrowed $14 from another family member and a friend. Similarly, Hamid had asked for $10 in wages in advance as a loan from the same employer guarding the funds Hamid was to send home. Conversely, Khadeja was serving as a moneyguard too, holding $20 for two women in her neighborhood trying to keep money out of their own homes and away from husbands and sons likely to spend it. The couple also owed $10 overdue rent to their landlord and $16 to a local grocer who had run a credit for them when they were a bit short on cash. Again, all of these were informal arrangements, not backed up by any legal contracts or documents. The one formal liability they had was a loan from the same MFI that held their savings.

This end-of-month snapshot shows a slice in time for this family. Yet rather than looking just at balances, we can also delve into the dynamics of their money management. The detailed bi-weekly tracking done by the *Portfolios* research team enabled following the money flows and other non-money barter-like transactions into and out of the household. The dynamics were as equally telling as the balance sheet about the complexity of the daily financial lives of the poor.

Adding up total flows in and out of the household over the year, the *Portfolios* team found that "Hamid and Khadeja 'pushed' $451 of their income into savings or insurance or into loan repayments, and 'pulled' $514 out of savings or by taking loans or agreeing to guard money for others. That total turnover—$965—is more than their total income for the year… about $840. So each dollar of income earned was subjected to $1.15 of intermediation—of being pushed and pulled through financial instruments of one sort or another."[3]

The flexibility that comes from this sort of **financial intermediation**, illustrated in Figure 2.3, lies at the heart of the demand for microfinance. Like Khadeja and Hamid, most poor people mainly use informal intermediaries such as family, shopkeepers, savings clubs among friends, neighborhood moneylenders and so on. However, these informal mechanisms have their own problems and risks, as we look into in detail in Chapter 4. Formal microfinance aims to do better. Moreover, microfinance can provide substantially broader service options that the informal players cannot hope to provide, like ironclad deposit security, ATMs or mobile money, among others.

Finance without Money

In addition to all these money-based tools, the couple—and in fact most of us, poor or otherwise—also similarly stored wealth in, lent and borrowed materials and goods as well as their labor, barter-like. Indeed physical assets

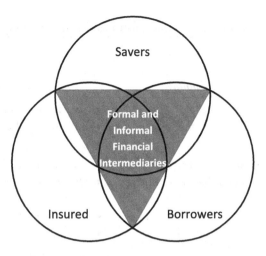

Figure 2.3.   Financial intermediation

make up the majority of stored wealth worldwide, in rich countries and poor alike. A house or a bag of rice stored holds value, as does a chicken or cow that can be sold if cash is needed.

Such tradable assets can be directly transactional too, bypassing cash, though usually with less so-called liquidity (i.e. speed or ease of use). A bag full of stored rice can be lent or borrowed from a neighbor to get through a hungry period before harvest and perhaps repaid in kind after harvest or by doing some work later. The poor do this sort of small scale reciprocal lending and saving with cash of course, but also food, salt, fuel for the kitchen, and on and on, for the majority of their "financial" transactions.

Marguerite Robinson, an anthropologist at Brandeis and Harvard, lists some of the ways the poor save and their advantages and disadvantages, as shown in Table 2.2. Convenience, access and liquidity are important, so there are upsides to using grains and livestock for farmers, wood for carpenters, wool for knitters, and transacting with neighbors. The downsides are particularly important in understanding the demand for formal microfinance. Cash can be stolen or burned in a kitchen flare-up; the neighborhood moneyguard might run off; livestock need feeding and might die; family or neighbors might fail to pay back; stored things need space and protection from the elements and thieves; and prices can fluctuate unexpectedly.

Table 2.2. Pros and cons of common forms of informal savings and lending

Form of savings or lending	Advantages	Disadvantages
Cash	• Convenience • High liquidity	• Security problems • Inflation/devaluation problem • Lack of return
Grain	• Some liquidity • Can be held until price rises • Can be sold in increments to smooth consumption	• Special storage needed • Quality deterioration in some cases • Risk of price fluctuation • Community expectation that grain will be lent or given in times of shortage
Livestock	• Generally high returns from propagation • Some liquidity • Animal by-products/labor	• Opportunity cost of taking care of the animals • Indivisibility • Risk of illness and death • Risk of price fluctuation
Raw materials and finished goods	• Can be purchased when prices low and saved for later • Can be occupation related (e.g. carpenters stockpiling wood)	• May deteriorate • Secure space needed to store • May go out of fashion
Gold	• Liquidity • Hedge against inflation • Serve as status symbols	• Security problems • Lack of return • Risk of price fluctuation
Land	• Source of livelihood (rural) • Base for enterprise, residence, or both • Investment value	• Titling difficulties • Opportunity cost of cultivation (higher income may be earned from nonfarm activities) • Regulation and taxation problem

(Continued)

Table 2.2. (*Continued*)

Form of savings or lending	Advantages	Disadvantages
Lending to others	• Generally high returns	• High risk due to generally undiversified portfolio • Labor demanding • High transaction cost of making and collecting loans
Deposits with savings collectors	• Security • Convenience	• Negative returns • Risk of losing savings with an unregulated and unsupervised collector • Lack of liquidity in some cases
Borrow from friends and relatives	• Low interest rate • Flexible loan size and payment schedule	• High social cost • Expectation that future credit request by others will not be turned away
Loan from local money lender	• Flexible loan size and payment schedule	• Extremely high interest rate • Personal safety threatened in some defaulting cases

Source: Robinson (2001).

The poor may also hold gold or other valuables in order to hedge against inflation and currency devaluation. The main advantage of holding valuables is that gold and jewelry are typically very liquid. However, they are also subject to theft. Moreover, when a community as whole experiences a shock—like a drought or flood—if everyone needs to sell similar valuable assets at the same time, markets get oversupplied, which lowers returns to the owners. For these reasons, holding gold and other valuables is an option mainly when other means are unavailable.[4]

The Need for Financial Services

Why do the poor need to do so many financial transactions using so many different tools? Clearly they must need to. They use them essentially constantly, and versions of the practices happen in every culture around the world. There are four basic financial needs that are, generally speaking, universal: the needs to (1) transact, (2) invest, (3) build assets, and (4) sustain consumption.[5] A typical person in a developed country has a wide array of financial services available to accomplish these, often in highly specialized ways, such as checking and savings accounts, mortgages, student loans, credit cards, home and car insurance, mutual funds, as well as wire transfers and online banking. Such broad availability is not the case in many developing countries, but the need is still present.

One of the main takeaways for the *Portfolios* researchers was that "the poor households we met actively employ financial tools not *despite* being poor, but *because* they are poor. ... lower incomes require *more* rather than *less* active financial management."[6] But why? As we will see, poor families need these tools and financial intermediaries to help them balance good cash flow days with bad days, short-term flows with long-term plans, consumption with investments, and personal needs with cultural obligations to family and friends; many of the same reasons, by the way, you have (for example, see the In Your Backyard Box 2.3 about college student Kevin).

The poor need and use financial intermediation for three very broad reasons: ensuring daily consumption, dealing with emergencies, and paying for big lump-sum expenses. We will look at each in turn.

Ensuring Daily Consumption

Most poor households face irregular, uneven income streams. A poor person may get a large inflow one period, and none at all in other periods. For example, workers in industries such as agriculture and fishing are extremely seasonally reliant. Farm workers earn the majority of their income during harvest, and little from farming during the down-season. As noted by the *Portfolios* researchers, farm workers usually seek urban employment during the off-season. It is common for a family member to move to a city to find work in order support the family back in the village (in turn creating demand for, among other financial service needs, secure ways of transferring money home).

In more urban environments too, self-employed people such as those who sell items in local markets also face fluctuating income flows. Income levels and fluctuation depend heavily on the nature and location of the work, and sometimes, the luck of the day. But families need to eat, ideally every day, not just when mom or dad has good days.

The process of spending less and saving during the up periods to cover needs during down periods when not enough money is coming in is called **consumption smoothing**. Without financial tools of some sort, income lulls mean sacrificing even basic necessities like food.

For a real example of the need for consumption smoothing, Figure 2.4, from *Portfolios*, tracks fluctuations over eight months for Pumza, a mother of four from Cape Town, South Africa, who earns her family's income selling sheep intestines. The top dark line is her daily business revenue added up each two weeks. The dashed line is her business expenses for buying the intestines, wood, and transportation. Two features are notable. First, revenues (before expenses) bounced from a low of less than $20 in some two-week periods to nearly $100 in others. After subtracting business expenses, her family's net income averages a little less than $1 per day per person. But it varies all over

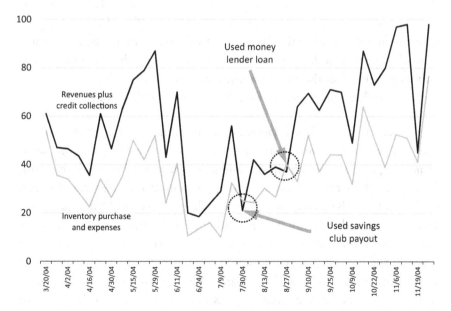

Figure 2.4. Revenues and expenses for Pumza, a sheep-intestines vendor, Cape Town, South Africa

Source: Collins et al (2009).

from less than 20 cents or so per person to nearly $5 each. Somehow she needed to feed the kids every day—not to mention buying new intestines and wood for her business—by saving on good days to cover those when there was only 20 cents each coming in.

The second feature of note is that in at least two of these two-week periods, Pumza spent more on her business than she brought in. Despite those losses, she still had to feed the family and run the household for those weeks, and still had to keep buying fresh inventory to keep selling. How? She took a loan from a moneylender and used funds she had accumulated in a savings club. These financial intermediaries, in this case both informal (and discussed more in Chapter 4), enabled her to do consumption smoothing she could not manage on her own.

It is not just the self-employed or seasonal workers who must deal with income uncertainty and fluctuations. Take the example, again from *Portfolios*, of Somnath and Jainath,[7] two brothers who worked at a garment factory, jobs in what economists would call the "formal sector." Working in the formal sector, though, did not guarantee steady income. Somnath and Jainath left their village and families behind to go find work in the Okhla Industrial Area, a major industrial zone in Delhi, India. The brothers found work in export garment factories, paid by the day or even by the piece. However, the amount of work they had to do varied day-by-day, and so did their income. Hired only as peripheral workers by a broker, their job was to work on "emergency orders" that the regular core workers at the factory could not do.

Together, Somnath and Jainath's earnings thus fluctuated between $53 and $85 per month during the busiest times of the year all the way down to nothing for four months in the middle of the year when work was slow. During this four-month break, nothing guaranteed that they could return to their jobs at the factory when seasonable business would tick up again. Jainath was told that he could resume his position only if he worked 12 hours a day, every day of the week. During this lull in their income, to cover living expenses the brothers borrowed over $120, mostly from a trusting landlord and a grocery store manager. They barely managed to get by until Somnath spent $4 to bribe his way back into his old position, only to lose it three months later. This example illustrates that not even a formal job guarantees job security or a steady income, particularly where seasonal variations in income are commonplace and labor laws are weakly enforced.

Box 2.1. In Your Backyard
Consumption Smoothing in Post-WWII Buffalo

Fergus was a college first-year student majoring in business and studying economics. His grandmother relayed this story of how informal finance worked to help her young family smooth consumption on days when funds were too tight, on the heels of the Great Depression.

One childhood memory that remains vivid is from the years shortly after World War II. My father [Fergus's great-grandfather] was employed by the U.S. Post Office and my parents had recently purchased a modest home in a suburb of Buffalo, N.Y. There wasn't much money, but our family lived much the same as our friends and neighbors. Occasionally, as payday grew near, we would be in need of bread for sandwiches, but there was literally not the ten cents left for the loaf. My mother kept a dollar bill in Hawaiian currency—a dala—given to her as a souvenir of her brother's service in the army. This was from before Hawaii was a state, and that bill from my uncle was a family treasure. Yet on those days we didn't have a dime in the house for bread, my mother would give me that dala *and I would walk down to the small family run food store where I'm sure everyone who walked in was a friend. In return for the Hawaiian dollar I left with the bread. In a day or two, after payday, my mother would redeem her treasured dollar from those kind people.*

Even this American family, homeowners with modest income and a steady job that put them among the then rapidly emerging middle class, used informal finance to deal with fluctuations in cash flows and fill the occasional hole.

Source: Marilyn Brady, personal communication.

Emergencies and Other Big Ticket Expenses

Beyond the need to pay for everyday small expenses like food and shelter, the poor also have to cover large **lump sum expenses**. As it turns out they do this surprisingly more often than we would think. But what do they spend those lump sums on? And how do they manage to do it with so little income?

Stuart Rutherford, founder of SafeSave, an MFI in Bangladesh, investigated for more than 30 years how the poor around the whole world use their money, and wrote several books about it. He identified three main categories of large lump sum spending needs: life-cycle events, emergencies, and investment opportunities.[8]

For example, weddings are a major **life-cycle event**, especially in some countries in South Asia (e.g. India), the Middle East or North Africa, where dowry systems make weddings especially costly. Other life-cycle events include funerals, religious celebrations, childbirth, education, and constructing a home (See the Dig Deeper Box 2.2 for examples on handling funeral costs). People also need to anticipate spending in old age when they might not be capable of working. Additionally, many of the poor have a desire to leave their heirs with inheritances, big lump sums near or after the end of life that require a lifetime of saving.

Box 2.2. Dig Deeper
Expenses and Funding Sources for a Funeral in South Africa

Table 2.3 illustrates just how complex it can be for the poor to pay for a life-cycle event, in this case a funeral and traditional *umkhululo*, a feast ceremony several months after a funeral. The total costs were in excess of two years of income for this South African family of five, who were living on $115 per month.

Table 2.3. Sources and uses of funds for a South African funeral

Sources of funds		Uses of funds	
		The funeral	
13 goats from relative	906	Slaughtered 10 goats for funeral	697
Cash contributions from relatives	279	Bought and slaughtered 1 cow for funeral	310
Cash payout from burial society	155	Food for funeral	449
Cash payout from funeral parlor burial fund	464	Coffin and funeral fees, provided by funeral parlor burial fund	465

(*Continued*)

Box 2.2. (*Continued*)

Sources of funds		Uses of funds	
Funeral parlor fund provision of coffin and funeral fees	465	Saved 3 goats for *umkhululo*	209
Savings club payouts	155	Save for *umkhululo*	279
Total	$2,424	Total	$2,409
		The *umkhululo*	
3 goats saved from funeral	209	Repaid store owner owed by deceased	108
Additional cash contributions from relatives	280	Slaughter cow (exchanged for 5 goats)	348
Saved money from relatives' funeral contributions	279	Bought 2 goats (for exchange for cow)	139
		Bought food for *umkhululo*	170
Total	$768	Total	$765

Note: US$ converted from South African rand at $ = 6.5 rand, market rate.

Because of the challenges to the poor of dealing with big expenses like this, specialized informal mechanisms have evolved for many purposes, such as burial societies or burial funds. A burial fund is a type of insurance that provides members of the fund with a fixed payout in the event of a death in the family. Each member of the fund pays a fixed sum in each period, insuring themselves against costly funerals. At the end of the year, if the total weekly payments exceed the total amount of payouts, the difference is redistributed to the fund members. In this family's case, such insurance paid nearly half the expenses. Generous family and a savings accumulation from an informal savings club made up the rest.

The burial fund is a simple way to plan for future events, but like any informal mechanism, there are downsides. If the number of deaths in a village is exceedingly high, then the fund could run into trouble. The problem can be reduced if there are a high number of members, but attracting a large number of members can be difficult.

Source: Collins et al (2009).

The second large lump sum category is emergencies, which may include illness, injury, theft, or the death of the household income provider. With small and irregular incomes, the poor are especially vulnerable to shocks such as these. Natural disasters such as fires and floods also fall under the emergency category. Finally, the poor must manage their money wisely in order to take advantage of potential investment opportunities. At any moment, an opportunity may arise to invest in an existing business, purchase land, or move a member of the family to an area where there is well-paid work.

To explore savings needs and behavior, a survey in India asked more than 63,000 households whether they saved and why. Nearly all did, and Figure 2.5 ranks their reasons.

In high-income countries, large sums of money for purposes like these can be easily moved and used with the swipe of a card or a click on a webpage. Incomes can be automatically deposited into an account and expenditures automatically deducted. Savings accounts and insurance policies are readily available as safety nets in the event of an emergency or other life-cycle events. These financial intermediary services allow for the consumption of food, clothing, and other needs when a family member dies, the home is damaged, or when there is a loss of employment. Similarly, the world's rich are able

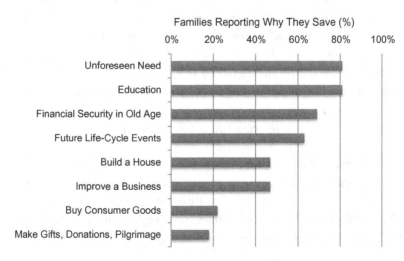

Figure 2.5.   Top reasons the poor save, India

Data source: Shukla (2010).

to invest and build assets in mutual funds and pensions, and to borrow to purchase homes and college educations, making it straightforward to invest in their futures.

As we have seen, the poor do these things too. While the poor do not typically enjoy the same ease of financial transactions as we do in rich countries, the fundamental principles of using financial tools for saving, borrowing, and insuring are the same.

Financial tools allow all of us to move our money around *across time*. In fact, savings, borrowing and insurance are all very similar conceptually, and largely differ only in the timing of cash flows. Stuart Rutherford shows us how similar these really are, with what he calls Saving Up, Saving Down, and Saving Through, which we explore in the next section.

Section in Bulletpoint

- Income streams for the poor are variable and uncertain.
- The poor need financial tools to smooth out consumption for daily needs.
- The poor also need ways to get larger lump sums for life-cycle events, emergencies, and opportunities.
- The poor use a variety of informal and non-monetary approaches to manage their financial needs.
- Financial intermediaries and financial tools provide flexibility for moving money around across time.

Discussion Questions

1. In developed nations, we keep most of our monetary assets in banks or financial investments like mutual funds. Hamid and Khadeja save their money using seven monetary methods. Where do they keep their money instead? What do you think are the reasons for the differences with how you keep yours?

2. Track your own cash flows in and out every day for one week (or better, one month) and try to note every formal and informal mechanism you use and for what purpose. Create a graph like Figure 2.4 that shows your own cash flows.

3. Have you ever used non-monetary forms of storing wealth, lending or borrowing? What were they? For what purpose?

4. Within the last week, did you do any consumption smoothing for small scale needs? How? Did you need to do it for larger-scale things within the last five years? How did that longer time frame make the tools you used differ?

5. Have you or your family used non-monetary forms of storing wealth? What were they? Compare those methods to methods used by the poor.

6. Contact the oldest living relative or friend you can, and ask them to tell you about any informal financial mechanisms they or their families may have used when they were young children, and how it worked. If you can, try the same question for someone from a developing country.

2.2 Informal Mechanisms of Savings, Lending, and Insurance

We have already discussed some reasons why the poor need to save and borrow. But without access to savings accounts or credit cards, how do the poor manage their money? The answer lies in the informal mechanisms of savings, lending, and insurance. **Informal financial mechanisms** are ways of handling incomes and expenditures in the absence of commercial banks or formal microfinance. Chapter 4 delves more deeply into informal finance, but we introduce a few main mechanisms here.

Informal mechanisms provide ways for the poor to manage their daily incomes and expenditures, but are limited in scope and lack the legal protections of formal, financial transactions. With a limited set of formal options, the poor are forced to use whatever means are available, despite whether or not it is appropriate for their financial needs. As we will see, informal mechanisms have their own challenges, and hence do not really solve the problem of limited access to financial services in developing countries. This leads to the global demand for microfinance.

Saving Up

In order to pay for expensive life-cycle events, emergencies, and investment opportunities, the poor must save their extra income, however small it may be. When you or they are **saving up** in typical bank savings accounts, you or they deposit a series of smaller sums over some period of time and can take a larger sum out at the end.

One example informal mechanism the poor use for saving up, but without a bank, is the **deposit collector**, illustrated in Figure 2.6. We'll explore informal mechanisms like *susu* collectors in Ghana in detail in Chapter 4. But briefly, under this scheme, villagers commit to a collector who comes regularly, maybe once a week, and collects small deposits and stores them safely. These deposits into the collector, in this instance say varying from $5 to $20 per week, are the smaller negative bars in Figure 2.6. After a certain number of deposits, perhaps 10 weeks totaling $100, the client collects the accumulated savings, the large positive bar on the figure, and can use the now large lump sum to make a purchase that would have been impossible with small payments.

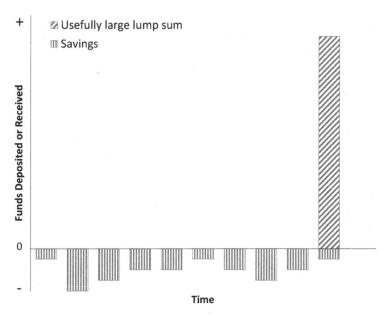

Figure 2.6. Saving up (i.e. savings)

The collector usually gets paid a fee, maybe $5 taken from the deposits, for offering the service. The client in this example would end up with $95 after 10 weeks. Although the fee paid creates, in effect, a negative interest rate for the saver, the poor are willing to save with the collector because they have few places to store their money safely. The poor are often unable to bank at commercial institutions, which can be long distances away and have high fees, unachievable minimum balances, intimidating paperwork, and other policies unfriendly to poor or illiterate clientele. Once villagers find a collector they can trust, they can be willing to pay high fees and are likely to start a new savings cycle as soon as the first cycle ends. Saving up is just one way in which the poor can transform their small amounts of discretionary income into a usefully large lump sum.

Saving Down

Another way to turn a series of small sums into large lump sums is **saving down**, as illustrated in Figure 2.7. You would probably call this pattern "borrowing" and then paying down the debt. So why call it a kind of "saving"?

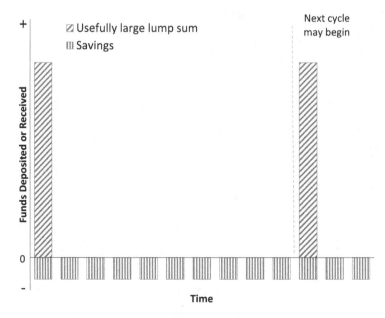

Figure 2.7. Saving down (i.e. borrowing)

Note that except for moving the diagonally-shaded positive bar in the savings up Figure 2.6 from the end of the cycle to the beginning, the cash flow pattern is basically similar. Only the timing of the lump sum is different. You can buy a costly cow or house by saving small sums up to get enough, or by borrowing a large sum and then repaying it in smaller increments over time. In other words, (ignoring interest) borrowing is just like savings where you get the lump sum at the beginning rather than the end. Figure 2.7 also shows the cycle starting again with a second loan taken after the first is paid down.

Informal saving down for the poor is exemplified in the model of the **moneylender**. We will meet a real moneylender, Satish Shetty, in Chapter 4. In short, the customer receives the large lump sum from the moneylender at the start of the agreement and agrees to a certain schedule of (deposit-like) repayments over a given period of time. An up-front fee is usually deducted from the disbursement. For example, a moneylender may loan $200 to a villager trying to start a business. Instead of loaning out the entire $200, the moneylender may only provide $180. The borrower will then pay back the full $200 in 10 $20 increments over time, with $20 being the fee for the service. The practice amounts to charging pre-paid interest on a $180 loan. If this example loan were paid back over 10 weeks, the effective annual interest rate (i.e. annual percentage rate, APR) would be more than 100%. If this were a loan paid daily (not uncommon in moneylending) for 10 days, the equivalent annualized interest rate is more than 700%!

Saving Through

A third essentially similar mechanism is **saving through**, seen in Figure 2.8. Once again, the only difference compared to either saving up or saving down is the timing of receiving the lump sum: this time in the middle. Insurance policies tend to have patterns like this. You pay a regular monthly or annual premium for your car insurance, say, and when you have an accident you get a large lump sum payout to help cover your loss. If you keep your policy after the wreck, the negative outflows for the premiums then continue.

Though car insurance is not very common among the poorest people, savings through is also the mechanism at work in something that is common among the poor all over the world, **Rotating Savings and Credit Associations (ROSCAs)**. We learn how they work in Chapter 4. But to

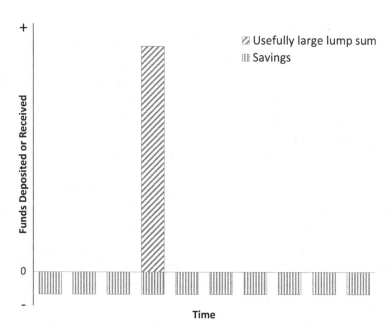

Figure 2.8. Saving through (i.e. insurance, or rotating credit & savings)

introduce them here suppose a group of, say, 10 members agrees to meet in a simple merry-go-round ROSCA for a certain number of periods. Every period, all 10 members of the group each make a contribution, say $15. Therefore, the "pot" will contain $150 every period. Members take turns taking the pot home. After 10 periods, the 10 members of the group have collected the pot once each and the ROSCA ends or a new cycle begins. The person who takes the pot home during the first period and then has to pay in the next nine periods, has a pattern like Figure 2.7; their payments are like saving down. Conversely, the last person to take home the pot will have saved up. Figure 2.8 would show one cycle of the ROSCA from the point of view of the fourth person in the cycle to take the pot. Over multiple completed cycles, the ROSCA works as a mechanism for all three, saving up, saving down, and saving through.[9]

In short, the process of saving through is very similar to the process of saving up or of saving down. If the cycle only happens once, the various timings of the payouts obviously make the three mechanisms different. However, if you imagine putting many of these charts end to end to end through many cycles of starting and repeating during a lifetime, the differences are difficult to find.

All three—saving up, saving down, and saving through—become processes that involve frequent, small contributions and an occasional large lump sum payout. Cash flows get combined or smoothed and moved around forward or backward in time to help people navigate variations in their financial situations. Financial intermediaries offering formal and informal forms of savings, borrowing and insurance help us all, including the poor, do this. Moreover, most of us need to mix all these simultaneously, as did Khadeja and Hamid who we met at the beginning of the chapter and Kevin, the college student we meet in Box 2.3.

Box 2.3. In Your Backyard
A U.S. University Student's Money Management

Kevin was a university junior, a math major with a minor in economics, when his professor asked each student in class to track expenses going out and money coming in, every day for a month. The professor also asked them to list the various financial tools they used to help manage their money and spending. Kevin's detailed chart (Figure 2.9) and list (Table 2.4) show that he used a wide array of both formal and informal financial tools. Moreover, he had very uneven cash flows, like most college students. As you see on Kevin's cash flow chart, money came in from his folks, a job and a rebate. But he also gave and got short-term loans from friends and received a small positive flow in when he forgot his wallet once and got the bagel anyway on credit from a friendly shop owner. He went and paid back a couple days later. Notice how financial intermediation allowed Kevin to move his money around in time, both backwards and forwards. Overall during the month he spent more than he brought in, using savings from earlier months and a credit card, postponing some payments. You may very well do similarly. Most of us in wealthy countries take such financial intermediation tools for granted.

(Continued)

Box 2.3. (*Continued*)

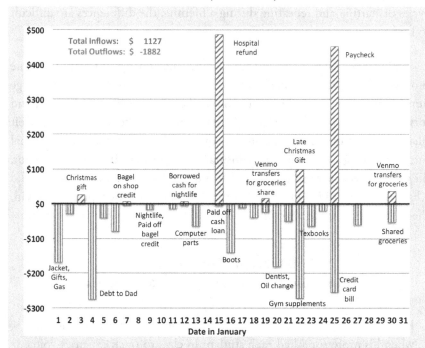

Figure 2.9. University student Kevin's daily cash flows for a month

Table 2.4. A university student, Kevin's list of financial tools he uses

Financial tool	Purpose
Cash stored in wallet	Enables cash transactions; a bit of wealth stored for short periods
Poker jar	Coins for playing poker with friends; transport & store some wealth
Credit cards	Transactions without cash (mainly to get cashback & points), for regular (gas, food, coffee) & special purchases (holiday gifts, textbooks, entertainment)
Checking account	Keeps savings & transacts safely & quickly over long distances & in large amounts (paying credit card bills)
Direct deposit	Summer paychecks went right into checking account

(*Continued*)

Table 2.4. (*Continued*)

Financial tool	Purpose
Lehigh Gold Plus card account	Works like debit card for purchases on campus & nearby shops; pre-paid so it also stores a small value as savings
Auto insurance	Protects against financial catastrophe in event of serious harm to car or liability for accident
Health insurance (parents)	Assured access to healthcare at the affordable cost of a co-pay
PayPal account	Receives money from strangers who purchased items I put up for auction & sale online (low, low prices!)
Student loans	Invest in my own human capital in hopes of a better career after graduation (Federal student loans)
Home equity line of credit (parents)	Partially pays for tuition & other costs of attending Lehigh (lower rates than other options)
Savings account (parents)	Prepares for emergencies and partially pays for costs of attending Lehigh
Mutual fund (529 accounts, parents)	Invests in stock market to partially pay for costs of attending Lehigh
Venmo account	Sends & receives money on cellphone from friends, to pay bets & share bills
Short-term personal loans	Things like: needed cash for nightlife over break (owed Dad); lend or borrow a few bucks from friends for transactions we're short for
Short-term in-kind loans	Roommates share the fridge & kitchen & we raid each other's stocks
Used textbooks & my electric bass	Currently storing (vast!) wealth; hope to sell to get some cash
Credit from merchants	Cellphone company bills me only after I actually use data over the limit; owed bagel shop when I forgot wallet but they still served me
Social obligations	Helped friend with homework, owes me dinner; I owe family help whenever needed, usually labor (like shoveling after blizzard last year)

The Demand for Microfinance

When needs discussed earlier for financial intermediation are not well met with low cost, convenient, secure options, the demand for microfinancial services arises. For instance, while ROSCAs are generally secure and provide a simple way to turn small savings into a lump sum, they provide less room for financial growth and long-term savings. And although it rarely happens, there is always a possibility that a member of the group may decide to run with the money without making their periodic contributions. Also, you may be out of luck if you need money but it is not your turn to receive the pot. But ROSCAs are only one form of informal financial management.

Similarly, informal deposit collectors are usually secure and convenient for the saver. The downsides to the agreement are negative returns for the saver, the risk of losing the savings with an unregulated collector, and liquidity problems. Recall that the saver receives a lump sum after making deposits for a certain number of periods. If the contract between the collector and the saver is strict, then the saver will be unable to use any of their savings during the term of the agreement. Moneylenders are also generally very convenient and can offer loan terms highly tailored to the needs of each client. However, as we will see in Chapter 4, they tend to be remarkably expensive, often charging annual interest rates in the hundreds or thousands of percent.

Therefore, among the world's poor there is a large demand for formal financial services, to which the phenomenal growth of many MFIs such as Equity Bank in Kenya (see the In the Field Box 2.4) over the past decades is testimony.

Box 2.4. In the Field
Equity Bank—Filling Unmet Financial Needs

Equity Bank today (Table 2.5) is a full-service, leading African bank that has grown exponentially year after year for more than 20 years. Equity Bank provides millions of clients throughout East Africa with savings accounts, money transfers, ATMs, agricultural loans, emergency loans, business development loans, and a variety of other services. The roots

(Continued)

Box 2.4. (*Continued*)

of that growth and success are firmly in microfinance. An insolvent firm about to go out of business, in 1994 the bank started innovating in microfinance, focusing on the unmet needs of low-income Kenyans for convenient and low cost small savings accounts.

Table 2.5. Equity Bank

Began microfinance operations	1994
Locations	Kenya; expanding in East Africa
Clients	7.4 million savings accounts; 0.7 million microloan borrowers (Dec. 2013)
Women as % of borrowers	29.4%
Self-sufficiency ratio	183%
Legal status	Commercial bank, stock traded

Equity Bank took a strictly market-led approach and is not supported by subsidies. As savings from its own clients grew, those same deposits allowed Equity Bank to provide more microloans. The bank also was innovative in using technology to manage large numbers of small accounts efficiently.

From humble beginnings designing financial services tailored for the previously unbanked poor, Equity Bank now provides nearly half of all bank accounts in Kenya and is rapidly expanding in nearby countries. It has become one of the world's largest microfinance institutions. Equity Bank and other large-scale MFIs have shown not only that microfinance can be profitable on the commercial level—Equity Bank's return on equity is nearly 30%, compared to the typical 10–15% for U.S. banks—but also that there are many millions of poor people who will utilize microfinance services where they are readily available.

Sources: Mixmarket.org; and Equity Bank Kenya: Our History, www.equitybank.co.ke/about/our-history.

Despite the impressive potential that microfinance presents, most of the world's poor still have little to no access. A conservative estimate is that about half the world's population still lacks access to formal financial services.[10] This is particularly true among the poor. As we saw in Chapter 1 (Figure 1.2), more than three out of every four of the poorest people in developing economies lack any sort of formal account at any financial institution. The numbers do not lie—there is significant room for the development of financial services in developing countries. Indeed, the steady decline in extreme poverty, which we discuss in the next section, is moving hundreds of millions of people into income ranges of thousands of dollars yearly, where financial services might be especially helpful in accelerating their rise out of poverty.

Section in Bulletpoint

- Although they have small incomes, the poor have the ability and need to save.
- The poor manage their incomes by saving up, saving down, and saving through.
- Informal mechanisms are helpful, but lack legal protections and have other challenges, so there is still a large demand for formal microfinance.

Discussion Questions

1. Saving up, saving down, and saving through can be used to model most financial services. For each of the three models, name at least one financial service you use that might be modeled that way, and briefly explain how it fits the model. Also name a system the poor use that matches each model.

2. This section briefly explains a few types of informal financial services used by the poor. Do you see any pattern (e.g. in costs or risks) in why the poor suffer from some drawbacks of those informal mechanisms? In what ways do traditional financial services improve on those drawbacks?

3. ROSCAs differ in which type of saving mechanism (up, down, or through) they create for different members, depending on where the member's turn comes in the cycle of receiving lump sum pots. Explain when each type of savings occurs in the cycle. Explain briefly what you think are the advantages and disadvantages of each type of savings and spot in the cycle, and why.

4. Why do most microfinance institutions charge interest rates on microloans? Why might those interest rates be relatively high?

5. Discuss how financial needs change over various stages of an individual's lifetime in a developed country. At what periods of life and for what purposes might the individual need to save up? Through? Down?

6. What unmet financial need do you have that an innovative financial tool might help solve? Briefly describe the problem and possible solutions (consider an app, new bank service, new kind of money, or whatever).

2.3 Patterns of Global Poverty

Where and How Poor Are the Poor?

Now that we understand some of the financial challenges for the poor at the individual level, we widen our lens to look at the broader patterns of global poverty. Most people have heard the term poverty before, and are familiar with its basic meaning. Poverty is having little to no money, assets, or material goods, and lacking basic necessities. However, this can mean different things to people in different countries, and sure enough, poverty exists in even the richest countries in the world. **Relative poverty** refers to income levels within a country being below a certain threshold in which it is difficult to maintain the standards of living enjoyed in that society. Those living in poverty in the United States, for example, may have significantly higher incomes than someone living in poverty in Nepal, but this does not mean they do not experience poverty relative to the living standards of most Americans. We will look at some relative measures later.

Absolute poverty, or destitution, on the other hand, is the condition of lacking access to the most basic human necessities, such as food, water, clothing, and shelter. But how poor is that? How do we measure it? **Poverty lines** are calculated for almost all countries, either by the country's government, or by an institution such as the World Bank. The World Bank sets relative poverty lines by taking a percentage of the average income of a country, and an absolute one by considering a group of food and non-food necessary consumption items, taking into account the cost of local foods and caloric needs.[11] Absolute poverty lines are set globally at two levels, one at $3.10 a day or less, and a second much lower at $1.90 a day or less for "extreme poverty." The World Bank estimates that there are more than 2 billion people worldwide living on $3.10 or less, of which about 750 million—more than one in 10 people on Earth—are living on $1.90 a day or less.[12] Clearly, poverty is a widespread problem.

The good news, thankfully, is that poverty has been decreasing remarkably and steadily for many decades. As Figure 2.10 shows, from 1981 to 2013, the proportion of people living on $1.90 a day or less (adjusted for inflation) declined more than 1 percentage point a year from close to half (!) the world's population to now below 11%. Amazing progress.

Figure 2.10. World's steadily declining poverty rate

Data Source: World Bank, PovcalNet database. http://iresearch.worldbank.org/PovcalNet/index.htm?1.

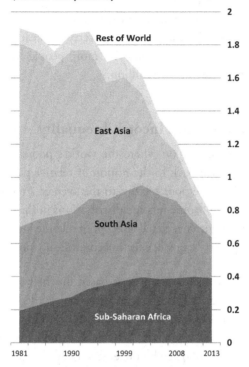

Population living on $1.90 or less (billions)

Rest of World

East Asia

South Asia

Sub-Saharan Africa

2
1.8
1.6
1.4
1.2
1
0.8
0.6
0.4
0.2
0

1981   1990   1999   2008 2013

Figure 2.11. Numbers of people in extreme poverty, by region

Data Source: World Bank, PovcalNet database. http://iresearch.worldbank.org/PovcalNet/index.htm?1.

However, that improvement, and poverty more generally, is not spread evenly throughout the world. As we see in Figure 2.11, poverty has historically been concentrated in South and East Asia as well as in Africa, and it can vary widely even between countries within a region. The decline within East Asia has been particularly extraordinary. Economic growth in China has contributed substantially to this decrease. In 1981, 84% of the Chinese population was living at or below the $1.90 poverty line. By 2002 that had fallen to 28%. Today, that number is around 6%.[13]

South Asia's poverty decline accelerated a couple decades after China's, driven largely by economic growth in India and Pakistan. The South Asian poverty rate has fallen to about one in four people, from three in five in 1981. Even so, large populations there mean that 400 million are still living in extreme poverty in South Asia.

Sub-Saharan Africa lies in stark contrast. The overall fraction of people in poverty there did decline slightly, from 53% in 1981 to about 43% by 2012. However, the population has grown faster, meaning that the actual number of Sub-Saharan Africans living in poverty has nearly doubled. Indeed for the first time, Sub-Saharan Africa has more people living below $1.90 than any other region, nearly 400 million.

Wealth Distribution and Income Inequality

Now that we have a handle on where the world's poorest live, in terms of absolute poverty, we turn back to the notion of relative poverty. The poorest individuals in the U.S. are poor relative to the average American, but would rank at the upper ends of some income distributions in the developing world. This highlights the important related concept of income inequalities—the fact that high levels of poverty can still exist in economically prosperous countries.

The World Bank classifies countries based on their average income per person. Just to get an idea of the range, the lowest recorded income per capita in 2016 was $618 for the Central African Republic, followed by $709 for the Democratic Republic of Congo, and $818 in Burundi. The highest recorded was $127,523 in Qatar, followed by Luxembourg at $105,882.[14] These values are adjusted to reflect how much they can buy in each country, referred to as purchasing power parity, and converted to dollars ($PPP), so you can think of the values in terms of what it would be like living in the U.S. on that amount of income.

Income is important for many things, of course, such as improving living standards like nutritious food, clean water, housing, and paying for education and healthcare. Because health is so dependent on many of the other standards of living, it is among the main measures besides income looked at to assess levels of poverty. Figure 2.12 shows each country as a dot sized relative to population and how those countries measure on income (horizontal axis) and health (vertical axis). As we see, health standards as measured by how long people tend to live is directly related to average income levels. Rich countries like the U.S., Japan, and most of Europe are clustered up in the top right: healthy and wealthy. The poorest countries—most of which are in Africa—tend also to be sickest, with the shortest average lives, clustering towards the bottom left on the graph.

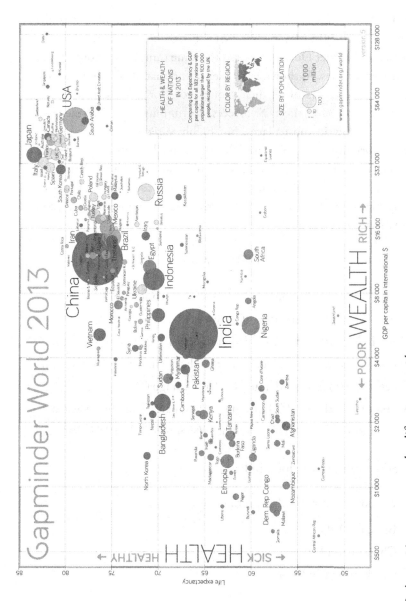

Figure 2.12. Average income compared to life expectancy, by country

Source: Based on a free chart from www.gapminder.org. Used under Creative Commons Attribution License.

Box 2.5. Dig Deeper
What's It Like to Live on $1.90 a Day?

It is difficult for most of us in rich countries to imagine what it is like to live on a $1.90 a day or less. MIT Economics Professors Abhijit Banerjee and Esther Duflo wondered the same thing and set out to find out in 13 countries. As shown here, they found that in poor households, half to three-quarters of all their money goes for food (compare that to the average 6% in the U.S.). Access to running water, latrines and electricity is low in most places, but highly variable across countries. Infant mortality is problematic. More detailed assessment in rural Udaipur in northern India found that while most poor households had beds, few had tables, chairs or bicycles, and almost none had fans or sewing machines. Illness and malnutrition were commonplace. Access to financial tools was not.

Among those living on $1.90 a day or less:

• Typical living arrangements: 6–12 people per household
• Food as % of total expenses: 56–78%
• Households with radio: 11% Udaipur; 30% Pakistan; >70% Peru
• Access to tap water: 0% Udaipur; <5% East Timor; 36% Guatemala
• Access to latrine: 0% Udaipur; 100% Nicaragua
• Access to electricity: 1% Tanzania; 30% Guatemala; 99% Mexico
• Infant mortality rate: 3% Indonesia; 9% South Africa; 17% Pakistan

Specifically, in Udaipur, India:

• Rate of ownership of other productive assets,
   o Bicycle: <14%
   o Chair or stool: 10%
   o Clock or watch: 50%

(*Continued*)

Box 2.5. (*Continued*)

o Table: 5%

o Cot or bed: ~100%

o Electric fan: <1%

o Sewing machine: <1%

• Adults go for an entire day w/out meal at some point in year: 37%

• Underweight adults: 40% females; 65% males

• Anemic adults (insufficient red blood cells): 55%

• Bedridden or doctor visit due to illness within last month: 46%

• Difficulty carrying out at least one "activities of daily living": 43%

• Have formal savings account: 6%

Source: Banerjee and Duflo (2007).

That said, per capita measures provide only an average income in a country and do not reflect how that income is distributed. Income varies substantially within countries. In the U.S., for example, average income in 2013 was $53,042 per person per year, yet tens of millions of Americans lived below the U.S. poverty lines of $11,490 for individuals or $23,550 for families of four.

Brazil had a gross domestic product (GDP) per capita of $15,038 ($PPP) in 2013, which puts it among what the World Bank calls upper middle-income countries. (You can find Brazil up near the huge dot that is China in Figure 2.12.) But Brazil also has notable income disparities. In fact, the poorest 20% of Brazilians get only 3.4% of the country's income, and 7.4 million Brazilians are living on $1.90 a day or less.[15] Meanwhile, the richest one-fifth account for three-fifths of Brazil's income. In fact, as we see in Figure 2.13, those richest 20% of Brazilians have average incomes slightly above the average middle-class American.

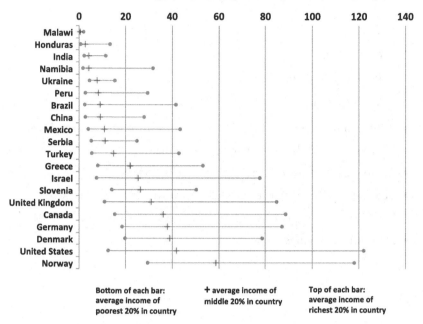

Figure 2.13. Income disparities in select countries, 2012

Source: Authors' calculations from data from World Bank, World Development Indicators, http://data.worldbank.org/indicator.

Figure 2.13 shows the differences in the income disparities between the richest 20% and poorest 20% in different countries. Malawi as we have said is among the poorest nations on Earth, and even the richest there have very little. Honduras is the poorest nation in Central America, but has a much wider income spread than Malawi between the poorest fifth and richest. Namibia, like Brazil, is particularly striking for its wide income gap. The poorest quintile there are worse off than average Hondurans, but the top 20% in Namibia live as well as the average Briton in the United Kingdom, one of the world's wealthier nations. The income spread in the United States is also very wide. The richest 60 million Americans live on nearly 10 times the average income each compared to the poorest 60 million. Nevertheless, poverty can be relative: that poorest fifth of Americans have average incomes similar to the richest 20% in India. Norway is richer yet on average, but has a significantly narrower income spread. The poorest quintile there live nearly as well as the average Briton too.

Section in Bulletpoint

- Poverty is not only a lack of money and material wealth, but also the lack of access to basic human necessities.
- The greatest reduction in poverty over the past few decades has occurred in East Asia, mainly China.
- Poverty worldwide has declined steadily for many decades.
- However, hundreds of millions remain living below the extreme poverty threshold of $1.90 income per day.
- Average income figures do not fully reflect the depth of poverty; income inequalities also matter.
- Poverty is not just measured in terms of income. Other indicators of poverty pertain to health, education, and nutrition.

Discussion Questions

1. Besides income, what other things would you want to look at to assess if a family is poor?

2. What is the difference between absolute poverty and relative poverty? Explain briefly: which would a philanthropist be most interested in reducing and why?

3. What might be some factors outside the control of an individual or a community that could affect poverty levels?

4. The poorest 20% of the U.S. have average incomes slightly higher than the richest 20% in India (Figure 2.13), yet why might we still think of those two group's experiences of poverty as very different? Who is better off?

5. Figure 2.12 is a snapshot of health and wealth in various countries in 2013. What did it look like in 1973? Or 1913? Use www.gapminder.org/world to map the trends over time. (The moving time-lapse charting feature is particularly illuminating.)

6. Trends in global poverty and health have been stunning over the past 30 years. Dig into those trends more yourself: on the internet, find three

different graphs or tables that illustrate some trends or comparative statistics you find insightful and did not know before. For each, write a brief (~200 words) blog you could publish summarizing and explaining.

Chapter Summary

There is a cyclical pattern to poverty. Without money, you cannot access education, and without an education you cannot get a high-paying, secure job, and without such a job, you cannot make much money. At the same time, without nutritious food or clean water, you cannot maintain good health and will fall ill, but without money you cannot access healthcare, and when you are ill you cannot work to make money. Similarly, without enough money to make business investments, you will have to make do continuing to earn a low wage, but if you continue at that low wage, you will never be able to make business investments that can improve your income and your financial stability and security.

It is these investments in health, education, and finances that the poor lack access to, and in part is what keeps them from pulling themselves out of poverty. The poor are generally incredibly hard working, but without access to financial mechanisms for saving, insuring, borrowing and investing, they have only little to show for their hard work. What microfinance provides more than anything else is simply access to services that enable and empower the poor by giving them financial flexibility for managing and growing their incomes and securing assets. The rest of this book will investigate the way microfinance works and how (and in fact whether) it serves the poor.

Key Terms

absolute poverty
An absolute level of income and consumption below which people cannot consume enough for minimum standards of well-being and health.

consumption smoothing
The process of spending less and saving during some periods to cover spending needs during other periods, facilitating more balance over time.

deposit collector
An individual or service that regularly, maybe daily, weekly or monthly, collects small deposits and stores them safely, allowing savings to accumulate into usefully larger sums; often charges fees.

financial intermediation
The process of facilitating money or asset flow between those with differing needs and goals; for example, enabling savers' deposits to be used for loans to borrowers or for payouts to the insured. Individuals or firms acting as financial intermediaries (e.g. moneylenders, banks, insurance companies, ATMs) often charge fees for such services.

informal financial mechanisms
Ways of facilitating monetary transactions (like sending funds, savings, lending and insurance) that do not involve banks or other legally regulated or legally protected systems; participants usually lack legal recourse if transactions go awry.

life-cycle event
A major milestone during the course of a lifetime that can entail a large lump sum expense, e.g. weddings, funerals, religious celebrations, childbirth, education, and constructing a home.

lump sum expense
A single, usually relatively large, payment; generally requires a means for turning a series of smaller accumulations into a useful larger sum.

moneylender
An individual or service that loans funds, often through private transactions outside the formal regulated financial sector. Loan terms and fees can be highly specialized and tailored to individual needs; sometimes but not always relatively costly.

poverty lines
The estimated minimun levels of annual income needed to meet basic needs for food, shelter and clothing; vary by country.

relative poverty
Poverty levels defined based on comparison to the overall levels of income and consumption in a country or region, and below which one cannot achieve the living standards of that society.

rotating savings and credit associations (ROSCAs)
Groups of individuals that each agree to make frequent, small contributions that collectively create a series of pooled funds, allowing each member in turn to receive one or more periodic usefully large lump sum payouts.

saving up, saving down, saving through
Alternative ways of turning a series of smaller pay-ins of money into a single larger lump sum, differing largely in the timing of acquiring the lump sum. Saving up first accumulates smaller sums over time, allowing a larger lump sum payout at the end; saving down pays the lump sum at the start (e.g. a loan); saving through pays the lump sum it in the middle.

Notes:

[1] Collins et al (2009).
[2] Collins et al (2009) pp. 7–8.
[3] Collins et al (2009) p. 10.
[4] Armendariz and Morduch (2010).
[5] Roodman (2012).
[6] Collins et al (2009) pp. 30–31.
[7] Collins et al (2009) pp. 43–44.
[8] Rutherford (2000).
[9] Rutherford (2000).
[10] Demirgüç-Kunt, and Klapper (2012).
[11] World Bank. Choosing and Estimating a Poverty Line. http://web.worldbank.org/WBSITE/EXTERNAL/ TOPICS/EXTPOVERTY/EXTPA/0,,contentMDK:20242879~menuPK:435055~pagePK:148956~ piPK:216618~theSitePK:430367,00.html
[12] World Bank. Poverty and Equity Data. http://povertydata.worldbank.org/poverty/home/
[13] World Bank. PovcalNet database. http://iresearch.worldbank.org/PovcalNet/index.htm?1
[14] World Bank. Data: GDP per Capita. http://data.worldbank.org/indicator/NY.GDP.PCAP.PP.CD
[15] http://povertydata.worldbank.org/poverty/country/BRA

Chapter

BARRIERS TO FINANCIAL SERVICES FOR THE POOR

"The financial lives of the poor are very complicated.... countless stories of people who had to forgo medical care or take their children out of school for want of a few dollars. The reason poor people face these agonizing choices is not just that they don't have enough assets. They also don't have access to a bank to help them use their assets effectively. If their savings are in the form of jewelry or livestock, for example, they can't very well chip off tiny pieces to cover routine daily expenses."

— **Bill & Melinda Gates**

Figure 3.1. Traditional banks have struggled to provide financial services to poor clients, some of whom live in places like along this winding dirt road in the remote Altiplano highlands of Peru

Half the world is unbanked. The unbanked do not use any type of formal financial service at all. Why? What has kept the poor from opening formal bank accounts to save for retirement, from getting health insurance or loans to build new businesses? The assumption used to be that the poor lacked the resources and needs. In Chapter 2, though, we saw that the poor can and do use a wide array of financial services, but largely rely on informal means. If hundreds of millions of people want these services, why do not banks and insurance companies offer them? Why does nearly everyone in Finland, Singapore and Australia have bank accounts, but more than 95% of people in Turkmenistan, Niger and Cambodia do not?

In this chapter, we will dig into barriers to providing financial services to the poor, and then in later chapters look into how innovative organizations are beginning to overcome some of those barriers. We start here with a brief background on the extent of access—or lack thereof—to financial services among lower-income people. We then turn to key challenges, some very real and others only perceived, both on the supply side from banks and other formal providers, and on the demand side from the poor themselves.

Our new understanding is not that the poor do not need the services, but rather that the business approaches aimed at wealthier customers in richer societies do not match up well with the behaviors of poorer clients and the realities of how and where they live. As Chapters 5–10 discuss, the microfinance sector has come a long way in addressing these challenges through innovation, yet much work remains.

3.1 Patterns of Access to Financial Services

The world is awash in bank accounts—there are more savings accounts in the world than people. Yet they are unevenly distributed. Half the world's adults are left out of banking entirely.

Which half? Figure 3.2 shows where those without any formal financial accounts live. High populations in Asia account for more than half the unbanked. However as Figure 3.3 shows, access rates as a share of population are actually better in Asia than in Latin America, Arab States or, particularly, in Africa. In Sub-Saharan Africa four in five adults lack any form of formal finance. In high-income countries, very few people go without.

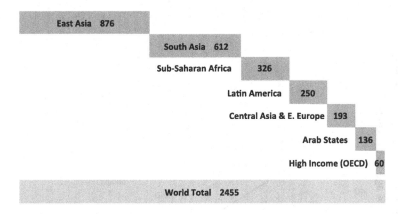

Adults Who Do Not Use Financial Services (Millions)

East Asia 876

South Asia 612

Sub-Saharan Africa 326

Latin America 250

Central Asia & E. Europe 193

Arab States 136

High Income (OECD) 60

World Total 2455

Figure 3.2. Populations lacking access to formal finance, by region

Data source: Chala et al (2009).

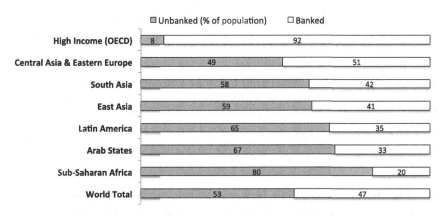

■ Unbanked (% of population)   □ Banked

	Unbanked	Banked
High Income (OECD)	8	92
Central Asia & Eastern Europe	49	51
South Asia	58	42
East Asia	59	41
Latin America	65	35
Arab States	67	33
Sub-Saharan Africa	80	20
World Total	53	47

Figure 3.3. Financial services use, by region

Data source: Chala et al (2009).

The access pattern is clearly related to poverty levels, as we can see in Figure 3.4. Countries to the bottom right, where most of the populations live in poverty, tend to have low financial access. In the Democratic Republic of Congo, the world's poorest country, 95% live below $2/day and only a few percent use banks at all. Rich countries up near the top left have nearly universal use of formal finance. In Finland and Denmark essentially everyone uses banks and hardly anyone lives below $2/day. In the U.S. the access rate is 88%. In short, bank accounts and other financial services are concentrated in rich countries.

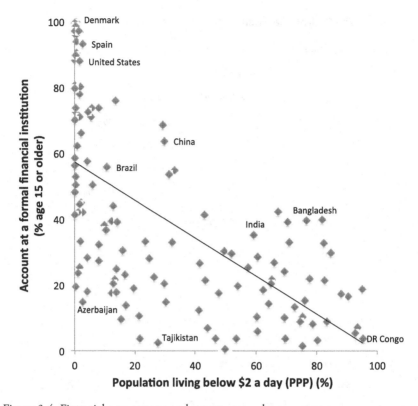

Figure 3.4. Financial account use and poverty rates, by country

Note: PPP, purchasing power parity, adjusts the value of local currency for local price levels.
Data Source: World Bank, Global Financial Inclusion Database.

The negative association between financial access and poverty, while strong, is by no means perfect. As Figure 3.4 shows, for example, China and Tajikistan have poverty rates similar to each other, yet the Chinese are 25 times more likely to use some sort of financial services than Tajikistanis, who rank among the very bottom handful of nations in terms of access.

Similar access patterns show up in the infrastructure that makes services convenient to use. As Table 3.1 shows, not only are adults in rich countries three to four times more likely to have bank savings accounts or loans, but also rich nations have 12 times the per capita availability of those checkout counter card terminals, and triple the ratio of ATMs and bank branches. That sort of connectivity is especially absent in remote rural villages throughout the developing world.

Table 3.1. Financial services gap between rich and low-income countries

Type of access	Developed countries	Developing countries
Number of bank savings accounts per adult	1.77	0.52
Number of bank loans to individuals per adult	0.82	0.22
Point of sale terminals per 100,000 adults	2,088	170
ATMs per 100,000 adults	78	23
Bank branches per 100,000 adults	24	8

Source: CGAP (2009a).

The gap is even more dismal for insurance. Less than 8% of the population in the poorest Latin America nations, 3% in Asia, and just 0.3% (not even 1 in 300 people!) in Africa had formal health, life, property or accidental disability insurance.[1] In 23 of the world's poorest countries, comprising a combined population of 370 million, there is no available microinsurance at all. Remarkably limited access indeed.

In the rest of this chapter, we explore why these gaps might exist. Some of the reasons are fairly obvious. Per potential customer, it costs too much to provide telecom networks and build bank branches in the remote reaches of the Amazon rainforest. Other hurdles are technical or regulatory, or have to do with psychology and how people behave. We will tackle those too. But as we will see, some barriers turn out to be based on what banks are learning are false assumptions.

Section in Bulletpoint

- Only half the adults in the world use any formal financial services.
- Access to financial services tends to be lowest in poor countries and for the poorest people within countries.
- Even among countries with similar levels of poverty, there is wide variability in access to financial services.
- The poor also have much lower access to convenient infrastructure like ATMs and point of sale terminals.

Discussion Questions

1. How accessible are basic banking services to you? Go to Google Maps (maps.google.com) and in the search bar type in something like "Banks near Hometown, Pennsylvania" using the name of your hometown and state or country. Count the banks and ATMs you could readily walk to, within one or two miles. Compare your hometown with other classmates'.

2. Search on Google Maps for "Banks Rwanda," which should return a map of the whole nation with dots for banks and ATMs. You may need to zoom in to see details. As you do, what do you notice about the geographic distribution of banks there?

3. People in the poorest countries tend to have the least access to financial services. Discuss whether and why microfinance institutions might or might not also have a hard time providing those people access.

Box 3.1. Dig Deeper
Do Global Investors Not Follow Basic Economics?

A basic economic concept is the law of diminishing marginal returns. You have probably experienced it yourself. Say you are hungry and head to the local pizza shop. After eating one slice your hunger decreases. Each subsequent slice quells your hunger a little less than the one before and may end up making you feel too full.

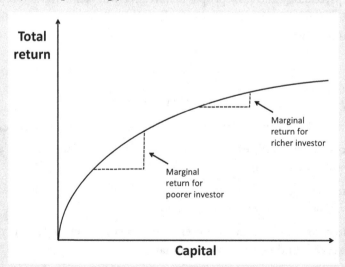

(*Continued*)

Box 3.1. (*Continued*)

What does this have to do with financial services for the poor? The same idea can apply to money. An additional dollar for people who already have plenty of money probably means less to them than an extra dollar for someone poor. What is one more dollar to Bill Gates? Move this idea to investments. You would try to invest first in opportunities with the best likely payoffs, while only accepting less attractive returns if you had additional funds to invest. In economic theory, as shown in the diagram, the early money (i.e. capital) to the left will make total returns to the investor rise faster than the investments over to the right. This rise-over-run slope is the marginal return to capital. It gets flatter as we move to the right—the marginal return per next dollar invested diminishes as you add more capital.

Here is the theoretic puzzle, then. Microfinance deals with the poor whereas normal banks loan money to richer investors. But the slope of that output vs. capital line is much steeper in the microfinance area towards the left. Testing this theory in the real world, economist Suresh de Mel from the University of Peradeniya and his colleagues at the World Bank and UC San Diego showed that poorer people in Sri Lanka indeed experience higher marginal returns per dollar invested in their businesses than people with more money. Anna Paulson of the Federal Reserve Bank of Chicago and the University of Chicago's Robert Townsend found the same in Thailand. Such evidence would suggest that investors around the world should jump at the opportunity to fund lower-income people because of the relatively higher potential returns.

It would seem odd, then, that banks instead direct funds to those who are less likely to get good payoffs, those with a lower marginal return. Yet the global empirical reality is that the rich, who already have lots of capital, get most financial services, not the poor. Why do funds not flow to those who might gain the most? Potential answers include a mismatch between needs and behaviors of the poor and of bankers, as well as transactions costs, risks, infrastructure problems, and government regulations that all can make the cost of doing business with these smaller clients higher, offsetting gains investors might receive from higher marginal returns.

Sources: Armendáriz and Morduch (2010); de Mel, McKenzie, and Woodruff (2008); Paulson and Townsend (2004).

3.2 Two Worlds: Formal Finance and Informal Markets

Financial service markets, like all markets, have demanders and suppliers. The poor, on the demand side, could use savings accounts or insurance or loans. Financial intermediaries, on the supply side, could charge fees for using ATMs or charge insurance premiums or interest on credit. Yet both the suppliers and customers must be willing and the costs attractive to both. Markets fail when for some reason one side or the other cannot or will not participate; preferences fail to align. Why then do financial markets for the poor fail? The short version is that there is a mismatch between, on the supply side, the business approaches used in the world of bankers and financiers and, on the demand side, the realities of the informal world of the poor. Let us dig more deeply.

Banking Business Models vs. the Informal Sector

Researchers at the World Bank asked people in poverty whey they do not use formal financial services. The two top replies? Not enough money, and too expensive.[2] Ask bankers and you would likely get the same answers: the poor do not have enough money and are too costly to serve profitably. They might add a third reason from the investment side: too risky. Three seemingly straightforward barriers for us to investigate: money, costs and risks. It turns out all three are real challenges, but proving less so than bankers might first have thought. We will explore all three in the following sections and address informational and regulatory barriers. But we will also see that some of the biggest barriers are behavioral. How the poor manage their funds day-to-day does not fit well with the financial products designed for traditional banking customers.

Dead Capital and the Informal Economy

Let us start with the money. The poor have more overall wealth than we might at first think, so there is a puzzle in why banks do not serve them well. In traditional financial businesses, big volumes of money flowing in and out can generate nice profits from small percentage service fees. In the U.S. alone, a trillion or so dollars per hour (!) flow through the banking system. Such high volumes, in turn, enable big investments in infrastructure, staff, new innovations, and so on.

Box 3.2. In Your Backyard
RiteCheck 12, South Bronx

Lisa Sevron and her students at the New School were studying alternative financial services used by low-income Americans. In class they discussed the check-cashing industry with Joe Coleman, president of RiteCheck. Professor Sevron asked him if she might work at RiteCheck as a teller, to better understand why so many people prefer alternatives to banks, despite high fees. She worked for four months at RiteCheck 12, a branch in Mott Haven, South Bronx. One of the poorest neighborhoods in the country, more than half the residents have no bank account. Excerpts of her experience:

Walk through any low-income neighborhood and it quickly becomes clear that check cashers and pawnbrokers are the norm, not the alternative. The financial lives of the poor and nearly poor don't operate according to the logic of mainstream institutions that serve the middle and upper classes. And RiteCheck 12's customers are certainly not naive or unable to sniff out a bad deal.… Most weigh the options and choose to use check cashers because they have found the other options unresponsive to their needs. Joe [Coleman] prefers the term "transactional" to describe his business. Transactions are what his tellers do all day (and night) long. From the RiteCheck window, I can see that our customers live close to the edge. People purchase one stamp, a $5, two-ride MetroCard. They cash their checks within a day or two of the date printed on the front.

Some reasons why many of our customers do not have bank accounts are obvious—they lack convenient branches or the hours don't fit well with their working lives. Others, like Carlos, have bank accounts but continue to use check cashers anyway. Carlos comes in frequently to cash checks of several hundred to a few thousand dollars for his small contracting business.… Why would Carlos pay nearly a hundred dollars to cash his check here…?… Today is Thursday, which means tomorrow is Friday; so Carlos probably has to pay his workers tomorrow.… If Carlos deposits his check in a bank, it will take a few days to clear—too late to deliver cash on payday.…

(*Continued*)

Box 3.2. (*Continued*)

Customers like Michelle come to RiteCheck to withdraw money from their Electronic Benefits Transfer (EBT) cards. The New York State Office of Temporary and Disability Assistance (OTDA) delivers cash and Supplemental Nutrition Assistance Program (SNAP) benefits on these cards…. RiteCheck charges a flat $2 fee for each transaction, and even though there are ATMs in the neighborhood where people can make two free withdrawals per month, Michelle asks me to take out $10 from her account. She will get $8 and pay what amounts to a 25% fee…. You can't take $8, or $27, out of the ATM. Most ATMs only let you withdraw amounts in multiples of $20, and these customers need every dollar they can access. They'd rather pay the $2 to get the $8 they can get their hands on than wait until their account builds up to $20. This is clearly logical, albeit expensive, behavior. It's expensive to be poor….

The banking industry and advocates for the poor argue that Joe and his colleagues across the country are taking advantage of low-income people, a criticism that implies that poor people don't know any better. But most of my customers know exactly what they are doing. Many have tried banks and rejected them. The fees are too high and they hit when customers don't expect them. They're not open when customers need them. They don't provide the services people want.

Source: Sevron (2013).

In corporate banking, the revenue, cost and risk management sides of the business are built around the needs and scale of transactions for customers like big business clients, pension funds, and the very wealthy. Fees are affordable as small percentages of large transactions but add up to a lot.

Another side of the industry, personal banking for everyday folks—like checking and savings accounts, credit cards, home mortgages, and small business loans—is less lucrative and involves smaller transactions with smaller fees than big corporate banking. But technology and economies of scale enable cost efficiencies in things as diverse as data management and hiring and customer call centers. The average checking account in the U.S. costs a bank about $350 per year to maintain.[3] But at a scale of more than 100 million U.S. households—nine out of 10—with checking and savings accounts, overdraft fees alone generated more than $30 billion and ATM fees generated $32 billion more. The average American household with credit card debt owes more than $5,700[4] on which banks charged average annual interest rates about 12% while simultaneously collecting billions in transaction fees from retailers.

In short, big banks are interested when there are trillions of dollars to manage. Microfinance so far, then, is as a whole roughly 10 times too small by these standards, with only hundreds of billions of dollars in assets, deposits and loans. With seemingly not enough scale, banks have been hesitant to enter markets for the poor. Harvard's Marguerite Robinson called this (in her view false) conventional wisdom the "penny economy view of the developing world."[5]

In reality, how much potential money is there among those billions of unbanked people? Too little despite vast numbers of poor? The short answer is there is plenty of wealth. The potential is huge. But—and this is a big BUT—the wealth is packaged differently.

One significant way financial markets for the poor differ is how the wealth is stored, in informal mechanisms that formal contracts and legal systems do not deal well with. The famous Peruvian economist Hernando de Soto estimated that in the 1990s the poor—when added up across the world—had about $10 trillion in assets trapped in what de Soto called **dead capital**.[6] That is a huge number that banks would ordinarily flock toward. It was at the time roughly the same as the total value of all the companies on the world's top 20 major stock markets (U.S., London, Tokyo, etc.) combined. It was roughly five times more than the total savings deposits in all U.S. banks added together. A $10 trillion asset base is plenty of wealth for banks to get excited about.

If the poor have so many assets, why have not banks tried to do business with them? Unfortunately for the poor, dead capital consists of assets, usually in informal sectors, that cannot be easily bought or sold or used as collateral, often because no documentation, legal paperwork or enforceable property rights exist to them. Housing built on land, for example, is often dead capital because legal systems have not assigned formal ownership to anyone—land just gets passed along in families or traded informally among villagers. Many of the world's large slums lack clear property rights. Millions of people have squatted in them, often for generations, building shacks and shops without any legally recognized ownership. De Soto estimated that "In Haiti untitled rural and urban real estate holdings are together worth some $5.2 billion. To put that in context, this sum is four times the total of all assets of all the legally operating companies in Haiti...and 158 times the value of all foreign direct investment in Haiti's recorded history...."[7] Without legal ownership documentation, mortgages cannot happen as done in rich societies to fund buying homes, paying school tuition, or opening new small businesses. In many poor areas, there are no street names or numbers, so the formal addresses needed to open savings accounts or get home insurance are missing.

Similarly, the informal businesses that the poor operate—market stalls, roadside stands, delivery services, and so forth—most often lack documentation and legal standing too, making financial contracts problematic for things like bringing in investment or arranging long-term supply. Activities in the so-called **informal economy** (sometimes called the shadow economy or gray markets) take place outside formally registered businesses subject to laws and taxes and legal contract enforcement. The world average is about 30% of economic activity in the informal economy. But as Figure 3.5 shows, in many developing economies more people actually work in the informal economy than in the formal sector, particularly women. In places like Bolivia and Peru, the informal economy is close to two-thirds of the whole. Hardly anyone there running a small market stall or roadside stand registers their business or reports income. Thus, the barriers are steep for enforcement of legal protections and contracts. Banks then avoid the informal sector, and do not serve it well. So, it is no coincidence that the microfinance industry has more women clients than men and has grown strongly where some of the highest informal employment rates occur, such in India, Indonesia, Peru, and Bolivia.

Why is there an informal sector to begin with? To get a flavor of why, think about your own economic activities. You may have participated in unregistered transactions yourself. Ever babysit or mow lawns for cash payments that neither side reported? Given the small sums involved even the most law abiding might think it is too much a hassle to record the wages, report them, and then pay and taxes on them. You also might not want to do the paperwork and pay fees to register for a business license and get business insurance. If for whatever reason you did not and you live in the U.S., then you were part of the estimated 8% of U.S. economic activity that is informal.

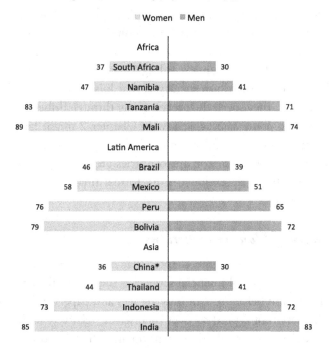

Informal employment as % of non-agricultural employment, by gender

Women   Men

Africa
- South Africa: 37 | 30
- Namibia: 47 | 41
- Tanzania: 83 | 71
- Mali: 89 | 74

Latin America
- Brazil: 46 | 39
- Mexico: 58 | 51
- Peru: 76 | 65
- Bolivia: 79 | 72

Asia
- China*: 36 | 30
- Thailand: 44 | 41
- Indonesia: 73 | 72
- India: 85 | 83

Figure 3.5. Informal employment shares in select nations

Note: * Six cities.
Data Source: International Labour Organization (2013).

Disincentives exist with big bureaucratic mazes to get things like business permits, file employment forms, or obtain health licenses. Similarly, where tax rates are very high, people are more likely to avoid paying taxes by not registering or reporting.

High levels of corruption and bribery are also directly correlated with high incidence of informal activities. High corruption can prevent a large portion of the poor from accessing formal financial and legal services if officials require pricey bribes to process required forms, and dole out favors only to connected elites. The alternative for the poor is the informal economy.

In many high corruption countries, obtaining a license to run a business with legal rights (and the accompanying access to commercial financial services) often requires large expenses and long waits. For example, the Peruvian economist mentioned earlier, Hernando de Soto, and his team tried to go through all the bureaucratic steps, standing in lines, filling out forms and paying fees needed in Lima, Peru to open a one-worker garment workshop, 100% letter-of-the-law properly registered. It took the team six hours per day for 289 days, plus $1,231, a sum exceeding 2½ years' pay at Peru's minimum wage.[8] The upshot of such bureaucracy is that business owners seldom put up with it. Instead, they speed the process along through bribery. This creates a problem for the poor, who as we saw in Chapter 2 might lack the funds even to feed their children regularly much less come up with two years' wages to cover bribes. The poor in corrupt countries are instead pushed into the informal sector, effectively excluded from formal finance, legal action, and government assistance.

The Primacy of Flow Transactions

We said at the beginning of the chapter that one of the main reasons the poor do not use traditional financial services is the lack of fit with their day-to-day activities and behavior. Not only are fees and paperwork problematic, but so is the design of typical services themselves: relatively high minimum amounts, required collateral, fixed repayment schedules over fairly long periods of several months or years, and so on.

Here it will help to introduce a bit more jargon to discuss the difference between **stock transactions** and **flow transactions**. When we think of a department store stocking its shelves, we are talking about the "stock" as a fairly large accumulation of goods all in one place at one time. To start a store, a storeowner would somehow need to finance purchasing that initial inventory. If the department store owner took out a loan for this purpose it would be so-called stock credit, a big chunk of credit for a one time big-ticket need. A machine shop owner might finance a costly piece of equipment, perhaps a new electric lathe, adding to the shop's stock of capital equipment. The mortgage for buying a house would also be stock credit, for housing stock. In all these examples, the stock credit finances occasional big-ticket expenses. As you might guess, collateral for a typical stock credit loan can often be the physical asset itself, e.g. the house, the cars, the machinery. Contract schedules over months or years make sense.

Contrast this to the needs of a woman in the informal economy selling fruit at her stall in a daily market. Each day or two she needs to replenish her fresh fruit supply buying from local farmers. The need recurs over and over. In Chapter 2 we met Pumza, a sheep-intestines vendor in South Africa. She had similar needs to keep acquiring a fresh daily supply of intestines, while also feeding her family whether or not her business generated enough profit in a particular week. Some weeks it did not, so she turned to short-term financial intermediation tools. These types of financial transactions are about the daily "flow" of money in and out of a household or business, not really about adding any sort of stock. Much of the everyday purchasing of gasoline and groceries by those of us who use ATMs or credit cards regularly would also fall into the flow transaction category. In short, flow transactions frequently recur.

Large swaths of the financial transactions of the poor living on the edge in the informal economy are flow rather than stock. Ensuring ongoing daily transactions is a high priority, as we have seen with Pumza and other poor families' stories in Chapter 2 as well as the RiteCheck story in this chapter. However, without the information and physical infrastructures available in wealthier nations, banks have a hard time offering services for flow transactions. Perishables like fresh fruit do not work well as potential collateral assets guaranteeing a multi-year loan that a typical bank might offer. Physical stock like housing or equipment as collateral only suffices if there is clear and legally documented ownership. And ATMs and credit cards only work where there are telecom networks to transfer data, lots of terminals, and reliable credit scores to evaluate potential cardholders.

Information Asymmetries and Agency Problems

Another central issue inhibiting financial services for the poor is called **asymmetric information**. Asymmetric information occurs when people on one side of a transaction have more or superior information relevant to the transaction than the other side. Without enough information, some market transactions can fail to occur that otherwise might be beneficial to both sides. For example, in poor regions people often do not have established banking or employment track records or bill payment histories—records readily available through credit score reports in rich countries. Loan applicants themselves would have far more information about their income streams, work situation, and potential history of paying bills than a bank could get. Lacking background on the borrower, a bank might hesitate to approve loans even if in reality the client would have been a perfect fit. In a similar vein, if driving records or health information are not available to insurance

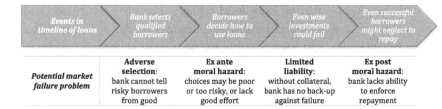

	Adverse selection:	Ex ante moral hazard:	Limited liability:	Ex post moral hazard:
Potential market failure problem	bank cannot tell risky borrowers from good	choices may be poor or too risky, or lack good effort	without collateral, bank has no back-up against failure	bank lacks ability to enforce repayment

Figure 3.6. Adverse selection, moral hazard and limited liability in a loan timeline

Source: Modified from Simtowe, Zeller, and Phiri (2006).

companies, individuals with big health problems and terrible drivers might flock to buy health and auto insurance, while healthy folks and careful drivers might not be able to get insured.

Asymmetric information problems arise in several flavors. As we explore various market failures, it will be useful to think about a basic timeline. The top of Figure 3.6 shows one for a loan. A similar framework applies to insurance and savings (though we leave diagramming those to you in the discussion questions). Banks who have funds to lend first need to select whether potential borrowers get loans. Then approved borrowers somehow use the funds, hope for some benefit or other, and are supposed to repay. We will look at the potential barriers at each of these phases.

By putting money at risk, the bank or insurance firm hopes to profit from fees and interest. They have to trust that a borrower invests wisely and can repay profitably, without really controlling what the borrower will actually do. Insurers have the same problem controlling their customers' behavior. Borrowers and the insured may behave differently than a bank or insurance company hoped, classic examples of what are known as **principal-agent problems**.

To help clarify this jargon, think of a sports agent who is supposed to negotiate deals for the benefit of a pro athlete. The agent acts on behalf of the principal owner of the valued athletic assets being put to work. Similarly, in credit or insurance markets the principal asset, the money, belongs to the lender or insurance firm. The lender or insurance firm is the "principal." Their customer is the "agent" who, by using the principal's funds, is essentially acting on behalf of the principal. In savings these roles are reversed: the bank is the agent acting with deposited funds that belong to the customer. As we will see, agency problems can occur in various phases of a financial relationship.

Adverse Selection

At left of Figure 3.6, the first agency problem is **adverse selection**. For loans, this problem arises prior issuing the loan. A potential borrower has some idea, perhaps for an investment in farm equipment, but lacks the funds. They propose how the loan will be used and how much they need. A key issue at this stage is assessing the riskiness of the borrower. Will they pay back? Analogously, insurance firms have to decide whether to insure someone. For savings accounts, the customer as principal has to decide whether a particular bank is a safe place to park deposits. We trust our savings bank will guard our deposited funds wisely. Yet, how might we know if some shady banker might steal our funds?

Let us focus for a moment on loans. To assess the riskiness of a borrower, a loan officer might consider several factors. Is there a high probability the borrower will make good choices in using the funds, use the funds as promised, work hard to make sure the investment succeeds, and make timely repayments? The officer also might assess the financial feasibility of any business ideas and the value of collateral offered as risk protection for the loan. The officer must also consider factors such as the state of the economy, the local context, the borrower's skills and financial discipline and family situation (spendthrift uncle needs the money for baubles?), and even gauge the possibility the borrower will just take the money and disappear.

The problem is that loan officers might not have enough information to assess all these complexities. In rich nations, credit agencies and well developed data reporting systems can help. However, such mechanisms are limited or nonexistent in developing regions. An institution can send a loan officer to rural villages in order to gather information; however, doing it independently can be a costly, particularly relative to potential returns from small-scale customers. Yet, without enough information it can be quite hard to assess a borrower's risk level. Which applicants should the bank approve? Are they high-quality borrowers or high-risk? Are they skilled entrepreneurs or naïve dreamers? Hard workers or slackers?

The loan officer needs to distinguish between risky and safe borrowers because another choice in issuing a loan is what interest rates to charge.

Low-risk loans generally have lower interest rates than loans with higher probabilities of failure. But if banks cannot tell the difference ahead of time, the same interest rate would apply to both. Interest rates might have to be set higher than actually needed for low-risk borrowers, potentially driving some of them away. The finance institution, not knowing how good a borrower can be, is in essence punishing safe borrowers with paying a higher interest rate in order to compensate for risky borrowers. If low-risk borrowers leave, the potential borrower pool drifts towards the riskier ones—adverse selection at work. The people who should be getting loans are priced out of the market. In short, without information on the quality of borrowers, due to adverse selection financial markets could fail to give loans to worthy borrowers. Indeed, if the extraordinarily high payback rate—better than mainstream loans—in the microfinance industry is any guide, the markets apparently missed hundreds of millions of potentially good borrowers for many years. Banks until recently severely underestimated the ability of the poor to repay.

A similar adverse selection challenge exists in insurance. If insurance firms cannot identify which drivers are reckless or safe, insurance prices would have to be set higher than needed to cover low-risk drivers, and some safe drivers might not buy insurance. The pool of those left buying insurance spirals ever riskier. Flipping the principal–agent roles the other way for savings markets, if savers cannot distinguish between risky and safe banks in which they might save, they might not be willing to pay as much, or avoid saving altogether. The resulting low fees and high interest rates banks would have to offer on savings accounts could drive the safest banks out of business.

Does the adverse selection problem mean that microfinance institutions must rely on luck in deciding which borrowers should be granted loans or given insurance? No, as we will see in Chapters 4 and 5, several mechanisms can mitigate adverse selection problems. For example, groups of people from one village might know a lot about each other. They could exclude risky individuals and obtain better rates. MFIs can also use various incentive structures such as progressive lending to encourage and reward good clients. Credit bureaus are effective too, like the one in Ghana discussed in Box 3.3.

Box 3.3. In the Field
Establishing Credit Bureaus in Ghana

Credit bureaus in the developed world collect and provide information about an individual's legal, credit and bill payment histories, providing services aimed at overcoming agency problems faced by financial institutions. Essentially every adult in rich nations is included in credit bureau databases. Banks and credit card companies regularly use these reports to evaluate potential clients. The services reduce independent costs associated with dealing with information asymmetries because standardized nationwide systems make the data available to any institution. Credit bureaus also benefit good clients because it allows them to build formal track records and establish themselves as safe customers. Good histories can make loans and insurance easier and cheaper to get.

Unfortunately, credit bureaus are hard to create in developing countries where it is difficult to keep track of the population and all their financial transactions. Individuals may have multiple banks or credit cards and pay bills to many companies. But nationwide data sharing systems are expensive and complicated to implement. Many financial organizations, especially small ones, in developing countries operate using basic spreadsheets or even paper ledgers. These rudimentary systems make sharing client data with other organizations cumbersome. Imagine trying from scratch to link all the widely different computer systems of all the banks and phone companies and shopping centers, and organize data on millions of individual transactions daily. Moreover, some developing countries have no systematic way to identify all their inhabitants—national identity cards or Social Security numbers—presenting another obstacle. In fact, Niger, Belize, Afghanistan and many other nations have no credit bureaus at all. As a result, large fractions of their populations cannot access formal financial services because banks hesitate to do business with people they do not have information about.

(Continued)

Box 3.3. (*Continued*)

There is progress, however. In 2007, for example, Ghana became the first nation in West Africa to introduce credit bureaus. The Credit Reporting Act 2007 created a set of standards allowing private companies to qualify as officially registered credit reference bureaus, collecting and disseminating consumer credit information nationwide under the supervision of the central Bank of Ghana. As one national official put it, the system was put in place to

> *ease credit referencing and also reduce information asymmetry, which has characterized the financial system.... The need for a credit reference bureau in the country arose from, among others things, the high loan default rate in the country which is crippling most banks and other financial institutions. It had been observed that some individuals were using the same collateral or documents to apply for loans in different banks and refusing to honor their obligation, leaving high non-performing loans, resulting in the collapse of some banks.*

By 2014, three private bureaus had been certified in Ghana and about 14% of adults and more than 200,000 small businesses were included in those databases. While coverage is not yet on par with the near 100% coverage in advanced credit bureaus, the Ghanaian government and central bank continue to urge all financial institutions to participate and share information on customers. They have particularly emphasized including the growing microfinance industry.

Sources: Daily Graphic, Ghana (2013) and World Bank Group (2014).

Moral Hazard

The next potential market failure issue featured on Figure 3.6 timeline occurs once borrowers begin to use funds. **Moral hazard** arises when financial institutions are dependent on, yet cannot directly control, how their customers actually act. It is difficult to keep track of whether the borrowers are acting in the best interests of the lender. Even if a person is a quality borrower, for example, extenuating circumstances may cause them to use the funds in ways other than originally promised. This is another type of agency problem. The borrower is the agent acting with the principal's money in ways inconsistent with the bank's intent—the "moral hazard."

Similar moral hazards exist for insurance companies, who can't directly control reckless driving by auto insurance customers, or unhealthy, risky habits from health insurance customers. Nor can savers control directly what a bank does with funds the saver deposits.

There are two types of moral hazard, ex ante and ex post, differing by when choices take place. Ex ante choices take place before the benefits from a project or investment are realized. For example, a borrower with a loan to buy a stand from which to sell crops could invest in the stand but not work hard enough to make it successful, losing the lender's investment. The borrower might achieve higher returns by working more, but choose not to—daily choices made before the end results of the crop stand investment emerge. Or, in an alternative form of the problem, the borrower could decide not to invest in the crop stand at all and instead choose a personal use not approved by the lender, such as home decorating. The idea is that once funds are given, it becomes costly to ensure they are used as approved. Similarly in insurance, a farmer protected by crop failure insurance might decide not to make much effort working the fields, preferring to let the crops fail and make claims against the insurance. On the savings side, an underhanded banker might take deposited funds and gamble on a long shot, risking a customer's life savings.

By contrast, ex post moral hazard (shown on the far right of Figure 3.6) refers to choices after benefits are realized. A borrower may have in fact used a loan well and realized high returns, but may not want the lender to know. Even if capable of repaying, it is possible the borrower would simply decide not to repay, or lie about whether they can, or move out of town where the lender can't find them. Similarly on the insurance side, insured farmers might hide successful harvests after the fact, but claim crop failure anyway. Some customers might fake injury to try to collect health insurance payouts. Sending adjustors to verify what actually happened is expensive, and insurance firms might conclude it is not worth it to offer the small microinsurance the poor might want. Reversing the principal–agent roles for savings, a banker who took your deposits and invested them for you in a successful venture might skip town with your proceeds.

Moral hazard can be more problematic in developing nations than in richer areas because of the difficulty in monitoring activities, keeping track of people, and enforcing contracts. Enforcement is harder where governments have less legal infrastructure, are less stable, and where people move around a lot. Indeed, ex post moral hazard is often also called "the enforcement problem."[9] The risk of ex post moral hazard is greater, for example, if it is straightforward to forge documents faking bankruptcy or accidents, or if large shares of the population migrate around regularly, making it easy to run off with someone else's money and disappear—when, say, swarms of migrant workers leave for extended periods during harvest, or in a mass migration amid political chaos.

Limited Liability

What can reduce risks of moral hazard? All these issues arise from information asymmetry; a company cannot know everything their customers know or do, and vice versa. Thus, getting more information from trusted third parties is one approach. To ensure safety for depositors, savings banks have to report reams of data regularly to oversight regulators on assets and use of deposits. Auto insurance providers usually require police reports of accidents and estimates from licensed insurance claims agents. Health insurers look to doctors' and hospital records. As we saw earlier, lenders might look to credit bureaus. Unfortunately, as we have also seen, such information sharing is far spotter in developing economies.

On the credit side, another approach exists too. For loans in rich countries a common answer is to require collateral. Being able to take something of value from the borrowers makes the borrowers liable for potential failures in how they use their loan. Liability creates incentives to use loans wisely and aligns the interests of the agent and the principal. However, the large informal sectors and high levels of dead capital mentioned earlier make collateral less applicable for dealing with poor clients in developing economies. Poor borrowers rarely own the land they live on and those assets they do have are likely to be in forms legally unsuitable as traditional collateral.

Lack of collateral or lack of an ability to assign clear property rights, together with lack of effective legal enforcement of contracts, leads to problems of **limited liability**. Without collateral or information on the borrower's actions, what guarantee does a bank have that it will be made whole if a borrower defaults on a loan obligation? The borrower does not have much to lose from bad behavior—their liability is limited—if there are no enforceable penalties for defaulting. Why not just take the funds and neglect to repay? Analogously with savings, without potential penalties, what is to keep a banker from running off with your deposits?

Moreover, even if loan collateral were possible for banks to require and take, it can be a moral issue particularly for MFIs because their borrowers are generally already poor. The MFIs are designed to help them. How would a loan offer feel having to go and repossess the only means of livelihood some poor family might have? Yet if word gets around a well-meaning MFI does not enforce collection on defaults, clients might suspect their liability is limited and treat loans more like charitable gifts. In fact, as recently as 2008 to 2010, politically fueled expectations of blanket loan forgiveness in countries as widely different as Nicaragua, India, and Morocco have proven severely counterproductive to the microfinance sectors in those countries as clients refused to pay back loans because they anticipated loan holidays. On the other hand, as we will discuss in Chapters 4 and 5, microfinance practices such as group meetings and progressive lending have proven effective ways to overcome the moral hazard, adverse selection and limited liability agency problems associated with asymmetric information.

Section in Bulletpoint

- The day-to-day financial behavior of the poor does not fit well with typical business practices of financial service providers.
- Much economic activity among the poor is in the informal economy, outside formally registered businesses subject to laws and taxes.
- The world's poor collectively have trillions of dollars' worth of assets, but not in forms legally useful for formal finance.
- Lack of good information or problems enforcing contracts can inhibit potential financial transactions because of moral hazard, limited liability and adverse selection.

Discussion Questions

1. Identify at least three of your own recent economic transactions in the informal economy, and briefly explain why you did not do them formally.

2. Can you think of ways government might try to improve possibilities for the poor to gain value from their dead capital? Search the internet for actual efforts along these lines, and briefly discuss pros and cons of several options.

3. Do you know anyone in a rich country whose majority of income comes from the informal economy? What are their reasons for being in the informal economy? How would you compare their reasons with those of the owner of an unregistered market stall in a poor country?

4. Figure 3.6 depicts a loan timeline and the agency problems at various event phases. Construct a similar event and agency problem timeline for insurance. Do one for savings too, remembering that the principal–agent roles are reversed.

5. Briefly discuss three choices you had made lately where your decision was subject to (a) moral hazard; (b) limited liability; and (c) adverse selection. What information might have helped overcome those, and what prevented you from getting that information?

6. Discuss the relationship between corruption and rates of poverty by comparing two online maps: Transparency International's corruption index by country (www.transparency.org/cpi2015/results) and World Bank's average income data (data.worldbank.org/indicator/NY.GDP. PCAP.PP.CD/countries?display=map).

3.3 Behavioral Barriers

So far we have dealt mostly with economic and informational barriers to financial services that institutions and the poor face. Other barriers, however, are social, cultural or psychological. We all behave in ways driven by the social norms and expectations of our communities, families and peers. No doubt you have had to deal with reconciling what your family wants with peer pressure, influencing your choices both positively and negatively. The poor and their financial behaviors are no different. Behavioral psychology also turns out to play an important role in how people make financial decisions. We human creatures are not always entirely rational.

Social and Cultural Norms

The role of family and friends is hard to overstate. In most cultures an individual's close friends and family are expected to help with needs and emergencies, spreading responsibilities across multiple households. Such expectations provide useful insurance-like diversification of risk. If your sister or best friend falls ill and cannot work, you chip in to help their kids eat or pay some overdue bills. We saw exactly this behavior with the financial diaries in Chapter 2. Extended family helped pay for a South African funeral; neighbors in Dhaka held savings as moneyguards for each other; a friendly Buffalo shopkeeper gave bread to a hungry family on credit for a "dala." Economists call interpersonal obligations like this **social taxation**.

However, social taxation can inhibit demand for more formal alternatives in poor communities. If family or neighbors will help handle emergencies or other needs, why put away money in a bank just in case? Aunt Beatrice and her stash of cash in her cookie jar can help us in a pinch, right? If we are struggling to cover expenses day to day, why pay for health insurance or save up in advance for groceries? In other words, social taxation can substitute for formal financial services and be hard for a bank to compete against in communities where cultural ties are deep.

Whether in cookie jars or elsewhere, cash is very liquid, i.e. quick and easy to use. Thus, cash is the most likely asset socially taxed. It is easier and more socially acceptable to ask a brother to borrow 50 bucks cash than to convince him to sell off his goat. For this reason, another tendency in the informal economy is to avoid storing too much wealth in cash or easily accessible savings accounts. If assets are too liquid, social taxation might be too easy. If every niece and nephew could come and expect handouts, Aunt Beatrice might not want to keep too much in that cookie jar or ATM-accessible savings account after all. With extra funds, she might instead prefer so-called semiliquid assets like a goat or jewelry or using a moneyguard. When she needs money, she can sell the goat or necklace, but her brother's kids would not be so tempted to drop by asking. Indeed, Kenya's Family Bank found ATM cards surprisingly unpopular among rural women who lacked household control, and hence were more subject to social taxation by husbands or other family members.[10]

Social traditions of using semiliquid assets instead can shrink demand for formal savings accounts. In one study, one of the main barriers to use of savings accounts among poor Latin American farmers was that they knew they could sell their livestock or pre-sell their crops for emergencies.[11] It was their second-choice mechanism for dealing with large financial needs. Help from family and friends—social taxation—topped the farmers' list. Use of actual formal savings accounts? Third place.

Other social barriers to formal finance stem from cultural traditions with respect to gender, race, religion, ethnicity, age and caste. For instance, financial regulations in India prohibit zero-interest consumer loans, at odds with Muslim Sharia prohibitions against paying interest on debt. In India too, business lending is often based on social ties within castes, and women from lower castes are far less likely to have bank accounts. We will explore gender-related issues in microfinance in greater detail in Chapter 7. But briefly, academic research has identified widespread evidence of various forms of discrimination that limit financial access. Even in rich countries, as you have no doubt heard, women on average earn less than men. Race creates similar wage gaps. All these sorts of discrimination reduce demand for financial services.

In research on financial access, lower-income individuals around the world also regularly report discriminatory experiences in banks—tellers ignoring or belittling them, managers requiring unattainable documentation or references, and so on. Hindol Sengupta, head of *Fortune* magazine in India, studied successful entrepreneurs from the lowest caste, the Dalits (aka untouchables). He reported that even though they were successful business owners, many avoided formal loans because as Dalits they feared discriminatory humiliation.[12] Since wealth and financial access tends to be concentrated among local elites, challenges of discrimination are exacerbated where corruption is high and political power is associated with kinship, race, and ethnic ties.

Psychological Tendencies

While discrimination and social taxation are conscious decisions, other barriers to financial behavior are more subconscious and psychological. Behavioral psychologists interested in economic choices have identified a number of psychological tendencies that reduce an individual's likelihood of using financial services.

Self-Control

We saw in Chapter 2 the irregular ups and downs in cash flows for the poor, which can make planning for longer-term savings or paying for insurance (i.e. saving through) difficult even under perfect circumstances. Putting money away requires some self-control, giving up consumption today to save for later. Unfortunately, psychologically many of us, rich and poor alike, tend to pay more attention to the near term than the long term. You have heard it: live for the moment, *carpe diem*! Why sacrifice now for the future? We have all probably acted like that, procrastinated, lost a bit of self-control, and perhaps occasionally regretted it in "shoulda" moments. It takes work, real mental effort, to plan ahead and to force yourself to avoid temptations and overcome impulsive urges.

We tend to make decisions that favor short-term outcomes because they feel more relevant right now, with what psychologists call a higher **momentary salience** of decisions. Things that might happen in some distant future tend have low salience, hence lower value. Economists call this reduction of values in the future "discounting." Excessive discounting can mean we assign far lower values to future needs and outcomes than we should in some fully rational sense. We are nearsighted in time.

For instance, in one famous experiment University of Oregon students were asked if they would prefer $15 right now or be willing to wait a year to get more, such as $30.[13] A year's patience would double their income. Some were patient, opting for waiting for $30, while others preferred immediate gratification and took the $15. Not yet irrational behavior, just different preferences for money a year later. It gets irrational when among those who were unwilling to wait, some switched preferences when the choice started at $15 four years from now vs. $30 at five. The 100% annual return was not worth waiting for this year, but would be in four years. Purely mathematical financial behavior should give us the same level of patience over one year in either timeline. Those students who switched choices demonstrated changes in the rate at which they discounted money over time, called **hyperbolic discounting**. It is psychologically easier to postpone consuming in the future than postponing now. The phenomenon is worldwide. In other studies, some Israeli students were hyperbolic discounters, as were some American 40-somethings, Vietnamese poor people, and poor Filipinos too.[14]

What does this have to do with barriers to financial services? If we have trouble with self-control, we may not save enough even when we know we should. A poor farmer who gets a big part of their yearly income all at once selling their crops after harvest knows they will need to save for feeding their family in winter, paying their kids' school fees due in a few months, or buying seeds to plant next spring. But those are far off in time, with low momentary salience. An impulsive farmer might spend too much now when all that cash is in their pocket, even when they know better.

If lots of people lose those internal mental conflicts with themselves— which research evidence suggests is true—then less demand exists than might otherwise for financial intermediation. One study done in collaboration with the Grameen-affiliated CARD Bank learned that despite many of CARD's microfinance clients wanting and intending to save, they had a hard time forcing themselves to actually meet their own goals.[15] The temptations to procrastinate savings and to overspend in cash-flush periods are real psychological phenomena that for the poor when combined with erratic income peaks and troughs creates an ever-repeating mental tug of war, in turn inhibiting use of formal finance.

Similarly, people aware of their own self-control problems might not want to save in an account either, even if they have funds available, if it were too easy to give in to temptation and take funds out to spend. Professors Nava Asraf, Dean Karlan and Wesley Yin, at Harvard, Yale and UCLA respectively, studied savings behavior in the Philippines and found that: poor women hesitated to open regular savings accounts if their funds were too easy to take back out.[16] Women who reported hyperbolic discounting were more likely to prefer an innovative, less-liquid, savings account version—designed specifically for the poor that explicitly limited their withdrawals. Interestingly, this preference suggests the women knew their own tendencies and that better, more poor-oriented, design of financial services might expand use. We will explore additional innovations along these lines in Chapter 6.

Mental Accounting

Like the Filipino women, most of us do try to find ways to impose some self-control on our own financial impulses. One key mechanism most of us use is to divide budgets into so-called mental accounts, regardless of whether we create actual separate bank accounts. We might think of day-to-day grocery money as one budget, reserving a second mental bin of funds for textbooks next fall term. Similarly, Hamid and Khadeja in Dhaka, the *Portfolios of the Poor* couple we met in Chapter 2, had several varieties of accounts they had tagged for different purposes. Another form of **mental accounting** is to categorize funds based on where they came from: regular income from work, a year-end bonus, inheritance from grandmother, and so on. To control ourselves, we treat each mental account differently—even though our money is in reality entirely fungible among them, i.e. can be spent for and from any category.

Similarly, over longer sweeps of time we might try to budget everyday living in one mental "current needs" budget and perhaps a second "stuff-of-value" category for less-liquid assets like a car, stamp-collection or livestock. Maybe we would think of the far off future needs like accumulating for retirement in a third "wealth" account. Liquidity differs between these in-and-out "flows" and stored-up "stocks" and importantly so does the mental ease with which we tend to spend them.

We have already seen that short-term cash flows are easier for people to spend than are less-liquid assets. Extending the idea one more layer, less-liquid assets like livestock or a car are still easier psychologically to let go of and sell off for funds than are mental accounts for long-range things like retirement. It turns out in experiments that after people set aside funds in those mental long-range accounts where we accumulate our "wealth," they are very unlikely to reach into them to pay for current expenses. In the U.S., for example, many people leave funds in retirement accounts, while simultaneously paying high fees and interest on loans for new cars and buying

Figure 3.7. This market stall vendor, selling used handbags in Kawangware, Kenya, like most of us probably uses mental accounts

everyday things on credit cards. Money in a one mental account for a stock of "wealth" is psychologically not nearly as interchangeable with flows of "current income" as it is in coldly rational reality.

The pattern is what economists call a **declining marginal propensity to consume**. In other words, in terms of likelihood we will consume more today, another dollar of current cash is most likely to get spent, semi-liquid assets are less likely, and income set aside in future-planning accounts is least likely to get spent.[17]

The flip side is if we do not spend our money, we save it in some form or other. Thus, we also psychologically behave with increasing propensity to save. Cash is least likely to get saved, and, once established, mental long run accounts are most likely to stay saved. Unfortunately, when someone is living day-to day on widely uncertain ups and downs in cash flows, like many poor people, then those long run future accounts are the most difficult to start putting money away for. When cash comes in in patterns that are difficult to predict or plan for, the psychological tendency is to think of that cash in a mental current account, easiest and more necessary (or salient) to spend now. Again, this leads to lower use of financial intermediation than we would see without the behavioral psychology of mental accounting.

Misestimating Risk

Psychological tendencies of yet another flavor also inhibit financial markets, particularly those related to insurance and saving for contingencies. As a general rule, people tend to not be very good at estimating risks.

First, there is simple denial, a false sense of security: it will not happen to me. Without laws that make auto insurance compulsory, for example, many of us in richer countries would not have enough car insurance even though driving is among the highest risk everyday activities. You probably know teenage drivers are particularly risky, but how many would voluntarily pay the high insurance rates if given a choice? Maybe you are like many of the rest of us in usually thinking we are better drivers than those other crazies on the road. But we cannot all be above average safe drivers. We each on average significantly underestimate the probabilities we will be in a wreck. We are similarly collectively in denial about health risks from smoking or overeating or sun tanning. We are aware these have risks, but many of us keep doing them anyway.

A second part of this tendency to misestimate risks is related to familiarity and control. Behavioral psychology suggests that people systematically underestimate risks involved in things that are familiar and over which we perceive we have some control.[18] Driving is familiar to many of us and we think we are more in control of the risks than we actually are. We tend not to experience wrecks too often ourselves, so we tend to underestimate the risks—until one actually happens to us. Then we tend to smarten up. In other words, when people make decisions based on their own experiences, we will give less weight than purely mathematically we should to familiar activities with risky possibilities that do not happen too often.

The challenge is similar with perceptions of formal financial services. Many poor people are much more comfortable with informal financial intermediation services (as we will describe in Chapter 4) than with banks or pension funds or insurance companies. The poor might not trust banks with their money because banks are unfamiliar and seem beyond control. We are social beasts, we humans, and if we have never dealt with banks our deep-rooted psychological tendency will be to have more confidence in our familiar neighbors and friends than in some strangers at a bank. Better the devil you know than the devil you do not. Yet the chance of a formal bank losing clients' money by going bankrupt or burning down is far lower than the chance of the same thing happening to a neighborhood moneyguard in the slum or a stash of cash in a tin box in a rural hut with open flames for cooking.

People will also tend to favor things they can see and touch over more abstract options. A goat as a savings mechanism for a farmer is easy to access, affordable and familiar, as is a neighbor serving as a moneyguard. The downside risks are less observable and more abstract, and as a result underappreciated. As measures of risk, a formal bank's financial strength or cash management security policies are similarly abstract and unobservable, so likely to be undervalued as well. As a result, a poor saver might choose a more risky informal option for their savings because they are familiar with it, even if they desire more safety over other features.

Section in Bulletpoint

- Social expectations that people will financially help family and friends in need can inhibit demand for formal finance.

- Discrimination in financial services is widespread globally.

- People tend to be financially nearsighted in time, overvaluing current spending relative to future needs.

- Current cash is psychologically the easiest type of asset to spend and also most susceptible to social taxation by family and friends, creating a behavioral challenge to save for the future.

- Using mental accounts helps people impose financial self-control.

- Most people are not very good at estimating risks and thus tend to underutilize financial services that might help mitigate risk.

Discussion Questions

1. Think of a recent time you were socially taxed. Briefly discuss how and why. Discuss whether the person who socially taxed you could have used formal finance to handle the need. Why didn't they?

2. Do you use mental accounting? Why? Discuss how interchangeable the money actually is between accounts compared to how interchangeable it is psychologically.

3. How often do you ask a friend to borrow a few dollars? How often do you ask a friend to sell an asset of theirs worth a few dollars so they could lend you that money? Is the former or latter socially easier? Why? What concept in the chapter does this illustrate?

4. You can do your own hyperbolic discounting experiment. Ask 10 people to tell you how much you would have to give them one year from now for them to prefer waiting rather than getting $20 right now. Then ask how much they would want to get five years from now to prefer waiting rather than getting $20 in four years. How many demonstrate hyperbolic discounting, i.e. are more patient in the future than in the present? Discuss briefly why you think they are?

5. Offering poor farmers insurance against crop failure has proven difficult for insurance firms. Funeral insurance for the poor has been more

successful. Discuss why this might be, combining ideas from sections 3.2 and 3.3.

6. Search the internet, or use your own experience, and find and write a blog (~400–500 words) about a specific real example from a developed nation that illustrates one of the main behavioral barriers to savings or insurance identified in this chapter. Be sure to note what specific barrier your example illustrates.

3.4 Problems of Costs and Risks

The second key problem we identified at the start of this chapter was costs. Both sides of the cost equation are important for the market: the costs to banks and other financial service providers delivering services to the poor and the costs to the poor for using them. Let us look first from the point of view of potential customers. Then we will move on to explore the costs of running financial services businesses.

Transaction and Opportunity Costs

Fees and other costs associated with formal finance can be prohibitively expensive for a poor person living on a dollar or two a day. Consider, for example, fees at Brazil's first and second largest banks, Bradesco and Caixa Econômica Federal (CEF). As Table 3.2 shows, to open a basic savings account in 2005 a new customer would have had to pay fees (1) to register with the bank, (2) to open the account, (3) to get checks, (4) for each withdrawal of funds, and (5) to simply check the account balance—all this on top of (6) savings account maintenance fees amounting to between $25 and $35 per year. These fees do not even include the required minimum deposits, tying up those funds too.

Roughly 14 million Brazilians in 2005 were living below $1.25 per day. For them, the annual maintenance fees alone would be on the order of a whole month's income. Imagine working a whole month every year just to pay savings account fees. Another study found the average total costs—fees for registration, materials, reference letters, IDs, minimum balances, etc.—just to open the most basic bank accounts in Benin amounted to 92 days working at Benin's minimum wage; in Uganda, 88 days.[19] It is easy to understand why so few of the world's poorest use such formal services, instead turning to informal mechanisms. Box 3.4 details similar **transactions costs** challenges for L.S., a poor farmer in India trying to obtain a small loan.

Table 3.2. Example fees (in Brazilian Real) in Brazil's biggest banks, 2005

Fees	Bradesco	Caixa Econômica Federal (CEF)
1. Initial customer registration fee	15.00	15.00
2. Fee to open savings account	0	15.00
3. Checkbook fee (10 checks)	6.30	3.30
4. ATM withdrawal fee	1.75	2.50
5. Balance inquiry fee (at ATM)	1.30	2.10
Balance inquiry fee (not ATM)	2.00	2.10
6. Monthly account maintenance fee	6.90	5.00

Note: In 2005, the exchange rate was about $1 = 2.33 Brazilian Real.
Source: Kumar et al (2006).

Box 3.4. Faces
L.S. Tries for a Bank Loan in Jaipur, India

L.S., a farmer, tends a small field near Jaipur, India. Speaking with Harvard anthropologist Marguerite Robinson, L.S. described his experience trying to get a loan of 5,000 rupees (about $150 then) from Regional Rural Bank. Cost after cost started piling up for L.S., and included not only several types of bank paperwork fees and bribes, but also transportation, payments to an informal moneylender, and the opportunity cost of time navigating bureaucracy:

Photo © Carol Mitchell. Used under Creative Commons license (lihttps://creative commons.org/licenses/by-nd/2.0/legalcode).

In order to get the signatures I needed for the loan application, I made four trips to see the patwari [village officer in charge of land records], and four trips to the tehsildar [revenue officer]. On the fourth trip to the patwari I could finally meet him. But I still could not get in to see the tehsildar. Then I asked a friend who is a relative

(Continued)

Box 3.4. (*Continued*)

of the tehsildar's servant to accompany me to the tehsildar's office. My friend came with me on my fifth trip. I paid the tehsildar's servant 25 rupees and got the signature. Then I had to make trips to two local banks and a cooperative in order to obtain "no dues" certificates [attesting that the applicant did not have outstanding or previously defaulted loans from these institutions]. Everywhere I went I had to pay. I had to find a loan guarantor and pay him 100 rupees. Next I went to the notary to obtain a "no encumbrance" certificate, for which the fee was 250 rupees. Including the transportation costs I paid 900 rupees in all. In order to pay these expenses, I borrowed 1000 rupees from a moneylender in my village for six weeks at 3 percent a month. However, my loan application was denied by the bank because the branch manager of the RRB did not have the authority to give loans outside the credit target. . . .

By the end of the process, then, L.S. was out 900 rupees in cash, plus interest to the informal moneylender, and the opportunity cost of many lost hours spent in what turned out a fruitless effort. High transactions costs indeed for a poor farmer.

Source: Robinson (2001) p. 211.

Beyond fees, convenience, time and hassle matter too. We saw in Table 3.1 that there are three times fewer bank branches or ATMs available per capita in developing countries. Getting to a bank or ATM is likely to be more of a problem. For example, a study in Kenya found that the average Kenyan lived 19 kilometers from the nearest bank branch.[20] As a result, transportation to get to a bank averaged more than $2.50 per trip. Opening a bank account makes little sense for poor Kenyans who might only want to deposit a few dollars per visit. A global survey similarly found that 20% of people without bank accounts say their main barrier is that banks are too far away.[21] Beyond the transport costs, the time to get back and forth (for rural villagers perhaps a half day or more) is also lost for other purposes such as working for wages or selling vegetables at the local market. Economists call these kinds of lost income opportunities **opportunity costs**.

Compare the Kenyans' 19 km bank access challenge to your own. How far might you have to walk to get to an ATM or bank? A few blocks? A couple miles? At Lehigh University in the city of Bethlehem, Pennsylvania, for example, students counted more than 50 ATMs and more than a dozen bank branches within a modest mile or two walk from campus; not to mention the ones right on campus itself.

Last Mile Problem and Complementary Infrastructure

If you live in a rich country, your bank may have installed its own ATMs in some locations you use, but you can also use whole worldwide ATM networks shared among banks. Most of us in rich countries can also use our credit and debit cards at terminals in stores almost everywhere; again a shared transactions processing network. Banks themselves share information among their own branches, with other banks, with credit bureaus, and with the government; all by using extensive telecommunications data networks of cables and central computerized interconnection systems. By paying fees to telecommunications companies, individual banks leverage these existing complementary infrastructures, which took many decades and literally trillions of dollars to develop, without having to build them from scratch. Yet large fractions of the poor live in places lacking much in the way of that sort of complementary infrastructure. Until the infrastructure in these regions catches up, financial intermediaries are on largely on their own.

Take a look at the photograph of the winding dirt road shown at the very beginning of this chapter. An MFI in Peru, Pro Mujer, uses that road to visit some of its microfinance customers, i.e. llama farmers living in the remote high altitude Altiplano region. In fact, that road ends before it reaches some clients, leaving only rough-hewn paths across saltpans and rocky desert. There are no cellphone towers, no telephone lines, no ATMs or stores with credit card terminals anywhere nearby that would enable banking services as we in rich countries know them. This lack of complementary infrastructure for delivering services, and the resulting prohibitive costs associated with reaching clients, is called the **last mile problem**. A bank that wanted to serve these customers would either have to establish a branch office nearby and somehow set up its own payment systems and communication infrastructure, or—as this microfinance organization did—send employees out on remote field visits lasting hours by motorbike. Horses or bicycles or canoes are sometimes used elsewhere for similar reasons; costly propositions when measured per client served.

The last mile problem pervades many cities too, especially high population slum areas. Millions of the world's poor live in slums where little public infrastructure of any kind—roads, water pipes, sewers—has ever been built, like Dharavi India, Cité Soleil Haiti, or Jembatan Besi Indonesia. Without complementary infrastructures, banks and other financial intermediaries cannot enter potential new markets alone. As we will see in later chapters, innovative financial service providers are teaming up with a range of alternatives, such as mobile phone providers, retail chains, and shop owners to find ways to tackle the last mile problem. Nonetheless, the problem is huge. And stubborn. Much, much work remains to develop low-cost delivery channels.

Challenges of On-Demand Access

Paradoxically, the same erratic money flow patterns that underlie the demand among the poor for financial intermediation cause fundamental delivery problems (and liquidity risks) for banks trying to supply those services.

We met Michelle, a customer at RiteCheck, in Box 3.2 earlier. She was willing to pay $2 to get $8 to use right away—a 25% fee—rather than wait to accumulate $20 to use an ATM for free. RiteCheck was quick, right in her neighborbood, open at unconventional but convenient hours, and served Michelle's immediate need for a small day-to-day transaction. Her behavior highlights a common theme for those living at the financial edge: among their most important financial needs are small, short-term transactions. She may not want to use that quick access all the time. Ready availability and frequency of use are not the same thing, and banks can hesitate to serve the poor because they mistake availability for high turnover in small accounts.[22] Nevertheless, when Michele does want access, liquidity and convenience dominate her choice of service provider.

Now, multiply Michelle's need for on-demand but unpredictable access by millions of potential customers distributed across big cities, slums, rural villages, mountains and jungles. That is a remarkably complex challenge. Big banks that serve richer clients pass on the high costs of the required infrastructures as transactions fees to their customer, but as we have seen such fees are big barriers for the poor.

CARD Bank, an MFI serving the poor in the Philippines, looked into how erratic money flow patterns affected savings account operations at its

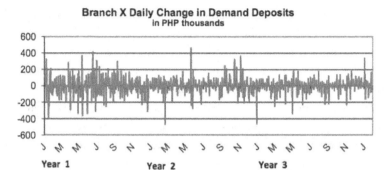

Figure 3.8. Daily deposits cash flow at a CARD Bank branch, Philippines

Source: Grameen Foundation (2012).

branch offices. Some days many more people wanted to deposit money into their accounts than to withdraw. On net, cash flowed in. Other days the bank had to give out more cash than came in. Usually the daily spikes and dips were more or less random, as we see in Figure 3.8, which shows for every day over three years the net positive or negative change in a single branch's deposits (shown on the vertical axis in Philippine Pesos).

The branch had to be prepared any random day to deal with a big net cash outflow or a big cash inflow, mostly in very small transactions. Bankers call this "liquidity management." Most days this branch went up or down less than 100,000 Philippine Pesos (about $2,300), but some days were five times that, randomly in either direction.

Enough piles of cash in small denominations had to be on hand to cover even the highest outflow days. It is a huge problem if a bank does not have enough liquidity to cover such days. If a bank ever failed to let savers withdraw their funds, it risks a crisis of confidence. People losing faith in their bank can be contagious, with runs on deposits, and banks can collapse quickly.

Yet cash sitting around providing occasional liquidity is then not available to invest, i.e. opportunity costs for the bank in missed investment income. This is a form of **liquidity risk**—too much liquidity harms profits. Moreover, banks in developing economies with unstable local currencies and ill-developed local stock markets have another liquidity risk in finding safe places to invest funds they do not need right away. A lack of places to invest in turn inhibits incentives to try to offer attractive savings deposit accounts to begin with. Where would a bank put deposited funds?

Transactions costs can be high as well. The branch had to handle hundreds of small denomination transactions as deposits came in. Tellers had to know how, managers and internal control operations had to ensure no fraud was going on, and computer systems had to keep track and connect all that information with CARD Bank's head office and Philippine regulatory oversight system. The head office then had to match all the random inflows or outflows across all the bank's many branches and other services like loans and investments.

Making all that work well drives costs up for a bank. A study of microfinance banks ADOPEM in the Dominican Republic and Centenary Bank in Uganda found the banks were paying somewhere between half to more than twice as much to manage small accounts than were actually saved in the accounts.[23] Most banks, facing costs like these to manage the erratic small transactions and account totals typical for poor customers, just decide not even to try. The liquidity management challenge helps explain in part why it is much more common, when financial institutions do serve the poor at all, to see them offer loans. Loan cash flows are more predictable. Banks can control when loans go out and dictate when payments are due.

Looking at the profit and loss statements for small savings accounts in isolation, it looks like ADOPEM and Centenary Bank were losing their shirts. Why do that? Pure charity for the poor? Hardly. The same study also found that the costs were more than offset by profits from other services for the same clients. Overall by attracting poor clients who used multiple services, the savings accounts paid off for both microfinance banks, adding 30% to total profits. In business jargon, the small savings accounts were "loss leaders."

Clearly, the large unmet demand among the poor for financial services leaves market opportunities for innovators like these two banks, or CARD Bank in the Philippines, and RiteCheck in the South Bronx. We will explore additional financial service innovations in later chapters.

Managing Risks

Financial companies worry a lot about risk. They should. You are no doubt aware of the financial meltdowns that lead to the Great Depression from 1929–1939 and the Great Recession in the late 2000s. Both were driven by mismanaged financial risks. Hundreds of banks and investment firms around the world went belly-up. Bank failure happens more often than you might think. In fact, there have been severe banking crises in more than 100 different countries since the 1970s, embroiling national economies and wiping out the savings and other assets of millions of customers.

We already mentioned liquidity risks, and financial firms face many other risks in developing nations as well: from credit defaults, from inflation or currency and interest rate swings (which can be big in weak economies), from macroeconomic crises in their countries, and so on. Corruption and political crises are all too common. Firms whose customers are concentrated geographically face similar other so-called **covariant risks**, that many customers might simultaneously suffer from wars or epidemics or droughts. Imagine running the insurance company when a typhoon wipes out your whole region.

Seemingly, the risks are high enough doing just normal financial business in such environments. It is unsurprising, then, that when considering offering financial services to the poor, banks and the governments that regulate them worry about piling on yet more risks from that sector. If a banker thinks about the uncertain incomes of the poor, compared to traditional customers it is natural to assume the poor are risker. How could the poor with such unstable resources regularly pay insurance premiums or put money away in savings, making it worth the bank's effort? How could the poor pay back debt, and when they default how can the bank collect collateral? Many poor cannot read and write, so how could they fill in the required forms, provide documentation or keep business records needed to assess their riskiness as bank clients?

Banking risk management is a world of written agreements, paperwork, contracts, documentation, background checks, collateral, credit scores, and on and on. It is a system built on the mores of the formal economy. Collecting all that documentation and background information drives up processing costs. That works, percentagewise, if clients have big accounts. For a loan of

$150,000, what is $200 in processing costs and legal documents? A bank that wants to apply the same process to tiny loan requests like $150 would not be able to afford to provide the service. Normal banking risk management schemes would not be cost-effective.

However, the conception of risk from the formal sector based on big-account clients breaks down when moving to services for the poor in the informal sector. Some critics say banks worry more than they should, mistaking informal economy transactions with risky transactions.[24] Suppose a $150 loan is not paid back? For a bank, so what? The business reality is a mere $150 would not matter to a big bank as long as large numbers of clients do not fail to repay. The bank would be better off letting go of the costly paperwork. Clients, like L.S. in Box 3.4 earlier, would be happier with simpler and quicker, and far more people might seek services. However, this upside-down formulation of the risk is inconsistent with most banks' existing risk mitigation procedures.

Risk mitigation is also important from the point of view of the poor themselves. People who have savings accounts at banks could lose their money if the banks collapse. This risk is one of the main reasons, along with the danger of broader economic crises, for what is called **prudential regulation**. Governments establish rules they hope will force banks and banking systems to be prudent in their activities in order to protect depositors and economies. The various rules govern things like how much debt banks can take on, how much cash they must keep in reserve, limits on risky investments they are allowed to hold, reporting to do to the government, and so forth.

Unfortunately, in many developing nations prudential regulations remain problematic and lack safeguards. If people do not have faith in the banking systems, because of corruption, or runaway inflation that erodes savings, or long memories of past banking collapses, then markets will fail to provide enough formal services. Potential customers hesitate to use banks in potentially unsafe banking systems, and banks hesitate to expand services in places at risk of crises resulting from weak oversight or unstable policies.

For example, in the late 1990s weak prudential oversight led to the collapse half the banks in Ecuador, one of the poorest nations in Latin America, in an environment of government budget shortages, plunging oil export prices and rapid currency devaluation.[25] First one small bank collapsed, and its depositors lost funds. This in turn led to a contagious run on other banks' deposits, a liquidity crunch, and eventually to the government freezing deposits. The economy collapsed and unemployment soared.

When income and jobs fall, the poor tend to suffer the most because, as we have seen, they tend to live on insecure and fluctuating income quite susceptible to broader economic shocks. There is evidence that the poor lose disproportionately in financial crises in another way too, because they have less information and fewer alternative financial options. Marina Halac, a doctoral student at UC Berkeley, and Sergio Schmukler of the World Bank found that small depositors in Ecuador's and similar crises tended to react much later to impeding crises than large depositors, leaving their deposits vulnerable longer.[26] This suggests information asymmetries and liquidity asymmetries as well. Wealthier people, who might be more in tune with risks brewing in financial systems, are more quickly able to move their money to safer places than the poor. The poor can suffer more as a result. To stabilize Ecuador's economy, the government had to abandon its own currency, the sucre, and adopt the dollar. When that happened, those small savers stuck with sucre still in banks when the government froze deposits ended up losing about 60% because the value of the sucre fell so much relative to the dollar. (Even so, with good liquidity management Ecuadorian MFI Banco Solidario weathered the turmoil, see Box 3.5.)

Subsidized Credit

A major, but counterintuitive, cost-related barrier to expanding financial access for the poor is subsidies. If the poor cannot afford financial services, would not subsidizing the costs of offering them help? Historically, many policymakers thought just that and viewed low supply of funds as a main reason why markets failed to offer financial services to the poor. After World War II, the idea became popular that governments should play a larger direct economic role by injecting resources to move countries from "developing" to "developed." In response, governments around the world created programs to subsidize credit, mostly in agriculture. Most developing nations had high fractions of their economies in agriculture, yet lacked advanced agricultural techniques. Theorists argued that one way to get farmers to adopt new agricultural practices would be to subsidize credit for better machinery, seeds and fertilizers.

Box 3.5. In the Field
Banco Solidario—Avoiding Economic Collapse in Ecuador

Table 3.3. Banco Solidario

Began microfinance operations	1996
Locations	Ecuador
Clients	395,047 borrowers; 88,171 depositors (December 2014)
Women as % of borrowers	51.2%
Self-sufficiency ratio	110%
Legal status	Commercial bank

Banco Solidario was Ecuador's first bank with an expressly social mission, to tackle the nation's poverty. It beat the odds during the 1998–2000 crisis and emerged among the strongest banks in the country, surviving in part because of effective liquidity risk management. The poor turned out to be less risky than mainstream banking customers. Its savers did not lose faith, nor did its main international investors, including the microfinance-focused ProFund. Here is what the Inter-American Development Bank had to say about how Banco Solidario weathered Ecuador's economic storm:

> *Ecuador's Banco Solidario was only two years old in 1998 when the country's economy began to spin out of control. The Ecuadoran economy was hit hard by extreme weather, a costly border war with Peru, sluggish world prices for its oil exports and a political crisis that saw the government go through three heads of state in rapid succession....*

> *In the midst of all this, Banco Solidario increased its lending to micro and small entrepreneurs a whopping fivefold, from about $4 million in 1998 to some $20 million in 2000. The proportion of its loans allocated to micro and small entrepreneurs went from 10 percent in 1998 to 60 percent in 2000, and it became Ecuador's*

(*Continued*)

Box 3.5. (*Continued*)

most profitable bank in early 2000. It was ranked as one of the country's five best banks [in 2006].

Four key factors in Banco Solidario's success are cited by Alex Silva, CEO of ProFund International, a major shareholder in the bank. First, Banco Solidario turned hefty profits by betting against the Ecuadoran sucre and trading in government bonds, which were sharply discounted during the crisis. Second, Banco Solidario's international investors, including ProFund, worked together to help it through the crisis with additional short-term financing, giving the bank much-needed liquidity and helping shore up its credibility in local capital markets. Third, Banco Solidario participated in a government-subsidized housing program that required low-income tenants to maintain savings accounts, thus providing the bank with yet more short-term liquidity. Fourth, the bank discovered that lending to microenterprises had its advantages, reinforcing, in Silva's words, "the institution's conviction not only that smaller clients are more resilient and withstand crisis better, but also that their payment ethics are better than those of larger clients."

Source: Kahn and Jansson (2007).

Yet after decades of loaning funds at very low interest rates through large state agricultural banks, governments across the world saw scant improvement in their agriculture sectors.[27] Unfortunately, the persistence of low-cost subsidized credit makes it hard for new competitors to enter and offer more services, restricting overall financial access by pushing out other options. Why go to a commercial bank for a loan if the government or a charity might give you one far cheaper? By competitively driving away potential alternative providers, subsidies thus worsen rather than improve the root problem for the poor: lack of enough financial intermediaries.

Access to subsidized low-cost funds also reduces the incentive for banks to try to attract savings deposits. Most banks take the deposits of their savings customers to invest or lend back out to other customers. But as we have just seen, offering savings accounts is costly. If lower-cost subsidized funds are available to lend out instead, the banks might not want to bother with offering savings accounts. While this may not sound too important, it inhibits innovation in developing savings account services that might better suit the needs of the poor.

A key problem with subsidized programs was that the credit rarely reached those who needed it most. The demand for subsidized credit is artificially large (who would not want nearly free government money?), but governments or charitable groups giving it out must limit the supply to keep from overextending limited budgets. Agricultural credit subsidies alone were eating up 2.2% of the entire economy of Brazil in 1980, for instance.[28] With demand too high, some mechanism—politics rather than markets— had to serve to allocate available funds. This is called **credit rationing**. Politics, power, and connections influenced who got the loans. While the loans were supposed to go to those in need and the most productive potential investments, the list of recipients instead often comprised family, friends, and supporters of those in office.

Across the globe, governments saw high default rates. Loose enforcement combined with favoritism led to many loans going uncollected. For example, University of Toronto Political Science Professor Lynette Ong found that political elites in China tended to use rural banks like blank checks to fund their own enterprises.[29] Bank officers risked losing their jobs if they did not approve loans for these individuals, or tried too hard to collect missing repayments or collateral. As a result, Chinese rural banks rolled up tens of billions of dollars' worth of unrecoverable loans, essentially went bankrupt, and were shut down by the government in 1999. Similarly, in the 1980s, loan repayment rates were a dismal 25% for Mexico's subsidized BANRURAL program.[30]

On top of this, some governments saw the credit programs as a means to garner political support. Since strict collection and foreclosure policies were unpopular, when election time rolled around politicians would, predictably, announce loan forgiveness periods, removing penalties or other downsides for not repaying. That limits liability and incentives to pay back. During one election cycle in Malawi, repayment rates to the government's subsidized Agricultural Credit Agency fell from near 90% to about 20%, bankrupting the agency.[31]

Widespread results like these led to rethinking of subsidized credit theories and helped usher in the era of microfinance. We will spend the rest of the book investigating how and whether microfinance works.

Section in Bulletpoint

- Fees and opportunity costs for using banks in some countries can amount to months' worth of income for the poor.
- Lack of complementary infrastructure like data networks and roads mean providing "last mile" financial access to poor people is costly.
- Facing volatile cash flow needs, the poor value convenient but small, short-term financial flow transactions, which can be costly for a bank to provide and create liquidity risk.
- To protect depositors and investors, banks and government regulators need to guard against economic shocks and other risks.
- The poor have proven less risky for banks than previously assumed, but can be disproportionately harmed by financial system failures.
- Subsidized credit policies for the poor, mainly in agriculture, have been disappointing, costly, and prone to credit rationing corruption.

Discussion Questions

1. Suppose a poor person went today to your bank to open a basic savings account. Find out what fees and minimum deposit they would have to pay. How many days would they have to work at legal minimum wage in your location to cover those?

2. One kind of prudential regulation is limits on interest rates that banks can charge on loans. Since banks are less likely to want to offer services when rates are low, what is the rationale for capping interest rates? Should we, as some microfinance practitioners suggest, relax rate caps to help MFIs offer more loans?

3. Using the idea of covariant risk, explain this puzzle: how can poor people in poor countries be good financial risks individually, but investing to serve them in poor countries still be unattractively too risky?

4. The reality is there is not nearly enough funding to subsidize all the needs of the poor for finance. Considering that credit-rationing corruption is widespread, discuss what mechanisms to allocate the limited financial service resources.

5. Government deposit guarantee insurance schemes reimburse customers' savings deposits up to certain limits if their banks fail. Some critics argue that limits that are too generous can create moral hazard, limited liability, and adverse selection problems, and that no bank should be "too big to fail." Do you agree? Discuss why or why not. (For help, this argument was prominent in recent cases of financial collapses in Cyprus and Iceland.)

6. The last mile problem in distributing services to the poor arises not only in financial services but also in healthcare, social services, transportation, retail and other contexts. Search the internet and identify at least three innovations for overcoming a last mile challenge, one in finance and two in other sectors. Briefly discuss how they work and any evidence of impact on the poor.

Key Terms

adverse selection
Happens if, when unable to tell the difference between good and bad options, choices disproportionally favor bad options: e.g. insuring mostly risky drivers; loaning mostly to risky borrowers; used car buyers getting mostly "lemons."

asymmetric information
Occurs when people on one side of a transaction have more or superior information relevant to the transaction than the other side.

covariant risks
Occur when many individuals are susceptible to similar risks at the same time, such as in droughts, storms, political chaos, and macroeconomic problems.

credit rationing
If institutions limit credit and demand exceeds availability at existing interest rates, non-market mechanisms allocate the credit instead; often politically driven and prone to corruption.

dead capital
Assets, usually in informal sectors, that cannot be easily sold or used as collateral, often because no documentation, legal paperwork or enforceable property rights exist.

declining marginal propensity to consume
As wealth or income increases, each additional dollar is less and less likely to be used for current consumption; conversely implies increasing likelihood of savings.

hyperbolic discounting
Changes over time in the rate at which future money is discounted; for some people it is psychologically easier to postpone consuming in the future than postponing now.

informal economy
Economic activities external to formally registered businesses subject to laws, taxes and contract enforcement; sometimes called the shadow economy or gray markets.

last mile problem
Exists where the final distribution link between service providers and end customers is disproportionally costly to develop.

limited liability
Situation in which the penalty or risk of loss to a decision maker is more limited than what is fully at stake in the decision; can lead to overly risky behavior.

liquidity risks
Risks stemming from not being able to meet immediate needs for cash quickly enough; also the risks to returns due to challenges in managing liquid assets.

mental accounting
Segregating current and future assets into categories between which money is treated differently, even if fully fungible in reality; can be used to foster financial self-control.

momentary salience
The perceived importance, at the moment of decision, of outcomes of that decision; many decisions favor short-term outcomes because they feel more relevant right now.

moral hazard
Arises when one side in an agreement has incentives to behave in ways contrary to the agreed interests of the other side, e.g. insured drivers claim fake accidents; problematic where information and contract enforcement are limited.

opportunity costs
The value of alternatives given up when taking some action or decision; e.g. time spent traveling to a bank is lost of other opportunities like working for wages; funds invested in one place forgo possible returns from investing elsewhere instead.

principal–agent problems
Occur when for one side (the principal) the outcome of an agreement depends on the actions or decisions of the other side (the agent), but the agent's self-interest runs counter to the principal's.

prudential regulation
Laws and rules governing things like debt levels, cash reserve requirements, investment risks, and information reporting, to ensure financial institutions and financial systems act in ways that safeguard depositors and economies.

social taxation
Interpersonal obligations, driven by social and cultural expectations, to give time and resources to help family, friends and community members in need.

stock and flow transactions
The former are economic exchanges, typically larger-scale, that add to physical stocks and long-term accumulations of capital, while the latter involve the everyday exchanges and short-term money flows that facilitate current consumption.

transactions costs
Fees and other costs involved in participating in economic exchanges.

Notes:

[1] Roth, McCord, and Liber (2007).
[2] Demirgüç-Kunt and Klapper (2012).

[3] Moebs Services (2014).
[4] U.S. Federal Reserve (2014).
[5] Robinson (2001) p. 250.
[6] de Soto (2001).
[7] de Soto (2001) pp. 30–31.
[8] de Soto (2001) p. 18.
[9] Armendáriz and Morduch (2010).
[10] Schaner (2014).
[11] Urquizo (2012).
[12] Sengupta (2014).
[13] Thaler (1981).
[14] Benzion, Rapoport, and Yagil (1989); Courtemanche, Heutel, and McAlvanah (2012); Anderson et al (2004); Ashraf, Karlan, and Yin (2006).
[15] Fiorillo, Potok, and Wright (2014).
[16] Ashraf, Karlan, and Yin (2006).
[17] Shefrin and Thaler (1988).
[18] Hertwig et al (2004).
[19] Deshpande (2006).
[20] Allan, Massu, and Svarer (2013).
[21] Demirgüç-Kunt and Klapper (2012).
[22] Robinson (2001).
[23] Westley and Palomas (2010).
[24] Rhyne (2009).
[25] Jácome (2004).
[26] Halac and Schmukler (2004).
[27] See, for example, Binswanger and Khandher (1995).
[28] Yaron, McDonald, and Piprek (1997).
[29] Ong (2006).
[30] Yaron, McDonald, and Piprek (1997).
[31] Yaron, McDonald, and Piprek (1997).

INFORMAL FINANCE

"The 'Susus' and 'Tontine' of West Africa, the 'chit funds' in India, the 'tandas' in Mexico, the partner in Jamaica or the legion of savings clubs and burial societies found in all parts of the world have operated for centuries."

— **Mary Coyle, Coady International Institute**

Figure 4.1. A savings and credit club in Ghana meets under a shady tree

Formal financial services are often missing in poorer areas. Before the emergence of microfinance institutions, the poor for the most part had only informal options for financial services. As we discussed in Chapter 3, to most banks and other mainstream financial service providers, poorer populations appeared to lack enough assets and be too costly and risky to serve profitably. Yet even without access to formal financial services, people participate in creative and innovative ways to accumulate savings and access credit and insurance through the informal economy.

We have already encountered in Chapter 3 one ubiquitous informal financial tool, social taxation: the interpersonal financial obligations we all feel to help family and friends in need. Social taxation serves as a form of informal insurance, spreading financial responsibilities across multiple households. Recall, too, from Chapter 2 that one of the main benefits of financial intermediation is facilitating our moving money across time, saving current income for use later or borrowing against later income for use now. An analogous interpersonal obligation is social debt or social reciprocity. If I do you a favor, financial or otherwise, informally I might expect a return favor at some time in the future; you owe me one. In that sense, social debt is an informal asset storing mechanism. I have stored up something informal of value for future use. You borrowed it for current use. I trust you will repay based on the strength of our friendship or family ties, i.e. **social collateral** rather than a physical asset as collateral. We are like our own tiny informal savings and loan bank.

Turns out that beyond social obligations there are many varieties of informal banking-like tools, some fairly complex, that have developed and been used for centuries among the poor around the world. In this chapter, we explore a number of the most widespread informal financial intermediation mechanisms. While services in these informal financial systems are not always efficient or stable, informal mechanisms often are the only options available to the poor. Hence, they are remarkably common. Informal financial intermediation mechanisms exist nearly everywhere and in every culture.

4.1 Savings Clubs

As discussed in earlier chapters, with few assets and erratic small income streams it is difficult for the poor to use banks and other formal financial services. Because there are relatively few secure locations to store cash or valuables, the poor often face challenges in saving for future expenses and investments. Without collateral and dependable income flows, formal loans for the poor are similarly often out of reach. To overcome these and other barriers to formal finance, many poor instead participate in savings and lending clubs, informal financial support groups that come together to save funds collectively. Forms of these clubs called rotating savings and credit associations, or ROSCAs, are discussed in the next section. ROSCAs trace their roots back at least as far back as the eighth century in China.[1] Today, they have become popular across the globe. In fact, participation rates in Sub-Saharan Africa range between half of the adult population to as high as 95% in some countries.[2] In addition to several forms of ROSCAs, a variety of other informal financial mechanisms exist, including moneylenders, deposit collectors, informal money managers, funeral insurance clubs, self-help savings groups, and many others.

Informal savings and lending clubs are typically managed by the participants involved, without outside help. Members of the clubs rely on trust and communal knowledge about each other's character as a sort of social collateral, ensuring all have regular periodic access to lump sums of funds. As we will see in Chapter 5, MFIs have leveraged the worldwide familiarity with these structures and have implemented similar models in their formalized financial services, adopting the social trust and communal information aspects of savings clubs in order to overcome obstacles of limited liability, moral hazard and adverse selection.

ROSCAs: Rotating Savings and Credit Associations

ROSCAs exist worldwide, going by names like *susu* clubs in Ghana, *hehui* in China, *chit* funds in India, *pasanaku* in the Andes, and *bajulojulo* in Sumatra. ROSCAs are a simple form of savings clubs that require participants to make regular contributions into a pool of communal funds. These pooled funds are then allocated in rotation to each group member in turn. One key objective of this system is to allow each member a chance to receive a lump sum of money to use for their needs, whether for larger household items, school fees for their children, or stock for their microbusiness. For this rotating system to work, members must each contribute their share. By the end of a cycle, everyone receives the benefit of a lump sum payment of a size that otherwise would be difficult to obtain on their own.

Basic ROSCAs

Figure 4.2 illustrates the operations of a basic ROSCA with five participants. Each large circle corresponds to a meeting between members, and each smaller bold circle signifies an individual who receives the funds during that particular meeting. For example in the third meeting of the cycle, the rightmost large circle, Noha receives the pot. In the fourth, Victor gets the pot. In a basic ROSCA, at each meeting period, each member contributes the same amount of money into the pot, which is then allocated to the chosen member of the ROSCA. The rotational cycle ends after the last person has received the lump sum, in this case after five meetings. These groups can often last for many years, rotating though multiple cycles.

For example, a ROSCA in Mexico may consist of members who gather once a month and put 50 pesos each into the pot. At a scheduled meeting, if there were five members, one would take the entire pot of 250 pesos. A month later, this group of five would meet again and each contributes another 50 pesos, giving 250 this time to the next member in line. This cycle continues until each member has received the lump sum. At this point, the process can either start over or end. Typically, new members cannot enter a ROSCA during a particular cycle but only at the start of a new cycle. This ensures everyone puts in and receives the same amount of money during the agreed duration.

ROSCAs meet frequently, usually weekly or monthly, some even daily, for several reasons. Meeting more frequently allows members to store loose

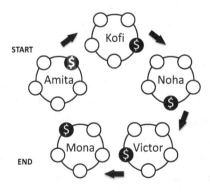

Figure 4.2. One cycle of a five-member ROSCA

Source: Modified from Rim and Rouse (2002).

change and extra cash more regularly in a safer and more secure location. Frequent group meetings also allow for shorter cash cycles, enabling the members to receive lump sums more often.

ROSCAs often consist of relatives or people who know one another and have already developed close relationships and trustworthy reputations, helping ensure that one member will not run away with the lump sum without contributing a fair share after their turn. Groups can be all women, or entirely men, or mixed, although mixed groups are somewhat less common. Sometimes such groups share a common entrepreneurial goal or skill, which allows each member to actively support one another's activities and to provide additional help and advice about business practices. Other groups consist of members from a common extended family, or a village, neighborhood market, religious society, or workplace—essentially anywhere relations are close-knit. Close relationships among members participating in a ROSCA act as social collateral, deterring participants from defaulting on their share.

In addition to these close-knit relationships, there is another implicit motive to contribute faithfully to the pot. In many small poorer communities, being labeled untrustworthy or a cheat brings shame that in some cultures can stay with the family for generations. Being considered undependable can hinder chances to access any other savings clubs that might exist in the community. ROSCAs may be the only form of savings institution available in a community. A member with a reputation for not contributing will no longer have any savings options left. Lack of savings could make many regular financial activities—saving enough to buy seeds and fertilizer during planting season for instance—difficult for the whole family.

Unfortunately, without legal protective measures to curb untrustworthy behavior the possibility does exist that participants might leave the group after receiving their lump sum. Since the pot is completely disbursed each period, there is no monetary safeguard against club deserters. In this sense, ROSCAs encounter issues pertaining to limited liability and moral hazard, discussed in Chapter 3. After their turn at receiving the lump sum, members have incentives to stop contributing to the communal savings pots, leaving other members at a loss. Additionally in a basic ROSCA, since each member contributes a set amount each period, funds do not grow like they might in savings accounts bearing interest.

Moral hazard problems are not insurmountable, however, as there are other ways to curb delinquent behavior. In order for ROSCAs to be successful, the number of participants is usually kept fairly small, around 5–15 members, and limited to extended family or close acquaintances, leveraging social collateral to defend against default as well as to enable distributing funds in a timely and efficient manner. Adding additional members lengthens the duration of the ROSCAs, which both stretches out the wait period for members to receive their sum and lengthens the period of time that those who have already collected must contribute to the pot before getting another lump sum. Although extremely large ROSCAs can exist, they are rarer because they require more formal management, such as a group overseer to keep track of the process. It is harder to socially know, trust and vet individual behaviors of larger numbers of people. And as the group size increases and cycle time gets longer, the momentary salience and self-control challenges noted in Chapter 3 suggest the probability that every member will contribute the full amount every meeting decreases.

ROSCA members who have proven inconsistent about contributing to the pot are not necessarily expelled from the group, but rather can be placed towards the end of the cycle, forcing them to wait longer before receiving funds. This method has the dual benefits not only of ensuring that riskier members contribute each period in order to ensure their share in the future, but also of rewarding the less risky participants by letting them collect their money first.

Members too negligent about contributing can be expelled from the group altogether. This possibility creates liability for poor behavior. We have seen in Chapter 3 that given their volatile and uncertain cash flows, the poor typically place high value on convenient, low-cost, repeated access to small transactional services. Where ROSCAs provide that access through repeated cycles, the risk of being excluded from future cycles can be a powerful dynamic incentive for good behavior during the current cycle.

Other Forms of ROSCAs

To hedge against some of the risks associated with basic ROSCAs, other forms of ROSCAs use slightly different operational frameworks.

Box 4.1. In Your Backyard
A ROSCA in New Jersey? Forced Savings at Work

In a small town in northern New Jersey, Michael Goldsmith, the owner of a landscaping company, has each of his employees participate in what he calls a "Forced Savings Plan." The office manager explains how their system works:

> *Every payday, we each put in $100. The boss held a master list of who would receive the 'savings' that week. Throughout the course of the summer, about 12 weeks, everybody received their enforced savings once. The savings were used for things like going on vacation, to send back home, etc. It felt like winning the lottery. It really did. Even though I was putting the money aside and it was my money all along, it really felt like winning the lottery. It was great.*
>
> *When you put a small amount away and then don't think about it, it's no pain, no fail. If everyone did this to save, put $25 a week into a bank account, they'd have a whole lot of money, but nobody thinks this way. I don't think there are whole bunches of people who do this type of savings program, not in this country, anyway.*

Source: Sue Hecht, Office Manager, personal communication.

In a **bidding ROSCA**, sometimes called an auction ROSCA, the members bid for how much extra they are willing to put in to receive the entire pool, with the agreement that the amount bid will be redistributed in the form of "interest" to the rest of the group. Suppose five members in Bangladesh are in a ROSCA where each contributes 100 Bangladeshi taka. They bid for the privilege of getting the first pot of 500 taka. If the highest bid is 50 taka, the 50 taka then gets redistributed as interest, divided evenly among the members, including the highest bidder. Each of the four non-bidding members will walk away 10 taka better off. However, they are still guaranteed the full 500 taka when their turn arrives if they wait to the end. The winning member receives 460 (500 − 50 bid + 10 share of bid) taka rather than 500; they are paying for the right to receive it first. This ensures that the person who takes the first pot is the person who values it the most, and the people waiting receive some interest on their investment. In later rounds, there are fewer people left to bid, so the bids tend to be lower. Such a system rewards people willing to wait, and is a straightforward way to determine the order in which members receive funds. Interestingly this type of ROSCA can attract both people more interested in borrowing, who would bid high early, and those interested in saving, who would wait and hence collect the bid payments as interest on their early contributions.

Since not all members may have the financial resources to bid for early access to funds but may need the funds just as desperately as other members, some ROSCAs instead incorporate a lottery system. **Lottery ROSCAs** allocate the funds by picking a name out of a hat or a similar method, ensuring that all participants have an equal chance of obtaining funds earlier.

Another strategy used in tighter-knit ROSCAs, and perhaps the most common, allows the group as a whole to decide which participant receives the lump sum. At each meeting, participants discuss to whom the pot should be disbursed and then proceed from there.

As Table 4.1 shows, the prevalence of ROSCA types varies, even within a country. Professors Tomomi Tanaka of Arizona State University and Quang Nguyen of the University of Lyon, studied ROSCAs in Vietnam. They found that in the southern part of Vietnam most of the ROSCAs consist of bidding ROSCAs. Interestingly, over 23% of participants said their group has had someone default. In contrast, most of the ROSCAs in northern Vietnam decide jointly who receives the pot of money, and only 13.3% have experienced a default in their group. Yet the northern ROSCAs tend to meet less frequently. Many other variations like this exist across regions and countries, so it is difficult to generalize about ROSCAs. The variations exist to suit the differing conditions and needs of the people participating and their economic, cultural and geographic environments.

Motivations for Joining ROSCAs

The poor join ROSCAs for a variety of reasons, summarized in Table 4.2. One major motive is that a person can attain a lump sum of savings that they would otherwise have difficulty accumulating in such a short period of

Table 4.1. Comparing ROSCAs in regions of Vietnam

	Northern	*Southern*
Method of determining order of recipients (%)		
Random	15.6	0
Bidding	2.2	94.1
Negotiation	75.6	2.9
Decision by leader	6.7	2.9
Total	100	100
Frequency of meetings (%)		
Every day	0	8.8
Every week	0	11.8
Every 2 weeks	0	11.8
Monthly	24.4	8.8
Every 3 months	17.8	58.8
Every 6 months	55.6	0
Total	100	100
Average number of members in ROSCA	13.6	23.8
Have members defaulted in past? Yes (%)	13.3	23.5

Note: Number of respondents in the North and South are 45 and 34, respectively.
Source: Tanaka and Nguyen (2009).

Table 4.2. Motives for joining ROSCAs

Motive	*Explanation of motive*
Early pot	To obtain and use the lump sum earlier than otherwise possible.
Household conflict	Participants (usually women) seek involvement within ROSCAs to distract them from daily activities and to find additional time away from husbands and domestic life.
Commitment to savings	ROSCAs present a clear, public, and disciplined approach to accumulating funds.

Source: Armendáriz and Morduch (2010).

time. We saw in Chapter 2 that just like the rich, the poor also periodically need larger than normal sums to spend on big items such as weddings, funerals, dowries, illness or disasters that may occur. ROSCAs offer a creative solution to dealing with these savings needs. ROSCAs prove an effective strategy for accumulating larger lump sums, which can be difficult as we saw in Chapter 3 in the face of the behavioral psychology of self-control, social taxation pressures, and without a safe place to store money.

This motive's drawback is that the probability of attaining the lump sum early depends on how many people participate in the ROSCA or how the selection process works for members to receive funds. At the same time, the more people who participate, the larger the pot. Moreover, the fact that every person in a cycle, except the very last one, is able to access the lump sum earlier than if they tried to accumulate it on their own serves as a large enough incentive to keep many poor participating. Thinking back to Chapter 2, only the last person receiving the pot in a ROSCA cycle is purely saving up (Figure 2.4). The first member in the cycle gets a stream of funds like pure saving down (Figure 2.5), while the rest are saving through (Figure 2.6), all of them getting their lump sum earlier than the pure saver. For all but the last in the cycle, it is using a commitment to save as a way to get credit.

Another widespread reason for participating is known as the household conflict motive. ROSCA activities generally require participants to leave their homes to attend group meetings, or to invite others into their homes, and as a result can help distract members from their daily lives. Going to a ROSCA meeting allows participants to not only manage their finances, but also socialize and discuss the occurrences in each of their lives. Thus, while ROSCAs serve a financial purpose in the lives of many, they may also serve as a social outlet, a way to meet others within the community, and perhaps a respite from tensions at home. This practice often becomes embedded within the culture of smaller, more isolated communities. This motive may be particularly attractive to women dealing with domestic challenges in the home, such as domineering husbands. We will explore gender-related issues in greater detail in Chapter 7.

Another motive, commitment to savings, can be further understood by examining how ROSCAs help the poor pre-commit to savings. ROSCAs serve as an efficient saving strategy for multiple reasons. First, costs for managing and safeguarding savings are minimal. The pool of funds does not need to be stored because the whole pool is allocated to a member of the group at each meeting. Furthermore, no obligation beyond the base payments exists, allowing every member to receive an equal sum during their turn. This keeps the process simple and leaves no room for confusion, requiring little or no record keeping. Secondly, ROSCAs are usually time bound, so each cycle has a clear beginning and ending term, making commitment to savings easier because the members can exit a ROSCA after the cycle ends.

Third, committing to a group of other people to pay regularly into ROSCAs is a low-cost convenient method for reducing liquidity; like the mental accounts discussed in Chapter 3, but with a public promise to other people. By agreeing to participate in a cycle, members agree to make an ongoing string of future payments into the scheme for the duration of the cycle. This enables members to impose some self-control on future pressures to spend, either their own temptations or requests from of family members or friends. The ROSCA locks funds away from immediate undisciplined spending urges and from social taxation pressures. As we saw in Chapter 3, the poor are well aware of their own near-term temptations and interpersonal social obligations and often prefer to reduce the liquidity of their cash flows. Aunt Beatrice can socially and psychologically more readily decline requests from a spendthrift nephew because the cash in the cookie jar has already been promised to her ROSCA friends. The public promise mitigates against social taxation or self-control pressures to spend with a social obligation to save.

One drawback of ROSCAs, and other group savings and lending mechanisms presented later, is the time involved. Meetings can last an hour or more, especially if groups are larger. All that time together with the time traveling to and from the meetings is lost for other possible activities such as working for wages or selling at the local market. So while their simplicity means the cash costs of ROSCAs can be small to nil, joining is not free. The opportunity costs of lost time can be non-trivial and a barrier to participating.

ASCAs: Accumulated Savings and Credit Associations

ASCAs are forms of savings and lending groups that are similar to ROSCAs. ASCAs are more complex than ROSCAs and as a result take on a somewhat more formal approach while still remaining part of the informal sector. Like

Box 4.2. Dig Deeper
What Are ROSCAs Used for?

Research has shown that ROSCAs come in handy for business investments or helping others in emergencies (i.e. social taxation). However, they are most commonly used for bigger-ticket family consumption purposes. In Ethiopia, upwards of 8–10% of the entire country's GDP resides in *equbs*, the Ethiopian equivalent of a ROSCA. Professor Abbi Kadir at the University of Leicester and Gamal Ibrahim of the United Nations found that many Ethiopians participate in *equbs* mainly for buying so-called consumer durable goods. Durable goods— things that last a while like electric lamps or kitchen pots—generally have bigger price tags than everyday food and other consumption goods. This table shows the primary purpose Ethiopian households used ROSCAs for:

Purpose	Members (%)
Buy consumer durables	45.2
Save	20.8
Start/expand business	17.4
Help friends and family solve problems	8.1
Buy food	2.5
Repay debts/pay water & electricity	1.7
Other (rent, education, build house, etc.)	7.1

Using ROSCA funds for business purposes ranks third on the list, after buying consumer durables and accumulating savings. The utilization of ROSCAS to accumulate larger sums than they could otherwise and for purposes outside of business investment suggests how the poor take advantage of informal financial intermediation mechanisms to better manage cash flows for improving their everyday lives. People in different locations may have varying motives for participating, but such informal mechanisms are a worldwide phenomenon.

Source: Kedir and Ibrahim (2011).

ROSCAs, ASCAs allow participants to funnel savings into larger pools, but unlike in ROSCAs, contributors can add or withdraw more flexible amounts of funds at more flexible times rather than only in fixed amounts at fixed times as ROSCAs require. As members save funds into the pool, those deposits are like buying shares in the ASCA. The more you put in, the more shares you own.

That difference compared to ROSCAs is important because another major difference is that groups running ASCA pools of funds often self-impose fees or interest rates charged on withdrawals from the pool, treating them like loans. Members determine what interest rates should be charged to each other. In the slums of Dhaka, for example, some ASCAs charge themselves what amounts to 60% annual percentage rate (APR) for loans from the pool, a rate which seems high to those of us used to rates in formal finance but is voluntarily and regularly paid among the poor to each other in Bangladesh.[3] Late payments can incur penalty fees as well. At agreed intervals, some or all of the fees and interest paid by borrowers gets paid out as dividends to members in proportion to their ownership shares. Savers are rewarded for enabling borrowers to get early access to funds. Some groups keep a portion of fees and interest paid as accumulated capital within the fund, expanding the pool available for future potential borrowers, just like a company retaining earnings to grow.

In short, those who join and form ASCAs become, essentially, shareholders and managers in the system, with the power to determine interest rates, loan and deposit sizes, late fees, and other requirements. Thus, this system functions a bit like a small-scale cooperative bank whose owners are the customers. Indeed, as we will see in Chapter 5, the methods used by informal ASCAs form the basis of the formal microfinance system called village banking.

ASCAs have evolved to incorporate different characteristics depending on the client base. Some ASCAs, for example, are time bound like ROSCAs, requiring members to allocate a certain amount of funds into the pool on a regular basis and have standards on the times funds can be withdrawn and when loans must be repaid. At the end of the agreed time period, saved deposits and retained interest and fees are distributed back to the members, and the group either dissolves entirely or some members can leave and new ones come in and another cycle begins. Other ASCAs are more flexible and do away with time restrictions, as we see in the next section. Either way, if members do not abide by rules, they can be removed from the ASCA, a penalty that—like in repeating ROSCAs—helps reduce moral hazard risks and create dynamic incentives for good behavior.

Non-Time-Bound ASCAs

Non-time-bound ASCAs generally allow members to join or leave without imposing specific cycles and participants can add or withdraw funds flexibly as well. In that sense, for members these can serve as informal mechanisms for either purely saving up, saving down, or saving through or some combination as needed. Pure savers can keep putting money in and collecting dividends. Pure borrowers can pay back over time, saving down, plus interest and fees. And, recall from Chapter 2 that saving through is like insurance.

Therefore non-time-bound ASCAs can potentially serve as a form of insurance, with the member paying into the ASCA pool until some emergency or other need arises for withdraw. The poor are no different than the rich when it comes to recovering from natural disasters, disease, and death and as a result also need to prepare for potential emergencies. Hence, investing in a fund that is not time bound but allows withdrawals whenever necessary serves this need.

In places like Thailand, for example, houses can be relatively insecure. Houses there and in many tropical countries are often made from bamboo hatch, which can deteriorate fairly rapidly with time, blow down in a typhoon, or catch fire if someone is inattentive during the common practice of indoor open flame cooking. Thus, non-time-bound ASCAs serve an immediate purpose as funds can be used to restore houses or help alleviate burdens in similar times of financial distress.[4]

In fact, some ASCAs are primarily organized as insurance ASCAs. They work using a model of saving through. At designated times, each member puts a small amount of money in a fund. When a crisis hits one member,

Box 4.3. Faces
Sugia Devi Uses Her ASCA Like Health Insurance

In the Gaya District, Bihar, India the Livelihood Pathways for the Poorest project helped 200 of extremely poor families organize into 17 so-called adapted self-help groups (ASHGs). Only 3% of participating families had enough money to eat thre meals per day; 92% were illiterate, and the majority of their income came from unskilled occasional labor. These self-help groups ran like non-time-bound ASCAs, enabling members to organize their own collective voluntary and flexible savings and loans.

Sugia Devi, a member of one of the groups, named the Barsha group, used the group as a sort of health insurance to help fund expenses related to cataract surgery. Not only did a simple few dollars' worth of ASCA financial intermediation help restore her eyesight, it raised the awareness of her husband and other men in the village to the benefits of participating in self-help groups. Here's her story, as told by the Grameen Foundation, one of the sponsors of the project:

> Sugia Devi from Barsha ASHG needed an eye cataract surgery to be done. In August, 2011, she learned that there was a free cataract surgery camp organized by a charity organization in Bodh Gaya, which is an hour away by bus. However, at that point in time, she did not have the money for the bus fare, but was able to take a loan of 100 rupees from her group's collective savings when encouraged by other ASHG members.

> After a successful surgery, her husband, Ramashish Manijhia, who had been opposing her participation in the ASHG, approached the project staff and the ASHG members and said, "I am very apologetic that I did not let my wife participate in the ASHG and discouraged her to save, the ASHG saved her eyes." This event marked a turning point in the attitude of men towards savings in the ASHG as it showed a tangible benefit.

Source: Grameen Foundation (2013).

they can withdraw funds necessary to cope with the crisis, and then pay back the money over time. Some groups charge interest, allowing the pool to grow and ensuring the pool can be distributed to another person during some future time of crisis. Thus, this kind of ASCA simultaneously provides insurance and accumulates saving and pays interest dividends to members. The informal insurance scheme can work well if only small fractions of members need payouts at one time. Unfortunately, the system is vulnerable to failure from covariant shocks, discussed in Chapter 3, such as if a typhoon wipes out every hut in the village.

Flexibility and Issues with ASCAs

The rigid schedule and pre-determined size of ROSCA payouts might not align well with a member's specific cash flow needs. By contrast, ASCAs that avoid a rigid structured payout schedule allow members to take funds out on demand. Compared to ROSCAs, this greater flexibility potentially benefits borrowers by allowing them to match the timing of withdrawals better with the timing of their needs or investment opportunities: you take out only what you need when you need it.

Because ASCA groups are self-governed, members often collaboratively develop group rules and procedures. As a result, the ASCA system can promote strong, cohesive engagement among group members. The collective decision-making tightens the group dynamic and the social cohesion can help prevent payment defaults. The team counts on all its members to step up. Since members have control over funds and have opportunities to weigh in on what the rules should be, incentives exist for participants to follow the rules once established. Additionally, like ROSCAs, many ASCAs consist of members who have close personal relationships outside of the financial group, helping strengthen cohesive bonds within the groups.

Although ASCAs have the ability to improve the lives of the poor who have few alternative financial options, weaknesses exist with the system, leaving room for more efficient and safer formal options. ROSCA funds are fully disbursed every cycle, but ASCA funds are not, requiring record keeping and a secure place for storing the money. Thus, operating costs and the risk of loss are higher in comparison to ROSCAs.

A common storage approach is a simple cash lockbox for storing accumulated funds and the group's records (as shown at the beginning of the chapter in Figure 4.1 from an ASCA meeting in Ghana). Someone, often a member elected by the group, must store and guard the box between meetings. Other members must trust the guard. The collective savings of the whole group is at risk should the person in charge of the box have less than honorable intentions. Some groups require two or three people with different keys to open the box. Theft by non-members who get wind of the accumulated cash and loss to accident or fire are also unfortunately common risks with cashboxes.

A related challenge is liquidity. The lockbox literally locks money away from friends and family and self-control impulses, which as we have seen can be beneficial. However, if only one or two people actually handle the money and record books it can occasionally be difficult to access funds from the box. What if they get sick or called out of town unexpectedly?

Bookkeeping and financial management also become more complex, requiring skills and time from certain individuals to ensure that operations run smoothly. Records must show who has saved how much, who owns what shares and who owes what fees and interest, together with calculated repayment schedules and dividend payouts. For example, Figure 4.3 shows individual record books from two members of the same ASCA in Ghana. Each stamped arrow indicates a deposit of 1 Ghanaian cedi (about 25 cents), which in turn represents one fractional share in the accumulated ASCA fund. Over the last seven weeks, one member put away two cedi weekly, the other five. The bottom of each page leaves room for calculating accumulated totals after additions and withdrawals. Devising and implementing an effective account keeping system like this that the whole group can trust is not simple. Finding an individual capable of managing the accounting necessary may be difficult in areas where ASCAs are popular and such skills are in demand, yet education systems are often weak.

Another considerable problem with informal ASCAs is that in most countries they are not regulated. The group agreements are not official legally enforceable contracts. Since ASCAs require oversight to ensure

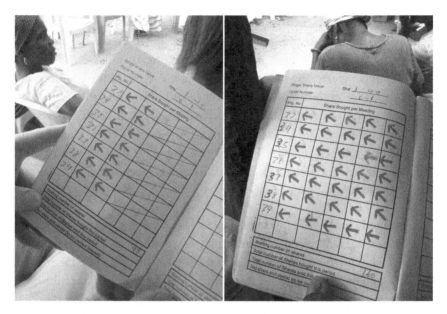

Figure 4.3. Record books for two members' shares in an ASCA, Ghana

funds are tracked efficiently, placing one person in charge of this job poses real risk. This person could potentially run off with the funds or mismanage them, leaving savings club members worse off than when the club began. As an alternative, employing a regulated institution or professional manager to run these informal collaborative structures could benefit members in the long term.

Aware of such disadvantages for people participating in informal finance, formalized MFIs take pieces of the ASCA model and seek to improve on the weaknesses. As we will see in Chapter 5, many MFIs' group financial services resemble the ASCA model, which clients might already be comfortable and familiar with, and add security and professional oversight and management. MFIs provide secure locations for storing funds, often with easier access by the clients. MFI personnel are responsible for managing the funds and generally already have well-developed record-keeping systems, overcoming many of the flaws of the ASCA system. The poor can spend more time with their families, working, or growing their skills and businesses.

Section in Bulletpoint

- ROSCAs and ASCAs are prevalent all over the world.
- They are run and owned by their members, and work thanks to the social collateral that exists between members.
- Motives for joining include creating lump sums, socializing, finding respite from household tensions, and pre-committing to savings.
- Issues of moral hazard do come up in these systems, but can be mitigated through incentives, as in bidding and lottery ROSCAs.
- ASCAs are more flexible than ROSCAs, simultaneously facilitating saving up, saving down, and saving through, and often charge interest and pay dividends.
- Non-time-bound ASCAs can function as insurance mechanisms.
- As group sizes increase, they often encounter more management, record keeping and moral hazard issues.
- Professional managers can help improve the efficacy of informal financial intermediation.

Discussion Questions

1. The early pot motive is considered among the key reasons people join ROSCAs. Briefly explain how this motivates people to join. Is this motive enough to hold a ROSCA together? Explain potential weaknesses of this motive and describe the process in which a ROSCA could unravel without other motivations.

2. Explain briefly what the household conflict motive is and to what group of people it mostly applies. Discuss how you think this benefits women. What might women get out of this motive that could be difficult to achieve without ROSCAs?

3. Explain briefly how the bidding ROSCA format can simultaneously benefit those members who want to wait and those who do not want to wait for their pot. What types of other financial transactions between these two types of bidding ROSCA members might be conceptually similar in terms of benefiting both sides?

4. Briefly compare and contrast a simple ROSCA to an ASCA. In your view, what are the key benefits and drawbacks of each of the two approaches? Which might you prefer to join, and why?

5. How is an ASCA a type of insurance? In what sort of situations might this function break down? How might formal microfinance solve this problem?

6. How do ROSCAs and ASCAs mitigate market failures such as moral hazard and adverse selection?

4.2 Savings Handlers and Credit Providers

External Managers

As we just discussed, in the informal sector it can become difficult for participants in savings and credit programs to manage their finances. Thus, external managers have evolved to help and assist the poor with the oversight of these financial tools. Some examples of managers include trusted individuals with skills and experience, non-governmental organizations (NGOs) and religious and other smaller, non-profit institutions with programs aimed at facilitating self-help financial intermediation among the poor.

External managers can serve as oversight for any pool of funds, but are most commonly seen in specialized ASCAs. As an illustration, some ASCA fund pools are created primarily for one purpose for all members participating in the fund, generally events that are likely to occur (e.g. the marriage of a child) or will definitely occur (death), yet at an unknown time. Pay-outs from these funds is dependent on the event happening, so the funds are like insurance policies.

In various cultures weddings and dowries can cost several years' worth of income for a poor family, requiring a means for accumulating large lump sums. Marriage funds are specifically designated for future marriage expenses and function so that many people can pool their funds. Because the accumulated money tends to be large relative to local incomes and the timeframes long for accumulating funds, such marriage funds may engage trustworthy outsiders to oversee and manage the ASCAs. A manager takes responsibility for safeguarding accumulated funds, transferring money to a member family when a marriage occurs, and ensuring that borrowed funds are repaid to the central pool.[5]

ASCA-like burial clubs have historical roots at least as far back as their use by the ancient Romans and Greeks. Like marriage funds, burial and funeral funds are an insurance device that is either time-bound or non-time-bound. Either way, a burial fund accumulates savings for funeral services and requires participants to set aside a sum of money that will be allocated to a member who experiences a death in the family. A non-time-bound fund grows over a period of time and allows for loan requests.

Figure 4.4 shows how this type of ASCA can work and how managers can play a significant role in the operation. In a burial fund, members allocate small, fixed amounts periodically into the pot throughout a long period of time. If within that time, one of the members experiences a death in the family, the member claims an agreed upon amount from the pot and uses it for their expenses. After the person claims the funds, some or all of the remaining pot is returned back to the remaining contributors as a rebate for their share. The cycle starts again as the receiver of the pot pays back their funds.[6] Managers collect and distribute the funds, and serve as the overseer to follow up with the member who withdraws the funds to ensure they pay back within the agreed periods.

Thus, managers can help ensure the security of the funds of the poor. At the same time, an individual manager can only manage so many accounts, and can

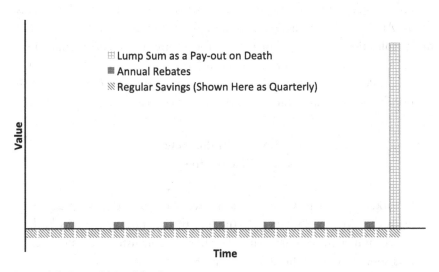

Figure 4.4. Annual burial fund

Source: Rutherford (2000).

face record keeping and enforcement issues without more formal infrastructures like computer networks and legal contract mechanisms. And unscrupulous ones could still run off with a group's funds. Therefore, institutions that formalize these informal savings clubs can help improve the availability and security of service as well as the management structure of these operations.

Deposit Collectors

We saw that several of the poor in Chapter 2 used other individuals as moneyguards, giving neighbors or co-workers small sums to store as a way to set aside funds for later and reduce the liquidity of saved cash without the fees of normal banks. A more structured version of moneyguards has evolved as well. Individuals who offer a service of collecting and holding small savings as for the poor, called **deposit collectors**, are popular among the poor seeking more regular and secure methods of saving. Deposit collectors act as a sort of personal bank, for a fee.

The basic scheme is straightforward. Typically, a collector visits clients at very regular intervals, daily or weekly, to collect a series of small deposits, often as small as 20 or 75 cents or maybe $2 each visit. Collectors usually come to clients at times convenient to the client, so clients avoid travel and opportunity costs of time lost doing transactions. The collector stores the collected funds, often in regular banks perhaps combined with other clients' funds. At the end of an agreed time period or number of visits, perhaps 20 or 30 collections, the collector returns the accumulated sum to the client, minus a fee—maybe one or two deposits' worth. As discussed in Box 4.4, deposit collectors in urban Ghana and in rural Benin alike take one daily deposit for every 30, amounting to a 3.3% service charge. Because of the fees,

Box 4.4. In the Field
Susu Collectors in Ghana

A market woman in Ghana typically sees her "banker" every day to deposit as little as 25 cents. At the end of the month, she gets back her accumulated savings, with which she replenishes her stock or buys something that she could not afford out of one day's profits. She

(*Continued*)

Box 4.4. (*Continued*)

sometimes requests an advance on the month's expected proceeds, but her banker may avoid lending because he lacks cash reserves or access to credit in case repayment is delayed.

This banker is an informal savings collector, known in Ghana as a *susu* collector. In Accra, over 500 of them have formed the Greater Accra Susu Collectors Cooperative Society (GASCCS). They play an important role in mobilizing savings in West Africa through their daily collection of deposits. Savings collectors contract with clients to collect a fixed amount daily (or at regular intervals), typically ranging from $0.25 to $2.50. In Ghana, this amount averages $0.73 a day for each client. At the end of each month, the savings are returned to the depositors; the collectors keep one day's deposit, or 3.3% of the monthly savings, as commission.

Collectors put the bulk of their daily receipts into commercial bank accounts, retaining some to return to clients who need funds before the end of the month and some for their own short-term business transactions. In one bank branch, such deposits reached 40% of total demand deposits. Nonetheless, bank managers, largely unaware of the collection activities of account holders, have done little to facilitate deposits by *susu* collectors. Collectors end up with net earnings of nearly $200 a month, or six times Ghana's average per capita income, with about 11% of their gross fees going to expenses like bank fees and transportation. Although collectors earn a satisfactory livelihood, they would like to increase their earnings by making more advances to attract more clients or by lending to non-clients (with a typical fee of 20% on a three-month loan).

Source: Steel and Aryeetey (1994).

people who save with a deposit collector usually experience negative returns on their savings. Nonetheless, many find this a better alternative than trying to accumulate savings themselves—again a means to improve security and alleviate self-control and social taxation barriers.

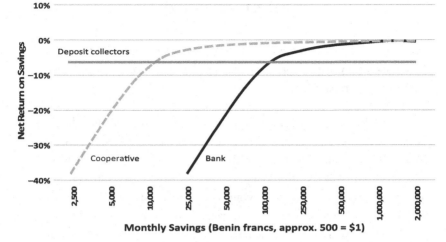

Figure 4.5. Net return on savings, by mechanism (Benin)

Source: Modified from Deshpande (2006).

Moreover, for saving small amounts collectors can be considerably less costly than paying fees and travel to use formal bank accounts. Figure 4.5, from a World Bank related study in a village in Benin, compares the net rate of interest (after fees and travel expenses) earned on various levels of monthly savings, across three different savings mechanisms.[7] Deposit collectors pay no interest on savings and instead take one deposit from each 30 as a fee, so the net negative return is the same, no matter how much the client saves—the horizontal flat line on the chart. By contrast, a formal bank—the solid curved line to the right—pays interest to savers, but costs the clients money and opportunity costs to go to a distant branch for services. The interest received does not make up for the costs enough to be a better option than deposit collectors unless the client is saving more than about $200 per month, equivalent to 120 days full-time work at Benin's minimum wage. Given that most of the poor in Benin earn far less than the minimum wage, formal finance is clearly out of reach. A local cooperative credit union, the dotted curved line, was better than the bank for small savers, but still required more than $20 monthly savings to be more attractive than a deposit collector.

In short, using deposit collectors is a simple yet effective method of small-scale saving that is safer than storing cash around the house where it can be stolen, or having non-liquid assets that are difficult to convert into usable cash. Having cash savings in one's direct possession also creates temptation for social taxation by friends and family or to use it for immediate personal consumption, such as alcohol or leisure goods, instead of leaving it for more important future needs. The moral hazard potential that deposit collectors might abscond with funds is limited by their need to maintain their reputations in the community if they hope to keep getting business. Having a good reputation may be hard to acquire in a community, but once a collector earns it, the informal financial intermediation service becomes a valuable asset both to the collector and to their clients.

Informal Moneylenders

While deposit collectors handle a client's own funds to facilitate savings, another similar informal personal service entails lending. Informal **moneylenders** are individuals within a village or region who lend to those who cannot obtain formal financial credit. For a price, moneylenders can lend either money directly or the use of useful assets such as oxen, fishing gear or sewing machines. Some moneylenders are known to charge exorbitantly high fees and interest rates, in many cases amounting to well beyond 100% APR and occasionally over 1,000%. The fact that so many millions of the poor are in fact willing to pay such high rates is not only testament to the value of the services but also evidence they have few alternatives to informal loans in times of need.

Often, tightly woven community relationships make moneylending possible, helping overcome the information asymmetry-related issues from Chapter 3. Compared to banks, moneylenders have access to more personal information about potential borrowers. Many moneylenders, not wanting to risk their investment unless assured that they will be paid back, will only lend to anyone they have met and know personally so they can gauge their riskiness as borrowers. Because moneylenders often come from the same communities as their clients, particularly in rural areas, they might also get to know their clients' families, friends and neighbors. To hedge against the possibility of default, they might do personal house visits, gauge the home life, visit the clients' market stalls or farms and otherwise keep tabs on the health of income sources, and interact regularly with families and neighbors. Should a borrower come into financial distress or otherwise have difficulty with repayments, the moneylenders may ask family or friends to help or pressure the borrower to repay, leveraging cultural norms of interpersonal social obligations and social taxation. In some cultures, the debt of one person is debt of the whole family, perhaps across several generations.

Because moneylenders can know their clients better than a bank might, they are able to specially tailor their services—individualized loan sizes, rates, durations, payback schedules, types of payments—to their clients' unique needs and situations. Existing clients and older borrowers tend to face lower interest rates, for example.[8] Personalizing services like deposit collectors, moneylenders might keep transactions and opportunity costs for their clients very low by coming directly to them at the most convenient places and times, perhaps at odd hours. Farmers might have to pay back only after harvest. Market sellers might pay only at the end of market days. People who get sick and cannot work for some period might get a temporary break from repayment, made up for later. Rather than in cash, a seamstress might pay back in completed garments the lender could sell. That flexibility and personal tailoring has real value to the poor. With few other options, they pay.

Providing convenient personalized services and keeping good information and tabs on borrowers take considerable time and effort. So, moneylenders—like the one in Box 4.5—tend to keep their numbers of clients relatively low

Box 4.5. Faces
Interview with a Moneylender

In an exclusive interview with a moneylender, Satish Shetty, operating in Yelahanka, Bangalore, a reporter from the magazine *Microfinance Focus* learned how this business is run and some of the practices that make moneylenders so common everywhere.

Q: When did you start moneylending and why?
A: I started eight years back. I had just suffered some losses in my bakery business, so I decided to enter this business.

(*Continued*)

Box 4.5. (*Continued*)

Q: How many customers do you have?
A: Around 15–20 borrow money from me every month.

Q: How do you market your service? Why do your clients choose to borrow from you?
A: Mostly through word-of-mouth. I don't run ads or anything of the sort. My clients come to me because my practices are similar to regulated norms. I don't charge them astronomical rates.

Q: So how does this money lending work? What interest rate do you charge? What type of interest is it? What collateral do your borrowers offer?
A: Well, I took training with some government officials before I started and run my business according to the practices I have learnt. I charge an interest rate of 3% per month....While familiarity with the person plays a role, I sign a legal document with the borrower that amounts to a contract. Also as a surety, the borrower gives me a blank check with his signature. If he doesn't pay the monthly interest rate for the entire period, then I cash the check, after taking interest rate into account. If the check bounces three times, I go to court. Similar to a bank, I hold their assets like mortgage.

Q: What is the average amount of money that you loan out? What is the fee that you charge?
A: I loan out anywhere between 10,000 to 25,000 rupees per person [about $200–$500], depending on what they want it for. And I don't charge any one time fees.

Q: What is your repayment policy? And what is your repayment rate?
A: I either have weekly collections or monthly collections depending on the borrower's job. If he's running a vegetable shop, or an auto-rickshaw then I charge weekly. If he's working a government job or some other place where he gets a paycheck only once a month, I collect monthly. The borrowers drop by my office regularly.

(Continued)

Box 4.5. (*Continued*)

When they don't I check on them. Usually most of the people I lend out to repay me within the specified time period. When they don't I take legal action. Sometimes they run away from the city, say if the auto had an accident for example, then there's nothing I can do. Suppose a guy owes me 10,000 rupees for a period of two years. I charge him 3% interest, so he has to pay 300 rupees interest per month. He can keep making payments of 300 rupees every month. If he pays back 2,000 rupees of principal say, then from the next month on, I charge 3% of 8,000 rupees, so then monthly he has to pay 240 rupees interest. So interest amount keeps on decreasing like that. If he makes regular payments, then I am flexible with time period of two years.

Q: What is your relationship with the people you lend to, professional or personal? What about the other lenders in the area?

    A: It's a bit of both really. At least once we enter into a transaction, I get to know them well. I don't really have much contact with other lenders.

Q: Is this your main business, or do you have other businesses?

    A: I have other businesses. This is only one of the things I'm involved in. In the moneylending business, I usually have a decent margin of profits, but if a couple of defaults happen in quick succession, and then I suffer losses. That happened a couple of years back.

Q: Are you satisfied with this money lending business?

    A: It's a business. But it helps people develop a means of sustenance, and it is under the purview of the government. So yes, I think I am doing a good job.

Source: Gullapalli (2010).

in order to know and serve them better and to maintain the useful social ties with the borrowers and their friends and families. The typical moneylender only serves between 20 and 80 individuals.[9]

Economics Professor Adel Varghese of Texas A&M University suggests that one way MFIs and banks might keep lending costs down and expand the number of clients eligible for financing is to consider teaming up with moneylenders, leveraging their more intimate knowledge of the community and potential clients.[10] With the moneylenders acting as agents for the bank, all sides could benefit. Borrowers could have higher likelihoods of receiving loans and at better rates and get more personalized services, the MFI or bank might attract more customers, and the moneylender would have a way to make extra money without overcharging and without placing their own funds at risk. Potential principal–agent problems do arise, however. The moneylender as agent could refer anyone to the bank claiming that they are a good risk, for example, or use their status in the community to pressure poor people into taking more loans than they can really afford.

Whether or not along these lines, better serving the billions of unbanked will nonetheless require many innovations of some sort or other. Innovative MFIs around the world are exploring ways to provide benefits and more flexible, tailored services like moneylenders, but at much larger scale and lower costs to clients. We will explore many of them in coming chapters.

How Much Do Moneylenders Charge and Why?

In South Africa, a typical loan from a moneylender carries an interest rate of 30%—not annually, but *per month*.[11] Rates like this are in fact commonplace worldwide. Figure 4.6 shows results of a summary of 28 studies of moneylender rates across 13 countries. The bottom line is that moneylenders are generally very expensive for the poor. Only 7% of reported moneylender rates were below 5% monthly (i.e. below 80% interest rate per year). More than one in five moneylender rates amounted to more than 100% a month. One in 10 exceeded 1,000% if calculated monthly, usually for very short-term loans like for a day or a week.

The demand for very short-term credit is particularly common among the poor. Why? Recall from Chapter 3 what we called the primacy of flow transactions in the informal economy. For example in one scheme found in Nicaragua a borrower would take a loan at the beginning of the day, perhaps 100 cordoba to buy enough daily fresh vegetables to sell in their market stall that day, and pay back 105 by the end of a day. Paid day after day that would amount to a 332% monthly rate. Similarly, in the Philippines, a

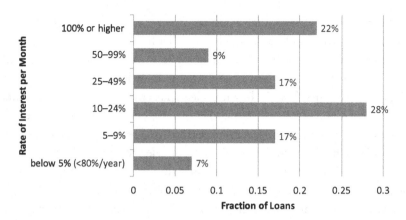

Figure 4.6. Effective monthly interest rates of moneylenders, 13 countries

Note: Interest rates are nominal. Average annual inflation was 3–20% for most of these countries during the study periods, and in all cases below 57%.
Source: Modified from Robinson (2001).

common agreement would be for a street vendor to borrow say, 1,000 pesos on Monday morning to buy dried fish from a wholesaler, and pay back 200 pesos every day for the next six days the rest of the week, an effective 149% monthly rate.[12] The moneylender facilitates the everyday flow of funds for these poor households otherwise unable to accumulate a lump sum 1,000 pesos on their own.

In another arrangement found in the Philippines a borrower might borrow 50 pesos and pay back 60 pesos by the end of a day. A 20% *daily* fee— a remarkable 23,638% if calculated as a monthly interest rate—is common not only in the Philippines but also throughout Asia and Latin America.[13] It is so common it has a widespread nickname: "five-six" in reference to the idea that six units are paid back for every five borrowed. In Indonesia it is called *sepuluh kembali duabelas* or "10 comes back 12."

The five-six idea is widespread in part because it is attractively simple, exactly suits the weekly cycles of market vendors everywhere, and is easy to understand; but it is a very costly form of credit. In understanding the willingness of the poor to pay such high rates, it probably helps to think of them as service fees rather than interest. The 20,000-plus percent monthly interest rate of five-six schemes is unimaginable for most of us in rich countries used to thinking in APR terms, but can be manageable when paid in 10 peso chunks (roughly 22 cents) after each day of market selling. Note how similar the willingness to pay five-six is to what we saw in Chapter 3 with the poor Americans using RiteCheck in the South Bronx. Customer Michelle was willing to pay a $2 fee to withdraw $8 out of her own account. Perhaps we might have nicknamed it four-five.

Box 4.6. In the Field
Moneylenders Help Migrants Begin Businesses in New Delhi

In places like New Delhi, where acquiring a formal bank loan requires a permanent address as well as proof of ownership for mortgage collateral, moneylenders have found ways to generate businesses for themselves and simultaneously help migrants moving from rural areas who are trying to start new lives in the city.

Even though over 30 million farming families now in the area are deep in debt, the government has had difficulties shutting down the operations of moneylenders. The services are popular. In fact, moneylenders have helped migrants not only secure loans to start up business in areas like the suburbs of New Delhi, but also have found ways to provide them with temporary shelter and other resources as they try to grow their businesses and establish new roots in their communities.

Generally, the moneylenders charge 10 rupees a day per every 1,000 rupees lent, 1% interest daily. Though this may sound high by formal banking standards, in informal markets where the average business owner earns around 150–200 rupees ($3–4) a day, it is not too much for moneylenders to ask for 10 rupees a day. These services are very much in demand because moneylenders are able to serve migrants in communities that do not have other financial options for new arrivals in search of fresh starts.

Source: Parashar (2008).

The poor would unquestionably be better off if they did not need to pay such fees regularly, but living on the fluctuating financial edge and without other affordable options necessitates it. As we discussed, most poor clients in the informal economy have no form of acceptable collateral and work under circumstances of substantial cash flow uncertainty, no steady work or no guarantee that their harvest will be successful enough that season to acquire efficient funds to pay back the loan. Thus, informal moneylenders work in risky environments where formal financers face cost and information barriers to penetrate the local ara.

It is that lack of options—the moneylender is like a local monopolist—combined with the convenience and the ability of moneylenders to provide services specially tailored for the unique needs of each borrower that enable moneylending fees to remain so high. The moneylender can gain local monopoly power several ways. They might be the only one in the village with enough funds. They could have the social stature and political power to keep would-be competitors at bay. They might control some key resource like land or the local mill. And they might be the only one able to overcome information asymmetry barriers with enough personal information on people in the community. In these situations, the poor are left with no choice but to borrow from the monopoly-like lender, locking in a cycle of debt and high fees.

Credit under Contract

A related common moneylending-like phenomenon is loans expressly tied with selling agreements. In these so-called **interlinked transactions**, or "credit under contract," the prices a buyer agrees to pay for output are tied with the terms under which the buyer provides credit to the seller. For example, in the narrative in Box 4.7, Economics Professor Muhammad Yunus talked about encountering one such arrangement in Bangladesh where a moneylender lends money to a weaver for raw bamboo with the expectation the weaver sells their finished woven bamboo stools to the lender for 2 cents more than loaned. On a larger scale, a study by the International Fund for Agricultural Development found that credit under contract is the dominant, sometimes the only, source of credit for poor farmers throughout eastern and southern Africa.[14] The study estimated that in just one sector in one country, Zambia's cotton sector alone, 150,000 poor farmers received a total of $10 million in credit annually to pay for inputs under contract to large cotton buyers. Another study by University of Leuven Professor Johan Swinnen and his colleagues showed that four out of every five cotton farmers in Kazakhstan had received finance from their buyers too.[15] Clearly, the practice of credit interlinked with output purchases is a global phenomenon.

Box 4.7. Faces
Weaver Sufiya Begum's 2-Cent Middleman Inspires Grameen Bank

When Chittagong University Economics Professor Muhammad Yunus, founder of the MFI Grameen Bank, was trying to uncover the major factors keeping Bangladeshis in poverty, he met Sufiya Begum living in Jobra, a village near the university. She spent nearly all her time, every day, weaving beautiful stools from bamboo. Yet she was unable to prosper, finding herself in a cycle of debt to her lender, left with barely enough to feed herself because the loans were contingent on the weaver selling all her wares to the lender. Yunus relates his first conversation with her.

She was in her early twenties, thin, with dark skin and black eyes, She wore a red sari and had the tired eyes of a woman who labored every day from morning to night.
"What is your name?" I asked.
"Sufiya Begum."
"How old are you?"
"Twenty-one." ...
"Do you own this bamboo?" I asked.
"Yes."
"How did you get it?"
"I buy it."
"How much does the bamboo cost?"
"Five taka." At the time this was about twenty-two cents.
"Do you have five taka?"

(Continued)

Box 4.7. (*Continued*)

"No, I borrow it from the paikars. *"*

"The middlemen? What is your arrangement with them?"

"I must sell my bamboo stools back to them at the end of they day as repayment for my loan."

"How much do you sell a stool for?"

"Five taka and fifty poysha."

"So you make fifty poysha profit?"

She nodded. That came to a profit of just two cents.

"And could you borrow the cash from the moneylender and buy your own raw material?"

"Yes but the moneylender would demand a lot. People who deal with them only get poorer."

"How much does the moneylender charge?"

"It depends. Sometimes he charges 10 percent per week. But I have one neighbor who is paying 10 percent per day."

"And that is all you earn from making these beautiful bamboo stools, fifty poysha?"

"Yes."...

I watched as she set to work again, her small brown hands plaiting the strands of bamboo as they had every day for months and years on end. This was her livelihood.... How would her children break the cycle of poverty she had started? How could they go to school when the income Sufiya earned was barely enough to feed her, let alone shelter her family and clothe them properly? It seemed hopeless to imagine that her babies would one day escape this misery.

Sufiya Begum earned 2 cents a day.

Within months Yunus founded Grameen Bank, now one of the world's largest MFIs.

Source: Yunus (1999) pp. 46–47.

How does it work? Many middlemen who deal with farmers or craftspeople such as weavers often serve as the main or only buyer or employer in an area, i.e. in jargon, a monopsony. The poor take loans from these buyers for, say, getting seeds, fertilizers, or raw materials for their crafts, in exchange for promising to sell their produce back to their lender–buyer. The loan repayment is deducted from the sale price. The lender–buyer then in turn acts as a middleman wholesaler, selling the products up the supply chain to retail vendors or other buyers. For instance, students and faculty from Lehigh University found a system where farmers in Kenya raised rabbits by getting feed and other inputs with credit linked to buyers who were supplying rabbits to hotels in South Africa. Large landowners who rent plots, often the main source of land and employment of farm labor, can play similar financial intermediation roles for tenant farmers.

The widespread use of interlinked transactions suggests the poor value the availability of this financial intermediation tool, and some research evidence—the Zambian cotton study noted earlier for one—suggests credit under contract done by large corporate buyers can improve the livelihoods of the poor, guaranteeing markets for their output and financing needed inputs they otherwise could not acquire. However, other research suggests that less scrupulous middlemen can instead abuse the unbalanced nature of the relationship.

Note that interlinked loans are generally for short term or seasonal flow transactions that repeat regularly, rather than longer-term stock investments in productive capital. The system can lead to repetitive dependence, often likened to indentured servitude and bonded labor. Local monopsony buyers or controlling landlords can control local trade flows and set prices for buying output, sometimes well below market prices because the poor often have no other location nearby to sell their goods. This system can perpetuate inequalities and discrepancies in society, forming a cycle difficult to break. If the farmer or artisan is not able to make sufficient returns to escape the need for another loan, their only option is to sell at the dictated price. Emergence of such bonded-labor vicious-cycles is often seen in areas with populations of low geographic mobility, meaning little direct access to markets and limited competition among either lenders or buyers, leaving borrowers little choice.[16] The opportunity costs to poor borrowers in the money and time repeatedly invested in repaying loans and fees could, with better financial intermediation options, otherwise have been devoted to savings, investment and consumption.

Section in Bulletpoint

- External managers oversee pools of informal savings and can help ensure that funds are secure and facilitate distribution, collection and proper record keeping.

- Deposit collectors agree, in exchange for fees, to safeguard savings and to come frequently to collect a series of small deposits, enabling the poor to accumulate savings.

- Moneylenders are prevalent everywhere in the world, giving the poor access to credit where formal financial institutions remain out of reach.

- Some moneylenders are known to charge extraordinarily high interest rates that create cycles of debt difficult for clients to break.

- However, the fact that the poor are willing to pay the high fees and the continued widespread use of moneylenders around the world suggests they provide services the poor value and need.

- Credit under contract arrangements, or interlinked transactions, ties the terms of loans to the terms of purchasing agreements.

- Some interlinked credit agreements are known to help the poor, while others can lead to vicious cycles of debt akin to bonded labor.

Discussion Questions

1. It is clear that deposit collectors are popular with the poor. Why do they exist when there are banks, ROSCAs and ASCAs available?

2. What are some of the common explanations for the exorbitant interest rates charged by some moneylenders? Why would someone borrow from a moneylender if they know that they will be charged such high rates?

3. How do you think moneylenders maintain their monopolies when there are other moneylenders close by, sometimes even in the same area?

4. This chapter said that credit under contract transactions can lead to indentured servitude-like practices. Explain how this might come about. Do you see microfinance as a solution to this? Why or why not?

5. What are some benefits that moneylenders can provide to people that formal banks have trouble delivering? How do moneylenders overcome some of the market failures that inhibit banks from serving the poor?

6. Clearly people around the world value moneylenders and are willing to pay for their services. But they can be remarkably expensive and usury. Write a well-supported opinion blog (~400–500 words) arguing whether informal moneylenders are good or bad for their communities. Support with links to real data, graphs and/or tables, etc. Address either developing economy contexts or developed economy issues (e.g. loan sharks, pawn shops, payday lenders, and check cashing are ongoing policy questions in some countries).

Chapter Summary

The poor around the world face financial intermediation needs perhaps even more central for their everyday lives than for the rich. With formal finance out of reach, they have developed a creative array of informal systems to fill the gap. They participate in ROSCAs and ASCAs in order to obtain large lump sums and as means of insurance. Deposit collectors facilitate savings for the poor and moneylenders and interlinked transactions expand their options to borrow. While some moneylenders and middlemen are justly criticized as abusing their power over people with few alternatives, many others are creating value for the poor by providing flexible and personalized services tailored exactly for their needs and situations.

Nevertheless, informal systems are by no means perfect. With their very informality and small scale come inherent weaknesses, risks and challenges for the poor. As we will explore through the rest of the book, innovative MFIs continue to look for inspiration in the way these many informal schemes function, combining some practices drawn from them with infrastructures from formal finance in quests to design more accessible and useful financial services for the poor.

Key Terms

ASCA
Accumulated Savings and Credit Association; more formal than ROSCAs, ASCAs function like a village bank in that they can grant loans and members can withdraw variable amounts at variable times.

bidding ROSCA
ROSCA in which members bid on how much extra they will contribute to the pool and the winner is able to withdraw their lump sum first, essentially paying higher interest for an earlier payment.

deposit collectors
Collect series of small deposits at very regular intervals, often daily or weekly, then later return the accumulated sums to the clients, minus fees; enable the poor to accumulate lump sums.

interlinked transactions
Transactions in which prices paid by a buyer for output are tied with the terms for the buyer providing credit to the seller; also called "credit under contract."

lottery ROSCA
ROSCA in which the order of payments is decided randomly or through a lottery system to ensure that each member has an equal opportunity to access earlier lump sums.

moneylender
Individual who provides loans to those unable to access formal financial credit; some charge exorbitantly high fees.

non-time-bound ASCA
More flexible than many ASCAs in not requiring repayment of borrowed funds within a specific time period and allowing participants to withdraw funds whenever needed; serves as a kind of insurance for disasters, death, or marriage; can be more complex to manage and often can charge high interest rates because it is convenient.

ROSCA
Rotating Savings and Credit Association; informal group self-regulated by members who each make regular contributions into a pool of communal funds, which is then allocated in rotation, enabling each individual to receive a lump sum payment of a size otherwise difficult to obtain on their own.

social collateral
Trust based within the strength of interpersonal relationships, friendships, family bonds or community ties, rather than on physical or monetary assets as collateral.

Notes:

[1] Yang (1952).
[2] Bouman (1995), and Anderson and Baland (2002).
[3] Rutherford (2000).
[4] Rutherford (2000) p. 47.
[5] Rutherford (2000) p. 62.
[6] Rutherford (2000) p. 65.
[7] Deshpande (2006).
[8] Robinson (2001) p. 193.
[9] Robinson (2001) p. 190.
[10] Varghese (2005).
[11] Collins et al (2009) p. 133.
[12] Robinson (2001).
[13] Robinson (2001).
[14] IFAD (2003).
[15] Swinnen et al (2007).
[16] Germidis, Kessler, and Meghir (1991).

Chapter

MICROLENDING

"I have been impressed by the power of a simple, small loan to those for whom fate and circumstance have resulted in disadvantage. Maintaining peoples' integrity and showing them trust, whilst facilitating a way for them to rebuild their own lives is such a meaningful way of alleviating poverty."

— **Queen Rania Al-Abdullah, of Jordan**

Figure 5.1. A solidarity group meeting: A fixture of microfinance worldwide

Microlending is a primary component of microfinance, and one of the most well known activities associated with the industry. Microlending has two basic models: group lending and individual lending. Due to the publicity of Muhammad Yunus and Grameen Bank's 2006 Nobel Prize, many people associate microfinance directly with the group-lending model, although as we have seen the industry stems far beyond lending to financial services of all sorts.

Nevertheless, the roots of the industry lie in group lending, so we shall start there. In this chapter, we will explore not only various flavors of group lending but also individual lending, and discuss the advantages and disadvantages of each. In particular, we will look at how in their lending practices microfinance institutions are overcoming some of the barriers to offering formal financial services to the poor that we identified in earlier chapters. In Chapter 6, we will move on to a similar discussion of savings, insurance and other financial services that are becoming increasingly common in the industry.

5.1 Group Lending

The idea of forming groups to gain better access to funds is far from a new invention. As discussed in Chapter 4, burial clubs, Rotating Savings and Credit Associations (ROSCAs), and other credit and savings cooperatives have existed in the informal sector for ages, bringing people and their own funds together for the members' benefit. Leveraging the worldwide familiarity people had with these informal financial collaboratives, during the 1970s MFIs built foundational strategies around the concept of formal lending to groups rather than to individuals.

Group microlending emerged in two different parts of the world. In 1973, Accion first began experimenting with solidarity groups in Latin America, and a few years later Muhammad Yunus began lending money to groups of women in Bangladesh through his experimental Grameen Bank Project. Success in those early trials by both organizations, which remain among the world's largest MFIs, fostered the global explosion of the microfinance industry over the following four decades. While some of the initial assumptions about why these early group-based systems of lending to the poor worked have since been questioned, there is no doubt that their success spawned the microfinance industry. They proved the poor were reliable and potentially profitable borrowers, and the world of mainstream formal finance eventually began to notice.

Group Lending Approaches

Group lending practices vary somewhat depending on the MFI and region in which it operates. For example, the Grameen Bank in Bangladesh maintains a group size of five members that are closely connected and know each other well. Groups affiliated with Accion in Latin American similarly tend to be 3–10 members. Experiments with models in Kenya by the non-profit organization Reach the Children suggested that larger groups of a dozen or more were more effective for them.[1] Larger still, FINCA's village banks can have upwards of 20–50 members. We will discuss the major group lending approaches that have emerged across the world of microfinance, and what makes the group approach effective. Though the methodologies vary, all the group lending practices are based on the common ROSCA-rooted concepts of group collaboration, social rather than physical or monetary collateral, periodic meetings, frequent repayments, and transferring responsibilities from the lender to the group members themselves. We will address individual lending later in the chapter.

Figure 5.2 categorizes group-lending schemes by two main differentiating features: degree of self-governance and sources of initial funds. We will learn more details on the main approaches below, but briefly to start, to the left are so-called solidarity group approaches. In two broad flavors described below, those pioneered by Accion and by Grameen Bank, solidarity groups are organized and formally overseen by the lending organization. Members take on various levels of responsibility running the groups, partial self-governance, but ultimate responsibility for managing the groups, setting procedures, and oversight of funds rests with the MFIs and their personnel. In Grameen-style groups, the members themselves become owners of their own mini-banks.

To the right on Figure 5.2 are group lending approaches that aim for full self-governance. Perhaps after an initial period of support and advice from an outside MFI or NGO, the groups take on full responsibility for all their own activities, establish their own procedures and rules, and own and manage their own funds. Some self-governed groups, like FINCA's "village banks"

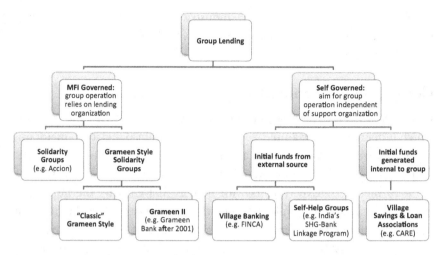

Figure 5.2. Approaches to group lending

Source: Modified from Waterfield and Duval (1996).

and formal "self-help groups" in India, both discussed later in this chapter, use loan funds initially provided by an MFI, NGO, government, church or other outside source, often adapting rules and procedures, bookkeeping guidelines, and materials suggested by those external sponsors. The sponsors, however, expect the groups eventually to mature, no longer need external oversight, and take over running all aspects of group operations themselves. In some cases, additional external loan funds continue to be available in an ongoing financial relationship with the MFI, while in others, particularly self-help groups, the support organization hopes the groups wean themselves from the need for external funds entirely.

Finally, on the rightmost branch of the diagram, other self-governed groups sometimes called village savings and loan associations (VSLAs) do not get outside funding to begin their lending. Instead, like ASCAs, they rely entirely on the members' own accumulated savings. Let us now look at the main alternative group lending mechanisms in more detail.

Classic "Grameen-Style" Group Lending

Although Grameen Bank is now using a different system, their original approach to group lending is often called **classic Grameen-style** solidarity group lending. A collateral-free approach to lending for the poor, it has been copied by numerous other MFIs worldwide, including many of today's largest. Under this model, self-selected groups of five are formed and rather than the lender requiring loan collateral from individuals, each group jointly guarantees the loans of its individual members. Members cannot be from the same family, but must be from the same village or neighborhood, well-known to each other, and the same gender. One of the members is selected as the "chairman" of the group, a position that then revolves among all group members. After undergoing training and learning about the policies of the MFI, approved groups can request their first loans. A minimum of five groups then forms a "center" (a *kendra* in Bengali) for holding joint weekly meetings with the MFI's loan officer. The groups in each *kendra*, in turn, became official parts, and legal owners, of the Grameen bank itself.

Before a new group can begin borrowing, members must begin meeting each week with the loan officer and putting away small amounts into savings accounts for at least four weeks. The compulsory savings requirement demonstrates their ability on a weekly basis to come up with extra funds like they will have to have to repay loans, while helping them begin to accumulate an asset. Once loan repayments begin, members must also continue to save an additional fractional supplement in addition to their repayment.

Members make individual loan repayments in public at each *kendra* meeting. This is an important aspect of the classic methodology as the public repayments may add social pressure from the community beyond the immediate five-person group.[2] The risk of being regarded as irresponsible helps ensure that the installment payments are made promptly and in full. The *kendra* also has the power to select its members; hence, if you or your group gets a reputation for not repaying, your entire group can be excluded from the *kendra* and thus unable to receive any additional loans.

The concept of social pressure is also applied at the group-level. Classic Grameen-style group lending uses the principle of staggering; i.e. waiting to give loans to some group members until loans to other members have been repaid. Originally in Grameen's case, loans were to two members of the group at a time. When these loans had been repaid, the next two members received their loans. The chairman of the group received a loan last, once all other members had fully repaid their loans. This method increases the social

Box 5.1. Dig Deeper
Historical Evolution of Formal Group Lending

As we see this chapter, today's global microfinance industry has adopted key components of
the workings of informal ASCAs. But embracing
the ASCA-like group credit system by formal
finance is not an entirely modern idea. One
of the earliest functioning formal ASCA-like
systems to exist was created by Jonathan Swift,
Irish author most famous for *Gulliver's Travels*.
Swift's Irish loan funds are today considered the historical original
collaborative microcredit in a mold similar to what we are familiar
with today.

An anti-poverty activist, Swift around 1720 started using his own
money to lend to Dublin's poor for their small business—without asking
for collateral or interest. As repayments came in the funds would be
loaned back out to others, ASCA-like. Swift's cooperative credit system
only required two other people to vouch for a borrower and be jointly
liable for the debt; substituting social collateral for physical collateral just
like today's microfinance industry. Eventually legally formalized by Irish
Parliament in 1823, the Irish loan fund system added formal savings
alongside credit and soon was distributing roughly half a million loans
annually to the poor throughout Ireland, without collateral, touching
one out of every five Irish families.

Later around the mid-1800s, Friedrich Wilhelm Raiffeisen, a
German businessman, was sickened by the exploitation of the poor in
rural areas in Germany. Like Swift, he sought to alleviate some of the
financial burdens of the poor by setting up cooperative credit and savings
unions, aka village banks, around the country to fuel investment in
agricultural settings to spur development within farming communities.
Credit, again like Swift's, depended not on collateral but on cooperative
shared liability among members. In what became known as the
sparkasse system, public credit unions backed by local and municipal

(Continued)

Box 5.1. (*Continued*)

governments, began sprouting up around the world, from people's credit banks (Bank Perkreditan Rakyat) in Indonesia to rural Latin America, Europe, and India. In particular, Raiffesien's *sparkasse* model formed the basis for the Peruvian municipal public credit unions, CMACs, a key component of Peru's world leading microfinance sector today. Similarly in India (including Bengal territory, today's Bangladesh), cooperative societies began sprouting up in the early 1900s through the support of the 1904 Cooperative Credit Societies Act, as the central government supported initiatives to extend ASCA-like village banking cooperatives to the rural poor.

Thus, historical formal group lending systems have existed in most parts of the world, indicating the potential of cooperative credit and savings exists across cultures.

Sources: Roodman (2012); Armendáriz and Morduch (2010); Global Envision (2006). Portrait from The Works of Jonathan Swift, D.D., D.S.P.D., in eight volumes. Dublin: G. Faulkner, 1746.

pressure within the group and enhances incentives for members to make good on guaranteeing each other's loans. If one member is unable to make an installment payment, the other group members know a default will have a negative impact on the group as a whole. If they do not make a repayment on behalf of a defaulting member, other members will not be allowed to receive loans of their own in the future. In this way, the liability for repayment is shared among all five members.

In practice what this joint responsibility often means is not that members actually end up paying each other's debts, but rather that they exert social pressure on each other to pay back, through open dialog, warnings, and occasionally with quite overt and harsh social sanctions. In other words, group pressure is a form of social collateral, which as we will see later can serve a way of dealing with issues of limited liability and moral hazard along the lines we discussed in Chapter 3. As Grameen's founder put it:

Group membership not only creates support and protection but also smoothes out the erratic behavior patterns of individual members, making each borrower more reliable in the process. Subtle and at times not-so-subtle peer pressure keeps each group member in line with the broader objectives of the credit program.... Because the group approves the loan request of each individual member, the group assumes moral responsibility for the loan. If any member of the group gets into trouble, the group usually comes forward to help.

— Muhammad Yunus, *Banker to the Poor*

A potential downside to the classic Grameen-style solidarity group model is that deciding which two members have the most pressing need for funds at any given time can cause tension within the group. Like in ROSCAs, not only do early recipients get benefits earlier, but also the liability to back up defaults falls on later recipients before they can benefit. Moreover, the members who have to wait for their loans may need to turn elsewhere if their needs are too immediate, perhaps to moneylenders or other competing MFIs. Debt for an individual with loans from multiple sources can spiral beyond healthy levels, leading to endless cycles of borrowing from one to pay off another.

On the other hand, if all group members repay without any problems along the way, they will qualify for increasingly larger loans in the next loan cycle. We have seen in earlier chapters how the poor generally value ongoing repeated access to funds to facilitate flow transactions. As a result, the incentive of **progressive lending**, i.e. the promise of larger future loans if early smaller ones go well, has proved to be perhaps even more of an incentive for repayment than the threat of social sanctions. Due to their effectiveness, progressive lending incentives are common not only in Grameen-style lending, but also much more broadly in group lending in general and individual lending too. For example, Figure 5.3 shows a loan officer from Pro Mujer,

Figure 5.3. Explaining progressive lending at Pro Mujer

an MFI lending in the Latin American solidarity group tradition (discussed next). He is introducing progressive lending using a stair steps metaphor during a training session for a new Pro Mujer solidarity group.

Solidarity Group Approach

Less-rigid than the classic Grameen system, the **solidarity group** approach nevertheless relies on the same underlying ASCA-like principles of small group peer pressure, regular meetings, no collateral, and cross guaranteeing. Solidarity groups are commonly associated with the practices of Accion International and its affiliates like BancoSol in Bolivia, so they are sometimes called Latin American solidarity groups, but the system is used widely all around the world. Borrowers form groups in which they jointly guarantee each other's loans. (As we will see later, however, increasing numbers of MFIs are dropping this joint guarantee requirement). Group sizes are more flexible than in the classic Grameen system, yet still tend to be small, usually consisting of between three and 10 members. Members assume various responsibilities like chair or treasurer. Regular group meetings with staff from the MFI, often weekly or monthly and often in each other's homes, enable members to make repayments and receive any new loans. Record keeping and money transfers are done in the open so every member can be assured all other members are adhering to agreed terms.

Because both systems draw on informal ASCA mechanisms, many aspects of the solidarity group methodology are similar to the classic Grameen approach. Group formation serves not only as social collateral to help guarantee loans without collateral but also to reduce the costs associated with administering individual small loans. However, a major distinction is that all members of solidarity groups can each have loans at the same time, rather than just two. This process eliminates some of the checks and balances of classic Grameen-style lending. With every member potentially having a loan, the total amount of credit outstanding will be comparably larger at any point in time. This increases the potential risk to the MFIs should a group collectively not be able to repay. Solidary group MFIs also generally take on central responsibility (and costs) for evaluating and approving each individual borrower, whereas those using the classic Grameen model evaluate loan worthiness at the group level. On the other hand, the terms are more favorable to group members who do not have to wait as long to receive credit. Moreover, the shared responsibility to backup each other's payments is distributed more equally across the whole group from the start, potentially reducing social tension.

Another major difference with the classic Grameen system is that solidarity groups themselves do not become owners or official parts of the MFI. Group members are simply clients rather than owners. We will see in Chapter 8 that this difference in ownership structure made the solidarity group approach the early norm among MFIs seeking to attract outside commercial investors.

Village Banking

In **village banking**, much larger—and self-governing—groups form to facilitate uncollateralized borrowing. John Hatch, the founder of the U.S.-based non-profit FINCA, created the method in a small village in Bolivia in 1984. Initially limited to Latin American countries where FINCA started, the village banking approach is now widely replicated and used in more than 90 countries.[3] Village banking groups are generally bigger than solidarity groups, sometimes as big as 20–50 members who are typically from the same neighborhood.

Each group of members forms an independent legal entity, a "village bank," which the members jointly own. Once approved, a group receives operational training and materials and an initial lump sum loan from the MFI. Each village bank entity then lends those funds on to its individual members, charging rates of interest and fees the members themselves collectively decide. Each village bank can set different rules, with guidelines from the MFI. Similarly, the members themselves, rather than the MFI, are generally responsible for approving individual loan requests. Typically, the members meet once a week to make installment repayments and engage in skills training, mentoring, and motivational activities.

As with other early group lending approaches, in traditional village banking every member is jointly liable for the loans of their peers. Because members are also owners of their group's village bank, if someone does not repay the owners suffer the loss. As a result, this transfers some of the risk associated with MFIs lending without collateral. The group collectively, rather than the MFI, has to bear the burden if an individual defaults on a loan. As members repay, the village bank accumulates those repayments

Box 5.2. Faces
Sherida Mkama, Tugeme Village Banking Group Member

Sherida Mkama lives in the village of Kamanga, Tanzania, with her husband and 10 children. She joined FINCA's Tugeme Village Bank in 1995 after learning of the opportunity through word of mouth. Though initially was hesitant to borrow money, scared she would get in trouble if unable to pay back her loan, she took out a loan of $50 hoping it would help her improve her family's income and begin the climb out of poverty. Sherida sold tomatoes at the local market, but had never had enough capital to expand her successful business because she needed all her proceeds to feed, clothe, and educate her many children. The initial and subsequent loans enabled her to expand her business and increase her productivity in growing and selling tomatoes, and to save for the future. According to Sherida, the village bank gave her "a newfound sense of hope and knowledge that, by her actions, she can determine her family's future."

Source: FINCA Client Stories, www.villagebanking.org/site/c.erKPI2PCIoE/b.2630021/k.A6B6/Our_Clients.htm.

and then it, as an entity not individual members, repays with interest what the group owes back to the MFI. Similar to the classic Grameen's savings requirement, in FINCA's specific system, as members repay loans they are also required to begin saving an additional 20% on top of what they owe. In other words, members simultaneously save up while saving down, slowly accumulating a formal savings balance.

The village bank accumulates those savings, together with interest and fees paid by members on their loans, into an ACSA-like asset base managed by the group as a whole. It might loan those accumulated funds back out, expanding financing for members and perhaps even for non-members, or might deposit them in a regular bank account or invest in something on behalf of its member-owners. In this sense, like an ASCA, the village bank entity maintains internal accounts for each member about their individual savings and borrowing and ownership share; but it also keeps a collective external account related to the entity's credit and interest owed to the MFI and any external assets jointly owned. Like with ASCAs, this account bookkeeping can be fairly involved, so the supporting MFI usually provides established procedural systems and helpful materials such as record books.

Once up and running, village banks tend to be fairly autonomous. They aim to become self-managed entities with the responsibility of everything from setting their own rules, interest rates, fees and fines, selecting members and appointing leaders, disbursing, depositing, and managing all funds, doing their own bookkeeping, and even chasing down delinquent payments. An officer from the MFI attends meetings to provide both education and monitoring assistance, playing a role similar to an auditor to ensure that the village bank's fund management is done accurately and effectively.[4] Despite the fact that the social ties might not be as strong among the village bank members as they are in the smaller solidarity groups, since the village bank can decide who gets to be a member, there is still peer pressure on the individuals to repay their loans.

As with solidarity groups, village bank group meetings facilitate transparency—and reduce information asymmetries—among members by making payment transactions open for everyone to see. Figure 5.1 at the start of the chapter shows a solidarity group's members sitting at a table together with their MFI's loan officer, watching each other receive or repay loans. As Figure 5.4 shows, some groups like this FINCA Peru village bank even use large, easy-to-see public ledgers that keep track of every members' payments and outstanding debt. The group's leaders and record keepers sit behind the table to the left, and each member in turn comes to the table to receive

Figure 5.4. Group transparency via public account keeping, FINCA Peru

or repay loans. For all to see, the big ledger gets updated in real time as transactions occur at each meeting, with special highlight marks for late and missed payments. (Note one member's young child running around in the foreground, illustrating how integrated into everyday lives group meetings can be; a chicken wandered through at one point too!)

Village Savings and Loan Associations

Except for their source of funds, **village savings and loan associations** generally operate similarly to village banks. Like village banks, VSLAs are self-governed and owned by members. The main difference is that VSLAs do not take external credit. ASCA-like, all money circulating in the group comes from the members' own savings together with the group's own accumulated interest and fee payments.

VSLAs are commonly affiliated with charity organizations. For example, CARE, Oxfam, and Catholic Relief Services each has large-scale programs aimed at the very poorest people, those who even MFIs have a hard time serving cost effectively. These external support organizations help initially organize the groups, often provide mentoring and training on recommended procedures, materials like lockboxes, bookkeeping documents, and the like, and help launch operations; but they do not provide any funds for loans.

Self-Help Groups

Another self-governing, joint-guarantee uncollateralized lending and savings mechanism is known as a **self-help group**. Owned by members, self-help groups are essentially formal ASCAs with formal links to a bank. Though extant across the world, self-help groups are particularly widespread in India, where the idea began, and as a result may in fact be the most numerous type of lending group, with several million groups in India alone.[5]

Like village banks, self-help groups generally utilize some external institutional source of funds—e.g. NGO donations, government subsidies, or bank loans—and initial organizational support. Like both ASCAs and village banks, self-help groups establish their own rules, fees and procedures, penalties in cases of default, and otherwise usually manage their own affairs and recordkeeping, perhaps with guidance from an NGO or similar external group. But unlike ASCAs, self-help groups use formal banks to deposit their collective savings and to get formal bank loans to supplement their own internal funds for lending. However, individual members do not have direct individual accounts or dealings with the bank. Rather, the group as a whole does, making members jointly liable for loans. Like in village banks, members have only internal accounts within the self-help group.

One key difference is that in village banking MFI personnel typically continue to participate in weekly meetings to facilitate ongoing auditing, education and assistance as needed. By contrast, self-help groups' relationships with their banks are typically more arms-length after initial startup phases. Unfortunately, given the financial and accounting complexities, a lack of ongoing external professional support can mean lax oversight and weaker fund management and record keeping than ideal, with an accompanying risk of loss through default, negligence or fraud. Records are often rudimentary hand-written ledgers like shown in Figure 5.5 from a self-help group in Zambia. One study of more than 200 self-help groups in India found that only 15% had complete and up-to-date, mostly error-free records; another 39% had moderately up-to-date records with limited errors; while fully 40% had weak records, out-of-date and error plagued.[6]

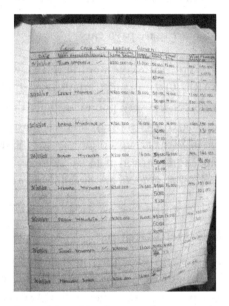

Figure 5.5. Handwritten loan records of a church-affiliated self-help group in Zambia

Half the groups were earning returns for members on their savings (though the majority was earning less than the rate of inflation), and fully 20% were actually losing money for their members.

To address recordkeeping, management and other challenges, in some cases self-help groups join formal federations that cluster multiple self-help groups. Federations can provide guidance, education and auditing services to member groups. Moreover, the federations, rather than single groups, then maintain direct interactions with the banks. Dealing with banks through federations of groups can mean larger-scale loans than any single group would get, enabling economies of scale and lowering borrowing costs.

Section in Bulletpoint

- Experiments with modern group lending approaches began in the 1970s by organizations such as Accion and Grameen.
- Instead of requiring normal collateral for loans, group lending usually employs joint liability and social pressure as forms of social collateral.
- The various approaches of group lending differ in group sizes, degrees of self-management by the groups, and in sources of funds.
- Progressive lending, the promise of larger future loans, has proved a strong incentive for repayment; perhaps more important than joint liability.

Discussion Questions

1. What are the main ways group lending differs from typical bank lending? Briefly, what do you think are the main reasons it does differ?

2. How do MFIs use group lending to manage risk?

3. How might group lending reduce transaction costs for an MFI trying to offer credit services to the poor?

4. Outline the key strengths and weaknesses of the various group lending approaches, including ways they motivate repayment.

5. What does "Classic Grameen-style" group lending mean? What are the main ways it differs from other group lending methods?

6. If you were running a charity organization, which group lending method might you prefer? Why? What method would you prefer if you were running a for-profit bank moving into microlending seeking potential profit? Why?

5.2 Group Lending as a Tool to Overcome Market Failures

Social Implications and Moral Hazard

In Chapter 3 we discussed how adverse selection problems, combined with moral hazard and limited liability from lack of collateral can cause problems for traditional banks offering financial services to the poor. The group lending approach in microfinance theoretically helps overcome those financial market failures by leveraging several related benefits that come from the social interactions among group members, thereby giving the poor access to loans they might not be able to get individually. We will explore the theory first, then dig a bit into emerging empirical evidence that some parts of the theory might not be the full story.

Figure 5.6 illustrates the timeline of key events in the life of a microfinance loan (that we first saw in Chapter 3, Figure 3.6) and how mainstream financial institutions face potential market failure problems at each step along the way. New here, the bottom row shows how the group lending approach might help mitigate those problems.

As we noted in Chapter 3, the potential problems start even before any loan might be given out. Banks face significant challenges in differentiating between borrowers who are likely to be reliable in repaying versus those borrowers who might shirk responsibility, make poor choices in how to use funds, not put in adequate effort, or just run off with funds with no intention of paying back. Before the microfinance innovation of joint liability in group

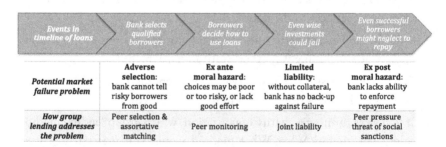

Events in timeline of loans	Bank selects qualified borrowers	Borrowers decide how to use loans	Even wise investments could fail	Even successful borrowers might neglect to repay
Potential market failure problem	**Adverse selection:** bank cannot tell risky borrowers from good	**Ex ante moral hazard:** choices may be poor or too risky, or lack good effort	**Limited liability:** without collateral, bank has no back-up against failure	**Ex post moral hazard:** bank lacks ability to enforce repayment
How group lending addresses the problem	Peer selection & assortative matching	Peer monitoring	Joint liability	Peer pressure threat of social sanctions

Figure 5.6. How group lending addresses potential credit market failure problems

Source: Modified from Simtowe, Zeller, and Phiri (2006).

lending, banks generally relied on requiring collateral and records of past repayment behavior in determining whether an individual was a risky or safe borrower. Yet many poor people have no such financial history, operating in the informal economy without previous access to banking, and lack assets in forms banks would consider for collateral. As discussed in Chapter 3, this creates an adverse selection problem for banks if potentially low-risk clients are driven away by the higher rates the bank might have to charge to cover costs associated with higher-risk clients, leaving the bank with mostly risky clients.

By contrast, responsibility for assessing potential borrowers in joint liability group lending falls largely on group members themselves—who might know the reliability and past behavior of their peers better than a distant banker could. They assess one another because they must be willing to form groups with each other. As we will discuss in the next section, a related potential benefit in letting clients form their own groups comes from the possibility of what is known as assortative matching.

Next in the timeline, once loans have been approved and given out, ex ante moral hazard stems from the uncertainty beforehand of what will actually result from the client's use of the loan and the negative influence on the result that poor choices might have. With no collateral on the line to lose, an unscrupulous client might slouch off if the banker is unable to closely and regularly interact and monitor the day-to-day activities of the borrower. Or an overzealous client may use the funds to gamble on a bad business idea with high likelihood of failure.

The group structure counteracts this risk through **peer monitoring**, where other members of the group and community can keep an eye on a borrower's investment decisions and effort. In an influential study, the Nobel Prize winning economist Joseph Stiglitz at Columbia University theorized that group lending helps mitigate moral hazard because it induces other borrowers to monitor their group members to make sure they use their funds wisely and do not default. [7] Peers in the group can help ensure a borrower uses their loan proceeds safely for the stated purpose, as opposed to other riskier purposes like gambling it away. Where a loan is for investment in a microenterprise, other group members can also keep watch that an individual puts good faith effort into generating returns from the loaned funds.

Figure 5.7. A self-help group's members look over each other's shoulders at a meeting

Peers have an incentive to monitor each other because the whole group assumes **joint liability**; that is, if your group member defaults, you have to help pay their share back even if their default is not your fault. So, each individual in a group has an incentive to help put pressure on other members, who in turn have a social incentive to behave reliably. Because individuals are concerned about how their peers view them, borrowers feel peer pressure to be in good standing within their group, and by extension their village. The threat of social sanctions also helps avoid another type of problem in Figure 5.6, ex post moral hazard, when banks lack enough leverage to enforce repayment terms even from successful borrowers. Individual borrowers would want to avoid shaming family or becoming social outcasts in the village, which might happen if other group members often have to make up missed payments on their behalf, particularly in cases when the borrower could have paid. Word of poor behavior gets around in small communities.

Joint liability appears to be particularly effective when combined with progressive lending at creating social incentives within the group to repay loans in full. Otherwise, members risk not qualifying for increased loans in the future. Therefore, members are more inclined to be heavily involved in knowing the other group members and ensuring they are reliable. In practice, as illustrated towards the end of this chapter in Box 5.3 on Grameen Bank's policy changes, MFIs are finding that progressive lending incentives might in fact be more important that joint liability itself. Indeed, for several reasons discussed later, many MFIs have begun dropping the specific joint liability requirement, while maintaining the group lending structure.

In summary, the social dynamics of group responsibility create a type of social collateral, which can make up for the lack of physical capital, like a title to land, that an MFI could repossess in the event of failure to repay. This social collateral is a key benefit of group lending. However, there are also some pitfalls, which we consider later in this chapter.

Gender and Group Lending

We will explore gender issues in microfinance in detail in Chapter 7. Briefly though, across all group lending approaches, women have proven to be more responsive to the incentive mechanisms of group lending, and thus more effective target customers for those MFIs focused on group lending approaches. As can be seen in Table 5.1, MFIs that use only group lending approaches such as solidarity groups and village banking have clientele comprised almost entirely of women, whereas MFIs that only lend to individuals, but not to groups, have a clientele gender balance near 50/50. The data suggest a strong correlation between the nature of an organization's lending methodology and the gender of its target clients. As it turns out, women are more influenced than men by the social interaction and social pressures associated with group lending. In particular, the concept of social collateral weakens for men, who appear to react less to the social sanctions created by groups, and face less social taxation as discussed in Chapter 4. The incentives and guarantees of repayment diminish.

Table 5.1. Gender differences among lending methodologies

MFI lending methodology	Median percent of women borrowers
Individual lending only	46.2
Both individual & solidarity group lending	64.9
Solidarity group lending	98.7
Village banking	86.3

Source: *Microbanking Bulletin* 19, December 2009, p. 48.

Why might this gender difference be true? One theory is that women and men differ in what is called labor mobility.[8] In developing countries, women are more connected to the household than are men. Additionally, women tend to work closer to the home and not travel as far as men do, making women more engaged in, and dependent on, the community in which they live. This makes peer monitoring among group members more transparent as the women can easily see what is being done with the funds of their fellow group members. But even more importantly, because of the closer ties women have with their community, social standing and reputation can be tarnished by the failure to repay loans. As a result of women's sensitivity to social sanctions, funds are misused less often and loan repayment rates are higher than they are for men.[9] Lending without collateral to poor women in groups has proven a good business bet. Interestingly, evidence also suggests that women also tend to invest more of their income in their families' nutrition, health, and education than do men. In the context of group lending then, targeting women makes both business and social-mission sense for MFIs, particularly where women's empowerment is among their goals.

Implications for Forming Groups

The jargon term **assortative matching** describes a theory of improved outcomes possible when borrowers select their own groups. The idea is that safe borrowers may tend to stick together, preferring to avoid people who they know might be risky borrowers. This avoidance would in turn force risky borrowers into separate groups.[10] If banks had a way to tell the groups apart, such segregation could create the opportunity to charge lower fees or interest rates for the safe borrowers and higher rates for the risky borrowers. Safe borrowers facing lower borrowing costs would be more likely customers, reducing the bank's adverse selection problem compared to if they had to charge rates associated with covering riskier borrowers.[11]

Table 5.2 shows a hypothetical example illustrating the potential efficiency of assortative matching. (These made-up numbers may at first seem a bit dense,

Table 5.2. Hypothetical example of two-person groups with a safe borrower

Two safe borrowers	*One safe and one risky borrower*
• Each borrows $100 at 35% interest	• Each borrows $100 at 35% interest
• Each succeeds and makes $200	• Safe succeeds and makes $200
• Each pays back $135	• If Risky succeeds (75% likely):
• Each goes home with $65	— Safe pays back $135
	— Safe ends with $65
	• But if Risky fails (25% likely):
	— Safe owes $200 due to joint liability
	— Safe ends with nothing

but it's not bad so bear with it; the payoff in our understanding will be helpful.) To keep this made-up example simple, suppose people all want loans of $100. Suppose also that the interest rate is 35%.

Let us say that a safe borrower will make a safe investment that will generate $200 for sure, and that a risky borrower will make an investment that might fail and become worthless, with say 25% probability. Suppose also that group lending requires two-person joint liability groups (for simplicity smaller than real groups tend to be). If both group members succeed, each member then owes $135 in total repayments, including the interest. If however only one borrower succeeds and the partner fails, suppose with joint liability the MFI requires successful borrower to repay an additional $65, for a total of $200, allowing the bank to just break even.

How might a safe investor choose a two-person group? As shown in Table 5.2, if two safe borrowers get together, they each invest their $100 loans in investments that become $200, each pays back $135 and each comes out ahead by $65.

The payoffs are different, however, if a safe borrower partners instead with a risky borrower. Safe still would always generate $200. When things go well for Risky, Safe again takes home $65 as before. However, Risky might fail and end up with nothing, thus unable to pay back anything. In case of a failure, the group then uses Safe's $200 to pay back. Failure by Risky would happen 25% of the time, so even though Safe always succeeds with her investments, because of joint liability Safe could expect to have nothing left 25% of the time. So Safe will be worse off sometimes if she joins a group with a risky borrower because she has to pay more should Risky fail. She would clearly prefer always to team up with safe partners and avoid the risk.

Overall then in this example, if Safe is free to choose group members she will always team with another safe borrower. This leaves Risky no choice but to team with another risky borrower (not shown on table); in other words, assortative matching.

What about the various outcomes from the point of view of the MFI? With groups of two safe borrowers at 35% interest, the bank always gets repaid $270 for its $200 investment, profiting $70. Similarly, with groups of two risky borrowers, if they both succeed the bank also profits $70. However, both might fail and leave the bank losing its entire $200, and in the remaining cases where one succeeds and the second fails the bank just breaks even.

Suppose the MFI has many such mixed-risk groups. Some get lucky and pay back profitably, and some are unlucky and cause the MFI to get nothing. We could estimate the various probabilities of various groups succeeding or failing. Suppose, again hypothetically, that there were 100 customers, half of whom are risky and half safe. The potential expected profits require a bit of probability beyond the scope of this book to calculate, but we would find that, after accounting for successful and unsuccessful borrowers, the MFI would expect to generate roughly $2,400 of profit, maybe a bit more or a bit less with luck. If instead the bank only used individual lending, the profit expected from the same 100 customers works out to be much lower, only about $1,800 plus or minus. With assortative matching, group lending helps the MFI make one third more revenue from the same set of customers. The poor can benefit from this too if it makes MFIs willing to provide more loans and/or to charge lower fees.

Strangers vs. Community and Friends: What Works?

When we think of microfinance, we often think of remote small villages, where the groups are all members of the same community who might have grown up knowing each other. As we have seen, such familiarity can help overcome the adverse selection problem. However, in bigger cities it can be challenging for this to happen. Potential borrowers may know very little about each other; they may not know each other's names, let alone what potential group members' risks are with investments. Also, there may be greater risk in a big city because it is easier for someone to borrow a loan and then disappear.

Under such circumstances, assortative matching may not work. Even so, Beatriz Armendáriz of Harvard University and Jonathan Morduch of New York University found theoretically that risky borrowers still gain from pairing with safe borrowers, just like with assortative matching.[12] But these researchers also looked into how the safe borrowers might in fact benefit from pairing with risk-takers, even though the simple model in Table 5.2 shows they can lose out by sharing a group with risky borrowers. The researchers found that in some circumstances safe types could gain if they team up with risky types. This is because the reduction in risk to the banks due to group lending might allow safe borrowers to get credit at lower interest rates than they would earn if they tried to get loans on their own. Lower rates are more feasible in urban areas as well because they are simply less costly per customer for banks to operate in. Higher population density and shorter travel times enables some economies of scale. Another researcher, Joel Guttman of Bar Ilan University in Israel, has shown that the positive effects of assortative matching might not hold if the models account for the potential dynamic incentives for good behavior over time provided by progressive lending.[13] Indeed, this may help explain the observed trend in actual practice towards individual lending by many MFIs.

Ultimately then it remains unclear, either in theory or in practice, which works better: working with your community members or complete strangers. There is probably no single simple answer. Each approach has pros and cons, and those appear to differ among different countries and cultures.

Section in Bulletpoint

- Group lending theoretically can help overcome several key market failures in providing financial services to the poor.
- The threat of social repercussions, such as losing good social standing in the community, creates incentives for borrowers to repay loans.
- Because group members are responsible for each other's loans, members monitor their peers' behavior before and after loans are distributed, thus reducing risks that arise from moral hazard.
- Social collateral can substitute for physical collateral for loans, reducing risks of limited liability.
- Assortative matching can occur when members self-select into groups. Low-risk borrowers can select each other, forcing riskier clients to form independent groups. Thus, MFIs can charge interest rates accordingly, reducing the need to cross-subsidize risky borrowers with safer ones, mitigating adverse selection problems.
- MFIs focused entirely on group lending have very high fractions of women clients. Evidence suggests women are more responsive than men to the social incentives of group lending.

Discussion Questions

1. How does group lending help avoid: (a) moral hazard, and (b) limited liability?

2. Discuss the concept of assortative matching. How does group lending alleviate the problem of adverse selection even though the bank remains unable to distinguish between risky and safe borrowers?

3. How are ex ante moral hazard and ex post moral hazard different? How are they similar? Think about your own experiences, and discuss a situation you faced a choice with potential moral hazard and explain which type it was.

4. How might progressive lending incentives make the potential benefits to the MFI from assortative matching less important? Explain.

5. In the U.S., it is illegal to discriminate by gender or otherwise in giving loans. Do you think the same rules should be applied internationally in microfinance? Explain arguments on both sides, and which side you agree with and why.

6. What are three main reasons that lending to women is beneficial for an MFI?

5.3 Limitations of Group Lending

Despite the fact that group lending has received much praise as a solution to some of the market failures microlending encounters, it does not come without flaws. Some of the major criticisms of group lending deal with the inflexibility of the loan terms, the potentially high opportunity costs and social stress for the clients, and issues of free riding, joint liability responsibilities, and the risk of collusion.

The Inflexibility of Group Lending

Group lending arrangements tend to be fairly rigid, in order to foster repayment discipline and to make management easier and more transparent. Generally in classic group lending, each group member will receive equal-sized loans of the same maturity. If all members have similar needs, this does not pose any major problems. But in many groups, financial needs can diverge. Members with separate microenterprises will inevitably experience different levels of success, or members can face different cash flow needs from family or health situations. Rigidly equal loan terms within the group then can limit some individual members, diminishing benefits they might receive.

We will look at individual lending a bit more later, but as can be seen in Table 5.3, average loan balances under group lending are significantly lower than average loan balances for individual lending. The more than 10-fold

Table 5.3. Comparing group and individual lending

	MFIs using solidarity group lending only	MFIs using individual lending only
Median loan balance*	$111	$1,404
Geography	Rural more than urban	Urban or high-density rural
Character check	Self-selection of group members Group formation process	Background check
Capital	Emphasis on human and social capital Examination of experience and skill	Evaluation of assets History of business Financial statements
Capacity to repay	Joint assessment with group Rough estimate of cash flow Focus on household	Rigorous financial analysis Focus on business and/or household
Collateral	Group guarantee Social collateral Compulsory savings	Pledge of asset Co-guarantors
Role of loan officer	Group formation Group meeting organizer Collection and disbursement	Business appraisal Loan supervision Relationships banker

Notes: *Average loan size from the *Microbanking Bulletin* 19, December 2009, p. 48.
Source: Modified from Benavides (2008).

gap suggests that as a borrower's credit needs grow, group lending becomes less and less desirable for that individual. As Harvard's Beatriz Armendáriz and NYU's Jonathan Morduch put it, "loan sizes are limited by what the group can jointly guarantee, so clients with growing businesses or those who get well ahead of their peers in scale may find that the group contract bogs everyone down."[14] In addition to different scales, some members may find they would prefer different loan durations as well, needing more flexibility in spreading repayment out over longer or shorter periods depending on the nature of their incoming cash flows.

Opportunity Costs

As we have seen, one of the benefits of group lending is that it lowers the overall costs to the bank by taking advantage of peer monitoring and economies of scale, effectively shifting many of the burdens from the bank to the borrowers. However, critics argue that to the customers, there are many direct and indirect costs associated with group lending. For example, the transportation and opportunity costs of travelling to and attending weekly meetings may be very high for some people.

In rural areas, where distances are long and transportation might be limited to walking, a poor borrower might have to give up several hours each way getting to a meeting. Add to this the meeting time itself, and group lending participants can lose half or even an entire day's worth of income generating activities to attend the group meeting. In many group lending schemes, these meetings occur weekly. This could result in the productivity loss of hundreds of hours annually. The productivity increases caused by the loan might not be enough to offset the opportunity cost of the lost time and earning potential. Where opportunity costs become too high, borrowers may forego trying to get loans altogether, and among those who do get loans group meeting attendance can suffer, hurting the related social incentives.

For example, Figure 5.8 shows a lending group meeting of BRAC, one of the largest MFIs in Bangladesh and the world. Despite its remarkable growth and success, BRAC found member attendance rates at its weekly group meetings often fell below 40%. When researchers investigated, far and away the most common reason clients gave for not attending was time lost.[15] BRAC groups are typically 30–40 members, and meetings typically last about two hours or more simply to get through loan transactions for that many members.

Figure 5.8. A BRAC lending group meeting, Bangladesh

Under circumstances of high transactions and opportunity costs for clients, informal moneylenders represent strong potential competition for MFIs offering group lending. Moneylenders are often quite adept at finding ways to decrease transaction costs for borrowers. As we saw in Chapter 4, moneylenders can decrease opportunity costs by making borrowing extremely convenient. They can visit the borrowers in their homes or places of work, at convenient times, visiting very frequently, or even on demand. However, moneylenders often offset this convenience to the borrowers by charging higher interest rates and fees—sometimes much higher.

This shifting of burden from the MFI to the borrower imposes yet other costs on borrowers as well, in the form of transferring to the borrowers some of the traditional responsibilities of a banking loan officer. Group lending tends to rely on the services of group members as group leaders, who organize the groups, find new members, keep records, keep cash boxes, host meetings and provide food in their homes, take time to track down late payments, and undertake other administrative responsibilities that banks would normally perform for their customers. In some situations, the added burdens might make potential borrowers less inclined to get a loan; simply to obtain a loan they may not want to be forced to form groups or be responsible for extra tasks. For instance, Gonzalo Afcha and Jerry Ladman of Arizona State University found that in Bolivia it was difficult for an early microcredit program aimed at rural farmers to find potential borrowers to lead their groups because these leaders had to spend a lot of time persuading other borrowers to accept the group lending rules.[16]

Free Riding

As mentioned previously, group lending transfers much of the risk of default from the bank to the group. In settings where group members know each other well and live close to one another, borrowers can efficiently select and monitor each other. However, in larger groups, such as village banks, and in urban or remote rural areas members might not know each other very well at all. Thus they may not be in any better position to monitor their fellow borrowers than the MFI. This reintroduces the moral hazard problem into the equation, and in some joint liability groups can encourage free riding by members who may take on projects riskier than they perhaps should. With the security of a group's joint liability, individuals may choose to take on greater risks or put in less effort than they would have under an individual lending scheme where they are solely responsible for their own loan. Joint liability creates a mutual insurance, a failsafe for a bad week or month. However, this mutual insurance may erode incentives to pick wise investments or work as productively as possible as borrowers become reliant on the joint-liability mechanism of the group.

Furthermore, the incentive of one member to work hard is undermined if they believe that the other group members are slacking or taking on greater risks, as they will still be liable if the other members default. Hence, effort-levels may decrease not only for the free rider, but also for the reliable borrowers.

Joint Liability's Double Edge

The joint liability approach has also been criticized as being too harsh. Under most traditional group lending strategies, all members are denied future credit if one member defaults on the loan. However, it is possible this may not be an optimal approach. If the source of a default is out of the borrower's hands—say through death, drought or illness—then the actual credit quality of the members has not necessarily diminished. For example, what if one group member falls ill and is thus no longer able to work or pay back the loan? The default is not caused by a lack of discipline or a failing investment idea. The rest of the group's riskiness and financial potential has not changed. It would thus potentially harm not only the group members themselves but also inhibit the broader economy to deprive the entire group of the access to credit.

Economists Tomas Sjöström of Rutgers University and Ashok Rai of Williams College suggested that this harshness of punishment can be reduced by cross-reporting.[17] Cross-reporting refers to the practice of loan officers seeking additional information from other borrowers about the member who is at risk of default. Depending on the reasons for default, alternative measures can be made that might be more efficient than complete exclusion, such as replacing the defaulting member rather than excluding the entire group from accessing loan services. As discussed in Box 5.3, Grameen Bank has taken extensive measures to address the issues of joint liability and improve its group lending practices through its implementation of Grameen II.

Joint liability also increases potential risks and costs for individuals in the group. While in a group, a borrower has to worry about the default risk of other members of the group on top of their own default risk. If the activities of peer monitoring and enforcing contracts are more or less costless, moral hazard can be mitigated. However, these activities are not costless in the real world even in small villages. Borrowers might end up spending much time and effort monitoring other members' spending activities and businesses, enforcing group rules, tracking down missing or late paying members and so on. So too, the likelihood of social taxation among group members is potentially strong. If a group member is having trouble paying back, another member known to have excess cash that week might be pressed by the group as a whole into covering the payments—much like Aunt Beatrice and her cookie jar cash from Chapter 3. Even the most conscientious members might decide to avoid such situations altogether, raising the possibility that adverse selection issues might arise again.

Box 5.3. In the Field
Grameen II and the Evolution away from Joint Liability

In 2001, Grameen Bank moved away from its original lending methodology by implementing what it called Grameen II. The development came as a result of the many criticisms of the rigidity and inflexibility of the loan terms under the classic Grameen-style group lending. By August 7, 2002, its last branch switched over to the new Grameen II system. Founder Muhammad Yunus described the changes in the following way:

> *In the Grameen Bank II, gone are the general loans, seasonal loans, family loans, and more than a dozen other types of loans; gone is the group fund; gone is the branch-wise, zone-wise loan ceiling; gone is the fixed size weekly installment; gone is the rule to borrow every time for one whole year, even when the borrower needed the loan only for three months; gone is the high-level tension among the staff and the borrowers trying to steer away from a dreadful event of a borrower turning into a "defaulter", even when she is still repaying; and gone are many other familiar features of Grameen Classic System.*

Interestingly, the Grameen II system completely eliminates joint liability, while retaining other benefits of working with groups. Yunus explained Grameen's new attitude towards cross-guarantees:

> *Although each borrower must belong to a five-member group, the group is not required to give any guarantee for a loan to its member. Repayment responsibility solely rests on the individual borrower, while the group and the centre [kendra] oversee that everyone behaves in a responsible way and none gets into repayment problem. There is no form of joint liability, i.e. group members are not responsible to pay on behalf of a defaulting member.*

While the method of requiring five-member groups remains intact, the function of the group is now more focused on support and monitoring, rather than acting as a guarantor of the loan to the bank.

(Continued)

Box 5.3. (*Continued*)

The Grameen II system is based on two types of loans: the Basic Loan and the Flexible Loan. New clients start off with the Basic Loan, which usually has a ceiling of around 5,000 Bangladeshi taka (roughly $65). To clarify, these are individual loans, and the group will not be punished if an individual member cannot repay. The terms are more flexible than before too, in that both the duration of the loan and size of repayment installments may vary depending on the specific needs of the individual (though they still repay at the interval of one week). If a borrower is unable to make proper repayments regularly, the borrower will be moved into a Flexible Loan instead.

Designed to help the struggling borrower get back on their feet, the repayment schedule spreads over a longer term, making it easier to keep up with. However, the loan size ceiling is significantly lower than for a Basic Loan. The goal is that the borrower will eventually be able to re-establish their creditworthiness and return to a Basic Loan. If the borrower still remains able to repay despite the more lenient terms of the Flexible Loan, the bank will eventually disqualify them from further membership.

Sources: Grameen Bank (www.grameen-info.org/bank); Armendáriz and Morduch (2010); Rutherford et al (2004).

Moreover, for those members struggling to pay, in joint liability schemes the resulting peer pressure and potential loss of social standing in a community can be stressful and economically and psychologically damaging to individuals and their families. A lively ongoing debate in the microfinance industry is whether MFIs are justified in using social pressures to reduce their own costs and risks. We leave deeper exploration of that debate for a discussion question.

The joint liability innovation helped alleviate former concerns by banks and investors that the poor would and could repay, which helped fuel several decades of growth in the microfinance industry. Nevertheless, given the weaknesses and concerns we just outlined, coupled with increasing evidence that individual liability might in fact perform just as well as joint liability (see the Box 5.4 in the next section), many MFIs, including Grameen Bank, have dropped the joint liability requirement. The industry has matured beyond experimental phases, discovering what works and trying to change what has been problematic.

Collusion Risk

Despite control mechanisms such as social sanctions and progressive lending schemes, there is always the moral hazard risk that a group as a whole will decide to collude against the MFI and not repay their loans. Research has produced diverging results on this issue depending on the region, making it hard to establish what type of group lending better reduces collusion problems. In theory, stronger social ties should make group members more responsive to social collateral, thus increasing repayment rates and decreasing the risk of collusion. In certain cases however, small groups with stronger social ties have been found to collude more often. Christian Ahlin of Michigan State University and Robert Townsend of the University of Chicago found that in the central region of Thailand, stronger social links among group members actually increased default rates, which implies that too much social capital can lead to collusion against the MFI.[18] Since, as we saw in Chapter 2, the poor generally need and value access to financial intermediation tools on a repeated and ongoing basis, one key mechanism that has proven very effective in inhibiting collusion is the threat of non-refinancing. By increasing the penalty of not paying back the loan (i.e. the penalty is lost future loans), the incentive to collude against the MFI is significantly decreased.

Section in Bulletpoint

- Group lending can be inflexible to the differing financial needs of different individuals or evolving businesses.
- Group lending shifts risks and the burden for some transaction costs, such as for transportation to weekly meetings and finding potential borrowers, from MFIs to borrowers.
- Opportunity costs in time and lost income for borrowers can be high for attending group meetings.

(Continued)

- Joint liability gives individuals a sense of default insurance, which may create incentives for some borrowers to slack or take on riskier projects.
- Due to free riders, hard-working members may then, in turn, become discouraged from participating or working productively.
- Strict joint liability has been criticized as too harsh and a cause of social and financial stress for clients; it may also thwart risk-averse borrowers or penalize groups for unique circumstances or actions of an individual at no fault of the group.
- Based on evidence repayment rates are not necessarily better, coupled with concerns over negative implications of social sanctions, increasing numbers of MFIs are dropping joint liability requirements.

Discussion Questions

1. In terms of incentives discouraging defaulting on loans, what innovations have microlending institutions been able to implement with their borrowers? How do those innovations help the MFI? The borrowers?

2. In what ways might group lending's joint liability policies be problematic? How are the policies beneficial?

3. How can "cross-reporting" help lenders and/or borrowers?

4. When one member defaults, is the threat not to refinance to the entire group too harsh? Discuss pros and cons from the point of view of the borrower and from the point of view of the lender.

5. Some critics of microfinance point out that group lending transfers many of the risks and costs from the bank to the clients. Is this fair to the poor? Discuss pros and cons from the point of view of poor customers.

6. Peer pressure and loss of social standing in a community can be stressful and both economically and psychologically damaging to individuals and their families. Are MFIs justified in using these social pressures to reduce their own costs and risks? This is a lively ongoing debate in the industry. Search the internet for evidence and arguments. Briefly argue and support with evidence both sides.

5.4 Individual Lending

Individual lending carried out by MFIs is similar to traditional commercial lending. Compared to group loans, individual loans offer clients more flexibility in the loan terms and payback schedule. They also carry the added bonus of individual accountability, allowing more-responsible borrowers to shed the burden of having to answer for their group members. This flexibility allows borrowers to use loans at their own pace and in keeping with the growth or other changes in their needs. On the other hand, without the social incentives of group lending, it is more common to see MFIs require some sort of actual collateral for individual loans. In this section, we will cover the current state of individual lending, trends in individual lending products, the costs associated with it and the issues it raises with respect to collateral.

MFIs often offer different kinds of individual loans to satisfy the varying needs of their clients. In general, loan structures differ in size, interest rate, and duration. Other requirements, such as providing proof of a business, tend to be consistent across loan classifications. For example as shown in Table 5.4, ACLEDA Bank in Cambodia offers three types of microfinance business loans called micro, small, and medium. The minimum requirements to qualify are the same for all three loans: clients must have their own

Table 5.4. Business lending products of ACLEDA Bank in Cambodia

	Micro business loan	*Small business loan*	*Medium business loan*
Loan period	• Up to 6 months for loan sizes up to $100 • Up to 12 months for loans between $100 and $1,500	• Up to 24 months for loans between $1,500 and $10,000	• Up to 24 months for loans between $10,000 and $30,000 • Up to 48 months for loans greater than $30,000
Interest rates	• 2.4% to 2.7% per month	• 1.5% to 2.0% per month	• 0.83% to 1.7% per month

Source: ACLEDA Bank, Cambodia: www.acledabank.com.kh.

residence, own a business, and already have at least 20% of the capital requested. However, terms and loan sizes vary greatly. Table 5.4 summarizes how ACLEDA classifies their microcredit. Many MFIs employ similar schemes to their individual microlending. As a screening process, some MFIs only offer individual lending to former group lending participants who have already proved reliable; a sort of graduation from group to individual loans. We will delve into the idea of graduation a bit more later.

Individual vs. Group Lending from the MFI's Perspective

As discussed in Box 5.4, evidence suggests that repayment rates can be similar whether loans are made to individuals or to groups with joint liability. So why

Box 5.4. Dig Deeper
Individual vs. Group Lending—Who Is More Likely to Pay Up?

Accumulating evidence questions whether or not group joint liability reduces default risks in microlending. Early theories, most influentially including by Nobel Prize winning economist Joseph Stiglitz at Columbia University, assumed group lending with joint liability helps alleviate risks on banks due to peer pressure within the group and community. Among the leading MFIs, groups paid back at very high rates, so many practitioners firmly believed the theory. However not much actual evidence one way or the other had been available until fairly recently. So, to test the theory, Xavier Giné of the World Bank and Dean Karlan of Yale University ran field experiments comparing individual to joint liability lending. What they found has since been reconfirmed by several other studies: joint liability does not necessarily make a difference in whether borrowers repay.

The researchers worked with The Green Bank of Caraga, which operates in the Philippines using group joint liability modeled on the classic Grameen-style system. Most "centers" of The Green Bank consist of around 30 clients, organized into five-person groups. Each group is responsible as one unit to repay loans before receiving another. Members are required to meet and make weekly payments, and to save some of

(*Continued*)

Box 5.4. (*Continued*)

their income in a pooled deposit fund. This helps the clients accumulate savings assets, but the bank also uses the deposit fund as collateral to partially offset default risk.

To compare results between group liability and individual liability, the bank agreed to shift the methodology for some borrowers to individual liability. Groups still met together to make payments, but some randomly assigned groups were not responsible for individuals who defaulted. As a comparison, other groups still partook in normal group lending. In this way, potential benefits of social interaction within all the groups remained, but for some groups there was no joint liability.

For both sets of borrowers, repayments were still expected weekly and individuals were still advised to save in their own accounts. In both sets too, loans were only issued to clients considered creditworthy. Over three years the researchers recorded activities of loan officers, surveyed clients in different groups, and tracked default rates, repayment rates, savings and deposits, loan sizes, and client retention for the bank.

Results showed similar repayment rates regardless of liability method. Similarly, both brand new and already existing clients were equally likely to default, showing that prior experience with joint liability did not necessarily determine how well an individual did in repaying loans. These findings imply that even though the social pressure incentives to repay a loan because of joint liability no longer exists, maintaining social reputation and preserving the chance of getting future loans nevertheless remain strong incentives.

However, these results were found over a relatively short period of time in a particular region of the Philippines. They may not necessarily apply in all regions around the world as diverse cultural and social factors interact, or over the long periods of time needed for substantial lasting impact on poverty. While growing numbers of MFIs have eliminated joint liability lending, it remains a very widespread practice.

Source: Giné and Karlan (2009).

then choose to offer one or the other? In making the decision, MFI managers try to balance the costs and benefits to the MFI with the needs of their clients.

Collateral is a major issue in microfinance. Many of the target clients, the poorest of the poor, do not have collateral. Group lending attempts to address this issue by introducing the idea of social collateral. Group members vouch for one another, providing the MFI with some assurance of repayment through the powerful force of social pressure. However, with individual lending, this social pressure is mitigated. While individuals may still fear earning a negative reputation by defaulting, their neighbors are no longer looking over their shoulders worrying about answering for unpaid loans. Therefore, individuals must either offer some sort of asset as collateral, or the MFI must assume a greater risk. A requirement of collateral assets to qualify limits the ability of individual loans to reach the poorest of the poor. The result, as we saw in Table 5.3, is that individual loans tend to be larger than for those in groups. Although the clients for individual loans are generally still poor, empirically they do on average tend to have somewhat higher incomes than the very poorest. For this reason, some MFIs, such as Bandhan as discussed in Box 5.5, offer specially designed programs targeted at the extremely poor, with the aim of helping them move on into other microfinance services.

Box 5.5. In the Field
Bandhan and Graduation among Loan Classifications

Bandhan is huge by microfinance standards (see Table 5.5). It is the largest MFI in India in terms of number of borrowers, and was the first MFI in India to transform into a fully licensed bank. In India more than a fifth of the population lives below the national poverty line. Bandhan classifies its borrowers into three groups: extremely poor, almost economically active, and economically active. By considering the various needs of their clients (100% women), and designing unique programs for different types of poverty, Bandhan has made substantive progress towards improving the lives of impoverished citizens of India.

(*Continued*)

Box 5.5. (*Continued*)

Table 5.5. Bandhan Financial Services

Began microfinance operations	2001
Location	India
Clients	5,409,866 borrowers (March 2014); was not yet licensed to take savings
Women as % of borrowers	100%
Self-sufficiency ratio	151%
Legal status	Commercial bank (transformed 2015)

Bandhan created a program for the extremely poor called Chartering into Unventured Frontiers–Targeting the Hardcore Poor (CUF–THP). CUF–THP specifically targets people who "lack the confidence to avail and repay loans or take the risk of initiating a business of their own." Candidates are typically beggars that cannot otherwise get a loan—even from microfinance institutions. This program exists outside Bandhan's regular loan services, and aims to allow borrowers to graduate into other microfinance programs. Through CUF–THP, Bandhan tracks the progress of these clients and transfers to them a set of assets while training them on how to use those assets to generate income. This way, they can join the ranks of the "economically active."

A step up the ladder, Bandhan offers microloans. Candidates are typically women without significant assets who earn less than $70 per year. Initial loans can range from $20 to $200, and increase in increments between $20 and $100. The borrowers differ from participants in the CUF–THP program in that they have skills that could potentially earn income and have confidence to take out their own loans. Thus borrowers may or may not actually be economically active, but are not seen as the poorest of the poor.

(Continued)

The last loan type is called the Micro Enterprise Program, for members who already have capital equivalent to the loan they are seeking, have already repaid a loan before, and are directly involved in an enterprise which generates income and employment. The Micro Enterprise Program allows people to enter a loan cycle to finance expenses in their entrepreneurial pursuits. These customers are those that have experience with microfinance and are very much economically active. Since these customers have proven abilities for generating income, they may borrow between $400 and $1,000. After each loan is repaid, their next loan may increase by up to $200.

Offering loan packages and graduation schemes tailored to the needs of their clients has proven successful for Bandhan, which has rapidly grown from a single branch establishment into one of the top handful of the world's largest MFIs (see Table 1.3). In addition to their corporate success, Bandhan is able to serve the poorest of the poor, women who are, unfortunately, often not served even by MFIs.

Sources: Bandhan, www.bandhan.org; mixmarket.org.

In addition to the collateral issues involved with individual lending, MFIs also face higher selection and enforcement costs. Whereas MFIs using group lending are able to rely on groups to select members known as reliable, MFIs making individual loans have no such help. Instead, they must screen possible clients individually, often requiring a home visit (like the one shown in Figure 5.9) to see the client's living and family situation and any business operations, and to take stock of potential collateral assets. They often also collect loan payments individually, which may mean recurring individual home visits not only to collect but also to ensure the loan is being put to proper uses. These visits and screenings increase the cost per loan, and when coupled with the additional risk of no social collateral, individual loans become potentially less appealing to MFIs. On the other hand, as Table 5.3 showed, individual loans tend to be larger, and thus more cost efficient since similar per loan costs can be spread over larger sums loaned out. Individual loans are also more common in urban settings than in rural areas, because the population density makes it easier for loan officers to visit many individuals per day.

Individual vs. Group Lending from the Client's Perspective

Individual loans provide more flexibility and growth opportunities for clients. Group lending typically constrains each member to receive the same size loan with the same duration and interest rate as all of the other group members. This may work well in the beginning if members' needs are similar. But if members' businesses develop at different speeds or their family situations evolve, more successful members or those in more dire circumstances may not be best served by one-size-fits-all loans. They might prefer to take out independent loans, for amounts best suited for them, with rates and repayment schedules built around their individual needs.

Figure 5.9. Loan officers from FUNED-OPDF, a Honduran MFI, visit a loan applicant's home during assessment

That loan tailoring flexibility, unfortunately, does not come without implications. In order for individual lending to be financially viable for an MFI, given potentially higher per-client operating costs and risks, the MFI might require more collateral or set larger minimum loan sizes or perhaps charge higher interest rates. These represent potential new challenges to poor clients, as their loans are now larger or more costly. If a client's business is ready to grow and they have proven their credit worthiness, then moving on to individual loans helps both the client and the MFI. If the client succeeds beyond that, they may be able to graduate to financing their business through more traditional commercial bank loans and climbing out of poverty. However, moving on too soon could lead to over indebtedness, and default.

Some MFIs only offer group lending, while others focus on individual loans. Many MFIs, however, offer both services, with the possibility that new clients start with small loans in the group lending scheme and progress on to individual loans as their businesses grow and their needs change. Other MFIs offer both services alongside each other, allowing clients to choose what suits them best. As a result, both lending methodologies remain solidly in use around the world, and in fact the financial services offered within both types continue to diversify as MFIs innovate in search of more sustainable balances of revenues to costs while also remaining dedicated to the poorest of the poor.

Graduation

Some critics of microfinance point to a lack of much graduation of clients, either moving from group lending to individual lending or from MFI lending to commercial lending, as evidence of the limited growth of clients' microenterprises and that microfinance is not helping its clients improve. We probe evidence on both sides of the impact debate in Chapter 9. Lack of graduation could also stem from MFIs wishing to retain their best and most profitable clients instead of graduating them to more traditional commercial banking, which in some cases might be less costly than microcredit for a client needing larger transactions.

On the other hand, lack of graduation of clients out of MFIs may also result from innovation by MFIs of new products more targeted at various types of client needs, the development and increasing professionalization of the microfinance industry as a whole (trends we dig into in Chapter 8). Or it may simply reflect the ever-present needs of the poor for small scale flow transactions in their everyday lives, which we saw in Chapter 2, that commercial banking is ill suited to provide. If microfinancial services offered are well designed and helpful, clients may grow attached to their MFI and may choose to stay with them instead of moving on. As clients' financial needs change or expand, they may simply shift to alternative products from the same MFI, out of perhaps a combination of both loyalty and the ability to access financial products well suited to their specific needs.

Section in Bulletpoint

- MFIs often offer different types of individual loans in terms of loan sizes, duration, and collateral requirements, in order to meet the varying needs and levels of poverty of their clients.
- Individual lending allows borrowers more flexibility to finance according to the changing needs of their family lives or businesses, rather than being constrained by the progress of a joint-liability group.
- Individual loans tend to be larger and targeted towards still poor but relatively better-off clients.
- Some MFIs offer both individual and group lending, enabling clients to graduate to individual lending if they maintain good track records.
- Critics censure microfinance because there has been limited graduation from group lending to individual lending and from microlending to commercial lending. Others argue that this lack of graduation stems from consumer loyalty and services better suited to poor clients' needs.

Discussion Questions

1. Why might an MFI's costs be higher for serving individual borrowers than group borrowers? How might they be lower?

2. Why could MFIs find it difficult to enforce repayment of individually borrowed funds?

3. Why would MFIs be reluctant to see borrowers graduate to more traditional commercial lending? Discuss the ethical merits, positive and negative, of MFIs keeping or graduating their most successful clients.

4. If your main goal in offering microcredit were empowering women, which method would you prefer, group or individual lending? Why?

Chapter Summary

While group lending is a traditional trademark of MFIs, more and more organizations are modifying their lending practices to reflect developments in the field and address key limitations of group lending. Theoretically, joint liability group lending practices can transfer some risks and transactions costs from MFIs to borrowers. Yet the joint liability scheme has come under increasing scrutiny regarding not only whether or not it is actually effective at reducing default risk, but also its potential for negative economic, social and psychological implications for already struggling poor clients. Other techniques such as progressive lending, frequent installment repayments, and periodic public meetings as a means to exert social pressure have emerged as apparently just as (or more?) effective in overcoming the challenges of information asymmetries, adverse selection, moral hazard and limited liability. The benefits, however, come with costs too. Public group meetings can be costly for clients to attend due to time and transportation expenses. Group and individual lending practices will surely continue to evolve and improve with the maturity of the industry as a whole.

Although there is an industry wide trend towards individual lending, due to its potential profitability for MFIs and greater flexibility for clients, it tends to not focus on serving the poorest of the poor. Individual loans are often larger and targeted towards those with bigger businesses, more assets and more income. Indeed, as discussed in Chapter 8, there is significant debate in the microfinance industry about the potential for so-called mission drift. This arises from the tension between, on one hand, the very real challenges of serving the very poorest in tough economic, political and physical environments and, on the other hand, the drive towards sustainable profits that could attract more investment and resources that could enable expanding services to more people.

More broadly, as we will see in later chapters some MFIs have been widely criticized for over-promoting borrowing in general, and as not much different than loan sharks in leading some of society's most economically vulnerable into endless cycles of debt from which they cannot escape. As one observer put the concern, "debts are *bonds*" binding the poor into poverty.[19] Thankfully, as we will explore next in Chapter 6, microfinancial services today have grown far more diverse than just loans, offering the poor a wide array of innovative and cost-effective financial intermediation tools to help them navigate their very real day-to-day financial needs and challenges.

Key Terms

assortative matching
Occurs when choosing potential group members if low-risk borrowers select each other, forcing riskier clients to form independent groups. May enable MFIs to charge interest rates accordingly, eliminating the need to cross-subsidize risky borrowers with safer ones. Addresses potential adverse selection market failures.

classic Grameen-style lending
Type of joint liability group lending in which small groups, usually five members, stagger their loan disbursements. Some borrowers have to wait for their peers to repay loans before they themselves can access funds. Clusters of groups form "centers" of roughly 25–40 clients to meet regularly with loan officers to repay and get new loans. Pioneered by the Grameen Bank in Bangladesh.

joint liability
Group members share the burden of member loan defaults, so each individual in a group has an incentive to help put pressure on other members, who in turn have a social incentive to behave reliably. Addresses potential limited liability market failures.

peer monitoring
Group members can keep an eye on one another's activities and behavior; resulting social pressure can help ensure a borrower uses loan effectively for the approved purpose and pays back, as opposed to other riskier uses like gambling it away. Addresses potential moral hazard market failures.

progressive lending
The promise of larger future loans if current loan is successfully paid off. Has proven a strong incentive for repayment.

self-help groups
Self-governed lending and savings groups, owned by the members, which operate much like informal ASCAs but are usually established with funds, training and other assistance from external organizations such as NGOs, churches or government programs. Particularly abundant in India.

solidarity group
A small group, usually three to 10 or so members, guarantee each other's loans in lieu of collateral. All members receive a loan at the same time. Pioneered by Accion in Latin America.

village banking
Larger more autonomous groups of roughly 20–50 form independent legal entities owned by members themselves; members gather regularly, often weekly, to save funds, disburse, repay, and manage loans, elect leaders, and set bylaws. As self-owners, the entire group jointly guarantees loans from the sponsor MFI. Pioneered by FINCA in Bolivia.

village savings and loan associations
Generally operate similarly to village banks in being self-governed and owned by members, but do not take credit from external sources. All funds come from members' own savings plus accumulated interest and fee payments. Commonly affiliated with charity organizations.

Notes:

[1] Kevin Clawson, Founder & CEO Reach the Children, personal communication.
[2] Yunus (2007).
[3] Polakow-Suransky (2003).
[4] Hatch (2004).
[5] Sinha (2006).
[6] Sinha (2006).
[7] Stiglitz (1990).
[8] Armendáriz and Morduch (2010).
[9] Armendáriz and Morduch (2010).
[10] Ghatak (1999); also van Tassel (1999).
[11] Armendáriz and Morduch (2010).
[12] Armendáriz and Morduch (2010).
[13] Guttman (2008).
[14] Armendáriz and Morduch (2010).
[15] Qayum, Samadder, and Rahman (2012).
[16] Ladman and Afcha (1990).
[17] Rai and Sjöström (2004).
[18] Ahlin and Townsend (2007).
[19] Roodman (2012) p. 176. Emphasis in original.

Chapter

BEYOND MICROCREDIT

"Imagine a world in which a farm couple in the highlands of Nicaragua saves enough money to provide for their old age, a slum dweller in Mumbai who falls ill gets medical treatment without sacrificing her life savings, and a snack vendor in Uganda borrows money and builds a small restaurant. Imagine that these examples are not special cases, but are multiplied hundreds of millions of times across the world."

— Elisabeth Rhyne, Managing Director, Center for Financial Inclusion, Accion International

Figure 6.1. Various windows offer a full suite of microfinancial services at ACLEDA Bank, Cambodia

Services provided by microfinance institutions (MFIs) extend well beyond lending, and encompass a wide range of financial intermediation. As we saw in Chapter 2, just like most of us, the poor need a portfolio of services for various purposes to navigate the financial complexities of their daily lives. MFIs continue to look for ways to better serve their clients in sustainable ways. Hence, the diverse array of additional services various MFIs offer aims to add not only revenues but also social returns by improving the lives of their clientele.

Given the diversity, this chapter cannot fully explore all the services MFIs now offer around the world. We will address microsavings and microinsurance in detail here, and look briefly at mobile banking and healthcare issues. We will also revisit market barriers from Chapter 3 that help us understand why these services might have been slow to emerge for low-income clients. While these services have only recently begun to reach the scale of microcredit, many economic development professionals believe savings, insurance and mobile banking might in fact have higher potential than credit for empowering the poor, with fewer potential downsides.

6.1 The Emerging Array of Microfinance Services

The microfinance industry is awhirl with innovation and new products, leveraging the widespread infrastructure the industry initially developed in extending credit. Figure 6.2 presents the myriad services aimed at individuals and small businesses, and a rough classification of product maturities.

As you can see, the list of services might well be mistaken for a list of normal middle-class financial services available in rich countries, from life, health and property insurance, to pensions, investment funds and even mobile phone banking. Yet in some places these services are now available to some of the poorest families. As we will explore, MFIs are beginning to find ways to specially tailor such services to better suit the needs of low-income households.

Over to the left of the diagram, the most broadly available services are group and individual microcredit, detailed in Chapter 5. Savings accounts and insurance bundled to cover microloans are also widely established. We investigate both later. At the other end of the product maturity spectrum, to the far right, early phase experimental programs are setting up pensions

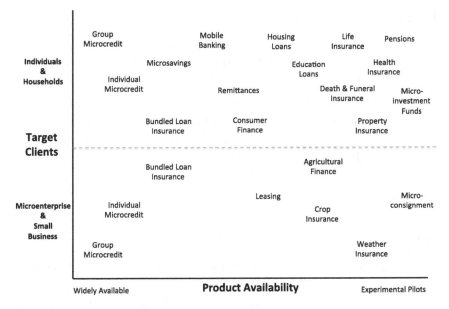

Figure 6.2. Microfinance product variety and availability

Source: Modified from Forum for the Future (2007).

and micro-investment funds for the poor. Crop and weather insurance for agriculture are also emerging, though proving challenging for insurers to operate sustainably, as discussed later. Focused insurance specifically to cover funeral expenses turns out to have been particularly popular where introduced and well suited to balancing the needs of low-income customers with business realities for MFIs. Loans for housing and education are also taking root.

A particularly promising and rapidly expanding area is banking services for the poor delivered directly on mobile phones, including mobile cash, deposit services, loans, and cash transfers. Mobile (i.e. branchless) banking might help MFIs solve some of the more vexing cost-related barriers we encountered in Chapter 3 to providing low-income folks access to financial services.

Section in Bulletpoint

- Although microcredit remains the most common service, MFIs increasingly offer a wide array of products, from saving and insurance to mobile banking, pensions, and even a few micro-investment funds.

Discussion Questions

1. Explain key reasons services like group microcredit and microsavings are far more commonly available than health microinsurance, or death and funeral microinsurance.

2. In what ways have mobile phones helped advance and expand microfinance services? What do you think are the main factors causing or enabling this change? Have your own uses of financial services been influenced by mobile phone technologies? How?

6.2 Microsavings

Why Do the Poor Need to Save?

A key reason microsavings took so long to develop was the misconception that the poor had no need and not enough money to save. Yet in previous chapters we discussed evidence the poor do in fact save, reasons why, and the informal mechanisms they use, such as livestock, deposit collectors, and rotating savings and credit associations (ROSCAs). The problem many low-income people face is not that they do not have money to save; it is simply that they do not have a convenient, safe, affordable place to save in the formal sector.

Morsheda Ahktar, a client of the MFI BURO Bangladesh, put her need to save this way:

> *Savings are important to all of us—more important than loans. Before I used to try to save a few paisa in the house, but we always spent it—a guest came, the children begged for an ice cream, or something else important came up—the money always went.... We need a secure place to put savings—somewhere outside the house, but where we can get access to them quickly when an emergency strikes.*[1]

While the demand for microsavings products should by now be clear, it is worth examining more closely their potential benefits. Figure 6.3 illustrates key benefits. First, we saw that even finding cash for day-to-day consumption flow transactions can be problematic without ways to store money to cover times when necessary expenses exceed current inflows (Figure 6.3a). In Chapter 2 we called this consumption smoothing. Similarly, we saw how the erratic nature of a low-income person's income leaves them vulnerable when facing sudden large lump sum expense, such as a medical bill or funeral

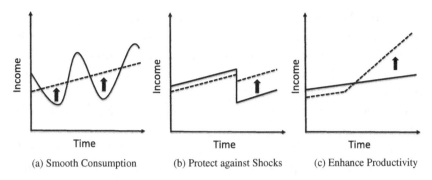

(a) Smooth Consumption   (b) Protect against Shocks   (c) Enhance Productivity

Figure 6.3. How savings can improve the lives of the poor

Source: Modified from Christen and Mas (2009).

(Figure 6.3b). Without effective savings mechanisms, the poor can find themselves struggling to dig out from debt in order to cope. Savings also can enable usefully large lump sums for stock transaction opportunities like productivity-enhancing investments in equipment, fertilizer, or education (Figure 6.3c).

This section reviews the positive effects expansion of savings can have not only for the poor but also for MFIs, some of the challenges of offering savings services, and how savings can be as important to microfinance as borrowing.

Types of Microsavings Services

People do not always wish to save in the same ways or for the same purposes. When MFIs offer savings, one challenge is choosing which savings products to make available. Among MFIs that take deposits, most (87%) provide simple savings accounts where clients can deposit money and might earn interest on the account over time.[2] Others offer more sophisticated products, such as fixed-term deposits, commitment savings products, and checking. Choices tailored to customer needs are central both for creating utility for the clients and sustainability of the savings programs for the MFI. Let us look over a few of the most common savings products tailored for the poor.

Compulsory Savings

As the name suggests, **compulsory savings** requires a borrower to commit to deposit a certain amount, often 10% or 20% of the loan amount, over a given time. Most often, compulsory deposits are paid over time bundled with regular loan repayments. Many clients like being forced to commit, appreciating the incentive for discipline in building savings assets. Recall from Chapter 3 the procrastination and self-control challenges many of us have that inhibit savings behavior. Similarly, the requirement to save can also help clients overcome social taxation pressures from family and friends. Sorry, cousin Constance, I cannot give you that money, I have to give it to the bank. Along those lines, as we will explore in Chapter 7, some MFIs believe mandatory savings can facilitate women's empowerment in cultures where men usually control money.

Requiring savings along with a loan also helps with limited liability, providing the MFI with some collateral to ensure repayment on the loans. The flexibility a client has to withdraw compulsory savings varies among MFIs, but in more rigid cases clients cannot withdraw the savings until their loan is repaid. The forced savings then acts as a kind of security deposit on the loan. If a client gets sick or has an emergency, the savings can be used to make loan repayments.

Figure 6.4 shows the idea in field practice, on an information poster hung up at each meeting of a lending group affiliated with the MFI Pro

Figure 6.4. Loan options with compulsory savings, Pro Mujer Peru

Mujer Peru. The first column lists possible loan amounts (*monto*), from 100 to 2,000 Peruvian nuevo sol. The second column adds the loan plus a loan fee (*monto con comision*). The third column shows the additional compulsory savings (*ahorro obligat*) to which clients must commit when taking a loan, in this case 20% of the loan amount including fee. The remaining columns show regular payment options, including interest and required savings, for various loan terms.

Some MFIs, including those using the classic Grameen system we saw in Chapter 5, required deposits starting before the actual loan itself. From the MFI's point of view, this ensures a track record and habit of the client managing money reliably enough to put some aside regularly. It is a step towards reducing the information asymmetry barrier to loans we discussed in Chapters 3 and 5.

Timing deposits with loan repayments means that loan officers can take both simultaneously at regularly scheduled meetings. This helps keep down costs and reduce the liquidity uncertainty that on-demand savings services can present for MFIs, as we explored in Chapter 3.

While MFIs point to the above benefits, many critics contend compulsory savings obscures from clients the true full costs of loans. A $100 loan with a required 20% savings, would effectively be an $80 loan, yet interest is charged on the whole $100. The effective loan interest rate is actually significantly higher than stated. Similar pricing transparency complaints aim at compulsory loan protection insurance too, as discussed later.

Voluntary Savings

By contrast, voluntary savings is what most of us in rich countries do when we save at our local banks. MFIs now offer a wide range of services for the poor who voluntarily want to save for short- or long-term needs. As we saw in Chapter 3, offering flexible on-demand savings tends to raise bank operating costs and risks. If clients can deposit or withdraw at any time, bank operations must accommodate many small transactions at unpredictable frequencies. Nevertheless, some pioneering MFIs have succeeded in mobilizing microsavings at large scale cost-effectively (e.g. BRI, Box 1.3, or Khan Bank, Box 6.1). Although individual MFIs create unique variations, the basic foundation for most savings products stems from one of three variations.[3]

First, deposits in **passbook savings accounts**, i.e. regular savings, are typically used to facilitate everyday transactions. Deposits might earn interest over time, but a main feature is liquidity; money is available for withdrawal as needed. In targeting the poor, many MFIs keep balance minimums low or in some cases eliminate limits entirely. As a way to keep costs in check and provide incentives to save more, the accounts often do not earn interest below a cutoff balance. For example, Khan Bank in Mongolia, where roughly a quarter of the population subsists on less than $4/day, offers a "current account" with a low minimum savings balance of 1,000 Mongolian tögrög (about $0.50). It requires no account-opening fee, but pays no interest. Khan Bank's "deposit account" does pay interest but has a higher but still relatively small savings minimum, 5,000 tögrög (~$2.50). Interest rates paid are even higher for larger accounts. Attracting larger savers, who might care more about getting interest, also can help the MFI offset the costs of servicing lots of small accounts.

A second foundational type, **fixed-term deposit accounts**, sometimes called time deposits, differ from passbook accounts in being comparatively illiquid. A fixed-term deposit account requires a commitment of a certain amount of money for a fixed period of time. Hence, savers use them for longer-term needs. Among the poor, a useful term is often a few months, although some depositors want to commit their money for longer. Over this period, the bank pays a fixed interest on the deposits. (You might be familiar with one type of fixed-term deposit accounts known as Certificates of Deposit.)

A fixed-term deposit account ensures the money is safe and untouched until a predetermined date. Penalty fees usually apply for withdrawals before then. In exchange for tying up the funds, interest rates paid are generally higher than for the more liquid passbook accounts. For instance, Mongolia's Khan Bank's six-month fixed-term deposit account in 2015 paid a 13% annual interest rate on minimum balances of about $10, compared to 6% on its passbook-like deposit accounts.

Fixed-term deposit accounts are popular, for example, among poor farmers to combat the lumpy seasonal swings of incomes at harvests and spending during planting season (see Box 6.1 on Khan Bank's "Herder's Deposit" fixed-term accounts). This strategy is not restricted to farmers, however, and is widely used by the poor to save for expenditure milestones such as weddings, school fees, and funerals. To facilitate everyday flow transactions, it is also popular to have a higher liquidity passbook account simultaneously.

Box 6.1. In the Field
Khan Bank—Mongolia's King of Microsavings

A former communist nation wedged between Russia and China may seem an odd place for a private commercial bank to become a world leader. Nevertheless, with 2.4 million savings clients, Mongolia's Khan Bank—established just after the fall of the Soviet Union—is now one of the world's top 10 in microsavings (see Chapter 1, Table 1.4), and the largest commercial bank in Mongolia.

By offering a wide variety of innovative low-cost savings options and other financial services specially tailored to its clients, Khan Bank has captured a huge market share: more than 70% of Mongolian households are customers. Accommodating different needs, Khan Bank has an array of passbook and fixed-term savings options with very low minimum balances, ATM access, checking and money transfer services, online and mobile phone banking, and various loan products. In short, despite its roots targeting Mongolia's poor rural population, it is a leading full-service bank.

Table 6.1. Khan Bank

Began microfinance operations	1991 (shortly after the Soviet Union fell)
Location	Mongolia
Clients (2015)	2.4 million savers; 358,910 borrowers
Women as % of borrowers	47.5%
Self-sufficiency ratio	118.5%
Legal status	Commercial bank

As an example of its product tailoring, in one variant for Mongolia's vast rural areas, Khan Bank offers a specially designed "Herder's Deposit" account, a fixed-term deposit account that pays the client interest each month rather than just at the end of the term. It targets

(Continued)

Box 6.1. (*Continued*)

clients (e.g. Figure 6.5) who want some money coming in during periods between episodic income flows, such as during long nomadic stays out tending livestock in the Mongolian steppe.

Figure 6.5. Khan Bank's fixed-term "Herder's Deposit" accounts are specially designed for the cash flow needs of rural poor like this camel herder in Dornogovi, Mongolia

Photo Source: © 2008 Angelo Juan Ramos; used under Creative Commons license (https://creativecommons.org/licenses/by/2.0/legalcode).

A third foundational type of account, which falls in between the previous two, is an interest-bearing **limited withdrawal account**. The name describes its function: it restricts the number of and/or amount of withdrawal in a given period. This helps the client mitigate temptation for too many spur-of-the-moment withdrawals. It is a middle ground flexibility that some clients like, while also for the MFI reducing potential transactions costs and liquidity risks associated with fully on-demand deposits. While passbook-like savings accounts may not pay interest below a certain balance, limited withdrawal accounts generally do not make this distinction. This enables savers with very little money to earn some interest. The account is typically used to save for short-term repetitive payments such as monthly rent or a weekly stock of goods to sell at market.

Commitment Savings

One area of ongoing experimentation and innovation in microsavings is designing services expressly grounded in social and behavioral psychology. Increasing numbers of MFIs are introducing what are called **commitment savings** services, sometimes known as "contractual savings." By building in incentive mechanisms to save small amounts regularly, commitment savings services aim to help the poor overcome the cash flow, social taxation, mental accounting, and self-control barriers to savings that we examined in Chapter 3. Clients who sign on agree ahead of time to put in a series of regular, typically fairly small deposits over a given time period in order to achieve a particular savings goal.

Committing ahead of time to achieve some specific future goal has proven effective in increasing savings among the poor. For instance, the MFI Opportunity International Bank Malawi undertook a pilot commitment savings program to see if it could help poor rural farmers.[4] Malawi's economy depends significantly on agriculture. But income flows for farmers are very cyclical. Large inflows right after harvest have to last the family throughout the year plus cover seeds and fertilizer for the next planting. Yet rural Malawians had little access to formal savings options. Consistent with predictions of behavioral psychology, researchers found that the farmers struggled with self-control and from social taxation, making it hard to save enough. So regularly would families go hungry in the months right before harvest that locals nicknamed it the "hungry season."

The commitment savings account allowed farmers to choose a target and select a date before which they could not withdraw funds. Most choose dates to coincide with the next planting season, a very salient and tangible future need, nicely framed in a mental account. The bank enabled farmers to pre-commit to automatic direct deposit payments into their savings accounts after they sell crops at local auction houses. They would not have to deal with holding cash. As we have seen in Chapter 3, future money is psychologically easier to delay using than current money. Thus, the pre-commitment to auto-deposits both helped the farmers reduce the temptation to spend cash and shielded them from social taxation pressure to share.

Did the pilot program work? Yup. Remarkably well. Farmers who used the commitment accounts invested 26% more on inputs for planting, sold

22% more after harvest, and were able to consume 17% more post-harvest than a control group without accounts. Farmers used their savings to invest rather than spend and got substantially more productive. The next hungry season was not so hungry for their families.

Although, as MFIs experiment, substantial variation remains in how these services operate, there are several common characteristics. Table 6.2

Table 6.2. Six key attributes of commitment savings services

1. Recurring savings
- Explicit commitment to save in a predefined plan is the essential element.
- The client commits to deposit the same amount on a daily, weekly, or monthly basis during a particular period.

2. Interest rates secondary
- Interest rate is usually a secondary factor; low-income populations' savings tends to be insensitive to interest rates.
- Instead, with commitment savings the client looks for features to help reach a savings goal.
- So, profitability for MFIs tends to be greater than that of on-demand transactional accounts but less than fixed-term deposits.

3. Time frame
- Fixed time frames; depend on the savings goal.
- Plans from three to 12 months are most common, but range to 24 or even 60 months.

4. Lower liquidity
- Plans tend to incorporate features that restrict liquidity.
- Many clients like lower liquidity as a way to discipline savings and reduce self-control and social taxation issues by hindering impulsive withdrawals.
- But too many restrictions can discourage adoption, so well designed versions also allow ways to access funds in case of need.

5. Savings goals
- Often designed for specific savings goals linked to events or future concrete expenses (e.g. school fees, Christmas savings, a household purchase).

(Continued)

Table 6.2. (*Continued*)

- However, also common to find plans without concrete objectives, which provides greater flexibility for clients to design features for specific savings goals.

6. Incentives

- To promote savings, plans often offer incentives to clients who achieve plan goals.
- Incentives might be lotteries, sweepstakes, gifts, or higher interest rates.
- Some plans provide helpful reminders (e.g. mobile texts), to nudge behavior.

Source: Modified from Martin (2013).

shows how Xavier Martin, an expert working with the Inter-American Development Bank, outlined key attributes of commitment savings services aimed at the poor.

Note how these characteristics of microfinance in practice dovetail with the theoretical discussion of behavioral barriers to savings in Chapter 3. For instance, restricting liquidity, through things like limits on withdrawals, no ATM cards, or penalties for early withdrawals, directly targets our self-control weaknesses by leveraging our declining propensity to consume when assets are less liquid. Similarly, letting clients establish and pledge towards particular concrete specific goals (e.g. save for school fees) takes advantage of our mental accounting tendencies. Rewards given only to those who complete their plans successfully increase the salience of the future, reducing our tendency to overly discount longer-term events.

The Benefits of Savings Mobilization

Though still lagging the availability of microcredit, microsavings services have gained substantial traction because of the potential benefits not only to clients but also for the MFIs themselves. A secure and convenient way for clients to deposit money, gain interest, facilitate liquidity for transactions and smooth consumption, and accumulate usefully large lump sums for investments or the inevitable big expenses in life, are all substantial benefits for clients MFIs can facilitate by offering savings services. So too, despite potential costs, risks and regulatory hurdles, MFIs see attracting deposits—in industry jargon savings mobilization—as a potentially good source of funds for loaning out in their microcredit operations, allowing the MFIs to do direct financial intermediation between their savers and their borrowers. As we noted in Chapter 3, some MFIs have also found that well-liked microsavings services can attract customers that will also then use and pay for other services the MFIs might also offer, such as money transfers, improving the MFIs' bottom-lines and attractiveness to investors, and reducing or even eliminating the need for charitable subsidies.

Benefits to the Individual

Because of the similarities we saw in Chapter 2 in cash flow patterns of saving up and saving down when repeated over many cycles, economic theory suggests that forward-looking households ought to be able to save their way out of needing credit if given enough time.[5] If able to overcome self-control challenges and avoid short-sighted spending, a saver will eventually not need borrowing to fill in day-to-day cash flow shortfalls—consumption smoothing—or for lump sum needs. Savings also provides an insurance-like cushion for covering emergency expenses. In this sense, lack of savings options could be a missing link in helping the poor better stabilize their family budgets, eat more regularly, reduce vulnerability to health problems, expand microenterprises, and invest in education.

Indeed, some experts believe microsavings will prove to be more important than microcredit, and suffer fewer downside risks like harmful debt spirals. We will examine evidence in more detail in Chapter 9, but briefly to illustrate: University of California, Los Angeles economists Pascaline Dupas and Jonathan Robinson found that four to six months after village women vendors in Kenya gained access to savings accounts, their daily private expenditures were 27–40% higher than women without such access.[6] In particular, the women with savings options were less vulnerable to shocks to their income from illness as compared to those without. The group lacking savings had to cut spending on their microenterprises during periods of sickness, harming income, but the savers were able to avoid such cuts.

Similarly, a two-year study of very poor clients of SEWA Bank, an MFI in urban India, indicated that those using either microsavings or microcredit had income grow at rates more than double those without access to microfinance. However, savers exhibited the highest increase in income of 17.3% over the time period, borrowers saw 16.2% growth, while non-participants' income only went up 6.8%.[7] As we will see in Chapter 9, other studies have found other improvements such as greater family food security among microsavers, less social taxation, and spillover of benefits from savers to others in their communities.

The informal savings mechanisms we explored in Chapter 4 lack the potential security that can be offered by a bank. The informal sector leaves savers open to risks simply because money is exchanged without formal contracts or legal enforcement. Furthermore, holding cash—an unfortunately common method of saving because it is cheap and convenient—simply is not fully safe, particularly in environments like slums where the poor tend to live. For example, the *Portfolios of the Poor* study we mentioned in Chapter 2 found that in a single survey year 11% of the surveyed poor households in South Africa suffered financial emergency from theft or violent crime.[8] Similarly in Bangladesh, 7% of *Portfolios*-surveyed households had emergencies because they were cheated or lost cash and 19% because they lost their home or property to fire or other forces—again all within just one year. In India, a remarkable 38% of surveyed poor families had financial emergencies from losing livestock or crops, common informal means of storing wealth. The *Portfolios* study year happened to coincide with particularly bad weather for that region's famers, but nevertheless the impact highlights the very real risks of informal savings mechanisms.

MFIs and banks can provide the poor with places where their money can be far safer, while still available to them when needed, often with better liquidity. Although it is common for the poor to store wealth via livestock, crops or other physical items, it is not as easy to turn these back into cash if a sudden need arises. Most regular savings accounts provide liquidity coupled with security because a customer can withdraw funds as necessary (except for fixed term, limited withdrawal, or commitment accounts). As an added benefit over cash hidden in the cookie jar, many MFI savings products offer interest on the deposits.

Organizations such as the Bill & Melinda Gates Foundation recognize the importance of savings and consumption smoothing, and have even offered millions of dollars in support to banks such as the Kenya Post Office Savings Bank (KPOSB) to help develop poor-oriented savings services. KPOSB offers voluntary savings and fund transfer services to nearly 2 million depositors, mostly low-income, such as small-scale farmers, traders, the ubiquitous *jua kali* fix-anything repairmen, and youth.[9] They offer a wide range of services including regular savings accounts, savings accounts tailored for groups, savings accounts designed for youth, fixed-term deposits, flexible limited withdrawal accounts that can lock and unlock deposits, a commitment savings program called *Save as You Earn*, money transfers, loans, credit cards, and even healthcare insurance.

Benefits for the MFI

The benefits that a MFI can gain from offering savings can be significant, but it is unquestionably a challenge. On one hand, many MFIs perceive offering savings as an uphill battle because of regulatory hurdles to become licensed to take deposits, as well as the potential high costs and liquidity risks associated with high frequency small deposits and withdrawals on accounts with relatively very low balances. On the other hand, as we have seen, savings products can enhance MFI revenues, particularly through cross-sales of loans and other products to microsavers, and by fees generated from the savings accounts.

For example, we mentioned in Chapter 3 the success profitably offering savings services at both ADOPEM in the Dominican Republic and Centenary Bank in Uganda. Reaching fairly large scale was important for cost-efficiency at both. By 2015, ADOPEM had about 200,000 borrowers and more than 340,000 depositors. Centenary Bank was similar in scale of borrowers, but had far more depositors, 1.3 million. Even though in both cases depositors are very poor and only maintained low average savings balances (about $330 at Centenary and $160 at ADOPEM), revenue at both institutions is more than enough to cover operating costs. Both institutions offer voluntary microsavings products and it turns out that their main sources of funding for all their services, including loan products, come from their own clients' microsavings. A World Bank-related study measured the additional costs necessary to maintain these two microsavings programs compared to the extra revenues generated. Turns out that despite the MFIs having to operate large numbers of tiny accounts, the profits generated on these microsavings accounts—in large part through cross-selling of other financial services to the same customers—was as high as 400% at Centenary and over 1,000% at ADOPEM.[10] As a result, approximately 30% of these companies' total profits were derived from their microsavings programs.

One daunting task is overcoming the initial high costs associated with developing a management system, infrastructure, and data network capable of handling a multitude of tiny savings accounts. Many MFIs charge clients an account fee, which can be particularly helpful if the cost of offering microsavings cannot fully be offset by fees on loans or by small savers purchasing other services. Centenary Bank charges small fees for its regular microsavings accounts, including roughly 50 cents U.S. monthly, enough to help cover costs but also low enough not to discourage many poor savers from using the services. The average monthly income of the poorest Ugandans, the one in five who live below the poverty line, is about $45 ($U.S. PPP).

As an added benefit, deposits can also be lent back out to other customers, potentially reducing financial costs for the MFI by providing a source of funds without the need to pay interest to external investors or bond markets. The interest paid to clients with savings accounts is most often less than the cost of procuring funds an MFI would otherwise need in order to provide loans. This gap can be particularly notable in developing economies, where global investors require higher interest rates to offset higher risks.

Finally, liquidity risks and costs have turned out to be manageable as well because MFI experiences have shown that the typical poor client does not withdraw large amounts of funds at one time, nor withdrawal all that frequently. Moreover, since the typical account is so small, there turns out to be lower risk that the MFI will not have enough funds to complete withdrawals for clients when necessary. Savings can be the source that MFI need for prolonged self-sustainability because of the fact that poor people will never be free of the need for a place to save their money.

External Challenges to Savings Mobilization

Several external factors significantly affect an MFI's ability to mobilize savings. Key challenges include regional stability, macroeconomic conditions, and government regulations.

Regional stability is arguably the most necessary. In countries torn by civil strife or war, microfinance programs can be extremely difficult, if not impossible, to run. MFIs do exist in very unstable countries, but encounter tough challenges. For example, according to the former chief economist of the Multi-National Force-Iraq, Colonel (and Lehigh University Professor) Frank

Gunter, microfinance programs have been tried as a tool for stimulating the economy of Iraq.[11] Operating in such an unstable region proved extremely difficult and costly, and the programs have never reached large scale, nor were they sustainable without substantial ongoing outside funding. Only in certain regions of Iraq where violence is less prevalent have microfinance programs seen modest success, yet even then requiring subsidization.

Another important factor is an enabling macro economy.[12] Generally, banks and MFIs thrive better where economies are growing, prices are stable, and where there are supportive regulatory environments. Such environments attract more local and foreign investment, have greater workforce participation, and have higher shares of good-paying jobs. In turn, healthy macro economies generally have better income growth opportunities for both wages and the microenterprises low-income people might operate.

Moreover, in times of prosperity people are more likely to have funds to save and to use other financial services, and are less likely to default on loans. MFIs then have incentives to expand and to innovate and compete to better serve clients. In the long run, increases in operational scale, competition and innovation can improve efficiency and decrease fees and improve interest rates for clients.

Keeping inflation in check is particularly central. In countries where prices or the value of the currency are unstable, investors experience high risks of losing the value of their investment as currencies depreciate quickly. Unanticipated inflation can lower real rates of return for MFIs, and can push MFIs to charge high interest rates to cover costs. Inflation also has an impact on a borrower's incentive to pay back a loan on time. If money is losing value fast, borrowers may have little incentive to pay back loans anytime soon. It is better to wait for what they owe to devalue.

In high inflationary circumstances like prices doubling every year or two—rates unfortunately common from time to time in some developing nations (e.g. Venezuela 2013–2015, Belarus 2011–2012, Angola 1991–2004)—the value of saved money erodes quickly, losing half its worth every time prices double. Imagine working at a bank and having your customers lose half their wealth in what they thought were supposed to be safe accounts. The poor (and rich too) would be better off investing their savings in tangible assets such as livestock, grains or jewelry they could later sell. In such environments, bartering can be a better alternative than exchanging cash. Banks and MFIs have difficulty surviving in these kinds of conditions. For example, in a mind-boggling bout of hyperinflation in Zimbabwe during 2007–2008 (see Box 6.2), three-fifths of all of Zimbabwe's MFIs failed. With hyperinflation, financial intermediation across time becomes completely pointless.

Box 6.2. Dig Deeper
Savings Is Futile—Hyperinflation in Zimbabwe

A prime example of bad macroeconomic conditions that can incapacitate a savings program can be seen in Zimbabwe. According to estimates by Johns Hopkins University's Steve Hanke and Alex Kwok, the annual rate of inflation during June 2008 exceeded 11 million percent, and by November 2008 was 89.7 trillion billion percent! Stores had to increase prices many times daily just to keep up. What cost 10 dollars one morning, could cost 20 or 30 by the end of the day, more than 1,000 a week later, and several trillion within a month. Mind-boggling.

To make cash transactions possible, the government had to print ever bigger values on bills (finally including a 100 trillion-dollar bill, Figure 6.6, with 14 zeros). When that was not enough they redenominated the currency by lopping off zeros—dropping a total of 25 zeros between 2006 and 2009. In other words, you had to have 10 million million million million pre-2006 Zimbabwean dollars to get one dollar of the 2009 currency. People began refusing to use the local currency at all. Eventually, Zimbabwe officially switched to using the U.S. dollar as legal tender.

Figure 6.6. An actual Zimbabwean bill, 2008

(Continued)

Hyperinflation kills the benefits of savings and all other financial intermediation services. Even if you would have somehow managed to save a trillion dollars, with inflation that fast you would be penniless in weeks. That bill in Figure 6.6? Worth only a few U.S. cents within months of being printed; it wouldn't even buy a city bus ticket. Today they are sold on the streets to tourists as novelty souvenirs; you too can be trillionaire!

Source: Hanke and Kwok (2009).

Thus, while MFIs have the potential to transform the financial lives of the poor in environments where they otherwise cannot get access to loans or other financial services, effective and stable monetary and fiscal policies are important enablers, as loose policies can scare away investments and eliminate growth opportunities for large swaths of a developing country's population.

A third important external factor that can inhibit the development of microsavings programs is government regulation. More often than not, MFIs are non-profit organizations like non-governmental organizations (NGOs) and church-affiliated groups, rather than formal, regulated banking institutions. Or at least many MFIs start that way. To protect depositors from losing their savings to potentially shady operators, governments universally require that any organization that wants to offer deposit services to customers be licensed, with operations monitored by government banking authorities.

Qualifying to become a licensed deposit-taking bank and then dealing with ongoing monitoring requirements is costly and time consuming. For example, Bolivia's BancoSol was an early MFI pioneer in moving from NGO to regulated commercial bank. In its first operating year in 1992, BancoSol found that complying with regulatory reporting requirements cost what amounted to 5% of its loan portfolio.[13] In other words, loan interest rates would have had to be 5 percentage points higher than otherwise just to cover that paperwork alone. In part this was a function of size: only about 15,000 borrowers at first. As the bank scaled up, this cost ratio fell to about 1% by 1998. A study of 30 MFIs in Peru similarly found costs related to banking regulation amounted to 3–4% of the MFIs' assets annually.[14] These sorts of costs have to get passed onto client if an MFI wants to be self-sufficient. For small institutions with limited numbers of clients, that would mean increasing what many think are already high loan interest rates for poor clients, seeming to run counter to most non-profits' social missions. Instead many NGOs do not try to qualify to take deposits. In short, one of the greatest barriers for many MFIs in mobilizing savings lies in the process of up-scaling into a fully regulated banking institution.

Note that many NGOs and smaller MFIs get around this barrier by partnering with existing traditional banks, or by helping clients establish their own savings mechanisms, such as self-help groups, that resemble the informal economy models discussed in Chapter 4. An alternative route is what is sometimes called "downscaling" by existing mainstream banks introducing products for low-income markets.

Another form of regulation that can deter offering microsavings is the regulation of interest rates, what are called **usury laws**. Usury laws aim to protect people from exploitation by unscrupulous banks or moneylenders charging extremely high rates on loans, or not paying fair interest on deposits. Oftentimes, however, these laws also inhibit the profitable development of savings programs. In order to cost-effectively mobilize savings, an MFI must charge higher rates on loans than given on deposits. In some places, however, usury laws cap loan rates at maximums so low or require interest paid on savings be so high that MFIs cannot cover costs. In such cases, overly restrictive interest rate regulation directly reduces the likelihood MFIs develop microsavings.

A less direct, and perhaps counter-intuitive concern is the presence of large-scale subsidies from governments and charitable donors who provide funds to MFIs. The well-meaning availability of cheap money can stifle incentives MFIs might have to mobilize savings. Innovation and implementation of savings services could slow if MFIs face no need to attract more deposits in order to expand other services. As we explore in Chapter 8, some proponents argue that MFIs need to grow to commercially viable sizes if they want to have large impact. They suggest that the best way for donors and governments to help the poor get access to financial services would be to subsidize fixed costs of ramping up MFI operations and infrastructure, rather than to give out loans below market rates. The argument is that too many low-cost services available because of subsidies can crowd-out the development and growth of commercial microfinance markets. Why would clients use commercial market services when subsidized ones are available more cheaply?

Section in Bulletpoint

- Microsavings services can help the poor smooth consumption, hedge against future risks, and accumulate useful lump sums, without debt.
- Some MFIs require compulsory savings for loan clients; a mechanism to mitigate information asymmetries and limited liability.
- Commitment savings products are designed to help clients overcome social and behavioral psychology barriers to savings.
- Some of the most successful MFI tailor design microsavings services to unique needs of different niches of low-income clients.
- Savings services can be profitable for MFIs, in part by attracting customers to other services.
- Large scale facilitates cost-efficient operations.
- Attracting deposits directly from savers to enable other operations like lending can be more cost effective for MFIs than external sources.
- Challenges in creating saving programs include high costs of becoming licensed, costly infrastructure, liquidity risks, economic and political instability, and overly restrictive usury laws.

Discussion Questions

1. What are some of the main reasons it is difficult for low-income people to save? Discuss from two points of view: first, the daily lives of those individuals; and, second, a financial institution's.

2. Of the three types of microsavings services, compulsory, voluntary, or commitment savings, which do you think might be most useful

to help overcome social taxation pressures from family and society? Explain why.

3. Do you think MFIs should be allowed to force their clients to save? Considering the pros and cons of compulsory savings, why or why not?

4. Discuss the main psychological and behavioral issues that commitment savings accounts attempt to address. Do you think they would help you overcome your own tendencies? Why or why not?

5. Why is it beneficial to MFIs to offer savings products, despite regulatory hurdles, high costs, and liquidity risks?

6. Some microsavings accounts pay no interest on deposits and charge fees. This practice essentially means negative return on savings for low-income people. Do you think that it is fair or ethical? Why would millions of poor people use these services anyway, despite negative returns?

6.3 Microinsurance

Why Microinsurance?

People in rich countries can find insurance for myriad scenarios, ranging from auto, home, health, unemployment, to even terrorism insurance. The wide variety of offerings essentially allows individuals to dial in a desired level of financial risk for seemly nearly anything. Singers insure their vocal cords; people insure pet dogs; you can insure against bringing home bedbugs while traveling. Worried your fantasy football player might get hurt in real life and hurt your fake team? Insurable.

The poor typically do not have access to such formal mechanisms to reduce their financial risks. Yet we have seen how their incomes and expenses can change unpredictably. Hence, development experts think that a lack of mechanisms to hedge against financial risks is among the main barriers to improving the economic security of the poor.

How does microinsurance differ from the everyday kinds of insurance those in rich countries are familiar with? Principally, the products cater to the different cash flow needs and capacity of low-income clients. Like microcredit and microsavings, the amounts of money involved are small compared with most insurance in rich countries. Depending on what is covered, microinsurance policies tend to a cost on the order of a dollar or two a month and potential payouts are modest as well. (For our purposes, we do not include insurance-like government social protection schemes such as welfare or national health care.)

Microinsurance serves two related roles: (1) help protect the poor from financial crisis, and (2) aid their productivity. The first is probably more obvious than the second. Insurance can be protective in that it can smooth out income flows in case of some external shock—for example a loss of property, death or illness of the family breadwinner, or in the case of farmers, poor weather. Where available, savings accounts or loans could absorb some financial hits. However, if a shock hurts the ability of a poor family to earn income for an extended period, microsavings might not suffice, and microcredit runs the risk of evolving into inexorable cycles of debt the family cannot pay off. Insurance serves as a safety net to catch vulnerable individuals before they enter that vicious cycle, which can otherwise erode benefits the poor might get from microsavings and microcredit.

Box 6.3. Faces
Opposite Shores—Health Microinsurance on Lake Victoria

"When Mary Anyango contracted typhoid in Kisumu Kenya, her family simply took her to her home village to die. Across Lake Victoria in Kampala Uganda, when Betty Waswa was bleeding to death after the birth of a child, she was taken to a top level hospital where she was treated and released in good condition to return home. Why the difference for these two, who both lived on about $2 per day? Health microinsurance. While Mary has passed, Betty insists that she would have died if it had not been for her health microinsurance policy."

Source: Noble and McCord (2007). Names changed for privacy.

OK for the first benefit, but the second? How can insurance be productive? Because insurance is "saving through" it enables the accumulation of usefully large lump sums. Much like savings accounts or loans, those lump sums are then assets that can be used productively. (See Box 6.4 on how Hope Community blurred the lines between productive loans and insurance.)

Similarly, by insuring borrowers or lenders from potential failures insurance can facilitate investments in risky productive assets like business equipment or fertilizer. Health insurance can also be productive. Many individuals living in poverty must deal with adverse environmental factors, such as tainted drinking water, which lead to health problems. Sickly individuals cannot work to their potential and often have a more difficult time keeping jobs or successfully running microenterprises, and in turn can struggle feeding their children and paying for housing or school fees.

Not only can these protective and productive features of insurance help clients, but they can also the MFIs. MFIs have found that effective microinsurance products can both generate good revenue and at the same time help clients better maintain cash flows and improve their ability to pay back loans and pay for other MFI services. Moreover, MFIs can offer insurance as additional financial intermediation services without adding much extra operating cost by leveraging their microcredit operational infrastructures— e.g. loan officers, group meetings, back offices, computer systems—and close connections with their clients.

How Widespread Is Microinsurance?

Until recently, microinsurance was not nearly as developed or widely available as savings or credit services available to the poor. Though there were thousands of MFIs or MFI-like institutions around the world, few offered many insurance products. Thankfully, that gap is closing rapidly in some places.

The sector is growing fast. As we see in Figure 6.7, by 2006 an estimated 78 million people had some sort of microinsurance in the 100 lowest income countries.[15] Roughly twice that many had microcredit in that same year (recall Figure 1.2). By 2009, the large insurance company Lloyds of London estimated that formal microinsurance had grown to cover around 135 million people.[16] Even so, coverage remained thin, only roughly 5% of what Lloyds believed was the potential overall low-income market for insurance, well in excess of 2 billion people. It left 19 of 20 poor people still without access. Then by 2012–2013, experts thought the sector had more than 260 million individuals covered, as Table 6.3 details. The scale now rivals the numbers of clients for microcredit.

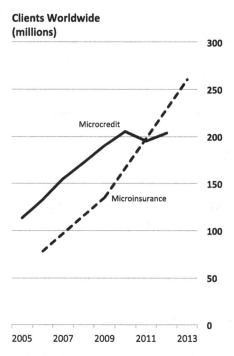

Clients Worldwide (millions)

Figure 6.7. Rapid growth of microinsurance 2006–2013

Data Sources: Microcredit Summit Campaign (2014); Roth, McCord, and Liber (2007); Lloyds (2010); Mukherjee et al (2014).

Unfortunately, availability is patchy at best; it is very uneven from country to country. India alone, with an estimated 111 million people with some form of microinsurance, accounts for about two-fifths of all the microinsured worldwide, thanks to laws requiring insurers to serve low-income customers and government subsidies for various forms of health, life, agricultural and livestock insurance targeting low-income people in the informal economy.[17]

By comparison, estimates for all of Latin America combined are in the range of 45–50 million, covering less than 8% of the population (see Table 6.3). Africa overall lags coverage of Latin America, with only about 4.3% of the vast continent's population using any form of microinsurance.[18] But South Africans heavily skew that ratio: more than half have microinsurance. By contrast, in Gambia in 2012, one estimate put coverage at only one person in 200; in Sierra Leone microinsurance was

Table 6.3. Global patterns of microinsurance

	Covered individuals & properties (millions)		
Type of risk insured	Asia & Oceania	Africa	Latin America
Life	83.9	33.9	32.5
Credit life	*	8.8	15.9
Accident	77.8	2.0	24.0
Health	29.2	2.4	10.3
Property	7.7	0.8	2.9
Agriculture	23.8	0.2	0.3
Measure	*Total coverage*		
Individuals & properties covered (millions)†	170.4	44.4	45.5
Coverage rate (% of population)	4.3	4.4	7.6
Top 3 countries by coverage rate (%)	Philippines 20.6 Thailand 13.9 India 9.0	Namibia 55.8 South Africa 54.4 Swaziland 12.0	Jamaica 20.9 Peru 18.2 Ecuador 18.2

Notes: * Included in line above, not separately reported. † Some policies cover more than one type of risk, so volumes by type add up to more than total individuals covered.
Sources: Mukherjee et al (2014); McCord et al (2013); McCord, Ingram, and Tatin-Jaleran (2012).

practically non-existent, 4,999 out of every 5,000 Sierra Leoneans lacked access.[19] Interestingly, Zimbabwe—infamous for recent hyperinflation—is also among Africa's microinsurance leaders, largely thanks to life insurance available to millions through mobile phone companies.

Table 6.3 describes global microinsurance markets in more detail. As you can see, life microinsurance is the most common in all three regions shown, covering from about half to three-quarters of all those people insured. Other popular forms include credit-life, health and agricultural insurance.

While some countries like South Africa and Namibia show widespread use of a narrow range of microinsurance products, most of the world remains underserved. Even the other top nations listed in Table 6.3 barely crack one in five people covered. Overall, despite recent growth, the vast majority of the world's poor lacks any formal microinsurance.

Who Provides Microinsurance?

In addition to MFIs, four other types of organizations attempt to meet the growing demand for microinsurance services, often teaming up to leverage each other's complementary skills and infrastructures: (1) commercial insurers, (2) community-based organizations (CBOs), (3) mutual insurers, and (4) NGOs. Insurers require an efficient mechanism to distribute insurance to the poor, capable of supporting a high volume of small financial transactions in addition to fostering client-insurer trust in convenient locations. Large mainstream commercial insurers have the resources to be fully regulated and professionally managed, thus they are the primary providers of microinsurance. While larger MFIs and NGOs have advantages in accessing the poor, understanding their needs, and serving as distributors, they often lack the ability to specialize in insurance.

Large commercial insurers provide the majority of insurance products worldwide. They dominate insurance markets serving richer customers, and now lead microinsurance markets as well. The companies have substantial resources, access to ways to spread risks across worldwide insurance pools, professional management and are registered under insurance regulations. However, they tend to lack good delivery channels to reach most low-income informal sector markets, just like we discussed earlier concerning major banks struggling to offer financial services to the poor. Partnering with other organizations like community groups, NGOs and MFIs help commercial insurers expand their market and outreach.

For example, MFIs like Spandana, BFIL and SEWA in India have partnered with local insurers. After all, why re-invent the wheel? Mobile phone providers are another rapidly growing set of distribution channel partners, not just for insurers but also for microfinance services of all sorts.

The second sort of microinsurance providers, CBOs are generally member owned and managed, but unregulated. This informal form of insurance conceptually mirrors the ASCAs we encountered in Chapter 4 or the self-help and village savings and loan groups of Chapter 5; all managed by the poor for the poor. As we saw, these informal mechanisms can provide a measure of collective risk sharing. However, most CBO organizers lack the skills and experience to provide cost-effective formal insurance at any substantial scale without partnering with more professional institutions. By teaming with commercial insurers, CBOs are now the most common channel of distribution for microinsurance in Asia, followed closely by MFIs.[20]

Third, mutual insurers are both professionally managed and regulated, and generally run like regular insurance businesses, but are owned entirely by their members. As a result, they have experience in financial activities and can have a close proximity to the poor. Because they do not have external owners to whom they need to pay dividends, they also can have more flexibility to offer services priced closer to costs, a potential advantage for low-income members. Mutuals are particularly prevalent in India in providing members with health insurance.

Fourth, outside of commercial insurers, the next largest type of providers by far is NGOs, such as trade unions, charity groups, and many MFIs. Yet these NGOs too tend to lack the professional skills and regulations to operate insurance directly on a wide scale. Instead, like CBOs they are increasingly serving as effective delivery channels due to their proximity to the poor. Since many NGOs utilize subsidies from donors and have deep social missions, they often provide subsidized health insurance to the poor, particularly those in deepest poverty for whom even basic microinsurance is financially out of reach.

Even so, most poor still live without any sort of access. Much experimentation continues in the field to find solutions on how to meet the high demand for healthcare coverage for billions among the world's poor.

Potential Market Failures and Microinsurance

Why does coverage remain so spotty, despite the growth? Offering insurance to the poor comes bundled with a number of potential information asymmetry and incentive problems that insurers need to overcome in order to offer relevant, quality products at affordable prices. Challenges include ones that all insurers (even in developed countries) face and additional problems unique to low-income informal sector markets. We have encountered many of these barriers before in Chapter 3, so here we will only briefly review them in the specific context of insurance and how insurers are beginning to overcome them.

Adverse Selection

As mentioned in previous discussions, adverse selection is one potential consequence of information asymmetry, and is especially relevant to any discussion on insurance. Studies have shown that an individual's demand for insurance correlates with that individual's self-assessed risk. The riskiest people are most likely to buy insurance; safe ones would not think they need it. If the insurer cannot distinguish and vary prices according to risk levels, ultimately insurers can end up with client pools dominated by risky clients.

For example, data from a Vietnamese health insurer indicated that healthy individuals were 41–55% less likely to purchase a policy.[21] If only sick people have health insurance, their insurance premiums would have to be much higher than if healthy people were also in the mix to help cover costs. As we will see later, microinsurers have begun trying to tackle adverse selection problems through mechanisms such as waiting periods, automatic enrollment, mandatory schemes, and enrolling whole groups at a time rather than having individuals self-select.

However, much room remains for experimentation and new ideas for ways to expand availability, particularly of health insurance for the poor. The bottom line problem is the cost of providing healthcare relative to the incomes of the clients. So far few programs outside India and China have found ways to be affordable enough, even after subsidies, for widespread uptake of health microinsurance. Many billions of the world's most impoverished remain without.

Moral Hazard and Limited Liability

In the context of insurance, moral hazard refers to how risk-insulated individuals have a tendency to take more risks than an insurer would view as appropriate because they face less downside, a problem we called limited liability. With the knowledge that some third party bears their risk, individuals may fail to take the same precautions that they would without insurance. For instance, a farmer with livestock insurance has incentives to avoid seeking medical treatment for ill animals—why pay for treating a sick goat when you could get a better, healthy goat? Additionally, clients may take advantage of their policy and seek costly help for things that could be resolved for less.

Strategies to combat moral hazard aim to reduce incentives to trigger insured events. Microinsurers try to structure contracts so clients share at least some of the risk. In property insurance, for instance, clients may have to pay a deductible before the insurer will cover larger losses. A crop insurance policy might cover 80% of the value of the loss, while the client must pay rest.[22] In the case of health insurance, many insurers require patients to copay some partial fee at the time of visit. Theoretically, this additional cost should make the client think more carefully about making claims that waste resources.

Fraud

Occasionally, insured individuals will take deliberate illicit actions to collect payouts. Fraud can occur at nearly every level of insurance, ranging from lying when agents screen clients for a new policy, to staging accidents on purpose, to claiming an insurable event has occurred when in reality it has not. Insurance firms have learned that claims verification provides an incentive for individuals to truthfully represent what happened. Unfortunately in developing economies with high levels of informal sector activity, corruption also tends to be high, and weak legal systems make both documenting verification and recourse in cases of fraud challenging. Fraud can happen on the supply side as well. Scam providers can collect payments and then fail to deliver promised insurance payouts. Hence, in most nations insurers are, like banks, regulated. Nevertheless, in high corruption counties, trust may not exist on either the demand or supply side, thwarting development of microinsurance markets.

Covariate Risk

Covariate risk describes the situation where a single event can cause an entire group of insured clients to collect payouts. Where risks are not independent of each other it is tough for an insurance firm to spread out the risks across a pool of clients. This concerns, for example, agricultural insurance products. A drought or an epidemic may wipe out all the crops in a region, leading all the insured farmers in that area to seek reimbursement. Insured homeowners after an earthquake or tsunami would behave similarly. Unless the region is small relative to the insurance firm's client base, the firm might be unable to make good on its promises to pay. Insurance providers can spread these sorts of risks by being large and geographically diverse or through what are called re-insurance markets. It might sound redundant, but insurers essentially buy insurance to cover risks they face from their own pool of insurance. Reinsurance markets can then spread risks across many regions, types of risk, and types of insurers.

Technical Challenges in Microinsurance

Developing the infrastructure and knowledge to provide insurance requires the use of complex mathematics and statistics to quantify the value of future risks and to set insurance prices to cover those risks while still attracting customers. A new microinsurer would have to tackle this analysis from scratch—requiring time, significant resources, specialized knowledge of actuarial techniques, and lots and lots of data. Yet data describing characteristics and risk profiles of low-income societies often are of questionable quality, further complicating the analysis. Large, established insurance firms have extensive experience analyzing market characteristics to develop and price insurance products— thus, it makes sense for a microinsurance program to take advantage of this specialization and partner with a large insurer.

Regulation also plays a key role inhibiting microinsurance from reaching the poor. In most places, in order to sell insurance, an agent must first obtain a license and have the government's approval to practice. The purpose is to protect consumers from the risk of losing their insurance money to badly managed or unscrupulous providers. But it creates problems on both sides. On the provider side, many MFIs and NGOs simply cannot afford the time or money to have their employees become licensed insurance agents. Similarly on the regulatory side, officials in low-income countries often lack the training and experience to effectively oversee the wide variety and large numbers of small NGOs and MFIs who might want to provide insurance. Regulations also result in complicated insurance policy documents and language, which in turn can be misunderstood or ignored by the often illiterate poor.

Despite these many barriers, we have seen that microinsurance is in a rapid expansion phase. Let us explore some of the main options now available, and examples of how they work. Key types include loan protection, life, savings-linked, health and agricultural microinsurance.

Loan Protection Insurance

Credit life microinsurance, also known as loan protection insurance, is arguably the longest-established practice in formal microfinance because it grew as a complementary, and often mandatory, coverage that is tied with a client receiving microcredit. A common practice among MFIs is to include a small fee on top of loan fees for insurance to guarantee payment of any remaining balances. The idea behind credit life microinsurance in its simplest form involves forgiveness of the client's outstanding debt in the event of the client's death. Relatives are then not responsible for repaying.

A version often called **credit life plus** adds a payment to the family of a deceased policyholder as well as debt forgiveness. For example, FINCA Uganda developed a credit life plus microinsurance product that covered clients for the duration of their microloan.[23] FINCA Uganda required the coverage for any microloan. Clients paid an additional 1% interest on top of the interest rate on their loan. In exchange, FINCA would pay off a deceased client's outstanding loan balance plus pay $700 to the next-of-kin for an accidental death or $175 if the death was not accidental (e.g. illness). That $700 for a life might not sound like much to those in rich countries, but it was more than 2½ times Uganda's average yearly income at the time.

MFIs that offer or require their clients to get credit life microinsurance enjoy a number of benefits. First, the services have proven profitable. A study of 511 different insurance providers throughout Africa found that payouts on credit life policies only amounted to 23% of paid-in premiums.[24] FINCA Uganda paid 45% of the fees it collected to AIG, a large international insurance firm based in the U.S., which in turn covered any payouts and loan repayments. The other 55% of the fees more than covered the MFI's extra administrative costs. In addition, since many MFIs team up with insurance firms to offer these products, the fact that an insurance firm will pay a client's debt reduces the MFI's risk that a loan not being repaid if a client dies. Moreover, the MFI thus avoids the costly and morally uncomfortable practice of trying to track down a low-income family to collect debt of the deceased.

Several characteristics of credit life products help mitigate potential market failures and help keep costs in check. Extra costs are limited because clients with this microinsurance also have microloans, enabling combining transactions and customer service for the two products. When mandatory, the coverage also addresses concerns of adverse selection. If all clients have to purchase insurance, theoretically high-risk clients will not dominate the risk pool. Healthier borrowers in effect subsidize riskier ones. Because life insurance requires a death to trigger a payout, the potential for moral hazard and fraud is contained as well. Death is more straightforward to verify than most insured events and few would do it intentionally.

Note too how FINCA Uganda helped overcome barriers from covariate risks by passing the risk from their clients in Uganda to AIG, a big firm that can spread risks across its diverse worldwide pool of customers, and that has more expertise in actuarial issues and in assessing, pricing and managing insurance risks than MFIs would.

Life Microinsurance

The array of life microinsurance options now extends well beyond credit life. Indeed, as Table 6.3 shows, some form of (non-credit) life insurance is now by far the most common microinsurance coverage. Flavors include funeral insurance, "savings life" insurance, "term life" insurance, among others.

Term insurance is a familiar type of insurance to most people in rich countries. If you drive a car, you probably have term auto insurance. You pay a premium that is fixed for a period of time, like one year (i.e. the "term"), in exchange for a guaranteed payout in the event of certain events. Under **term life microinsurance**, if a death occurs during the term the payout goes to relatives or other designated beneficiaries. At the end of the term, the policy and guarantee expire. If you want to continue the coverage, you must renew the policy, but the fees and/or payout may change. (By contrast, "whole life" insurance premiums and payout guarantees remain fixed for the client's lifetime as long as premiums are paid.)

While term life insurance is typically for individuals, some MFIs and insurance firms offer group term life policies. A group of low-income individuals come together and get a single policy that covers all of them. Group term life microinsurance can be an attractive option for microcredit groups, ROSCAs and similar clubs. The mechanism spreads the burden of keeping up with paying regular premiums across all members, reducing the risk that an individual's policy might lapse due to payments missed due to some erratic cash flow.

Funeral microinsurance is very similar conceptually to term life. However, the distinction—perhaps driven more by marketing than by any innate difference—is consistent with the mental accounting tendencies we discussed in Chapter 3. Funeral insurance is essentially term life insurance marketed as covering funeral and burial expenses up to a certain level. A family could use a term life payout exactly the same way. But we may be more willing to put money aside (i.e. save through) if marketing focuses our attention on funerals in our mental accounts. The salience of the lump sum need is likely to be especially high in cultures where funerals and related ceremonial gatherings can be very costly relative to income; just like weddings. You may recall Box 2.2 in Chapter 2 shows funeral expenses in South Africa adding up to more than two years' income for the low-income family. In the face of such large costs, combined with the ongoing death toll from the AIDS epidemic in South Africa (where 18% of adults are HIV-positive), funeral insurance for low-income families has been particularly popular there. It is even sold in retail packs just like gift cards next to candy bars at local shops and grocery stores (Figure 6.8). In fact, the 24 million South Africans covered by funeral insurance make up 60% of all the life microinsurance across Africa.

Savings-Linked Microinsurance

One challenge MFIs and other microinsurance providers face is the hesitancy of many low-income individuals to pay premiums to cover things that might not occur. If the insured-against event, say a death, accident or health crisis, does not happen within the time period term of the policy (or for some reason the individual cannot continue to pay premiums and lets a policy lapse) they would get nothing tangible in return for any premiums paid. It can feel like wasting money.

Savings-linked insurance is a combined mechanism that helps overcome such concerns by linking insurance to some sort of savings, so that a client builds up a usefully large sum by the end of the policy even if the insured event does not happen. For example, one version, savings life microinsurance (sometimes called endowment policies), insures against death but also simultaneously builds up a savings balance that the client can take when the policy matures, even if they do not die. In a variant

Figure 6.8. Funeral insurance packaged for retail shops, South Africa

Source: © 2009 Guttorm Flatabø. Used under Creative Commons license (https://creativecommons.org/licenses/by/2.0/legalcode).

called savings completion insurance, a client establishes some target level of savings to accumulate by some future date, and agrees to make regular small deposits into the account that would add up to that target, plus pay additional small insurance premiums with those deposits. The premiums pay for a guarantee that if the client dies before the end of the term, the family will get the full target savings amount anyway, even though it would not have yet been fully saved up. If the client lives, they retain their accumulated savings. In some versions, early withdrawals, perhaps with a penalty fee, are permitted along the way as well, simply reducing the guaranteed savings available at the end.

Some providers also allow microinsurance clients to take out microloans, using as collateral the payout value of their insurance policy. As a result such policies become a combination of insurance, savings and credit all intertwined.

Let us look at some specifics from one of these interwoven policies, with an additional complexity that it targets groups. The Indian insurance firm

Bajaj Allianz offers a combined savings and life insurance policy, called *Sarve Shakti Suraksha*, aimed at groups such as the self-help groups so popular in India.[25] The policy has proven very popular, attracting more than 3.5 million clients. A group signs up for a single master policy, within which group members agree to each put in regular installments totaling a minimum of 500 rupees (about $8) annually for a minimum of five years. Members then get group term life insurance plus pension-like savings investment accounts that, after insurance premiums and account management fees are deducted, accumulate and earn market returns. An early withdrawal of an individual's whole accumulated account is possible, but incurs an early withdrawal penalty (7% during the first two years, declining over the subsequent three to 5% then 3% and 0%). Bajaj Allianz also allows microloans of up to 85% of the accumulated value of an individual's policy.

The availability and usefulness of complex policies like this illustrate how similar saving up, saving down, and saving through are conceptually, and how each can play a role (sometimes simultaneously) in helping low-income and rich people alike cope with the short- and long-term ups and downs of their income flows. (Box 6.4 illustrates a similar blurring of saving

Box 6.4. In Your Backyard
Hope Community Blurs Lines of Insurance and Loans

In Chapter 2 we saw the similarities in cash flow patterns between saving up, saving down (e.g. loans) and saving through (e.g. insurance), the patterns differing primarily only in the timing of the usefully large lump sum. Field experience with microfinance in New Orleans in the aftermath of Hurricane Katrina demonstrates how the lines can blur between loans and insurance.

In 2005, Hurricane Katrina caused unprecedented destruction in New Orleans: death tolls near 2,000 and $80 billion in damages. Making matters worse, many who lost homes and small personal businesses lacked insurance. People lost everything they had worked their entire lives for. In response, the Hope Community Credit Union teamed up with the MFI Accion USA to use microfinance to help New Orleans victims.

(Continued)

Box 6.4. (*Continued*)

How? Providing what they called small business recovery loans. People needed capital to restart their small businesses. To expand the number of people who qualified for loans, Hope and Accion looked beyond credit scores and other traditional screening metrics, to things like character references and site visits. The recovery loans were typically small by U.S. business standards, they averaged about $8,000, and short-term, with repayment terms from as short as two months up to 60 months. The loans aimed at mom and pop businesses such as restaurants, landscapers, or day-care services, and came with consulting-like assistance from specialists.

Billy Boy Arceneaux experienced this first hand. He had been running his own business making crab nets, but ended up living in a temporary FEMA trailer after Katrina. Here is how Hope and Accion USA described him:

Billy Boy lost everything he owned to Hurricane Katrina, including his prosthetic leg. But he never gave up hope on putting his life back together and reestablishing his small business, Arceneaux Net Company. A fourth-generation crab net maker who learned the trade from his father, Arceneaux can make over four dozen crab nets in one hour. He sells his nets in small stores throughout Hancock County. To fulfill his most recent business contract, however, he needed working capital.

Arceneaux's story of misfortune had been heard by Mississippi Governor Barbour's First Lady, Marsha Barbour, William Richardson, President and CEO of the Mississippi Hurricane Recovery Fund, and several other key players, and led them to action. Together they assisted him in helping to secure a contract to produce thousands of crab nets to be sold at Wal-Mart.

The contract with Wal-Mart, however, might have turned into a missed opportunity had he not approached the recovery loan fund offered by Accion USA and Hope. Arceneaux was approved by Accion USA and Hope for a loan to buy additional webbing, wire and bags.

Sources: Sherwin (2007) and Accion USA (2006).

through and saving down from New Orleans). The point helps reiterate what we mentioned in Chapter 1: financial intermediation, whether for the rich or the poor, fundamentally simply serves to enable people to move money and cash flows back and forth across time in ways they could not do on their own.

Health Microinsurance

Of all the types of microinsurance, health insurance arguably has the greatest potential for substantial social welfare gains for the poor. Heath and poverty are tightly intertwined. If a family's main earner falls ill and cannot work, a family can quickly find itself trapped in a downward poverty spiral. Indeed, health expenditures are a main direct cause of poverty: the World Health Organization estimates that 100 million people annually worldwide fall into poverty because of the cost of healthcare.[26] Health microinsurance, then, is fundamentally aimed at both financial security and ensuring access to healthcare services. More narrowly for MFIs, poor health is one of the leading reasons clients cannot repay microcredit loans. Good health enhances productivity and earnings potential.

Despite the obvious benefits of offering health insurance to the poor, the challenges of designing and implementing relevant, affordable policies that can cover costs—which for very sick people can be high—make it perhaps the most difficult type of insurance to deliver sustainably. In Table 6.3, only about one in six of the already limited number of individuals with any sort of microinsurance has health coverage; that ratio falls threefold to about one in 20 in Africa.

Conditions in every country differ, e.g. disease prevalence, access to care, and differing quality of care. Wide variation in these factors make it difficult, perhaps near impossible, to design a universal health insurance package that works everywhere. As a result, an extremely wide variety exists across health microinsurance programs. For insurers, the actuarial task of setting insurance prices and estimating possible future costs are problematic too because the availability of medical statistics is limited in many developing countries. It is then hard to predict how often the insurer might have to pay for various treatments. Additionally tough, adverse selection poses a particularly big problem for voluntary health insurance.

Although there are many schemes for providing health microinsurance, several approaches are well established. Among them are (1) partnerships between commercial insurers and MFIs and NGOs, (2) insurance through community-based groups, (3) insurance programs run directly by healthcare providers, and (4) government social welfare programs. Government social programs include, in some countries, universal health care provision, and may include partnerships with private insurance firms and private medical facilities. Government social microinsurance programs, such as those in China and India encompassing hundreds of millions of low-income individuals, cover by far the most people. However, we here focus on non-government programs.

What's Covered? Balancing Costs and Demand

A key challenge of offering health insurance lies in design: what types of services should the insurance cover at what price? It is a balancing act between costs and clients' demand for a broad range of healthcare services.

Perhaps the most cost-effective method to improve health involves preventative care services. By educating individuals about concepts such as water sanitation and through active interventions like inoculations and distributing mosquito nets, insurers could effectively treat their clients before they fall ill. Ideally, a quality preventative care policy will empower clients to make healthy decisions and give them the tools to do so, ultimately helping them avoid needing care in the first place. However, abstract prevention tends to be far less tangible or salient than more pressing day-to-day spending needs or treating immediate acute problems, so clients are often hesitant to pay enough to cover the costs of preventive insurance.

When the poor do get sick, accessing healthcare relates directly to income flows and the ability to pay. Often, low-income individuals facing uncertain cash flows will put off seeking help and hope that an illness will go away on its own. In developing countries, infections such as malaria, tuberculosis and gastrointestinal problems make up the majority of illness faced by the poor. These infections, if diagnosed and treated early, are readily treated and offer very positive outlooks for recovery. However, should individuals postpone treatment, infections can worsen, requiring progressively more expensive treatments. In severe cases, the inability to pay can effectively be a death sentence.

Many policies address the costs associated with inpatient hospitalization. Considering that hospitalization occurs infrequently and unexpectedly and can run up a large bill, insurance is well suited for this task. Policies can cover a select few aspects of hospitalization, such as emergency surgery or maternity care, ranging to covering all reasons for admission. For example in Jordan, the MFI Microfund for Women partnered with Women's World Banking to launch the country's first health microinsurance program.[27] Called "Caregiver," the insurance is automatic and mandatory for all the MFI's microcredit clients, a feature designed expressly to overcome adverse selection issues and to enable enough scale to spread risk across a large pool of clients (more than 90,000 by 2012).

The MFI labeled the program "gap" coverage, filling gaps between the nation's healthcare system for the poor and the full costs to the client. Clients pay premiums of about $1.50 per month with regular loan repayments. To keep costs in check, the insurance is focused. It does not cover everything, such as outpatient visits or long-term treatment for chronic diseases like cancer or HIV/AIDS. But it does cover what the MFI's clients thought were high priorities: hospital fees and related costs, including for maternity. Such fees had previously kept many from seeking care. It pays up to $14 per night for as many as 45 nights of direct hospital expenses per year, and also indirect costs related to those stays like transport, meals and—most notably—income lost from not being able to work or run a business. The initial pilot program in 2010 with one branch in Jordan proved so popular and effective that Microfund for Women rolled it out nationwide by 2012.

The positive experience in Jordan notwithstanding, focused hospitaliz-ation coverage insurance has not proven universally popular. Earlier programs in India cost less than $1 per month yet had disappointingly low take-up, and failed to reach sustainable scale. Why? Researchers from the International Labour Organization found that, in part, it was because the insurance was voluntary not mandatory, and also because the infrequent uncertain events it covered lacked salience for clients.[28] The MFI clients in India reported that that compared to routine care or ongoing treatment for chronic problems like diabetes, infrequent emergencies requiring hospitalization were more likely to be covered by informal, family and friends. In other words, informal social taxation substituted as insurance in paying for hospital stays.

Hence, a next level of microinsurance involves covering outpatient services, like visits to a clinic and for medicines. Some insurers only cover local clinics, enabling low premiums in exchange for typically lower-quality services. For instance, many local clinics can diagnose a client's illness but may not have resources to treat them. That said, where quality local clinics do exist, covering outpatient treatment may prevent clients' illnesses from progressing to the point where hospitalization is required. We tend to think of outpatient care as less problematic financially than more acute illnesses that require checking into hospitals. Yet perhaps counterintuitively, when World Bank researchers investigated it turned out that the poor were three times more likely to fall into poverty because of paying for outpatient expenses than for hospitalization.[29] The NGO Freedom From Hunger compared the pattern to an "unceasing dropping tap of healthcare expenses."[30] Lots of smaller expenditures add up to much more of a problem than the occasional crisis.

Indeed, low-income individuals in India were far more interested in microinsurance for routine and outpatient expenses than for hospitalization.[31] Their informal networks of friends and family were less likely to be willing to help pay for routine or ongoing recurring expenses for chronic problems than for emergencies. Unfortunately, from an insurer's point of view outpatient coverage is much more challenging and costly. Claims for hospitals are infrequent, and so claims processing is reasonably manageable. Only about one in 20 of the clients in Jordan made claims in a given year for the hospitalization insurance. In comparison, if outpatient expenses were covered, most clients would likely visit a clinic or pharmacy few times annually for something routine. By one estimate there could be 50 times as many outpatient claims annually if microinsurance covered those costs.[32] Processing can quickly become cost prohibitive. Moreover, the likelihood of fraud or moral hazard is more limited for hospitalization too, since hospital stays require admission screening by medical professionals. One innovative approach, pioneered by MFIs like Pro Mujer in Latin America, is for the MFI to offer select outpatient healthcare services like checkups and routine prenatal care directly to clients.

Some health insurance policies, particularly some government social programs, cover treatment for chronic illness such as cancer or diabetes. Unfortunately, offering coverage for chronic conditions deepens the adverse selection problem, and can quickly cause costs to rise. Thus many non-government programs omit chronic illness coverage, aiming instead for scale and sustainability in what they do insure.

Box 6.5. In the Field
"Bima ya Jamii Is the Best!"

"Lameck and his wife Faith live in a rented room divided by a curtain in Huruma, a suburb East of Nairobi. Lameck makes a living by selling second hand shoes at the Gikomba market in the same area.

As soon as Lameck heard about the Bima ya Jamii insurance he was impressed. 'They spoke about how the insurance would help us pay for hospital bills—and how it would take care of the family if there were any problems. Before, I had never thought about buying insurance. I was more preoccupied with paying the existing bills. But since my wife was expecting a baby I had started to think differently. No one else but God knows what will happen tomorrow,' says Lameck.

Their first son, Ian, was born just before the New Year and there were unforeseen complications during the delivery. The hospital visit cost 20,000 KSH—a lot of money for the family—it's the equivalent of approximately four months of expenses.

The usual way to get money for unforeseen expenses is to ask one's family, friends, neighbors or your own SACCO [self-help group] for help. 'It is quite embarrassing to go around asking for money—Bima ya Jamii is the best!'—Lameck says and laughs.

To be on the safe side, Lameck had saved money before the birth was due. He wasn't sure that the insurance would work. He will now use the savings to pay for his son's school fees in the future.

Lameck describes his satisfaction as follows: 'I felt like I had eaten a whole goat when the insurance company (Cooperative Insurance Company of Kenya) told me that I didn't need to pay anything.'"

Source: Mutua (2010).

Adverse Selection and Health Insurance

Voluntary health insurance carries large adverse selection problems. Healthier individuals may pass on coverage, while riskier individuals and those already sick might flock to it. This produces a risk-biased pool of clients, which increases costs to the insurer. As we have seen in the Jordan program earlier, the most common antidote is mandatory coverage for large groups. Another problem: unnecessary clinic visits. Why not go if they're paid for by insurance? To combat this, insurers introduce co-pays to discourage superfluously seeking medical aid. Yet social-mission-driven MFIs continue to debate the efficacy of using co-pays as a mechanism to reduce insurance abuse. Grameen Kalyan, Grameen Bank's health insurance program, supports the use of co-pays—interestingly not for their abuse reduction but instead to imply a higher quality of care for their clients:[33] Others fear that high co-pays or deductibles may discourage low-income clients from seeking treatment and preventative care. If so, the insurer might see increased costs down the road as the illness escalates. The Union Technique de la Mutualite, based in Mali, has developed a potential solution to the co-pay problem by organizing village savings and loan association-like cooperative member-owned "mutual health organization" groups specifically designed to provide insurance that covers co-pays.[34]

Why Isn't Health Microinsurance More Widespread?

The USAID identified four key reasons health insurance has been slower than other services to emerge in microfinance.[35] As Table 6.3 showed, the combination of these factors has limited offerings of health insurance thus far. First, as a supply-side consideration, health insurance has significantly more nuances than credit-life insurance, making it more expensive to design and implement; and potentially less profitable. The likelihood of adverse selection raises cost risks higher than most insurance firms have been willing to accept given the limited pricing potential for low-income clients.

Second, the quality and accessibility of healthcare have resulted in reduced client demand for health insurance. Unless a client lives within close proximity to a clinic they can incur prohibitive transportation costs. For those in remote villages, transportation can significant time as well as money—that is if transportation is even available. Additionally, the poor quality of many local clinics dissuades individuals from purchasing policies. If you doubt your local clinic, why pay to cover visits?

Third, little reliable healthcare data exist which would allow insurers to determine fair market prices for coverage. Without such data, many insurers will not even consider offering a product, or set high prices in response to absorbing unknown risks. Considering their clientele, insurers recognize that they will have a harder time selling more expensive policies to the poor, providing further negative incentives for offering health insurance.

Finally, the design of the product itself can reduce demand. Policies that do not meet the needs of clients, such as offering coverage for non-local diseases, will turn away potential clients. Additionally, some policies come with restrictions that will not work for poor clients. For instance, some forms of coverage require clients to find funds to cover their own care first, followed by reimbursement. Clients without enough available cash up front can postpone seeking medical aid, potentially leading their condition to escalate, scarcely better off than individuals without insurance. While more complex to implement, microinsurance programs that do not require client to front funds prior to care better suit the cash-flow realities of the lives of the poor.

Agricultural Index Microinsurance

Considering that large fractions of the populations in low-income countries work in agriculture, and given the importance of secure food supplies for the health and well-being of the world's poor, mechanisms to help poor farmers deal with agricultural risks clearly have positive social implications. Unfortunately, market failure challenges of moral hazard, fraud and adverse selection have proven difficult to overcome.

Imagine offering insurance on livestock. If the fluctuating market value of a farmer's cow or goat drops below the insured value, the farmer has little incentive to keep the animal healthy or alive. Why not just collect the insurance rather than incur the costs and hassle of feeding and veterinary visits? Similarly for working crops in the field, why work hard to maximize crop yields if insurance will pay anyway? For the insurer, the challenge of monitoring crop yields or goat deaths on large numbers of very small farms make offering widespread microinsurance cost-prohibitive. Covariate risks of draught or diseases raise the risk levels for regional insurers as well. To succeed, spread risks and achieve economies of scale, agricultural insurance schemes need to be reach large numbers of clients.

To overcome the very real market failure problems, insurers have been looking for innovative ways to help small-scale farmers mitigate agricultural risks like bad weather or crop disease. So far the one gaining the most traction has been **index insurance**, which offers payouts to all policyholders in a given region provided a condition, the index, is satisfied. Agricultural insurance indexes typically either measure weather or average crop yields.

To see how this works, let us consider rainfall insurance, one specific form of weather index insurance. An insurer will place rainfall gauges throughout a region, and monitor rainfall during the term of the contract. For instance a rainfall index microinsurance policy piloted by the World Bank for small-scale farms in the Ukraine had a cutoff of 50 mm of rainfall in a region with normal rainfall around 80 mm during growing season.[36] For every 5 mm below this cutoff, an insured farmer received 100 Ukranian hryvnia (about $20) per hectare. For the insurance, farmers paid a premium of 40 hryvnia ($8) per hectare.

A second version of index insurance is an area yield index. Rather than investigating every individual farm for crop yields, a sampling compares average crop yields at locations throughout a region to historical yields and pays if the index falls below some established cutoff.

Index insurance appeals to insurers because its structure limits potential market failures. The fact that farmers cannot influence the weather effectively eliminates potential fraud and moral hazard. Additionally, the risk of bad weather remains constant regardless of the number of farmers, or the characteristics of the farmers who purchase policies—eliminating adverse selection concerns. Operating costs are limited as well, since payouts to all policyholders are based on the index, not on individual damages. The insurer needs only monitor rainfall gauges or sample plots, eliminating the need to pay agents to inspect individual farm production.

Interestingly, not only farmers can purchase agricultural index insurance. In certain cases, individuals who do not work in the field but have other professions related to the weather, such as traveling traders, have purchased index insurance. While these people will suffer no direct crop losses as a result of adverse weather, their livelihoods might nonetheless depend on farmers' success. No crops, no crop trading. It can thus be attractive to hedge bets, and still receive payment if the weather satisfies the index condition.

While the idea sounds great on paper, poor farmers have not yet demonstrated much enthusiasm for index insurance. Farmers may view index insurance as having a low value. For instance, rainfall index insurance implies a strong correlation between rainfall and incomes. Farmers may not agree, as a great distance from the gauge or differing land and soil characteristics of the region may impact their bottom line. If a client works 20 miles from a rainfall gauge, they may experience different rainfall levels as compared to the farms close to the gauge. This may result in the farmer experiencing better weather than the gauge, where the farmer will collect a payout without incurring any losses. On the other hand, if the farmer experiences worse weather than the gauge, the farmer will lose their crops, while not collecting a payout.

Jim Roth and Michael McCord, among the world's leading experts in microinsurance, highlighted the difficulty insurers have in convincing the poor of the merits of basic index insurance. They described the difference between crop insurance and index insurance: "...we will pay you the value of your crop loss" as opposed to index insurance "...if there is low rainfall at a weather station 100km from your home during x period we will pay you y for every mm less than z mm of rainfall."[37] This abstraction makes index insurance not only somewhat more difficult to understand, but also reduces its salience psychologically, as we saw in Chapter 3, compared to events that are directly visible and concrete for farmers. Thus insurers have to devote substantial resources to educating clients.

As a result of all these difficulties, agricultural microinsurance has been slow to emerge. Note in Table 6.3 that outside of Asia, it is the least likely form of microinsurance by a wide margin. In Africa and Latin America only a few hundred thousand individuals have any sort of agricultural microinsurance, compared to more than 40 million insured for other things. Only in India, with more than 20 million farmers insured, has any semblance of scale begun to emerge. Nearly all existing agricultural insurance programs remain heavily government subsidized.

India is unique in large part because of government's emphasis on finding ways to make agricultural insurance work at large scale. To encourage experimentation by insurers and take-up by farmers, the government required any farmer who got government-subsidized agricultural loans to get agricultural insurance. Moreover, every insurance company was required to derive a specified minimum fraction of revenue from rural areas.

Experimentation was widespread. One investigation suggested that for every pilot insurance scheme that succeeded, eight failed.[38]

Mongolia's index-based livestock microinsurance program is an interesting case too.[39] While client numbers are not high, with only 19,500 poor herders covered as of 2014, the scheme is innovative and potentially instructive for designing programs elsewhere. Based on a successful pilot program funded by the World Bank and the government of Mongolia, the scheme combines private market insurance—herders pay premiums to private insurance firms—with a government guarantee to help the insurance firms cover years with extreme losses. Seven local insurance firms are now participating.

Winters in Mongolia's steppes, where temperatures regularly drop below −40 °C (same as −40 °F), can be brutal on livestock. Semi-nomadic poor herder families make up about 30% of Mongolia's population. Between 1999 and 2002, extreme winters and summer droughts killed nearly one-third of Mongolian livestock. The index insurance scheme developed in the aftermath is fairly simple and transparent to herders. Indexing across whole geographic districts mitigates moral hazard and the risk of fraud. Officials count the total livestock of each species in a given district. Herders bear their own risks for small losses. But if across a whole district more than 6% of a given species perish during the year, all insured farmers collect payments, irrespective of what happened in their individual herd. Private insurance firms then cover losses up to 30% of the herd. To help overcome covariate risk for the insurers, in very bad years when livestock morality is beyond 30%, the Mongolian government steps in to make up the difference.

In summary, MFIs continue to seek ways to expand services beyond lending to create healthier, more empowered, financially stable clients, who in turn benefit MFIs with revenue from both primary and non-financial services. With the experience of pioneers like India and Mongolia, agricultural microinsurance appears poised to follow life insurance as the next expansion wave. As MFIs experiment with insurance, savings, and other services, they aim to create and scale up sustainable programs that are both attractive to clients and socially and economically beneficial to the communities in which they operate. As we move forward to Chapter 7, we will learn more about how microfinance and the services offered can have a particularly strong impact on women and their economic and social roles in their families and communities.

Section in Bulletpoint

- Microinsurance has grown to roughly the same scale as microcredit, with hundreds of millions of clients; but country coverage is uneven.

- Micronsurance, i.e. saving through, can complement savings and microcredit among financial tools for low-income individuals.

- Commercial insurers supply most policies, either directly or in partnership through other organizations with connections with the poor such as MFIs, NGOs, and community organizations.

- Key barriers to microinsurance include fraud, moral hazard, limited liability, adverse selection, covariate risks, and high operational costs.

- Insurers have introduced a diverse range of products tailored to low-income clients; term life microinsurance is widespread, as are credit-life, savings-linked, and funeral insurance.

- Health and agricultural insurance have proved more problematic to scale up, despite potentially high benefits for the poor.

- Health and agricultural insurance remain dependent on subsidies.

Discussion Questions

1. Why do the poor need access to microinsurance products?

2. Why has health microinsurance, with its high demand, failed to achieve as rapid an expansion as other forms?

3. In what ways could having insurance cause market failures?

4. What are the main potential problems that an insurer must address when insuring the poor? Provide examples of mechanisms that insurers and MFIs use to deal with those problems.

5. How do microinsurers mitigate typical insurance-related market failures, such as adverse selection, moral hazard, covariate risks, and behavioral psychology challenges like salience and hyberbolic discounting?

6. Suppose you were running an MFI considering introducing micro-insurance for your clients. What design features and types of events insured might you prefer to offer, and why? If you had to pick only one insurance type to offer for the poor, which would it be and why?

Key Terms

commitment savings
Sometimes known as contractual savings; clients agree ahead of time to put in a series of regular, deposits over a given time period in order to achieve a particular savings goal; grounded in social and behavioral psychology to help overcome the cash flow, social taxation, mental accounting, and self-control barriers to savings.

compulsory savings
Requires a borrower to commit to depositing a certain amount over a given time period in order to receive a loan; often 10–20% of the loan amount.

covariate risk
Occurs if events (e.g. droughts) can cause entire groups of insured clients to collect payouts, so that risks are not independent of each other; makes it difficult for insurance firms to spread risks across a pool of clients.

credit life microinsurance
Loan protection insurance that forgives a client's outstanding debt in the event of death; a widespread microfinance practice, a small fee added to loan fees guarantees payment of remaining balances.

credit life plus
A version of credit life microinsurance; adds a payment to the family of a deceased policyholder as well as debt forgiveness.

fixed-term deposits
Sometimes called time deposits; requires a commitment of a certain amount of money for a fixed period of time, over which the bank pays a fixed rate of interest; certificates of deposit (CDs) are familiar versions in some countries.

funeral microinsurance
Essentially term life insurance marketed as covering funeral and burial expenses up to a certain level; a family could use a term life payout exactly the same way, but the name leverages mental accounting and the high salience of funeral expenses in some cultures.

index insurance
Offers payouts to all policyholders in a given region provided a condition, the index, is satisfied, irrespective of individual circumstances; agricultural insurance indexes typically either measure weather or average yields; helps reduce moral hazard and fraud.

limited withdrawal accounts
Pay interest on deposits, but restrict the number of and/or amount of withdrawal in a given period; help clients mitigate temptation for spur-of-the-moment withdrawals.

passbook savings accounts
Regular savings accounts that take deposits and can earn interest; the money is available for withdrawal whenever necessary to use for current purposes.

savings-linked insurance
Combination that ties insurance to some sort of savings, so a client builds up a usefully large sum even if the insured event does not happen; one version, savings life microinsurance, insures against death but simultaneously builds a balance the client can take when the policy matures, even if they do not die; blurs lines between saving up and saving through.

savings mobilization
The effort by MFIs to attract deposits; a potentially good source of funds for loaning out in microcredit operations, allowing MFIs to do direct financial intermediation between their savers and their borrowers.

term life microinsurance
Premiums fixed for a set period in exchange for a guaranteed payout if death occurs during the term; the policy and guarantee expire at the end of the term, and fees or payout may change for renewal the next term; usually for individuals, but some MFIs offer this to groups.

usury laws
Restrictions on allowable interests rates; aim to protect people from exploitation by banks or moneylenders charging extremely high rates on loans, or not paying fair interest on deposits; if too restrictive can inhibit availability of microfinance.

Notes:

[1] Wright (1999).
[2] http://www.spblog.org/2010/02/mfis-financial-products-and-services-an-overview-of-sp-report-data. html
[3] See Ledgerwood and White (2006).
[4] See Brune et al (2011) and Tantia and Comings (ca. 2011).
[5] Armendáriz and Morduch (2010).
[6] Dupas and Robinson (2013a, b).
[7] Chen and Snodgrass (2001).
[8] Collins et al (2009).
[9] www.postbank.co.ke; and http://reports.mixmarket.org/mfi/kposb
[10] Westley and Palomas (2010).
[11] Gunter (2009).
[12] See Ahlin, Lin, and Maio (2011).
[13] Christen and Rosenberg (2000).
[14] Christen and Rosenberg (2000).
[15] Roth, McCord, and Liber (2007).
[16] Lloyds (2010).
[17] Mukherjee et al (2014) and Churchill and McCord (2012).
[18] McCord, Ingram, and Tatin-Jaleran (2012).
[19] McCord et al (2013).
[20] Mukherjee et al (2014).
[21] Armendáriz and Morduch (2010).
[22] Curchill.
[23] From Armendáriz and Morduch (2010), based on Cohen and Sebstad (2003).
[24] McCord et al (2013).
[25] See Bajaj Allianz (2010).
[26] Xu et al (2007).
[27] See Women's World Banking (2012).
[28] Pott and Holtz (2013).
[29] Berman, Ahuja, and Bhandari (2010).
[30] Quoted in Pott and Holtz (2013) p. 4.
[31] Pott and Holtz (2013).
[32] Pott and Holtz (2013).
[33] Radermacher, Dror, and Noble (2006), reported in Armendáriz and Morduch (2010).
[34] See Fischer, Sissouma, and Hathie (2006).
[35] Noble and McCord (2007).
[36] Roth and McCord (2008).
[37] Roth and McCord (2008) p. 23.
[38] Mahul, Verma, and Clarke (2012).
[39] See World Bank Group (2015) and GFDRR (2011).

Chapter

GENDER ISSUES IN MICROFINANCE

"Ensuring that women do not lose out in access to microfinance as institutions grow is vital. There are 30 years of data showing that women put more of their loans than men do into education, healthcare and nutrition, that their children stay in school longer and have longer life expectancy."

— **Mary Ellen Iskenderian, President & CEO,
Women's World Banking**

Figure 7.1. "My new income means I can spend money on my daughter the way I think is best, without waiting for husband's approval." Feroza, tailor & self-help group member, Balkh province, Afghanistan[1]

You may know the famous quote of the Chinese revolutionary Chairman Mao Zedong that "women hold up half the sky." Clearly, he had not yet heard of microfinance. Most microfinance clients are women, three out of every four worldwide. Some microfinance institutions (MFIs), including some of the very largest in the world, exclusively serve women. Of Bandhan's 5.4 million clients in India, 100% are women. So are every single one of BFIL's 6 million clients. Fully 96% of Grameen Bank's 6.7 million members were women, as are 98% of the CARD Bank, Inc.'s clients in the Philippines, and 94% of Compartamos Banco's borrowers in Mexico. Indeed, the majority of microfinance institutions provide services expressly designed to address women's needs.[2] Some MFIs like Women's World Banking and Pro Mujer highlight their gender focus right in their names.

The industry is very gender lopsided. But it is not uniformly so. In this chapter we explore microfinance's gender distribution patterns, some exceptions to the women-rule rule, and key rationales for the overall emphasis on women. We also look into the implications of that intentional bias. It turns out that the impact microfinance has on women, and through them their families, differs substantially than on men, as does the impact on job creation and business growth. In short, gender issues are central in understanding how the microfinance industry works and why.

7.1 The Focus on Women

The two most comprehensive compilations of data on MFIs show that women accounted for 75–82% of all microfinance clients around the globe in 2013.[3] The more than 3–to–1 gender ratio has been fairly steady for many years, despite rapid expansion in size and scope of the industry.

But why so gender unbalanced? Is there more demand from women because microfinance is more attractive or relevant for women? Are women more likely to be poor? Are women better business customers for MFIs? Is there a socio-cultural women's empowerment movement at work? As we tackle these questions and others in the following sections, we will see it is in fact all of the above.

Regional Patterns

Let us begin by looking at gender patterns in microfinance regionally around the globe. As has been true in our earlier dives into microfinance data, Asia drives the overall global statistics. We see in Figure 7.2 that women dominate MFI customer bases for microcredit in Asia, particularly in South Asia where more than 93% of borrowers are women. We saw in Chapter 1 (Table 1.3) that five of the six largest MFIs in the world are in India or Bangladesh, and all five—Grameen, Bandhan, BFIL, ASA, and BRAC—target women.

But Eastern Europe and Central Asia look quite different, with men predominating. The largest MFI there, Mongolia's Khan Bank, serves 45% women; the second largest, Access Bank in Azerbaijan, only 21%. Latin America and Africa show middle ground balances near 60% women. Note that this

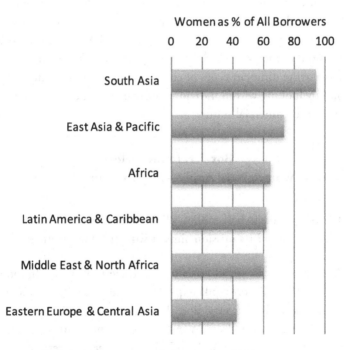

Figure 7.2. Gender balance in microcredit, by region, 2013

Data source: Mixmarket.org.

chart only looks at borrowers, not including microsavings or microinsurance. Unfortunately, no comparably detailed gender data exist for those other microfinance services.

Another notable pattern in gender balance emerges when we compare types of MFIs and their style of operations. Recall from Chapter 5 (Table 5.1) that among MFIs using only solidarity group lending, the median share of women borrowers was nearly 99%. Village banks averaged 86% women. By contrast, the median MFI doing exclusively individual lending lent to more men (54%) than women.

Commercialization and Gender

In Chapter 8, we will investigate details on how, as the microfinance industry grew over the past several decades, it evolved towards a commercial approach. **Commercialization** broadly means that many leading MFIs are now run more like market-oriented businesses operating in mainstream capital markets than like charitable organizations. That commercialization trend has had gender-related implications. Commercially-focused MFIs appear to include greater fractions of men among their client bases. We can see this in two ways: first by comparing different types of commercial and non-profit institutions, and second by looking within individual institutions at changes among those who alter their commercial status.

Box 7.1. In the Field
Only Women Need Apply—MBK Ventura, Indonesia

All of MBK Ventura's half million clients are women. So are nearly all its employees. Why? Its mission aims at women's empowerment.

A deep Asian financial crisis took a huge toll on the Indonesian economy in 1997. Poverty spiked quickly as many near-poor households fell back below the poverty line. Dr. Shafiq Dhanai and his wife, Elizabeth Sweeting, who lived in Indonesia as consultants for economic development, saw the need to help Indonesia's very poorest.

(Continued)

Box 7.1. (*Continued*)

Table 7.1. MBK Ventura

Began microfinance operations	2003
Location	Indonesia
Clients (2015)	555,732 borrowers; not licensed to take deposits
Women as % of borrowers	100%
Self-sufficiency ratio	146.6%
Legal status	Non-bank financial institution

In 2003, they launched a small microfinance institution, *Mitra Bisnis Keluarga* (MBK), meaning "Family Business Partners." At the time, about half of Indonesians fell under the $2 dollar per day poverty line. The founders aimed explicitly to empower poor women to improve their livelihoods and escape poverty. Since its founding, MBK Ventura has served exclusively women in the poorest 25% of households. Early on, MBK hired an all-women staff. The founder was the only male. The emphasis on hiring women field officers continues today. Dr. Dhanai believes that female staff not only can work more closely with the female clients but also are more connected in helping other women in their society.

In contrast to many MFIs that have diversified their product offerings, MBK still has only one: basic loans using the Grameen group-lending model, for business investments in the range of $150–300. (A version introduced in 2012 is compliant with Muslim Sharia prohibitions against charging interest.) MBK's female field officers visit potential clients and assess the household's assets and sources of income. Potential clients must fall under 25th percentile income threshold and use loans for income generation.

MBK Ventura has proven very successful, with near perfect repayment rates (99% or higher every year), and cost-efficient. The

(*Continued*)

Box 7.1. (*Continued*)

MFI grew from a meager 2,400 borrowers to 101,300 within four years, and then to more than half a million by 2015. MBK Ventura's efforts and efficiency were recognized by the Microfinance Information Exchange (MIX) when in both 2008 and 2009 MIX ranked MBK the number one MFI worldwide in overall performance in the categories of outreach, transparency, and efficiency. MBK has continued in its mission to serve exclusively women customers because it believes women are more vulnerable to subsisting on the economic edge.

Sources: MBK-ventura.com; Mixmarket.org.

Table 7.2. Comparing gender mix and scale across types of MFIs, 2012

MFI legal status	% Women borrowers	Median number of		Mean number of	
		Borrowers	*Depositors*	*Borrowers*	*Depositors*
Regulated commercial bank	63	27,470	65,951	274,921	371,439
Credit union/ cooperative	42	2,421	7,889	9,671	33,174
Non-bank financial institution (NBFI)	76	12,857	0	90,156	20,643
NGO	79	8,697	0	85,717	105,236

Data source: Mixmarket.org.

First, Table 7.2 categorizes different MFIs by their legal status. As we noted in Chapter 6 when discussing microsavings, some MFIs have transformed from NGOs into regulated commercial banks. Others remain exclusively non-profit NGOs. In between there are **non-bank financial institutions** (NBFIs) that do not have full banking licenses but nevertheless provide some commercial financial services like microlending and money transfers; in most countries they are usually regulated too. Legal cooperatives and credit unions are generally bank-like operations owned and governed by members for their own benefit, rather than for profit.

The table compares the gender mix and measures of the average sizes across these MFI types. Overall NGOs and NBFIs have the highest fractions of women borrowers, at 79% and 76%. For MFIs that are commercial banks, by comparison, women comprise a notably lower share, 63%. At first blush, then, it might seem that the trend towards commercializing services might hurt women's access to microfinance.

However, despite lower fractions of women, in terms of absolute numbers of women served, commercial banks are much bigger on average, particularly when it comes to providing savings services, which few NGOs or NBFIs are licensed to do. Table 7.2 looks at two measures of average size, medians and means, for borrowers and for depositors. Half the MFIs in each category are larger and half are smaller than the medians. The median bank serves 27,000 borrowers compared to fewer than 9,000 for NGOs. The median bank has nearly 66,000 depositors, while NGOs and NBFIs show zeros because most legally cannot take deposits at all. The means are substantially larger, due to the strong skew in the size distributions. A few huge MFIs with millions of clients pull those averages way up.

Credit unions and cooperatives tend to be small and overall do not make much of a dent in global statistics. In total they serve more men than women, reflecting that many of the largest are affiliated with labor or trade-related organizations in sectors like manufacturing where men tend to dominate workforces.

The second way we can see the gender-related impact of commercialization is by looking at changes among those MFIs that transition from an NGO into a regulated commercial bank, a process known in the industry's jargon as **transformation**. Women's World Banking followed over seven years 27 institutions that transformed from an NGO into a regulated bank, and compared them to a control group of 25 others who had not switched.[4] Among MFIs that commercialized, the share of women clients fell post-transformation. On average, two years before transformation women comprised 88% of the institutions' clientele. This decreased to 60% five years after transformation. The control group went the other way, increasing from

72% to 77%. However, the now-commercialized institutions grew much more quickly, and diversified their offerings more too. As a result, they ended up serving more women overall relative to the control group, and ended with double the number of savers. In sum, the now-commercialized MFIs added men clients more quickly than adding women, but because they achieved substantially greater scale they still provided more services to more women than the non-transformed MFIs.

Section in Bulletpoint

- In most of the world, women dominate the microfinance customer base.
- Male microfinance clients outnumber females only in Eastern Europe and Central Asia.
- MFIs focused on group lending methodologies, including many of the very largest MFIs in the world, overwhelmingly serve women.
- Non-profit NGOs have substantially higher fractions of women clients than do MFIs that are commercial banks.
- However, because banks are bigger on average, banks serve more women overall than non-profit MFIs.

Discussion Questions

1. Why might Eastern Europe and Central Asia be the only region with more male clients in microfinance than females?

2. The introduction says the majority of MFIs offer services specially targeting women's needs. What special financial needs might women have compared to men? Different non-financial needs?

3. Is it ethical that the majority of MFIs favor women and design special products targeting women's needs? Should men be left out? Why or why not?

4. Write a blog (~500–750 words) you might post online addressing both the pros and cons of the microfinance industry's explicit gender bias. Argue in favor of one side, but acknowledge and perhaps challenge the other side.

7.2 Why the Focus on Women? The Demand Side

To summarize in one sentence the statistics we have seen so far: women clients dominate microfinance, particularly in Asia; women dominate MFIs that are non-profit NGOs, and solidarity groups and village banks; the share of men, while still the minority, grows for commercial banks and MFIs offering services to individuals. But why? Why do the majority of MFIs in most regions of the world target women? Poverty-related gender issues are a complex mix of interrelated factors, many of which vary by culture and economic context. The challenges for poor women are manifold. Though we cannot do full justice to that complexity in a few pages, we will cover a range of the most important factors.

We have some clear clues already: the changes in gender strategy by early pioneers driven by results working with groups in the field, and the fact that men jump aboard more in individual lending and commercial services. It appears, then, that both demand-side and supply-side forces are at work. Let us look at each side in turn.

Why Might Women Demand Microfinance More Than Men?

The complex multifaceted intertwining of poverty and gender not withstanding, the first part of the gender imbalance story is straightforward: demand for microfinance services begins with lack of access among the poor to alternative forms of formal finance. If women have less access to alternatives, they might be more likely to want the services MFIs offer.

Figure 7.3 compares the rate of access of men to women to formal financial services in various regions. In every region, men use banking and formal financial services of all types more in general, in turn suggesting less access for women to alternatives to microfinance. The gaps are particularly striking in the Middle East & North Africa, where men are 1.77 times more likely to use formal financial services than women, and South Asia, where the ratio is 1.64. Recall too that Figure 1.1 back in Chapter 1 showed the poorest people are far less likely to have access in general. A person who is both poor and female, then, is doubly disadvantaged statistically.

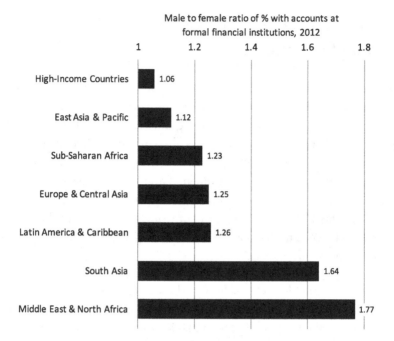

Male to female ratio of % with accounts at
formal financial institutions, 2012

Figure 7.3. Gender gaps in financial access, by region

Data Source: Demirgüç-Kunt and Klapper (2012).

The next piece of the microfinance gender imbalance story is simple as well: poor people are more likely than higher-income folks to need microfinance, and women are disproportionately likely to be poor in many parts of the world. According to the United Nations Development Programs, women and girls comprise an estimated 70% of the world's poor.[5]

In a similar vein, Mayra Buvinić and Geeta Rao Gupta of the International Center for Research on Women did a comprehensive review of research in 61 developing countries and found that in 38 of those studies households headed by women were more likely in poverty than households headed by men.[6] In Brazil for example, female-headed households are 30–50% more likely to be in poverty. Similarly, given the prevalence of microfinance in India it is worth noting that studies show a higher rate of poverty there too among households headed by women. But culture and context differ so widely there is clearly no single universal relationship between gender and poverty. Fifteen of those studies showed relationships between only some categories of female-headed households and some measures of poverty, but not others. In eight of the countries, there was no evidence of gender imbalance related to poverty at all.

Wage Gaps and Informal Economy Financial Patterns

Poverty is higher in some places among women in part because when women work in formal jobs, their average earnings tend to be lower than men's. The International Labour Organization tracks gender inequalities in wages and income around the world. Figure 7.4 illustrates the **gender wage gap** for select developing economies, shown as a percentage of men's earnings. We see for example, that in Argentina women are paid about 27% less than men on average. Roughly half that gap (gray) is due to differences in education, experience, sector, and other characteristics related to labor markets. By contrast, in China, essentially none of the 23% gap could be explained by gender differences in labor characteristics. In Brazil, the negative (gray) part of the bar means that women, according to their experience and other characteristics, should have 10% *higher* average wages on average than men. Yet the black bar shows women actually get paid nearly 25% less there, meaning the overall wage gap, after adjusting for labor characteristics, is nearly 35%. (Gender wage gaps are hardly unique to the developing world. By comparison in the U.S., a recent study by Cornell University Professors

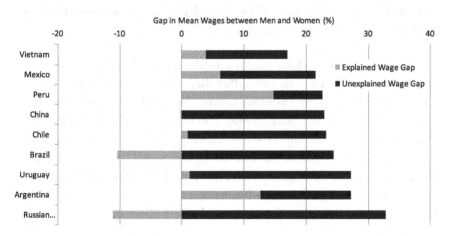

Figure 7.4. Gender wage gaps in select developing countries, 2014

Data Source: ILO Global Wage Report 2014/15.

Francine Blau and Lawrence Kahn found the unexplained wage gap was about 9%, of a total gap near 20%.[7])

A related pattern that helps explain our microfinance gender imbalance puzzle is participation in the informal economy. We saw in Chapter 3 that people working in the informal economy face a substantial mismatch between their day-to-day financial lives and the financial products designed for traditional banking customers. We have seen how cash flow patterns in the informal sector also tend to be more flow transactional—like the day to day flows in and out of market stalls—rather than larger scale stock investments. Thus, informal economy financial needs are well aligned with the typical weekly meetings and small-but-frequent installments seen in self-help groups, village banks and solidarity groups. Thus, microfinance, which typically targets the informal sector, may be particularly attractive. Figure 3.5 showed that women are more likely to work in the informal economy than men; this is true across nearly every region and culture. Informal economy work tends to pay less than formal sector jobs, and lacks other benefits that might come with a job, like union representation, healthcare plans, and pensions.

Women are also less likely to own land or other property, both because of their higher rates of informal sector participation and because of cultural prohibitions. This makes collateral for loans, and even formal addresses that mainstream banks need to open savings accounts, harder for women to provide. As we have seen, MFIs have designed products specifically to accommodate such barriers to traditional finance.

Moreover, among those working in the informal sector, the types of enterprises women tend to run differ that those run by men. Women's businesses tend to be in different sectors, be smaller, be less productive (see Box 7.2), grow less, and employ fewer other people than men's. For example, Box 7.2 mentions types of self-employed business in Sri Lanka. Bicycle repair shops there are essentially exclusively run by men; lace-making enterprises by women. Those working in male-dominated sectors earn more on average. Women's businesses, because they are smaller, also tend to generate less cash flow that might help them qualify for regular bank loans.

Box 7.2. Dig Deeper
Are Women More Capital Constrained?

One of the hopes of proponents of microfinance is that access to finance will help improve client incomes. The assumption is that constraints on access to financial intermediation services limit the possibility of productive investments by the poor. We briefly explored the idea of diminishing marginal returns to capital in Box 3.1. If true, reducing **capital constraints** should improve incomes, and if women otherwise face more restrictions they should gain more from extra capital than men.

To test this idea and compare how the impact of financial constraints differs between women and men, a landmark 2009 study investigated how an influx of new money affected microenterprises in Sri Lanka. Economist Suresh de Mel from the University of Peradeniya, and his colleagues David McKenzie at the World Bank and Christopher Woodruff at UC San Diego, found significant disparities between men and women. The gender gap could not be fully explained by factors such as skills, training, or entrepreneurial propensity.

The team worked with poor Sri Lankans with assets lower than 100,000 rupees (about $1,000) who were self-employed either in retail and sales or in manufacturing and who had no employees. Half the participants received grants of cash, and half got equipment. Of all these grants, two-thirds were worth $100, the remainder $200. The size and type of the grant received were determined randomly.

Recipients were subsequently interviewed over a three-year period about their incomes and expenses, profits, changes in capital stock, and inventories. Interviewers also sought additional information about the participants' backgrounds, skills, attitudes towards risk, and work histories to explore the importance of confounding variables.

The researchers were surprised to find that women on average earned no statistically meaningful extra income from the inflow of extra capital.

(Continued)

Box 7.2. (*Continued*)

On the other hand, men on average increased income by about 8% of the grant, whether the grant came in the form of cash or equipment.

What might explain this difference? Since participants were all self-employed, one possibility is differences in who decides to pursue self-employment. Perhaps the self-selection process differs by gender. Another explanation involves the types of businesses the participants pursued and the profitability of those industries. Some types of self-employment in Sri Lanka, such as bicycle repair shops, are dominated by men, and others by women, e.g. lace making. The study found that those working in male-dominated industries invested and earned more.

Even so, a large gender gap remained even after the researchers adjusted for the types of businesses. If women were indeed more capital constrained to begin with, the findings ran counter to the hypothesis of diminishing marginal returns. So, we are left a puzzle of why the women were less productive with this extra dose of capital.

Source: de Mel, McKenzie, and Woodruff (2009).

Section in Bulletpoint

- Women might disproportionately demand microfinance for several reasons:
- In every region of the world, men have more access to formal financial services than do women.
- Women and girls account for 70% of the world's poor.
- Women are more likely to work in the informal economy and own fewer assets, hindering their access to formal finance.
- Women on average earn less than men and work in jobs and sectors that pay less but also have cash flow cycles better suited for group microcredit models.

Discussion Questions

1. How does the gender wage gap affect microfinance? In which countries might the effects be most important? Why?

2. The large differences among regions in women's relative access to financial services, shown in Figure 7.3, suggest that cultural differences in social expectations, gender roles, religion, and so on, play a big role. Should microfinance institutions be trying to change culture? Is that an appropriate role for financial services? Discuss arguments on both sides.

3. Women themselves choose to work in jobs or businesses that pay less, so aren't gender wage gaps OK? Do you agree? Why or why not?

4. Do poorer countries tend to have higher gender wage gaps than richer ones? The data for Figure 7.4 are available online in the International Labour Organization's "Global Wage Report 2014/15" (Figure 37) and in spreadsheet form at http://www.ilo.org/gwr-figures. Briefly discuss whether the developed economies appear to have higher, lower, or similar wage gaps compared to developing economies. Which country has the largest "actual" wage gap? Lowest? Which country has the biggest "explained" wage gap?

5. Imagine you are in charge of designing a specialized financial service for women where you live. Briefly, what might that service be and why? What financial needs do women in your area have that might differ from men?

7.3 The Supply Side: Why Do MFIs Prefer Women?

Are Women Better for Business?

One reason MFIs have focused on women is pure business. It turns out that women are less risky borrowers. Interestingly, the focus on women was not always central, neither in solidarity group lending nor in village banking. Grameen Bank's initial solidarity group lending efforts in 1976–1978 had only about 20% women (Figure 7.5). But loan repayment rates early on were not healthy, and women proved more reliable. As a result, by 1985 Grameen began to officially target women. The Bank scaled up rapidly thereafter and its gender mix cracked 90% women within five years.

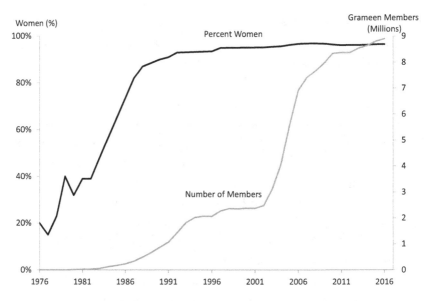

Figure 7.5. Grameen Bank's membership & gender mix, 1976–2016

Data Sources: Grameen Bank & Mixmarket.org.

Another early pioneer, FINCA founder John Hatch, in his first village banking lending experiments in Bolivia, similarly started mainly with men.[8] FINCA switched to women early on too, driven in part by differences in occupations and cash flow patterns. The men, Hatch found, tended to use the funds in farming, where long harvest cycles made it difficult for them to get cash regularly enough to make weekly repayments. Women were more typically market traders, with daily or weekly sales turnover. Short-term financial terms offered by most MFIs better suit the more transactional financial flows of women.

It is not just the pioneers of decades ago who found women to be better risks. The trend still holds true today: MFIs that focus mainly on women have better loan repayment rates. In a 2011 study of several hundred MFIs throughout the world, Professor Bert D'Espallier at the Hogeschool-Universiteit Brussel in Belgium and his colleagues found that the higher the fraction of women clients, the lower an MFI's fraction of loans written off as uncollectable, after controlling for other factors.[9] In a related study in 2013, the same researchers found that MFIs not focused on women had about a 40% higher rate of borrowers **in arrears**, i.e. behind in their repayments, than those focused women.[10]

This gender difference in repayment rates is consistent with the idea that women have fewer alternative sources of financial services. With fewer other options, women would not want to risk losing financial access altogether. If they fail to repay a loan that they do manage to get, they may be left out in the future. Hence, the incentives diminish for the types of moral hazard behavior we discussed in earlier chapters. As discussed in Chapter 5, lack of alternatives might also help explain why the technique of progressive lending appears to work well for maintaining repayment incentives.

In addition to differences in occupations, cash flow patterns, and incentives for maintaining continuing access, another reason for better borrower risk among women might have to do with how they respond to social incentives of group lending methodologies. In their early pilot programs both FINCA and Grameen found women responded better to working in lending groups than did men. Box 7.3 presents a similar disappointing result

Box 7.3. In the Field
All-Male Lending Flops at Sinapi Aba, Ghana

Sinapi Aba Savings and Loans is one of the largest financial institutions in Ghana exclusively oriented towards the poor. It began as a non-profit NGO giving microloans, and in 2013 legally transformed into a registered non-bank financial institution in order to be allowed to offer savings services. In 2015, the MFI anticipated fully funding all its lending activities entirely from the deposits of its own clients, nine in 10 of whom are women, rather than relying on external sources.

Table 7.3. Sinapi Aba Savings & Loans, Ltd

Began microfinance operations	1994
Location	Ghana
Clients (2015)	201,739 depositors; 142,701 borrowers
Women as % of borrowers	89.6%
Self-sufficiency ratio	97.3%
Legal status	Non-bank financial institution; non-profit

(Continued)

Box 7.3. (*Continued*)

Early on when it was called Sinapi Aba Trust, the MFI experimented with the gender mix of its lending groups. Here is what researchers Susy Cheston and Lisa Kuhn from Opportunity International reported about what happened when Sinapi Aba tried all-male groups:

After running a successful women's Trust Bank program, Sinapi Aba Trust began forming men's Trust Banks in mid-1998. By the second loan cycle, the all-male Trust Banks were already performing worse than the all-female Trust Banks in terms of arrears. By mid-2000, arrears in the men's Trust Banks constituted 20 percent of the total arrears of the Trust Bank clients; the arrears rate in all-male Trust Banks was 2.5 times that of all-female Trust Banks.

Among the reasons for the higher arrears cited by Sinapi Aba staff were the fact that male clients were often in direct competition with each other and were apt to take risks like selling their goods on credit. Staff also reported that men's groups were more difficult to control and did not have a positive attitude toward meeting attendance. They also noted that the men were not committed to the mutual guarantee of the group even though its importance was stressed to then. As a result, Sinapi Aba discontinued all-male Trust Banks and now serves men primarily through its individual lending program and as a minority in mixed Trust Bank groups.

Sources: Mixmarket.org; Cheston and Kuhn (2002).

with lending to men in groups at Sinapi Aba Trust in Ghana. The result, as we have seen, is seen that MFIs that focus on women are more likely to use group-lending methodologies like solidarity groups and village banking. Indeed, some of the very largest MFIs, with many millions of women clients each, such as Grameen (96% women borrowers) in Bangladesh, Bandhan (100% women), BFIL (100%) and ASA (92%) in India, were all built on variations of the solidarity group model.

Why might group methodologies work better with women than with men? In Chapter 5, we explored the idea that the social collateral stemming from group peer pressure and peer monitoring can help mitigate limited liability and moral hazard. There is some evidence that women may be more responsive than men to that sort of peer pressure for maintaining their reputation within their groups and communities.[11]

Does this lower borrowing risk for women translate into better business results for MFIs? While intuitively it might seem that it should, the reality is more complex. We saw earlier that female-focused MFIs are more often non-profit organizations with broader, socially oriented goals. Their clients tend to be poorer, with resulting smaller average savings accounts and loan sizes. A related characteristic is that women-focused MFIs are also more likely to offer more than just financial services, such as education or healthcare services or empowerment training.

This combination of broader services, smaller average account sizes, and non-profit orientation results in higher operating costs. Professor D'Espallier's team found that MFIs focused primarily on women spend, on average, 21% of their assets on operations, compared to only 18% for those not so gender focused. On net, then, despite women's better repayment histories, the research team could find no statistical difference in key bottom line business results like return on assets whether MFIs focused on women or not.[12] Nor was there any difference in interest rates charged on loans.

It appears that focusing on women and offering them more services while servicing women's smaller-scale accounts does not necessarily hurt the bottom line or mean worse prices or fees for customers. Women repay better, and the higher operational costs are driven by differences in how the organizations chose to work, not by gender itself. It is an appealing have-cake-and-eat-it-too proposition for MFIs with socially driven missions because strategic emphasis on social mission clearly also lies behind the focus on women. In particular, beyond bottom-line business issues, two broad socially oriented motives also drive MFIs towards women: potential impact on families and women's empowerment.

The Family Impact Motive

Though poorer on average than men, women tend to spend more of what money they do have on their children and families—on food, health, housing, and (in some cultures) education. The pattern seems fairly universal as evidenced by studies all around the world, in Brazil, in Mexico, in Cote

Box 7.4. In Your Backyard
Kids' Hunger in America—Father Doesn't Know Best?

The preference that women show in spending more on their children and families than do men is not just a poor country phenomenon. The same pattern shows up in rich countries too, including the U.S.

Professor Catherine Kenney, a sociologist at Bowling Green State University, looked at what happens in low-income and moderate-income American families when Mom manages the money compared to when Dad does. Turns out the kids eat better and go hungry less when Moms make those decisions.

Dr. Kenney looked at more than 1,000 two-parent families living in or near the edges of poverty, those most likely to have challenges feeding their kids—so-called children's food insecurity. She analyzed how children's food insecurity depended on whether the mother, the father, or both together made the main decisions about how to use the family income. In a survey, parents reported the extent to which they had to have their kids skip meals, cut back on the size of meals, or otherwise go hungry because of lack of money.

When fathers controlled the money (either alone or jointly with the mother), American low- and moderate-income kids were far more likely to be food insecure. Remarkably different. The odds of children's food insecurity were more than twice as high compared to when mothers alone controlled the family income.

Source: Kenney (2008).

D'Ivoire, and many other places.[13] As we see in Box 7.4, it is true even in wealthy countries like the U.S. This relative bias that women have towards improving the living standards of families is attractive for those MFIs seeking to have broader social impact.

For example in a widely discussed early study of the impact of micro-credit, Economics Professor Mark Pitt of Brown University and Shahidur

Khandker of the World Bank found that microcredit to poor families in Bangladesh helped increase their household consumption, whether the credit went to men or to women.[14] But the impact differed by gender. The improvement in a family's consumption was more than 60% higher on average when the loans went to women than when they went to men. A related study by the same research team found that the children of women microcredit recipients were healthier on average than those of non-participants.[15] The same kids' health advantage was not found if the credit went to men.

Similarly, Women's World Banking did in-depth studies in four countries (Bosnia and Herzegovina, Dominican Republic, Jordan, Morocco) exploring barriers poor women face in running businesses as compared to men.[16] Wide cultural variations from country to country notwithstanding, several gender differences relating to families were more general and helped explain disparities in business size and use of money.

First, among those who run their own enterprises, women on average spent less time on their businesses than did men, so they make less money. Why? In large part because women spent much more time on household responsibilities such as caring for children, cooking and cleaning. That gender disparity in household division of labor is even true when comparing women and men employed in full-time jobs. Numerous time-use studies around the world show that, in poor countries and rich ones alike, on average women end up working more hours than men. Many of those hours are unpaid household activities for the family.

This tendency towards families not only inhibits earnings potential, but also suggests that women are more likely than men to seek ways to better facilitate everyday flow transactions for household needs—for consumption smoothing and protecting against irregular income shocks. Indeed, the non-profit Microfinance International tracked financial diaries of poor women and men in Malawi.[17] One central finding was that Malawian women generally handled more of the little daily household financial transactions, but men controlled big transactions. In other words, women have more need for comparatively small and short-term financial intermediation tools—needs well aligned with what MFIs offer.

Second, women reinvested less of their business earnings back into the businesses, preferring to prioritize spending on children. This combination of less time and less investment limited the growth potential of women's businesses compared to men's, but the women tended to see their businesses as supplemental household income rather than the main source. The Malawian study found a related pattern that in running their enterprises, men tended to make more purchases and spend much higher amounts than did women.

Indeed, third, Women's World Banking found that women were more likely to want to limit business growth on purpose in order to keep the activities lower profile and less time consuming. Time spent on the business tends to lead to heavier workloads for women, given their responsibilities around the home and in caring for children and elderly parents. Researcher Linda Mayoux found that African microfinance practitioners reported that a lack of alternatives like daycare services to help tend children and the elderly could be substantial source of added stress on the women running businesses, with adverse effects on the children and elderly.[18] Another reason women preferred keeping it low profile was a behavioral dynamic within households: some women thought the more money they brought in, the less their husbands would feel responsible to contribute for the family.

Fourth, another reason women's businesses were smaller than men's had to do with locating in less productive places, those not necessarily the best for attracting customers. Again it is a conscious choice. Women wanted their activities closer to home, to facilitate child rearing and reduce transportation needs, particularly in cultures where women traveling on their own is discouraged or even prohibited. Many women operate their businesses right in their home. The close-to-home location preference also suggests that women might place higher value on the convenience of MFIs' financial services compared to traditional banks, such as field officers coming to places of work or holding solidarity group meetings within the neighborhood. Women's tendency to stay near also means they are more likely than men to be able to attend group meetings and makes it easier for group members to monitor one another. Closeness also helps MFIs keep monitoring and field officer travel costs lower.

One benefit of the tendency of women towards smaller scale investments than men is that MFIs might appreciate the lower risks. Women's smaller types of businesses that generate income tied to daily household activities are good fits for smaller savings accounts and short-term flow-transaction loan products, which we have seen are the mainstay of solidarity groups and village banks. Larger businesses, and larger, higher-risk financial transactions such as capital investments, tend to be better suited for individual lending and closer matches for the collateral and size requirements of mainstream banking.

The Empowerment Motive

Women's empowerment is an explicit motive of many MFIs. In fact, empowering women is second among four core themes of the Microcredit Summit Campaign, one of the leading industry organizations championing microfinance worldwide.[19] Fully 60% of MFIs surveyed had specific goals for women's empowerment or gender equality, and most offer women's empowerment services of some sort in addition to financial services.[20]

MFIs have embraced this mission beyond ameliorating poverty because it is clear from numerous studies that various forms of gender discrimination across myriad cultures limit not only women's access to financial services, but also more broadly restrict a host of income related opportunities like education, higher-paying occupations, and so on. Such discrimination generally reflects deep cultural norms about gender roles.

For example, some cultures prohibit women from independent financial transactions. As recently as 2013, surveys by the World Bank found multiple Middle Eastern and South Asian nations, such as Pakistan, where women cannot get loans unless co-signed by men.[21] In some countries, like Ghana and Nepal, family assets like bank accounts are not jointly owned by spouses, meaning women can bank only what they earn themselves. Some types of jobs are off limits to women as well, by cultural tradition or law, restricting earnings potential. By law in Kazakhstan, women cannot be welders or lumberjacks or process raw cotton fibers.

Figure 7.6 was put together as a guide for microfinance practitioners by Linda Mayoux and Maria Hartl, experts on gender dimensions of microfinance. They show three key channels and potential virtuous cycles through which microfinance might enhance women's empowerment across various socio-economic contexts. The channel towards the left includes mechanisms that might improve well-being within the household and family. The center channel shows potential economic empowerment impacts

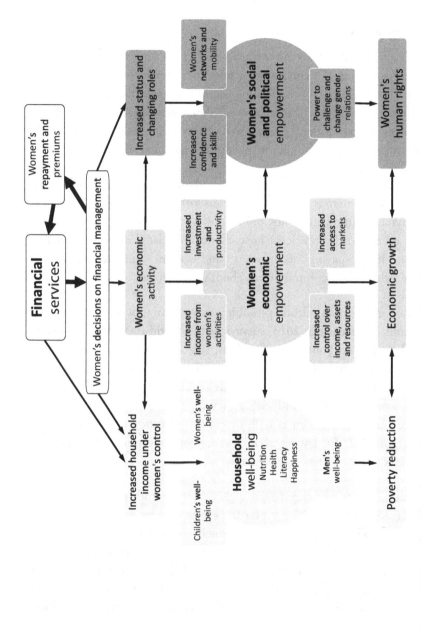

Figure 7.6. Microfinance and women's empowerment: Potential benefits

Source: Mayoux and Hartl (2009). Reproduced with permission.

on women, while the right channel illustrates possible social and political empowerment effects.

MFIs attempt to foster women's empowerment in all three channels through enabling women's access to otherwise out of reach financial tools. MFIs also aim to improve women's control over financial decision-making, so-called **financial autonomy**. In many places, compared to men women have less control over family money and assets. If women gain more income or more independent control, since women tend to invest more in their families, the household channel can improve nutrition, health, education and overall welfare for not only the women but also their kids and spouses.

Indeed, a long-term study of more than 2,000 women who had gained access to microcredit in Bangladesh investigated the potential impact on the women and their families.[22] Compared to non-participants, women involved in Bangladeshi microcredit programs had greater say in household choices, more control over savings, more say over how to use money, and greater independence in deciding to buy things. They also had broader social networks, more freedom to travel outside the home, and communicated more with their husbands about family planning and parenting.

Some MFIs have specifically designed products in ways to improve women's control over assets. Grameen Bank in Bangladesh, for instance, offers women microfinance loans with longer-term payback periods for acquiring housing or land.[23] To qualify for the loans, the woman must register the land and house in her own name, not a male family member's as might be traditionally. In this way, the MFI seeks to increase women's control of assets and improve their income security. The requirement has the added benefit of reducing husbands' likelihood of divorcing or abandoning their wives and families, an unfortunately common trigger driving women and children into poverty because men are often their families' principal wage earners.

Moving on to the center economic empowerment channel in Figure 7.6, it suggests that if women gain access to financial options, they might invest more, expand or start new businesses, and earn more on their own than otherwise. For example, a 2014 study by the World Bank, based on 20 years of following microcredit-using families in Bangladesh, found that increasing women's borrowing elevated their workforce participation three times more than for men.[24] Contributing more income to the household could improve their stature within the family and increase control over their own finances and investments in their children. In that same World Bank study, not only were women with access to microcredit more likely to be earning income, but also expanding women's borrowing by 10% was also associated with increases of approximately 8% in school enrollment by their children. With hundreds of millions using microfinance, if this pattern proves more generally true the long-term economic impact through women's investment in children's education might be substantial indeed.

Another example effort along the financial autonomy lines is the Credit and Savings Household Enterprise (CASHE) project in India. Cultural traditions in India often require large dowries paid by a girl's parents to the family of the groom. CASHE developed a pilot microcredit service aimed at adolescent girls.[25] Parents can get microcredit loans to enable their daughters to buy productive assets to help them earn income. Being an income producing member of the family can help the girls delay pressure for marriage. And if and when they do marry, the bride has an asset to bring with her, which in turn can reduce the culturally-expected size of the dowry her family needs to pay.

Another issue related to women's role in society and the household has to do with the fact that in many cultures women have less freedom of association with people outside their families, and suffer more domestic violence. We saw in Chapter 4 (Table 4.2) that household conflict was one of the widespread motives women cite, together with improved financial autonomy, for why they join informal finance groups like ROSCAs. Because microfinance group lending methods borrow from those informal traditions, similar household conflict motives help explain the preference some women have for microfinance. Group lending participants generally must leave their homes to attend meetings, or may be expected to invite group members into their homes. Husbands also may have to cede some control over family finances if a woman commits publicly to other group members participating with an MFI. As outsiders of members' families, MFI personnel and group members might also play a role identifying or dampening potential cases of domestic abuse. Thus, particularly for women, MFI group meetings can serve not just financial purposes, but more: as social outlets, ways to meet others, and perhaps respites from tensions at home and domineering husbands.

Greater income and financial autonomy might also lead, in the rightmost channel in Figure 7.6, to improved self-esteem, to more interactions and respect in the community, and to enhanced social stature and political voice. If large numbers of women make progress along these fronts, gender role expectations might change at a larger cultural level as well. One suggestive bit of evidence along these lines comes from India's many self-help groups, which we encountered in Chapter 5. Self-help groups are self-managed by the members, so many women in rural villages gain experience organizing groups, running meetings, keeping records, and so on. Moreover, the members, particular those leading the groups, apparently are visible and politically active in their communities. One study found that one in five self-help groups in India had at least one woman who had been elected to some local public office.[26] Likewise, 30% of the groups had pursued some sort of community action, like improving health care, education, water systems, or the environment. In other words, the women were politically empowered.

Further, some MFIs expressly aim beyond the empowerment potential of financial access in and of itself by offering additional non-financial services such as education, occupational workshops, childcare and healthcare, and other benefits. For example, Figure 7.7 shows a loan officer from the MFI

Figure 7.7. Self-Esteem Training, Asociación Arariwa Group Meeting, Peru

Asociación Arariwa in Peru doing an educational workshop with a lending group, discussing self-esteem and ways women can foster and hinder it. This idea of MFIs providing arrays of social services beyond financial tools is sometimes referred to as **microfinance-plus**.

Potential empowerment has an added advantage for the MFIs themselves: the possibility of hiring women clients who demonstrate particularly good skills. As we noted earlier, women in many regions have fewer job opportunities than do men, so MFIs with empowerment agendas often like to provide employment options. For example, we saw in Box 7.1 a commitment to hiring exclusively women field officers at MBK Ventura in Indonesia. Similarly, Box 7.5 illustrates the empowering effects of microfinance on a former microfinance client hired by the MFI Pro Mujer in Bolivia. Hiring women is not entirely selfless for MFIs either, since women's wages tend to be less than men's, helping MFIs control costs. Possibly as importantly, former clients generally come from the very communities the MFIs serve. Closer culturally and geographically to customers than other staff might be, former clients might better understand their community's needs and be more trusted by customers.

Box 7.5. Faces
Amalia Aramayo's Climb from Poor to Empowering at Pro Mujer

Pro Mujer is an MFI in Latin America focused on women's financial independence, health and leadership. Nearly all their clients are women, and empowerment is a central mission. Here is how they described the empowering impact of microfinance on one of their clients. It is a story of a 16 years' climb from poverty to mentor and Master's degree:

From the beginning, life in Bolivia was challenging for Amalia Aramayo. She and her mother were poor and often hungry and cold.... Amalia's stepfather was domineering and easily angered. To keep the peace, Amalia became quiet and withdrawn. As a

(*Continued*)

Box 7.5. (*Continued*)

child, Amalia never imagined that one day she would have the confidence not only to take control of her own life, but also to act as a mentor and leader for other women looking to improve their lives....

As Amalia grew into a young woman, she wanted so much to provide support for her whole family, especially her mother. But her only possession was a sewing machine. She dreamed of becoming a seamstress but could not afford to buy fabric or thread. When she saw a Pro Mujer sign in her community, Amalia made the most courageous and important decision of her young life. She joined 25 other women to form a Pro Mujer group.... With her first loan of $100, Amalia bought sewing supplies and opened her business.

Over the next two years, Amalia's business flourished as she bonded with the other women in her Pro Mujer group. Amalia came to value more than Pro Mujer's help with her business—she became passionate about Pro Mujer's message to women that they must develop their sense of self-worth and true potential and understand their rights.

After two and a half years as a seamstress, Amalia turned over her business to her mother and approached Pro Mujer for a job helping other women fulfill their dreams.... "I was shy, but they said I'd be good at the job," she remembers. "They assured me I could learn to do it." And learn she did, working to inspire women to reach for higher goals than they ever thought possible. Early on, she found the courage to enroll in college even though money and time were in short supply.... "I remember taking my baby to classes, working all day, and falling asleep over my textbooks," she recalls. "I got so discouraged and tired. I considered quitting, but co-workers at Pro Mujer convinced me not to give up."

(Continued)

Box 7.5. (*Continued*)

Fourteen years later, Amalia still works for Pro Mujer in Bolivia, where she is now a global trainer. The timid young girl is gone. She is now powerful, proud, confident, and happy. Amalia lights up when she describes training new employees to understand clients' needs and help them improve their lives. "Pro Mujer clients are strong women, able to overcome many challenges," she adds. "But they need someone they trust to tell them they will succeed. It was Pro Mujer's trust in me that helped change my life. I now do that for other women."

Figure 7.8. Amalia recently returned to finish her university studies and in April 2014 received a Master's degree in economics. She wrote her thesis on the benefits of microcredit for women

Source: Pro Mujer Two-Year Report 2012–2013.

Might Microfinance Dis-empower Women?

We might think of Figure 7.6 as a set of complexly interlinked hypotheses, drawn from scholars and practitioners, about different ways empowerment might happen through access to financial services. Belief in that potential has been compelling enough to drive large swaths of the microfinance industry to embrace the empowerment mission. However, a countervailing view argues that some or many of the links in the chain of hypotheses may not prove true. Microfinance may instead, at least in some contexts, reinforce prevailing gender roles, unequal power relationships, and other inequities. Perhaps counterintuitively, some of the most vocal critics of microfinance as a tool for women's empowerment have come from the feminist movement. Because we might otherwise expect feminists to embrace efforts to foster women's empowerment, the incongruity itself gives serious weight to the concerns. Add that many of the concerns are grounded in empirical evidence from the field, and they are well worth exploring.

A first line of critique has been whether or not there is good empirical evidence for the various empowerment effects claimed. For example, an evaluation team from Maastricht University and elsewhere reviewed 25 studies that purported to explore the impact of microfinance on women's control over household spending.[27] The evaluation found more than half those studies lacked strong methodologies or rigorous theoretical frameworks. Moreover, a meta-analysis combining data across the various experimentally rigorous studies found there was not enough evidence to say the impact of microfinance on women's control over household expenditures statistically differed from no impact. A number of other studies did show small magnitude effects, but the team considered them only "quasi-experimental" and thus less rigorous or well controlled.

Another suggested weak link is evidence that even though on paper women may be listed as the clients, often their husbands or other male household members end up receiving the financing. Men might use funds from savings accumulated by women. If microcredit becomes available to women, husbands or in-laws may put pressure on women to take out loans, and to use funds that otherwise might go to the family to pay back. Women may take out loans in order to give them to their husbands, or men may leverage their authority in the household control whatever money women earn. A 1996 study in Bangladesh, for instance, found that of 275 women only 18% controlled their loans, and about 22% had zero control.[28] More recently in a similar study of 90 women with loans in India in 2011, Elena Bridgers reported that women themselves had been the decision maker in only 26% of cases.[29]

In some reported cases men have apparently worked directly with male loan officers to take out loans in their wives' names, without the women's knowledge. For example, one study from the mid-1990s in Pakistan investigated in detail the use and control of 31 microloans to women. Only seven were actually controlled by women; men controlled 16 without involving women in the loan process; the remaining eight were loans that women were completely unaware had been taken in their names.[30] In cases like these, then, is microfinance empowering the women, or simply enabling men control of more resources? On one hand, from a skeptical viewpoint we worry about rewarding repressive patriarchal behavior. For instance, that same study mentioned above from the Philippines found that when men got access to microcredit directly, the women in their households actually ended up with less empowerment several years later as measured by control of resources and family decisions like moving or how to raise the children.[31] On the other hand, a more optimistic view might suggest that at least some women, although not a majority, were controlling things despite cultural norms to the contrary. And even those women that did not were at least now a necessary party in the financial transaction, nudging empowerment forward. Effects supporting both viewpoints might be simultaneously occurring.

Similarly, even if women are able to make more decisions about how to use money, they may simply repeat gender-role reinforcing choices. Women's businesses and jobs earn less, on average, so women may just continue investments in lower-income, smaller options. Indeed, one bit of evidence that microfinance may be replicating gender biases is that women's microloan sizes are smaller on average than men's. Not only might women's business needs be smaller, but also larger loans often require collateral, which women tend to lack, particularly where they are not allowed independent ownership of property.

MFIs, then, by providing primarily small loans helpful mostly for flow transactions—because that is what works well in solidarity groups—could be perpetuating women's subordinate status. Counterintuitively perhaps, the direction of causality might instead run the other way: from empowerment to microfinance. It may be that women who are already somewhat more empowered than average are the ones who seek out microfinance to begin with, perhaps to pursue activities they would normally be doing anyway, hence reinforcing cultural gender roles.

A related potential downside of different gender tendencies has to do with productivity and economic growth. The near term economic growth potential from microfinancial services for women is likely lower than if those same resources went to men. Why? Because average women invest less in businesses and women's businesses are smaller, hire fewer people, and tend to concentrate in lower-value-added added industries. A World Bank study in 2013 found the productivity of women-owned enterprises to be about 6% less than men's on average, due differences in the sectors, smaller average sizes of the enterprises, and lower investment in equipment.[32]

To the extent that economic development is a principal goal, it is feasible that the gender bias of the microfinance sector could be inhibiting the poverty-reducing growth and job creation impact, at least in the near term. Unfortunately, evidence one way or the other of longer-term impact of microfinance on growth is lacking. The large majority of studies of the impact of microfinance have looked only at a short time period, such as a year or few years of evidence. Over longer periods it may be that women's greater investment in children's education and health, when accumulated across millions of families over timeframes like decades, might generate longer-term productivity and employment gains that outweigh the short-term gap in business investment and job creation compared to men.

That long-term potential, however, is also uncertain for several reasons. For one, another potential weak link in the empowerment chain is that if women use financing to run their own microenterprises, they may need labor and help, either within the business itself or for household work like care for the young or elderly, which they may get from their children or other unpaid family members. The kids, particularly girls, might not then go to school, and dis-empowering cultural traditions of unpaid family labor and constricted female education might get reinforced.

Evidence on microfinance and schooling is somewhat mixed pro and con. A study in Bosnia and Herzegovina, for instance, found older teenage school attendance dropped about one-fifth on average for low-education families who got microcredit compared to those who did not.[33] The teenagers worked dozens of more hours in the family business instead. Yet an extensive review of various studies found that many more showed positive impact than showed negative influence.[34] For example, Jorge Maldonado of the Universidad de los Andes in Colombia, and Claudio Gonzáles-Vega of Ohio State University, found that families in Bolivia who had been using microfinance kept children in school about half a year longer on average than families without microfinance. Other studies found that the availability of various forms of credit and insurance in villages helped families better weather unexpected holes in their income flows, enabling them to keep paying the fees needed to keep kids in schools.[35]

A related criticism of the empowerment potential of microfinance stems from how MFIs themselves use their client women's time and labor. As we saw in Chapter 5, women comprise the large majority of members of solidarity groups, village banks and self-help groups. Such groups require regular attendance at group meetings, which may last several hours plus time to travel to and from. Group members are sometimes responsible for bookkeeping and other administrative functions, and are often expected to use their social relationships to pressure delinquent borrowers to repay. Critics of microfinance suggest these expectations simply transfer responsibilities from MFIs to the women, amounting to unpaid female labor. Supporters of the industry point to the voluntary nature of participation in such groups and that savings and lending group systems mirror informal mechanisms like ROSCAs that many cultures have used voluntarily for generations. Nevertheless, the gender bias of microfinance could be reinforcing cultural norms that women's time and work, whether in the home, in groups, in jobs, or in the community, is not valued as highly as men's.

Similarly, women who run their own microenterprises are then generally not working in formal wage jobs. It may be that self-employment is necessary because no wage jobs are available to them. However, having microfinance options might to some extent divert some women from seeking wage jobs in larger scale businesses like manufacturing that might otherwise be more productive and pay better than self-employment, again perpetuating gender-biased cycles of low income.

The relationship between formal wage employment and economic well-being is strong. Figure 7.9 is somewhat complex, but well worth a close look. Using survey data from 137 low- and middle-income countries, the World Bank looked at the relationship between women's employment and national income levels. The lines on Figure 7.9 show the average women's share of employment in various types of work, in both formal and informal sectors, and how that share changes with the level of income across countries. Although there is much country by country variation above and below these lines across cultures and social gender roles, the average relationships are instructive.

A first key point to take away from this graph is that women account for about 40% of the labor force overall, a ratio that is fairly consistent across low- and middle-income nations (light gray line in the middle). Thus work, per se, is not really the empowerment issue; lots of women work to earn

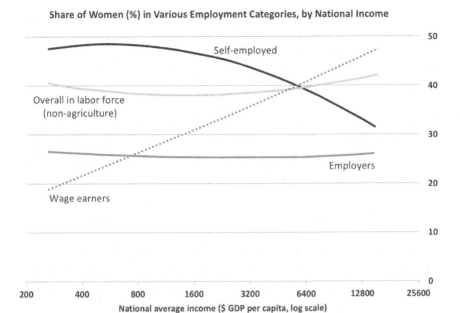

Share of Women (%) in Various Employment Categories, by National Income

Self-employed

Overall in labor force
(non-agriculture)

Employers

Wage earners

50

40

30

20

10

0

| 200 | 400 | 800 | 1600 | 3200 | 6400 | 12800 | 25600 |

National average income ($ GDP per capita, log scale)

Figure 7.9. Women's employment patterns change with national income

Note: Excludes agriculture.
Source: Hallward-Driemeier (2013).

money. Rather the issues are the sectors and types of work. By contrast, note how the share of women in wage jobs (dotted line) rises fairly steadily from below 20% on average in the poorest nations to almost half in middle-income countries. Wage jobs are typically steadier sources of income and better paying than are informal options. Women's opportunities for earning regular wages clearly rise as economies grow. Indeed, women's share of wage jobs actually outpaces their overall labor share in the richer countries on the graph. (Note, however, the graph does not include the richest countries, with average incomes above about $20,000.)

An opposing trend of interest is self-employment (black line). In low-income nations, women tend to be disproportionately concentrated in self-employment. Women account for about half the self-employed on average in low-income nations—a substantially greater share compared to women in the overall labor force. But women's self-employment ratio falls below a third on average for middle-income nations.

Women's share is lowest among those who create jobs for other people, e.g. are employers (bottom darker gray line). Only slightly more than a quarter of employers are women, in both low- and middle-income nations, much lower than their overall participation in the labor force. In other words, men's businesses account for most jobs.

One final line of serious concern about the gender impact of microfinance has to do with intra-household conflict and domestic violence. There is some evidence that in some cases financial and social tensions within households can increase with microfinance. Men may try to control or steal funds women put away for the family. Women's control over savings accounts or money from loans might create jealousy from her husband or other male relatives.

The domestic tension challenge may be particularly acute with microcredit. Pressure to pay back loans can lead to disputes within the home over the uses of family income. In a study in one rural Bangladeshi village, anthropologist Aminur Rahman, then a doctoral student at the University of Manitoba, lived for nearly a year in a rural village where Grameen Bank had been active for many years. He found that domestic violence increased for women microcredit clients.[36] He discovered that even though Grameen Bank's loans were to women, the majority got loans because their husbands requested it; 40–70% of Grameen Bank loans in the village were actually being used by men. Moreover, fully 70% of surveyed women reported that getting microcredit led to increased violence or aggressive behavior in their households, while only 18% reported decreases.

Pressure from husbands on their wives to take out loans might in and of itself create disagreements within the household. Then any sense of jealousy, of the husband losing financial control, or struggles to make loan repayments could raise tension further. Stuck in between, on one side, MFI officers pressuring women to repay loans and to track down other delinquent group members, and on the other side husbands who expect to control the money and women's choices, the women might prefer if the men themselves were responsible for accessing financial tools.

Dr. Rahman undertook his study in the late 1990s before Grameen Bank made major changes in its microcredit practices (i.e. Grameen II), and was only in one village. It may therefore not be generalizable to other situations. Nevertheless, similar findings across several studies like it led to ongoing

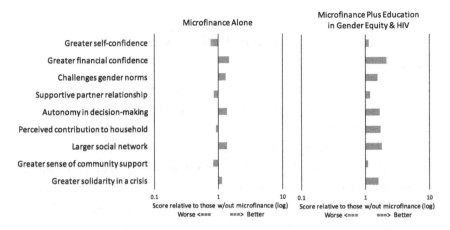

Figure 7.10. Impact of microfinance plus education on South African women's empowerment

Source: Kim et al (2009).

substantial cautionary introspection by the industry about the realities of the women's empowerment potential of microcredit, and fueled a push to broaden into microsavings and other services that might not have the same negative implications as debt. As we saw in Chapter 5, with Grameen II, Grameen Bank changed its practices in major ways.

In another example of efforts towards change, one experimental program paired microfinance with gender equity and HIV education in an impoverished district of South Africa. As Figure 7.10 suggests, while microfinance alone had mixed and limited measurable impact on measures of empowerment, the combined (microfinance-plus) program resulted in reduced levels of domestic violence against participating women, together with improvements in multiple other measures of women's empowerment such as financial confidence, gender norms, autonomy in decision-making, and greater social network membership. The program also proved a cost-effective way to improve women's health and life expectancy, in large part by reducing physical and sexual violence against women by more than half.[37]

The debate on microfinance's impact on women's empowerment is vigorous and continuing. So too are efforts to improve microfinance's benefits for poor families more generally, along multiple dimensions. In Chapter 9, we will explore evidence on whether or not those hoped-for impacts are happening.

Section in Bulletpoint

- Women have proven less risky customers for MFIs than men.

- MFIs focused on women tend to have higher operating costs because the MFIs are smaller and offer wider ranges of services; yet, bottom-line business results are similar.

- Moral hazard may be more mitigated for women than for men because women are more likely to lack financial alternatives yet also more likely to face repeated needs for small scale flow transactions.

- Evidence suggests women are more responsive to the social collateral of peer pressure and peer monitoring in microfinance groups.

- Women's businesses tend to be smaller than men's in part because women spend less time on their businesses, reinvest less money, and choose less productive locations; favoring family needs instead.

- In many places, compared to men women have less control over money and assets, and lower social mobility and status.

- Many MFIs aim to improve women's empowerment by improving women's well-being, control over resources, and social status.

- Women's opportunities for wage jobs rise as economies grow.

- Critics contend that microfinance might hurt women's empowerment by reinforcing existing cultural gender roles, increasing tensions within households, and transferring MFIs' risks and costs to poor women in groups without paying them for their time.

Discussion Questions

1. Some MFIs favor women because they tend to reinvest more in their families than men do. Does this policy help alleviate poverty and empower women?

2. Group lending is a common practice in microfinance. Why might group lending work better with women than men?

3. Do you think it is a problem for achieving the goals of microfinance that men's businesses on average generate more employment than women's? Why or why not?

4. MFIs have been accused of passing on to their women clients too much risk and time responsibilities. In lending groups, members may be responsible for managing the groups, attending meetings, monitoring each other's behaviors, chasing down delinquent payers, and so on—all without compensating the women. Do you think this fair and reasonable or unfair taking advantage of poor women? Why?

5. Imagine you work for an MFI that decides to offer financial services exclusively to women. Create a list of pros and cons for the MFI from both the supply/cost side and the demand/revenue side.

6. Suppose you are asked to innovate new or modify microfinancial services to reduce the risks of dis-empowering women. Briefly discuss two ideas you might suggest, and why.

Key Terms

capital constraints
Limits to how much money is available for spending and investment in a given time period; because of discrimination and gender role norms, women may be more capital constrained then men, but empirical evidence is mixed.

commercialization
Refers to how MFIs, as they move towards self-sufficiency and scale, tend to run like market-oriented businesses participating in commercial capital markets rather than relying on donors and government subsidies.

financial autonomy
Control of and independence in making financial decisions such as spending, saving, investing, and borrowing; often taken to include independent ownership of property; in many places women have less financial autonomy than men, sometimes by law.

gender wage gap
The difference between what men and women get paid, usually as a percentage of men's average wage; can be adjusted for differences in education, skills, experience and other characteristics; alternatively called the gender pay gap.

in arrears

Describes loan accounts where borrowers are behind schedule with repayments.

microfinance-plus

Aiming to increase impact on poor families, many MFIs add non-financial products and services, such as other education, occupational training, childcare, and healthcare; expansive versions sometimes labeled microfinance-plus-plus.

non-bank financial institutions

Sometimes known by their acronym, NBFIs do not have full banking licenses but provide some commercial financial services like microcredit, insurance or money transfers; regulated in most countries, but usually under different rules than banks.

transformation

The process by which an MFI changes from an NGO into a regulated bank or similar commercial financial institution; often aimed at enabling the MFI to attract deposits and expand services; a principal pathway to commercialization.

Notes:

[1] Feroza, Tailor, Balkh province, Afghanistan ©2015 Hand in Hand International, www.hihinternational.org. Used under Creative Commons license, http://creativecommons.org/licenses/by/4.0/
[2] Pistelli, Simanowitz, and Thiel (2011).
[3] Microcredit Summit Campaign (2014) estimated 75% of all clients of reporting MFIs were women at the end of 2012; and MixMarket.org database showed 82% of borrowers in 2013 were women.
[4] Frank (2008).
[5] UNDP (1996).
[6] Buvinić and Gupta (1997).
[7] Blau and Kahn (2006).
[8] History based on interview with Hatch by Roodman (2012).
[9] D'Espallier, Guerin, and Mersland (2011).
[10] D'Espallier, Guerin, and Mersland (2013).
[11] Goetz and Sen Gupta (1996) and Rahman (1999).
[12] D'Espallier, Guerin, and Mersland (2013).
[13] See reviews in Kenney (2008) and Blumberg (1988).
[14] Pitt and Khandker (1998).
[15] Pitt et al (2003).
[16] Frank (2008).
[17] Stuart, Ferguson, and Cohen (2011).
[18] Mayoux (1999).

[19] See http://www.microcreditsummit.org/about-the-campaign2.html
[20] Pistelli, Simanowitz, and Thiel (2011).
[21] IBRD (2013).
[22] Pitt, Khandker, and Cartwright (2006).
[23] Mayoux and Hartl (2009).
[24] Khandker and Samad (2014).
[25] Mayoux and Hartl (2009).
[26] Sinha (2006).
[27] Vaessen et al (2014).
[28] Goetz and Sen Gupta (1996).
[29] Bridgers (2011).
[30] Harper (1995).
[31] Pitt, Khandker, and Cartwright (2006)
[32] Hallward-Driemeier (2013).
[33] Augsburg et al (2015).
[34] Chua (2010).
[35] Jacoby and Skoufias (1997).
[36] Rahman (1999).
[37] Jan et al (2011).

THE EVOLUTION OF COMMERCIAL MICROFINANCE

"There is no Grameen Bank of vaccination. One does not hear of organizations sprouting like sunflowers in the world of clean water supply, hiring thousands and serving millions, turning a profit and wooing investors. Yet one does in microfinance.... More than any other domain of support for the global poor, microfinance comprises spectacular indigenous institutions."

— **David Roodman, Center for Global Development**

Figure 8.1. Competition among commercial microfinance firms drives advertising, like this promotional poster for Financier a CREAR in Peru

Microfinance, as an industry, has rapidly evolved since the mid-1990s. Changes were so fundamental they amounted to what Harvard University's Marguerite Robinson called the "microfinance revolution."[1] What was initially a niche sector of mostly small, non-profit, donor-dependent efforts aimed at poverty alleviation, is today a full-fledged global industry. The large majority of microfinance clients worldwide are customers of large-scale, self-sustainable microfinance institutions (MFIs) not reliant on subsidies. Indeed, most of the largest MFIs now are commercial firms seeking profit for owners and investors. They raise funds in international financial markets rather than relying on subsidies, and offer a variety of financial products, well beyond just microcredit.

The transition from charity to commercial industry is largely unique in international development, not seen in other target fields like education, health, infrastructure, or the environment. The result has been the development of private firms, many created and owned locally, that employ hundreds of thousands of people and serve hundreds of millions in economies that often struggle to grow.[2] Poor microfinance clients now have access to what one observer suggests is "basic banking service that is often more reliable than the education and health services that they commonly encounter."[3] This chapter explores that evolution, and how and why it happened. We will also explore some widely held concerns about potential negative consequences, the dark side of the commercialization of microfinance.

The cornerstones of commercial microfinance are profitability, competition, and effective regulatory oversight. Commercial MFIs aim not only to fight poverty, but also to generate profit for owners. Early pioneers demonstrated the potential for profitable commercial MFIs operating at large scale. That profit potential attracted additional investors and banks to the sector, thus increasing competition. Commercialization proponents argue that competition puts pressure on MFIs to innovate, to develop better financial products that customers value, and to keep costs in check, fees low, and interest rates attractive.[4] A wider array of financial services becomes more affordable for more people, expanding resources available for the poor.

Industry jargon calls this the **double bottom line**, i.e. creating both financial returns to shareholders and social returns to the community. The approach puts microfinance squarely amid **socially responsible investments**. The commercial microfinance industry gains access to funding from investors, and that ability to attract resources enables greater outreach to the poor.

On the surface, the impact of commercialization might seem like a strictly positive development. However, there are numerous criticisms that boil down to the question of **mission drift**: is it possible for an MFI to keep its clients' best interests in mind and reach out to the poorest of the poor, while at the same time seeking the highest possible return to shareholders? Is it right for wealthy investors in rich countries to make profit from some of the poorest people in the world's poorest countries? The social mission debate remains active and heated.

8.1 Profitability, Transformation and Scale

Demonstrating MFI Profitability

We will discuss three fundamental phases of the transition of microfinance into a commercial industry no longer dependent on aid: (1) demonstrating MFI profitability and scaleability; (2) development of an ecosystem of financial intermediaries channeling commercial investments into microfinance; and (3) emergence of international markets for selling and buying stocks and bonds of MFIs.

The first phase involved demonstrating that MFIs could be profitable and self-sustaining without subsidies, and that they could scale up to be of mass market interest to investors. When the concept of microfinance was emerging in the late 1970s and 1980s, a few institutions were already taking a "financial systems approach" to microfinance.[5] A few pioneering MFIs, such as Bank Dagang Bali (BDB) in Indonesia, began charging fees and microcredit interest rates that, together with keeping loan losses in check, enabled their own revenues to cover all their costs—what is known as independent **self-sufficiency**—while simultaneously ensuring affordability for their clients. In the 1980s, another Indonesian bank, Bank Rakyat Indonesia (BRI), was the first to profitably operate a large-scale microfinance banking system, without relying on donors.

At the time, this was unusual because the microfinance industry was in its formative stages. Most MFIs depended heavily on subsidies for survival. Instead, as we learned back in Box 1.3, BRI succeeded by leveraging its ability to take deposits from its clients, turning its clients' deposits around into microlending. Regulated banks have the legal ability to mobilize savings deposits as a source of funds, but early microfinance savings products had not yet been well developed. They were rarely generating enough deposits coming in to meet the demand for microloans going out.

These institutions at the forefront proved that MFI financial viability beyond the charity of donors was possible. Yet not until the 1990s did commercialization of the industry truly take off. For example, Box 8.1 describes how the Cambodian refugee aid organization ACLEDA morphed in the late 1990s from a charitable non-governmental organization (NGO)

Box 8.1. In the Field
From Tragedy to Transformation—ACLEDA Bank, Cambodia

Even in an industry littered with stories of fast growing MFIs, ACLEDA Bank stands out. ACLEDA began as a charity dealing with humanitarian tragedies in the wake of the Khmer Rouge regime, which murdered millions of Cambodians in the 1970s. ACLEDA refocused exclusively on microfinance in 1996. It became a commercial bank in 2000, legally able to take deposits, which fueled growth. Since then, it has grown at double-digit rates every year, including in the 2008–2010 global financial crisis (Figure 8.2). By 2015 it served nearly 2.5 million clients, mostly poor women. ACLEDA aims to become not simply a microfinance provider but Cambodia's leading commercial bank, period. It recently launched subsidiary operations in neighboring Laos and Myanmar, both among Asia's poorest nations.

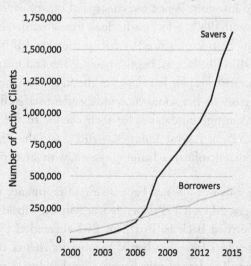

Figure 8.2. Growth in client numbers, ACLEDA Bank, Cambodia, 2000–2015

(Continued)

Box 8.1. (*Continued*)

Table 8.1. ACLEDA Bank, Plc

Began microfinance operations	1996
Locations	Cambodia, Laos, Myanmar
Clients (2015)	2.45 million savers; 408,349 borrowers
Women as % of borrowers	53%
Self-sufficiency ratio	154%
Legal status	Commercial bank

Dr. Ira Lieberman, founding CEO of CGAP, and colleagues point to ACLEDA as a prime example of the potential benefits when nonprofit MFIs transform into legally regulated commercial banks:

Origins. ACLEDA originated from the tragedy that befell Cambodia with the assumption of power by the Khmer Rouge in 1975. The International Labour Organization (ILO) and Care International recruited the company's management from refugee camps on the Thai-Cambodian border. Although initially targeting demobilized soldiers, the program quickly grew to assist refugees, widows, and other displaced persons of the war.... In 1996, a liquidity crisis forced ACLEDA to decide between offering business-development services and providing financial services—microfinance—to its constituency. The General Assembly of the Association decided to unify ACLEDA's agencies into a single unified institution and focus on microfinance. With funding from the Swedish International Development Cooperation Agency and USAID growth was substantial, such that the portfolio increased five times between 1996 and 1999.

Transformation. ACLEDA began the process of transformation to a bank in the mid-1990s and finalized the legal transformation into a bank in 2000. Since 2000, both the loan portfolio and savings have grown at an incredible pace: savings at a cumulative growth rate of 137% and loans at a cumulative growth rate of over

(*Continued*)

into a commercial bank. Access to deposits resulted in explosive growth. Similarly, Box 8.3 explores ProFund, launched in 1995 as the first venture capital fund that exclusively targeted microfinance. ProFund proved private investment in commercial MFIs could be profitable over the long haul.

These days, commercially oriented MFIs provide the majority of microcredit and other micro financial services, including the vast majority of savings accounts, fostering large-scale outreach to hundreds of millions of poor people. To reach this scale, MFIs needed large amounts of capital, much more than could be obtained solely from donors. MFIs like BRI in Indonesia and, later, BancoSol in Bolivia and (controversially) Compartamos Banco in Mexico proved that profits could be made. That proof opened doors to other mainstream commercial sources of capital beyond client savings deposits, such as external private investment funds, debt financing, and public stock offerings. Deep-pocketed private investors got interested. By the end of 2014, microfinance had attracted an estimated $31 billion in cumulative investments across international borders, about a third from private sources.[6]

The track record of profit also led existing big multinational banks like Citicorp in the U.S., Canada's Scotiabank, and Spain's BBVA, among others, to move down-market into microfinance, often partnering with organizations already active in the sector.

These shifts and resulting flow of big money enabled MFIs to expand rapidly and completely changed the industry, in both hopeful and troubling

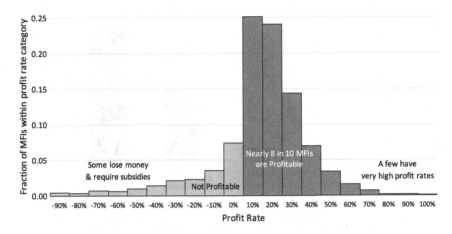

Figure 8.3. Distribution of profit rates, MFIs worldwide, 2012–2014

Note: Excludes MFIs in the extreme tails, reporting profits (losses) exceeding 100% (−100%).
Data Source: Microfinance Information Exchange, mixmarket.org.

ways. By 2014, as shown in Figure 8.3, nearly eight in 10 MFIs were operating profitably.

Transformation of Non-Profits into Regulated Banks

Regulated, profit-seeking MFIs are at the center of the commercial industry. In fact, some suggest that growth of the industry hinges on these organizations' ability to attract and absorb investment funds and expand their services. Hence, as Box 8.1 suggested for ACLEDA bank, in addition to showing profitability, another main plotline in the commercialization story has been the formal legal and financial process by which MFIs move from being non-profits to regulated banks.

As shown in Figure 8.4, the number of formal, regulated for-profit institutions in microfinance grew rapidly starting in the late 1990s. In 1997, Mayada Baydas, Douglas Graham and Liza Valenzuela at Ohio State University were able to identify only 18 financial institutions in microfinance that had formally registered as regulated banks or commercial non-bank financial intermediaries. These included some that like BancoSol had been NGOs and then transformed into regulated banks, and others like BRI in Indonesia or Standard Bank in South Africa that were traditional banks that went down-market and developed microfinance operations. Four years later in 2001, Valenzuela counted 70 such profit-seeking regulated commercial

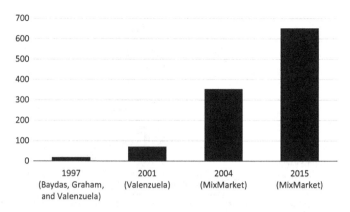

Figure 8.4. Growth in number of regulated, for-profit MFIs, 1997–2011

Sources: Baydas, Graham, and Valenzuela (1997); Valenzuela (2001); mixmarket.org

organizations. By the end of 2011, the Microfinance Information Exchange listed 635. Some of the most successful include Compartamos Banco in Mexico, BancoSol in Bolivia, Equity Bank in Africa, BRI, and the ProCredit Group (see Box 8.7).

Why would an MFI want to go through the lengthy and expensive **transformation** process of regulatory hassles, paperwork, computer system changes, and so on needed to become a regulated bank, subject to government oversight and rigid requirements? There are a number of potential benefits. In well-regulated markets, these can include lower fees and better interest rates for clients, creation of more financial products, better management and internal governance, greater institutional sustainability, and—importantly for achieving large scale—increased access to the world's huge capital markets.

Regulated MFIs can generally offer a broader range of financial services, creating economies of scope otherwise unavailable. In most countries, NGOs and other non-regulated MFIs are restricted by law from taking deposits. This restriction prevents non-regulated microfinance institutions from offering savings and microinsurance products to their customers. As discussed in Chapter 6, these products have grown increasingly popular in recent years and may be even more important than credit in combating poverty. Beyond savings and insurance, regulated institutions can offer other services that require being part of formal financial systems, like international remittances, electronic payments and transfers, ATM cards, and mobile money. Diversification of income streams for the MFI can, in turn, help reduce the MFI's risk from downturns or market fluctuations in one segment or another.

However, as noted in Chapter 6, savings and other products can require greater infrastructure for MFIs and costs per transaction can be significantly higher. As a result, such product line expansions typically do not happen until an MFI has not only transformed but also reached sufficient scale and sustainability on which to build. More about scale follows, but achieving economies of scale and scope can be mutually reinforcing.

Another benefit of actively pursuing a double bottom line is that the necessity to turn a profit and be transparent in reporting to regulators and investors instills financial discipline and efficiency incentives that may be absent in unregulated MFIs, subsidized programs, or charitable organizations. Commercial and regulatory pressure for better decision-making puts a premium on improving and professionalizing management, information systems, and institutional governance.

All these benefits—management, efficiency, transparency, oversight, lower risk—are attractive to external investors. Another major benefit of transformation, then, is enhancing an MFI's ability to access commercial sources of funding. Funding is arguably the single largest constraint on growth if MFIs are limited to charitable donors or local investors, particularly in developing economies without robust financial markets. Big international commercial investors are unlikely to be interested without the assurances that come with well-regulated institutions. Regulatory oversight and reporting requirements can reduce risks of an MFI facing financial crisis or bankruptcy from things like over-indebtedness and underperforming investments, and also limit the chances of corruption or fraud.

Potential investors value clear, standardized and independently verified information about MFI financial and social performance. Lack of reliable information about a particular MFI's operations discourages investment, even if the MFI has the potential of being profitable. Relieving this constraint stimulates substantial growth and economies of scale and scope. Countries with more developed reporting frameworks, such as Peru and Bolivia, have much greater capitalization than countries lacking them, such as Nigeria.

The Distortion Potential of Subsidies

One tenet of advocates of commercial microfinance is that heavily subsidized MFIs can undermine the growth of commercial microfinance. NGOs that are heavily subsidized and have no shareholder interests to take into account have weaker incentives for efficiency or innovative change. Well-meaning but inefficient operations can linger while absorbing resources that might be better used elsewhere. As noted in Chapter 3, another effect of subsidies is that they can undermine competition and distort prices in the market place. If an MFI subsidized by donors can afford to charge interest rates and fees below real costs, other MFIs might find it hard to enter and compete in the market.

Commercialization supporters' reasoning is not that all subsidies are bad, just that subsidies would be better utilized in ways that avoid price distortions. Subsidies used to fund start-up costs or technology development costs, rather than subsidizing interest rates or fees, can help an MFI get on its feet and develop the operational proficiency required to become a self-sufficient institution in the long-run. Subsidies can also encourage innovation and experimentation with new types of financial services, improved approaches to serving customers, better management techniques, and staff training. Subsidies likely also are needed to ensure financial access for some clients who may never be commercially viable to serve, such as those in abject poverty or in accessible remote locations.

Achieving Scale and Mass Outreach

Commercialization proponents argue that without attracting commercial, profit-seeking investors, the microfinance industry could never scale up enough meet the $250 billion estimated global demand for microcredit loans.[7,8] Achieving outreach to the world's billion extremely poor people means MFIs need to find ways to serve mass markets and drive costs per client down.

As Table 8.2 shows, MFIs that seek profits tend to grow to serve more clients than non-profit MFIs. For-profit MFIs tend to have larger loan sizes

Table 8.2. Scale metrics of for-profit vs. non-profit MFIs

Median values of	For-profit MFIs	Non-profit MFIs
Number of loans outstanding	21,031	12,668
Average loan balance per borrower	$855	$537
Number of depositors	56,155	26,404
Total assets ($millions)	23.9	9.6

Note: Data set includes more than 1,000 MFIs serving 95 million borrowers and 87 million depositors in nearly 100 countries.
Data Source: Mixmarket.org; data for December, 2013.

as well. Since many of the costs of processing loan transactions are similar no matter the loan size, MFIs with larger average loans tend to be more cost efficient, spending a lower fraction of funds on operating costs.

However, as we explore in our discussion of the social mission debate later, this difference in loan size is also a key point in criticisms of commercialized MFIs. Larger loan sizes may reflect a profit-seeking move to somewhat better-off clients, away from the risk and cost of tiny loans for the neediest. As we will see, larger average loan sizes could help or hurt the social bottom line, depending on the details of how an MFI's portfolio of loans changes.

Note the values in Table 8.2, showing that the median-sized MFIs have numbers of depositors or loans in the tens of thousands, reflect large numbers of fairly small MFIs. However, as Table 8.3 shows, small MFIs only account for a few percent of clients. The vast majority, more than four of every five microfinance clients, save and borrow at just a few hundred MFIs with hundreds of thousands or millions of clients, levels where the benefits of scale are particularly pronounced. Worldwide by 2015, 368 MFIs reported serving at least 100,000 or more depositors and/or savers.[9]

A quick look back at Table 1.3, which listed the largest MFIs, shows a dozen with more than a million borrowers. Not shown are a dozen more MFIs, mostly in South Asia, also with more than million borrowers. As we see in Table 8.3, half of all borrowers do business with those two dozen million-plus client MFIs. Eighteen of those 24 million-plus borrower MFIs are for-profit. More than two-thirds of all other microcredit borrowers are

Table 8.3. Measures of outreach and efficiency, by MFI scale

MFI scale (active borrowers)	Small (less than 10,000)	Medium (10,000 to 100,000)	Large (100,000 to 1 million)	Very large (more than 1 million)
Share of total number of MFIs (%)	51	39	12	1
Share of all borrowers (%)	1.4	12.6	35.8	50.2
Share of all savers (%)	2.9	17.6	46.1	33.4
Average real interest rate + fees (as % of loan, inflation adjusted)	28.9	24.9	21.1	13.5
Profit margin (% of revenues)	−14.8	9.8	10.4	19.8

Notes: Data set includes more than 1,000 MFIs serving 95 million borrowers and 87 million depositors in nearly 100 countries. Profit, expense and interest rate averages are medians within category. Interest & fees row reports "Yield on Gross Portfolio," using real rates, adjusted for inflation.
Data Source: mixmarket.org; data for December, 2013.

clients of MFIs above 100,000 clients. A similar pattern emerges for savings (Table 1.4). About two dozen MFIs have more than a million depositors. Two decades earlier, only a single MFI, BRI had reached the million-depositor scale. By 2015, BRI alone had 43 million savings clients (Box 1.3).

We see in Figure 8.5 that MFI costs per client are lower at larger scale, falling from a median of $250 per borrower for small MFIs with fewer than 10,000 clients, to $17 per borrower for those very large MFIs with millions of clients. With lower costs come higher profits. As shown in Table 8.3, the average small MFIs operate at a loss, bringing in less revenue than they cost to run. By contrast, average profit rates for mid-sized MFIs are about 10%, and rise with MFI scale. Also note in Table 8.3 that the pattern of increasing profit with scale occurs despite the larger institutions charging lower average interest and fees, a benefit for their customers. Small MFIs average nearly 29% rates of interest and fees, adjusted for inflation, compared to 13.5% for the very largest.

You may be wondering how institutional efficiency, while good for the MFI, is good for the clients. Is there a link between operational efficiency

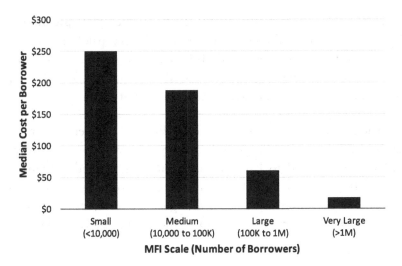

Figure 8.5. MFI costs fall with scale

Data Source: mixmarket.org; data for FY 2014.

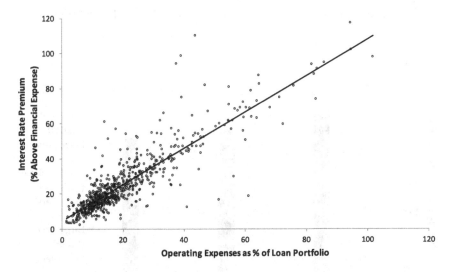

Figure 8.6. Loan interest rates and fees charged rise with operating costs

Data Source: mixmarket.org; profitable MFIs only.

and benefits to borrowers? Figure 8.6 illustrates the relationship between interest rates and fees charged to microcredit customers and MFI operating efficiency. The figure includes only MFIs that turn a profit. We can see how MFIs with higher operating costs tend to charge higher interest rates and fees.

The figure uses on the vertical axis what is called the real **yield premium**, the inflation adjusted rate of interest and fees the MFI gets paid for loans above and beyond the financial costs the MFI paid to acquire the loaned funds. Cost-efficient MFIs, the large cluster towards the bottom left of the graph, charge much lower premiums above their own cost of funds.

In addition to covering cost of funds, MFIs need to cover risk exposure, such as credit, foreign exchange and currency risks, discussed later. Mature and larger MFIs tend to have better risk mitigation methods, and can afford tools to mitigate those risks. Risks that are not mitigated are passed on in part to borrowers in the form of higher interest rates. Thus, robust risk management is beneficial not only to the institution, but to borrowers as well.

The overall effect of all these advantages of scale for the clients may best be summarized in Figure 8.7. It shows that the large-scale MFIs in India charge, on average, 6–8% lower rates of interest than MFIs that remain small-scale, except for on the smallest microloans (those below 5,000 rupees,

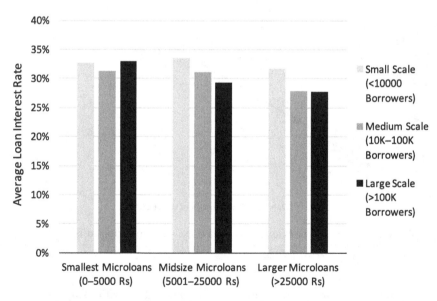

Figure 8.7. Average loan interest rates fall with MFI scale, India, 2010–2014

Data Source: Microfinance Transparency, India Country Data, www.MFTransparency.org; average interest rate is effective annual percentage rate (APR), including all fees (not inflation adjusted).

roughly $75). The figure also shows that bigger microloans incur lower rates no matter what size the MFI is.

In summary then, increased scale and efficiency help commercial MFIs operate sustainably and profitably, without reliance on subsidies and donor funds, ensuring their longer-term ability to serve the poor. Moreover, it is a potentially virtuous cycle: competition combined with scale efficiencies enables lower prices that attract more clients, which attracts investments and yet greater scale, increasing competitive pressure to keep prices low.

Efficiency and Pricing Incentives in Competitive Markets

The potential efficiency and pricing benefits of profit-seeking competitive markets are the holy grail for proponents of microfinance commercialization. Evidence from the Bolivian market, for example, suggests regulated commercial MFIs competing for customers potentially benefit poor clients through lower interest rates and fees on microloans, higher returns, lower fees and fewer restrictions on savings accounts, and lower microinsurance premiums.

Bolivia is widely considered one of the most competitive microfinance markets in the world. It was essentially the first country where microfinance became fully integrated with the traditional full-fledged financial sector. Leading the way, Bolivia's BancoSol was the world's first fully commercial for-profit MFI and the first to attract significant international commercial investment. By 2016, BancoSol, together with other commercialized Bolivian MFIs (Banco FIE, Banco Los Andes ProCredit, and Banco Prodem) have become four of the strongest and most efficient MFIs in the world. Competition among them and a host of more than 20 other aggressive competitors meant that Bolivia could boast some of the world's lowest microcredit interest rates.

Figure 8.8, from Richard Rosenberg and colleagues at the Consultative Group to Assist the Poor (CGAP), shows the interest rates charged on microcredit loans in Bolivia from 1992 through 2007, comparing traditional commercial banks and MFIs. Increased competition and commercial focus brought MFI loan interest rates down by more than two-thirds in 15 years, from near 60% early on to about 18% by 2007. Rates have roughly stabilized since. That means that microcredit customers in Bolivia were paying rates

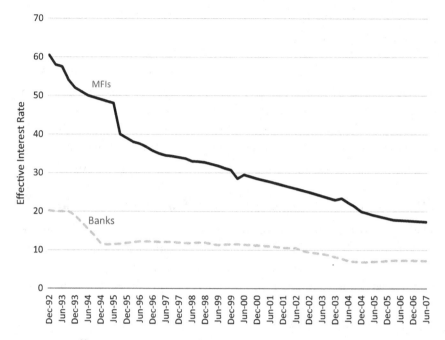

Figure 8.8. Effective interest rates on loans in Bolivia, 1992–2007

Source: Rosenberg, Gonzalez, and Narain (2009).

similar to or better than what many Americans and Europeans pay on their credit cards, as we explore in Box 8.2. Interestingly, responding to the competitive pressure from microfinance, interest rates at Bolivia's traditional banks were also driven lower. (A financial services reform law passed in 2013 in part requires Bolivian MFIs to cap microcredit loan interest rates at 11.5% within five years.)

Though the competitive efficiency story is a compelling argument, and the commercial industry is now serving hundreds of millions of poor clients, many pro-poor voices continue to raise serious concerns. We will look at some of the most heated criticisms later. Criticisms of commercialization are in part about cost: are fees unreasonably high to be charging the poor? Where banking regulatory systems work well, they can help protect consumers and create incentives to prevent abusive pricing. Unfortunately, as discussed next, high rates remain problematic in countries where competition is limited or regulatory oversight is weak.

Other criticisms arise over efficiency in alleviating poverty. Given that billions of dollars have been invested in fighting poverty through microfinance, does microfinance actually help the poor? As we will see in Chapter 9, the evidence on impact is decidedly mixed. Additional skeptical questions have to do with ethics, i.e. in the face of uncertainty about whether microfinance really helps the poor, is it ethical for stakeholders to get rich from investing in MFIs built on putting poor people in debt? The pro-microfinance argument is that the credit and other services are productive and can be used by borrowers to climb a rung or two on the wealth ladder. We will learn in Chapter 9 that some impact assessments support this; some do not.

How Much Does Microcredit Cost?

The Bolivian experience is illustrative of the potential of well-regulated competitive markets to keep the prices the poor pay for microcredit in check. But how do those Bolivian interest rates compare to what the poor are paying for microcredit elsewhere around the world? Have other markets become as competitive? The answer is both yes and no. Some markets are now even more competitive, others substantially less so.

The Microfinance Information Exchange collects data on the interest and fees each MFIs earns as a percent of its loan portfolio. While this measure differs from the main loan-cost metrics used by traditional regulated banks in the United States and Europe, such as annual percentage rate (APR), an MFI's "gross yield on loan portfolio" approximates what clients pay on average at each institution.

By weighting each institution's average rate by its number of borrowers, Figure 8.9 estimates how many people are paying what interest rates (including fees). Since inflation can vary considerably from developing nation to developing nation, the figure uses real interest rates, i.e. adjusted for inflation; the nominal interest rates clients are charged, and which are reported in some studies, are higher by whatever the inflation rate in the country is. The data includes more than 1,000 MFIs worldwide in 2013–2014. These MFIs collectively had 95 million borrowers across almost 100 countries.

Figure 8.9 gives a sense of how costly and variable average microcredit real interest rates and fees are around the world. While this technique is

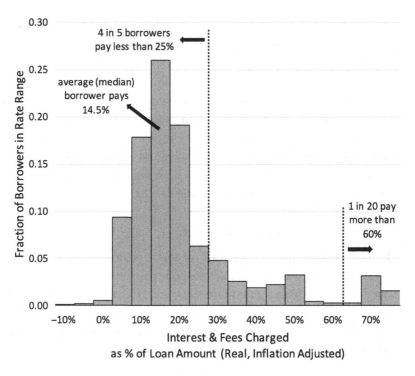

Figure 8.9. Microcredit interest and fees charged worldwide, 2013–2014

Data Source: Mixmarket.org; Gross Yield on Loan Portfolio (Real), weighted by number of borrowers. Data set includes more than 1,000 MFI serving 95 million borrowers in nearly 100 countries.

unable to capture interest rate variation among different loan products within individual microfinance lenders, within-institution is not the main source of variation in rates borrowers face. It is across institutions. Even more importantly, the major variation is differences in loan prices from one country's markets to another's.

As we see, the average (median) microcredit borrower paid about 14.5% in interest and fees, in real terms. The large majority, about four of every five microcredit borrowers worldwide, were with institutions charging less than 25% real interest and fees on average. Again, these rates are adjusted for inflation in each country—a difference averaging about 6.6% during that period.

How do these microcredit prices compare to other types of loans? High compared to mortgage rates homeowners in most rich nations pay, to be sure (and high even compared to mortgage rates some of these same MFIs offer locally). Yet we have seen how unlike mortgages or car loans, many microcredit loans are unsecured, not backed by anything but social collateral within a solidarity group (discussed in Chapter 4) or an MFI loan officer's trust in the borrower. For a closer match, we can compare what people pay on similarly unsecured small loans, such as on credit cards, which are similar (Box 8.2).

**Box 8.2. In Your Backyard
How Much Do U.S. Credit Card Borrowers Pay?**

Americans owe about $700 billion on their credit cards. Like much microcredit, credit card loans are generally unsecured, not backed up by some asset the bank can come repossess if a borrower fails to repay.

How do the interest rates charged on these unsecured loans in the U.S. compare to rates charged to microcredit clients? Figure 8.10 shows what American families paid on their credit cards in 2013. To facilitate comparison, it uses the same scale as Figure 8.9 for microcredit.

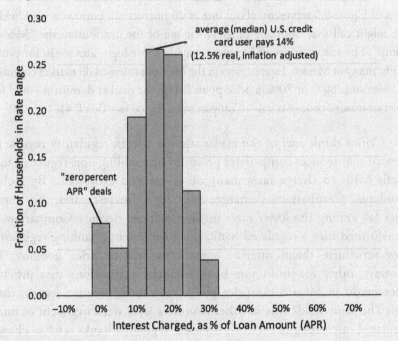

Figure 8.10. U.S. credit card interest rates, 2013

(Continued)

Box 8.2. (*Continued*)

Note how similar Figure 8.10 looks to the left part of Figure 8.9. The average (median) American family paid 14% APR on their credit cards in 2013. Inflation in the U.S. was about 1.5% then, so the inflation-adjusted real rate Americans paid on credit cards averaged about 12.5%. The average microcredit borrower in 100 poor countries paid 14.5%, about two percentage points higher than the Americans. Interestingly, if we look only at South Asian markets, where most of the largest MFIs operate, the microcredit real interest rates there in 2013 averaged 12.9%, remarkably close to what everyday Americans paid.

Data Source: U.S. Federal Reserve, 2013 Survey of Consumer Finances.

Unfortunately, much higher microcredit rates do exist. That bump to the far right of Figure 8.9 represents about one in 20 microcredit borrowers worldwide. We might call that troubling bulge at the tail of the distribution the "Mexico bump." The vast majority of borrowers paying those high rates are in for-profit MFIs, many in Mexico. Interest rates in the Mexican microcredit market continue to hover near 60% or 70%, a price point led by the market dominant—and for obvious reasons controversial—Compartamos Banco (see Box 8.4).

Critics think part of the explanation is a weak regulatory regime in Mexico that reduces competitive pressures by enabling non-regulated for-profit MFIs to charge rates many observers find exorbitant. By global standards, Compartamos charges very high interest rates. Yet those rates are among the lower rates in their market. Because Compartamos transformed into a regulated bank, the government's banking regulators now scrutinize them, offering some resistance to price gouging. In contrast, other for-profit non-bank financial institutions that provide microcredit in Mexico can price gouge even more because, legally, they can. The same holds true in other countries with weak oversight of non-regulated microfinance services: licensed, regulated banks tend to charge less than for-profit non-banks.

Without that Mexico bump, the world's microcredit real interest rate histogram would look remarkably similar to the U.S. credit card one in Figure 8.10. In short, for better or worse, most microcredit lenders across 100 of the world's poorest countries are only about as usury and consumer-abusive as American banks' credit cards in one of the world's richest societies.

In summary, commercialization's effect on interest rates is dependent on effective regulation and market competitiveness. Effective regulatory oversight promotes norms of pricing transparency, fiscal discipline, and customer protection that institutions must legally follow, which when coupled with competitive pressures, can help drive managerial decisions and corporate strategies towards lower prices for clients. When an MFI becomes a regulated commercial bank, responsible to both shareholders and to regulators, its for-profit mandate coupled with a social mission improves incentives for better managed, more responsible, more impactful institutions.

Section in Bulletpoint

- Most commercial microfinance institutions actively pursue a double bottom line, meaning they seek both social and financial returns on investment.
- The first phase of the evolution of commercial microfinance was demonstrating profitability and potential for mass scale.
- In the 1980s, Indonesia's BRI was the first MFI to operate profitably without donor support.
- Today, about eight in 10 MFIs are profitable.
- BancoSol in Bolivia was the first to attract significant international equity investment.
- Competition drove a three-fold reduction in prices to poor Bolivian microfinance clients.
- Potential benefits of commercialization include efficiencies driven by competition and scale, lower loan interest rates, higher returns to savers on deposits, creation of further financial products, and greater institutional sustainability.

(Continued)

- Good regulatory systems and information transparency are fundamental to competitive and cost-efficient microfinance markets.
- Heavily subsidized MFIs can undermine commercialization by distorting market competition.
- Microcredit borrowers in competitive markets now pay real interest rates in the teens, similar to rates on U.S. and European credit cards; however, rates are much higher in some markets, such as Mexico.

Discussion Questions

1. What are the main reasons behind the trends in the evolution of the microfinance industry into full-fledged mainstream commercial business?

2. Should commercial MFIs pursue a double bottom line? Briefly argue pros and cons.

3. Muhammad Yunus, founder of Grameen Bank, argues strongly against commercial microcredit in particular. Box 8.6 later shows one of his editorials. Many of his other thoughts are widely available online. Search to find some of his other main points and briefly summarize them.

4. Do you think that MFI scale and self-sustainable commercial operations benefit the poor? How? In what ways might those trends harm the poor? Develop your argument, with supporting background evidence, in the form of an opinion blog you might post online or a newspaper editorial.

5. Are the rates and fees charged for microcredit too high? Why or why not? How high would be too high? How low would be fair? Why?

6. Pick a country where you would like to know more about the microfinance industry. Within it, pick an MFI. Discuss briefly the environment for the microfinance industry in the country, e.g. its size, how developed and competitive it is, and key social, regulatory or economic issues in the country or region that affect MFIs. Then outline your specific MFI's history and mission, target clients, types of services offered and anything else you find interesting. How has the overall environment affected that specific MFI? (A good online source of ideas for institutions is www.mixmarket.org, a searchable database of MFIs by country. Click on "Profiles and Reports.")

8.2 The Ecosystem of Intermediaries

We have seen that the first phase of the evolution of commercial microfinance was the demonstration of profit potential, which attracted commercial investors. But potential alone would not have been enough to channel mass-market-scale investments to MFIs. International capital flows of that magnitude require a whole ecosystem of financial intermediaries and information providers. Microfinance's evolution from a fledgling, donor-dependent industry to a fully incorporated component of the global financial system involved global banking institutions and investment funds, as well as organizations that provide various information and related professional services for the industry. That ecosystem's emergence has been a second key phase of the commercialization story. Thanks to this ecosystem, the industry worldwide now has substantially more funding from private investors than from government or charity sources.

International Financial Institutions and Investment Funds

International financial institutions and private investment funds provide the majority of the capital for the commercial microfinance industry. While in the past, most MFIs relied on government subsidies and charitable donations to expand their services, many now can turn to private investors or **international financial institutions** (IFIs), which are large international banks—i.e. chartered collaboratively by multiple countries—that focus on development issues. MicroRate, a leading microfinance investment rating organization, reported that by 2012 about 500 MFIs were of the quality that global investment markets seek.[10]

IFIs and similar development-oriented financial institutions include global, multilateral entities like the World Bank, regional institutions like the Inter-American Development Bank or the Asian Development Bank, or even national organizations like the Netherlands Development Finance Company, KfW Development Bank in Germany, or the Brazilian Development Bank. IFIs channel mostly public funds, and sometimes private capital through public-private partnerships, to foster development across the globe, not only in microfinance but also in energy, environment, infrastructure, health, human rights, cultural preservation, and so on. Microfinance and other financial access initiatives are only part of what they do.

Although IFIs may have for-profit mandates, compared to private investors, they usually are willing to get lower rates of return on their investments. In addition, IFIs often offer grants designated for technical assistance programs to help MFIs improve operations or address other needs. In theory, publicly supported IFIs should target riskier investments and projects, filling gaps by investing in beneficial opportunities that might not draw purely private investors. Some critics contend, however, that IFIs keep investing in lower-risk MFIs, using public funding, leaving less attractive options for private interests.[11]

On the private side of this financial intermediation ecosystem, mainstream big banks and brokerage firms have shown interest in microfinance investment and in servicing the steadily growing industry. Their resources, combined with expertise in managing debt and equity financing, have proven helpful for many MFIs. A few of the most active global investment banking institutions involved in microfinance include Deutsche Bank, Morgan Stanley, Credit Suisse, and Citigroup.[12]

Perhaps even more important, by 2016 there were at least 113 independent **microfinance investment vehicles** (MIVs), entities that are Wall-Street-like investment funds in behavior, but orient investments towards microfinance and other social investments.[13] These investment funds have played an increasingly important—and now dominant—role in the supply of microfinance capital, bringing more than $8.5 billion into microfinance worldwide. As Figure 8.11 shows, about half of these funds have come from private large institutional investors, and about a third from public sector development agencies. Until 2009, public aid sources were the majority share of funding to the sector. Now, commercial rather than charitable interests drive the industry.

MIVs include several types, shown in Table 8.4. For instance, ProFund, incorporated in 1995, was the very first investment fund to prove that microfinance equity investments could generate healthy returns (see Box 8.3). It drew international attention to microfinance's potential and set the stage for attracting future investors. Since then, new

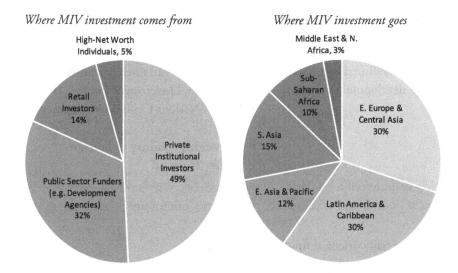

Where MIV investment comes from

High-Net Worth Individuals, 5%

Retail Investors 14%

Public Sector Funders (e.g. Development Agencies) 32%

Private Institutional Investors 49%

Where MIV investment goes

Middle East & N. Africa, 3%

Sub-Saharan Africa 10%

S. Asia 15%

E. Asia & Pacific 12%

E. Europe & Central Asia 30%

Latin America & Caribbean 30%

Figure 8.11. Microfinance investment vehicle fund sources and destinations

Data Source: 2016 Symbiotics MIV Survey.

investment funds have emerged every year, peaking with 18 new funds launched in 2010 alone.[14]

Many investment funds target particular issues or regions. For example, the Higher Education Finance Fund—whose investors include IFIs like KfW and Norfund, as well as Deutsche Bank, one of the world's largest commercial banks—aims to promote the expansion of microfinance into loans for higher education for lower-income students, by financing (mostly) MFIs in seven Latin American nations. Similarly, the AfriCap Microfinance Investment Company is the first private investment fund in Africa, and has focused on enabling African MFIs to build capacity and become more attractive to other private investors. The Leapfrog Financial Inclusion Fund specifically targets microinsurance.

In terms of patterns of where the funds go, the largest 150 MFIs or around the world get almost 60% and the top 500 (i.e. with assets >$10 million) absorb 94%.[15] Regionally, Eastern Europe and Latin American attract the most investment, followed by Southern and Eastern regions in Asia. Though Africa's share so far has lagged behind other regions, the investment climate is increasingly attractive: MIV investments in Africa more than tripled from 2010 to 2015.[16]

Table 8.4. Example microfinance investment vehicles (MIVs)

Type	Examples
Funds established by public-sector development agencies	• Inter-American Development Bank's Multilateral Investment Fund • United Nations Capital Development Fund • Norwegian Ministry of Foreign Affairs' Norfund
Non-commercial funds that aim at promoting microfinance	• Accion Gateway Fund • Calvert Community Investment Notes
Commercially oriented funds balancing both return and promoting microfinance	• ProFund • AfriCap • Leapfrog Financial Inclusion Fund • ShoreCap International
Commercial private funds seeking returns for investors	• Oikocredit • Grey Ghost Microfinance • MicroVest • responsAbility • Symbiotics

Source: In part from Microcapital Funds Universe, www.microcapital.org/microfinance-funds-universe.

One main reason for the differences among regions is relative stages of maturity of their microfinance markets. African microfinance is in an earlier phase in the cycle than is Latin America or Eastern Europe. At early, immature stages of market development the MFIs involved tend not to be big enough or well managed enough to attract private interest. When the system works well, publicly subsidized IFI financing can help mitigate early risks, provide technical assistance to help nurture management and infrastructure, and establish credibility that attracts private investors (again, see Box 8.3 on ProFund). This market maturity cycle—IFI-led early risk taking and infrastructure development, in turn stimulating private investors—has held true not only in the geographic sense of markets, but also in the sense of types of underdeveloped products and services, such as markets for microinsurance or education microloans.

Box 8.3. In the Field
ProFund—Demonstrating MIVs' Investment Potential

ProFund was the first private, profit-seeking investment fund in microfinance. It invested exclusively in MFIs. Inspired by the first fully commercial for-profit MFI, BancoSol of Bolivia, ProFund's founders were motivated by a deep-rooted belief that private investors could be drawn to microfinance if shown that investments were profitable and poor people could be credit worthy. Before then, in the 1990s, the sector had no commercial investment track record. Most of the industry's funds came from non-profit, government, or similar development-related sources with social missions, rather than profit-seeking investors.

Looking to fill that gap, ProFund began in 1995. ProFund sought not only profits for its investors but also to demonstrate to others that providing financial services to the poor could not only sustainably pay for itself but return a profit. The main original sponsors were the non-profit Accion International, the Canadian investment firm Calmeadow, the private foundation FUNDES in Switzerland, and the French development agency SIDI. Other socially oriented investors soon joined, and a total of 19 investors collectively put in $22.5 million to launch the fund.

The focus was mainly on generating returns. However, it quickly became apparent that this was only possible if the MFIs themselves were well managed and effectively organized. This led ProFund also to emphasize technical assistance to the MFIs and to get involved directly in hands-on governance.

Through investment and advising, ProFund fostered numerous high-profile successes, demonstrating profit and commercial potential via several different mechanisms: transformations from NGOs to banks; public-private partnerships; commercial down-

(Continued)

Box 8.3. (*Continued*)

scaling of mainstream banks into microfinance; and even public stock offerings.

ProFund invested in 13 different MFIs in 11 nations in Latin America and the Caribbean, including MiBanco, now the largest MFI in Peru, and Compartamos, today the top MFI in Mexico and among the first MFIs in the world to sell shares on pubic stock markets (Box 8.4). ProFund was instrumental in helping both MFIs transform from roots as NGOs into commercial banks. MiBanco was established in public-private partnership with the Peruvian government, but with purely commercial ownership. Another key success included the transformation of the NGO Enlace Sociedad Financiera in Ecuador into the commercial Banco Solidario, now one of Ecuador's top two MFIs. Along a different trajectory, ProFund worked with Haiti's largest bank, SogeBank, to go down-market into microlending, launching an MFI called Sogesol. As a founding partner, ProFund gave SogeBank equity investment, loans, and managerial assistance.

When ProFund liquidated after 10 years, as planned, it generated an 6% average annual return for its investors, especially notable given political instability and currency volatility in Latin America during the period. More importantly, the demonstration effect clearly worked. Within a year after ProFund closed in 2005, at least 20 other private microfinance funds were actively investing in Latin American microfinance.

Source: Oberdorf (2006).

By making private debt and equity investments—an equity investment in an MFI by one of these funds averages about $4 million—these organizations have enabled MFIs to expand their outreach to serve millions of more clients. At the same time, they pave the way for socially responsible investors by proving the feasibility of achieving the double bottom line in microfinance.

Information Providers and Other Professional Services

Another group of organizations within the industry provides professional services. This group includes information providers such as credit bureaus, data aggregators, and ratings agencies, and other professional service providers like microfinance networking organizations and think tanks that provide advice and promote best practices.

The industry over the years has made improvements in transparency and standardized reporting of information. Among the most important of the evolving information services has been the integration of MFIs into national credit bureaus. For instance, we saw in Box 3.3 that Ghana's national credit bureau started in 2007. The first credit bureau in West Africa, it emphasized including MFIs in a national system of standardized reporting and sharing information among banks and other regulated financial institutions. Such systems make better information about clients available to MFIs, which helps reduce risks that clients become over-indebted, helps reduce transactions costs for processing new clients, and improves abilities to manage loan portfolios; all of which makes MFIs more attractive to commercial investors.

Such information sharing has value enough that in countries without national credit bureaus, some MFIs have collaborated and voluntary created them. One example comes from Ecuador.[17] In Ecuador, all regulated banks have to report to a credit bureau. However, credit bureau services were not available to the more than 800 non-regulated MFIs in the country. This led Red Financiera Rural, a collaborative industry association of Ecuadoran MFIs, to develop a plan to partner with an existing mainstream credit bureau, called Credit Report, to jointly launch a microfinance-specific credit information exchange. Started in 2005 with just 37 MFIs participating in a pilot project, it worked: credit default rates fell 2 percentage points within the first 16 months. Within a few years, 274 Ecuadoran MFIs had joined, of which 204 were non-regulated and had no legal obligations to report yet found participating beneficial nevertheless.

Other information providers similarly help increase transparency on MFIs' financial and social performance, as well as on interest rates and fees charged to clients. A few other of the most prominent include the Consultative Group to Assist the Poor; its affiliate the Microfinance Information Exchange; the Microcredit Summit Campaign; Microfinance Transparency; and SymInvest. They also help establish performance benchmarks for MFI managers and investors seeking best practices. They provide information at all levels of the industry, from statistics on poverty, to microfinance impact assessments, to microfinance industry growth measurements, to assessments of investment environments and changes in industry focus. Some information providers focus on single topics, such as the Microinsurance Network, a forum on issues solely related to insurance services for low-income populations. Others are broad.

Ratings agencies are another service group important for microfinance investment. As outsiders who independently assess the financial strength and social performance of MFIs, they provide much needed industry transparency for international investors. There are four main specialized microfinance ratings agencies: MicroRate, Planet Rating, M-CRIL, and MicroFinanza Rating. Collectively they have issued ratings on thousands of MFIs.

All four of these agencies evaluate two types of measures: institutional and social. Institutional ratings are similar to the ratings on mainstream banks from Standard and Poor's or Moody's. These ratings evaluate financial performance, credit worthiness, and long-term institutional stability. Social ratings in microfinance evaluate an MFI's ability to put its social mission goals into practice, using metrics such as market penetration and depth of outreach to the poorest, inclusion of various groups such as women, ethnic minorities, and so on.

Beyond microfinance-specialized ratings agencies, some of the world's largest ratings agencies for all types of investments, including Standard & Poor's, Moody's and FitchRatings, have issued ratings on dozens of MFIs as well.

Another group of supporting organizations, as discussed in Chapter 1, are microfinance network organizations, which have been helpful among other things in connecting MFIs with international investors. Network organizations, such as Women's World Banking (WWB), are groups of affiliated, but independent, partner MFIs, often spanning the globe. WWB has 40-member MFIs in 29 countries.

Network organizations generally work through a central office with experienced staff to provide technical and managerial assistance to member MFIs, facilitate the sharing of best practices, and help arrange financing. There are more than 130 microfinance network organizations around the world. Many are in single countries, such as COPEME, a network of more than 60 institutions in Peru, the REDMICROH network of 26 MFIs in Honduras, or the AMFOK association of 37 MFIs in Kazakhstan. Others are regional, like Pro Mujer in Latin America or PAMIGA in Africa. Large worldwide networks include Accion International, FINCA, Grameen, and ProCredit Holding, all of which we have seen in "In the Field" boxes scattered throughout this book.

Section in Bulletpoint

- The growth of the microfinance industry has been fueled by commercial MFIs' ability to attract investment and expand services.
- A second key phase in the evolution of commercial microfinance has been the development of an ecosystem of financial intermediaries channeling commercial investment into the sector.
- MIVs play an important role in channeling investments to the sector; as the first MIV, ProFund was particularly instrumental in proving the feasibility of achieving the double-bottom line in microfinance.
- Five hundred or so MFIs around the world absorb nearly all the commercial investment; most MFIs are not yet attractive to private investors.
- Publicly funded international financial institutions such as the World Bank often support riskier and earlier-stage investments than commercial interests; but some critics say they crowd out opportunities for private investors.
- Information providers such as credit bureaus and rating agencies, together with microfinance networking organizations, help promote industry transparency and establish and spread best practices.

Discussion Questions

1. Suppose you were a socially responsible investor looking for double bottom line results. In deciding which microfinance organization to invest in, what main measures, results, or characteristics would you look for in that MFI before you invest? Briefly explain each and why. Would it matter if you were trying to invest money for your retirement?

2. Explain how the information services of credit bureaus and rating agencies help investors. In what ways do those information services help the poor?

3. In what other ways—besides financial—might microfinance investment funds like ProFund be able to help an MFI?

4. Let us explore recent trends in the microfinance investment sector. The Symbotics Group publishes an annual report on MIVs. Find online the most recent version. Review the report and identify at least four trends over time that you find interesting; summarize them and briefly assess why you think they might be happening and if you think the trends are good signs or are concerning, and why. (The 2016 version is here: http://symbioticsgroup.com/wp-content/uploads/2016/09/Symbiotics-2016-MIV-Survey-Report-1.pdf.)

5. Pick one microfinance network organization you want to know more about (there are more than 130, including Accion, WWB, Pro Mujer, FINCA, COPEME, etc.). From online or other sources, develop a roughly 500-word overview of that organization, what it does, its history, size, the MFIs it supports, regions where it works, and evidence of the impact it might have had.

8.3 Accessing International Capital Markets

As mentioned earlier, access to capital markets is perhaps the single largest factor in the commercialization of the microfinance industry. In the previous section we discussed the types of institutions that fund MFIs, primarily through private equity investments or loans. Yet those private investors would not be nearly as numerous or deep-pocketed if they were unsure of their ability to get their money in and out at times of their choosing. In other words, what makes mature international capital markets really tick is liquidity, the ability of investors to buy and sell marketable securities, e.g. stocks and bonds. The emergence of international markets for microfinance securities, then, has been the third main phase of the industry's commercial evolution.

MFIs can get funding from capital markets in several ways, including private equity, selling new shares of their stock through public stock markets (called public equity), or by selling bonds, so-called commercial debt. Each has different implications for the institutions engaging in them. Private equity refers to private ownership investments, not loans or grants, in MFIs made by individual, institutional, and public-sector investors, such as the IFIs and MIVs. Of the total investments into MFIs made by IFIs, MIVs and private funds, less than one-fifth are in the form of equity. Most MIV funds engage in a mix of equity and debt investments, with emphasis on the latter.

Although important to MFI growth, private equity sources of funding are not enough to integrate mature MFIs into the global financial markets. Mainstream commercial financial intermediaries, like big banks or insurance companies, can access global capital markets for funding via selling public equity and commercial debt. These days, some MFIs have matured to the point where they can do the same.

Public Equity

By far the most publicly visible and most controversial, yet least common, source of funding for microfinance has been stock markets. **Public equity financing** refers to money put into a company by investors who buy shares of ownership, often called equity, entitling them to a portion of assets and profits. The shares in the company are bought and sold on a public stock market and are available to individual investors. The company receives financing when the shares are initially created and made available for sale on the stock market through an **initial public offering** (IPO), or what is known as "going public." In addition to their IPOs, sometimes companies in later years issue and sell more shares, called secondary offerings.

Part of the reason that public equity financing is advantageous is that it provides investors with good liquidity. Because shares of stock can be bought and sold at any time on open stock markets, it is easier to get money in and out than with other forms of investment. Early investors know they will have the ability to sell their shares whenever they want to "exit." This flexibility can attract more investors and lead to better share prices paid to the MFI than for less-liquid options. If investors are not sure they will be able to sell their shares easily, there is more risk involved. So, they tend to be less willing to pay higher prices for the shares—the lower price reflects the so-called "illiquidity discount."

However, IPOs are a major undertaking and commitment by an MFI. Before engaging in a public equity offering, a company must first reach a level of scale and profitability attractive to investors. They also need to have solid accounting systems in place and the ability to regularly share reliable information about their financial health and results to both their investors and government regulators.

As a result, in microfinance (and most industries) IPOs are a limited phenomenon.[18] Through 2015 only a couple dozen MFIs had done IPOs or otherwise gone public by listing on stock exchanges. Half of those were tiny IPOs on the Nepal stock exchange, with shares sold generally only to Nepali citizens.

All the IPOs combined have raised about $1.5 billion for various MFIs around the world; less than 4/10 of 1% of that was in Nepal. Table 8.5 lists the rest. As we will see in the next section, compared to that IPO total, more than five times more funding has come into MFIs through corporate borrowing.

BRI was the first microfinance-focused bank in the world to go public, raising $489 million in 2003 as part of a partial privatization program by the Indonesian government selling off government owned banking operations. In a much smaller transaction, BRAC Bank in Bangladesh raised $13 million by selling half its shares to the public in 2006.

Back in Chapter 2 (Box 2.4), we saw that Equity Bank in Kenya went public in 2006, which it did by listing on the Kenyan stock market shares already held by clients and employees. The value of the company has increased rapidly, averaging more than 50% per year for eight years, from its initial $87 million to about $1.5 billion by 2015.

Box 8.4 discusses Compartamos Banco going public in 2007. It has been perhaps the most famous and controversial of all microfinance IPOs.

Table 8.5. MFIs listed on public stock exchanges

MFI	Location	Year	Value of offering ($ millions)	Notes
BRI	Indonesia	2003	489	State bank Partial privatization
Equity	Kenya	2006	87	Listed existing shares, none new
BRAC	Bangladesh	2006	13	
Compartamos	Mexico	2007	474	
NMB	Tanzania	2008	41	State bank Partial privatization
SKS	India	2010	358	Renamed BFIL, Bharat Financial Inclusion Ltd
NPF	Nigeria	2010	23	
Fortis	Nigeria	2012	50	
AG Finance	Philippines	2013	4	
Zuoli Chuangke	Hong Kong	2015	44	
Yetu	Tanzania	2015	3	
GetBucks	Zimbabwe	2016	3	
Equitas Holdings	India	2016	327	33% new shares
Ujjivan Financial	India	2016	134	40% new shares
13 IPOs in Nepal	Nepal	2012–2016	6	11 raised below $350,000 each
Other announced				
Bandhan	India	2018	n/a	

Sources: Lieberman et al (2009) and author's compilation from MFIs' stock filings or press releases.

Box 8.4. In the Field
Compartamos Banco—Big IPO, Big Controversy

Compartamos Banco is one of the great success stories as a commercialized MFI, but also one of the most controversial.

Founded in 1990 in Mexico as an NGO, its early years were typical of many NGOs, relying on grants from aid organizations such as USAID, the Inter-American Development Bank, and CGAP. It also received loans, credit guarantees, and equity from its founders, management team, and several outside investors, including the World Bank, ProFund (see Box 8.3), and microfinance pioneer Accion International. In fact, Compartamos is a member of the Accion network of MFIs (see Box 1.4).

Between 1996 and 2000, Compartamos expanded by 24% a year to 64,000 clients. Compartamos then switched in 2000 from an NGO and became a for-profit company and a regulated financial institution. After the switch, client growth rates nearly doubled so that by the end of 2006 Compartamos had 600,000 customers with loans totaling $271 million.

Table 8.6. Compartamos Banco

Began microfinance operations	1990
Locations	Mexico, Guatemala, Peru
Clients (2015)	2.86 million borrowers; 233,685 savers
Women as % of borrowers	88.2%
Self-sufficiency ratio	135%
Legal status	Commercial bank, publicly traded

This growth and associated profitability allowed the bank in 2007 to complete an initial public offering of its stock, selling about 30% of its shares to the public. The IPO raised about $474 million for Compartamos's initial investors. Note however that no new shares were issued. The IPO involved only selling existing shares owned by early

(Continued)

Box 8.4. (*Continued*)

investors. The proceeds went to those principal shareholders rather than to the bank itself.

The IPO was commonly viewed as a huge success; but for whom? The early investors, certainly. The non-profit Accion International, for example, made $143 million from an initial $1 million invested. An astonishing gain by any standard. The overall estimated average gain for early investors was an amazing 187% *annual* return. Yet the success story is mitigated by the fact that poor customers were paying interest rates above 80% a year. Even by 2015 rates remained in the 80% APR range (helping account for the Mexico bump).

Compartamos has been vigorously criticized by many, notably Grameen Bank founder Muhammad Yunus, for exploiting the poor to generate profits for its shareholders. The truth probably lies somewhere in between Yunus and equally vocal proponents of commercialization. Most of the return the initial external investors received from the IPO was reinvested in development-related efforts, and the bank's outreach increased significantly to millions of poor clients, without relying on subsidies. But the question of how much interest is too much remains.

Sources: Lieberman et al (2009); mixmarket.org.

The next major IPO in the timeline, SKS in India, raised $358 million when it went public in 2010. SKS (now called BFIL, Bharat Financial Inclusion Ltd) was a huge and rapidly growing MFI, then reaching about 5 million poor women in India. We noted in Chapter 7 that 100% of BFIL's borrowers are women. The IPO marked a significant milestone as the first microfinance IPO in India, arguably now the largest microfinance market in the world. Initial trading in August 2010 valued the company at an unprecedented $1.6 billion, and early investors gained handsomely. The company struggled through a crisis in Indian microfinance (Box 8.8) that started shortly thereafter, fueled by political fallout from its IPO.

Its share price fell dramatically, then slowly climbed back to about half the initial value by 2015. Like Compartamos, BFIL has been controversial, not just because of the issue of rich investors profiting from charging high interest rates to the poor. It also came under fire because of complaints about aggressive marketing and sales tactics, and concerns over unseemly pressure that some loan officers—who in some cases get paid more if they sign up more customers—were reportedly putting on clients.

Beyond a few smaller banks that went public in 2012 to 2015, the most substantial IPOs after SKS/BFIL were also MFIs from India. Two more of the very largest MFIs in India, Equitas Holdings and Ujjivan Financial, went public in 2016. Each boasts millions of clients, and the hundreds of millions of dollars in their IPOs rival their main competitor BFIL. A fourth very large Indian MFI, Bandhan (see Box 5.5), also announced plans to go public by 2018.

In short, despite their limited number and associated controversies, most microfinance public listings have been successful, some dramatically, from both the MFIs' and the initial investors' points of view. That track record, combined with the increasing numbers of IPOs beginning in 2013, suggests that further growth in microfinance public equity offerings is sure to come.

Commercial Debt

Debt securities, sometimes known as fixed-income financing, are currently the most common form of microfinance investment, making up more than four-fifths of all capital from microfinance investment funds.[19] This type of financing can be broken down into two segments: local bond issues and international debt issues.

A local bond issue occurs when an MFI sells bonds to local investors. Bonds are essentially an IOU, a contractual promise to repay. That promise is backed by the MFI itself. In 2002 and 2003, for example, Peruvian MFI MiBanco issued 50 million Peruvian nuevo soles worth of local bonds (about $14.5 million) in order to fund the bank's growth, and sold the bonds to investors within Peru.[20] Local bond financing is safer than international debt issues because no risk of foreign exchange or currency value fluctuation is involved. However, it does require the availability of local investors with enough funds, which can be a challenge in countries lacking deep traditional financial sectors.

International debt financing is cross-border, with loans usually made by large global banks and investment funds to individual MFIs. These loans differ from local bond issues in their typically larger sizes, complexity, and risk. International capital markets are enormous and loans provided through them are usually very large as well. Only top-tier MFIs with strong track records, good balance sheets, and transparent financial reporting, and that are well-rated by ratings agencies—i.e. those 500 or so investment quality institutions noted earlier—qualify for international debt funding. As Box 8.5 shows, from an investor's point of view microfinance international debt investments have proven surprisingly steady performers

Even before Compartamos Banco leveraged public equity markets, it was a major early benefactor of commercial debt securitization. About the same time and size as MiBanco's local bond issue in Peru, in 2002 Compartamos issued 200 million Mexican pesos in local bonds to private investors in Mexico. That set the stage for a 2.5-times larger debt issue in 2004, when Compartamos sold 500 million Mexican pesos (worth ~$43 million at the time) in bonds to international investors. Because this was early in the emergence of commercial microfinance, investors were wary.

Box 8.5. Dig Deeper
Microfinance Debt's Surprisingly Steady Performance

Invest in some stock or bond, and over time the value can rise or fall. But most investments do not earn exactly the same rate all the time. Some years are worse than others; there is volatility, meaning risk for investors.

With both returns and volatility in mind, look at Figure 8.12, from analysts at Symbiotics, a leading player in microfinance investment funds. It shows the changing value of investing $100 in five different types of investments over 10 years, 2003–2013.

(Continued)

Box 8.5. (*Continued*)

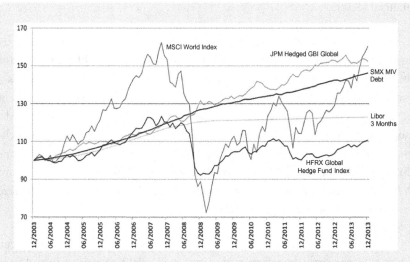

Figure 8.12. Risk and return comparisons for microfinance debt investments

Source: Dominicé, Holmegaard, and Narayanan (2014).

The MSCI World Index—a portfolio of stocks from developing nations—had the best 10-year return on the chart. If you sold at the end of 2013, you gained about 60% over the 10 years. But along the way the ride is a risky roller coaster. Had you needed to sell in 2008, you would have instead lost nearly 30%. With high volatility, high risk.

The investment type ending lowest, global hedge funds, fluctuated too, but not as wildly, with lower downside risk. The tradeoff for the lower risk: a paltry 1% or so average gain per year. An even lower volatility, but also low return investment, was the lightest-shade line that ends second lowest. It shows "LIBOR 3 Months." LIBOR is the acronym for the rate banks pay each other for short-term loans— steady, low risk with very little fluctuation. The problem was, once the Great Recession hit in 2008 those interbank rates essentially flatlined. Policymakers at the U.S. Federal Reserve drove short-term interest rates to near zero. Banks' short-term lending investments would not have lost money, but stopped making much return at all.

(*Continued*)

Box 8.5. (*Continued*)

Now, consider the darkest line, the SMX index of microfinance bonds; i.e. loans by commercial investors to MFIs. Like LIBOR, commercial microfinance debt shows remarkably little volatility. It was very low risk. Yet unlike the interbank index, microfinance debt investments climbed steadily, right through the Great Recession. Overall, the microfinance debt investment gained almost twice as much as LIBOR, and with hardly more risk. In fact, it performed almost as well (+46%) as the second highest-ending option, a basket of major non-U.S. bonds (+52%), but with almost none of the latter's volatility.

Hoping to help establish a track record for microfinance debt securities, the World Bank's International Finance Corporation, an IFI, stepped in to guarantee about a third of the debt. The guarantee limited the investors' downside risk should Compartamos default. Five years later, Compartamos again went to international debt markets, borrowing three-fold more, 1.5 billion pesos. This time however, with a track record of profitability and its IPO completed, there was no need for a World Bank guarantee. By that time, commercial investors were willing to bear the full risk, providing another example of the role IFIs can play in demonstrating microfinance investment worthiness.

Loans given to MFIs by large international banks and funds are often denominated in widely accepted stable or "hard" currencies, like U.S. dollars, Japanese yen, or euros rather than local currencies. From the MFI's point of view, that increases foreign exchange risk; they could end up owing more if their local currency devalues. For these reasons, some industry experts believe that the ratio of international debt to local debt and equity financing will decrease in the future.[21]

That last point raises one further example service that has emerged to support the industry; high inflation and associated big fluctuations in currency value are unfortunately common characteristics of developing countries. To attract investors, it can be useful to hedge against these risks. Currency hedging is essentially like buying insurance against fluctuations.

But currency hedging can be expensive, particularly for minor currencies, and may not even be possible in some of the more under developed and risky markets in which MFIs operate.

One effort aimed at reducing this currency risk barrier to the expansion of microfinance is MFX Solutions, a company started in 2009 by a group of microfinance-related organizations who saw the industry's growing need for currency hedging services. MFX remains the only firm specifically dedicated to offering currency hedging products—covering 45 currencies as of 2016—to investors seeking social impact. The majority of their customers are microfinance investors, MIVs in particular.

Investing MIVs who opt to hedge often are willing to pay for the insurance-like products because they want to fund MFIs in the MFIs' own local currencies. It is mostly a social-mission decision, even for profit-oriented investors. From a purely profit-seeking point of view, the expense of hedging means it usually makes more sense for MIVs to invest in dollars rather than local currencies. But using local currency instead of dollars is of interest to social-mission-oriented investors because it is ultimately cheaper for the MFIs—who then do not have to worry about any risks or expenses from currency trading—and also for the micro borrowers, because the MFIs do not have to raise prices to pass on currency risk. Without the insurance of hedging, using local currencies would put the investing MIVs' portfolios at risk. This is a good example of the tensions social investors face between social and financial bottom lines.

Section in Bulletpoint

- The third main phase of the industry's commercial evolution is the ability of investors to buy and sell MFI stocks and bonds on capital markets.
- Commercial MFIs can access capital markets through corporate debt issues and through both private and public equity financing.

(Continued)

(Continued)

- Selling equity shares provides investors with greater liquidity, but public offerings are, so far, uncommon in microfinance. An institution must first attain an attractive level of scale or profitability before it can offer shares to the public.
- Global banks have made substantial microfinance investments and also provide services helping MFIs issue debt and sell shares.
- When issuing commercial debt, local financing is safer than international because there is no exchange rate risk; but that requires a domestic financial sector of a large scale often lacking in developing nations.
- Private equity refers to private investments in MFIs made by individual, institutional, and public-sector international finance institutions.

Discussion Questions

1. In terms of setting goals and helping the success of an MFI, how and why might it matter who owns it? How might different kinds of owners differ in how they measure success of an MFI?

2. What are some advantages and disadvantages for an MFI to go public?

3. Do you think IPOs for microfinance banks go against the socially motivated goals of microfinance? Are the missions of profitable IPO banks like BRI and Compartamos still well-aligned with the socially responsible principles that they were founded on? Why or why not?

4. Some developing countries are politically unstable. Some risks not discussed in this chapter are socio-political: political unrest, war, corrupt government institutions, and so on. How do you think these types of risks might affect the microfinance industry's ability to grow and mature? How might those risks influence investor's decisions? Do you think stability is necessary for an MFI to be sustainable?

8.4 The Social Mission Debate

Do the poor benefit or lose from profit-seeking, commercial microfinance? It has been one of the most hotly contested issues in the field of microfinance. The central concern is that profit-seeking organizations could lose focus on serving the poor. Can profit chasers really keep the best interest of the poor front and center?

Grameen Bank founder and Nobel Peace Prize winner Muhammad Yunus has been one of the most vocal critics of commercialization, as his *New York Times* editorial in Box 8.6 suggests.

Box 8.6. Faces
Muhammad Yunus—The Loudest Voice in Dissent

Grameen Bank founder Muhammad Yunus is one of the most outspoken critics of commercialization. This editorial, among his most influential, appeared in the *New York Times*.

Sacrificing Microcredit for Megaprofits
By Muhammad Yunus, January 14, 2011.

Dhaka, Bangladesh. In the 1970s, when I began working here on what would eventually be called "microcredit," one of my goals was to eliminate the presence of loan sharks who grow rich by preying on the poor. In 1983, I founded Grameen Bank to provide small loans that people, especially poor women, could use to bring themselves out of poverty. At that  time, I never imagined that one day microcredit would give rise to its own breed of loan sharks.

But it has. And as a result, many borrowers in India have been defaulting on their microloans, which could then result in lenders

(Continued)

Box 8.6. (*Continued*)

being driven out of business. India's crisis points to a clear need to get microcredit back on track. Troubles with microcredit began around 2005, when many lenders started looking for ways to make a profit on the loans by shifting from their status as nonprofit organizations to commercial enterprises. In 2007, Compartamos, a Mexican bank, became Latin America's first microcredit bank to go public. And this past August, SKS Microfinance, the largest bank of its kind in India, raised $358 million in an initial public offering.

To ensure that the small loans would be profitable for their shareholders, such banks needed to raise interest rates and engage in aggressive marketing and loan collection. The kind of empathy that had once been shown toward borrowers when the lenders were nonprofits disappeared. The people whom microcredit was supposed to help were being harmed. In India, borrowers came to believe lenders were taking advantage of them, and stopped repaying their loans.

Commercialization has been a terrible wrong turn for microfinance, and it indicates a worrying "mission drift" in the motivation of those lending to the poor. Poverty should be eradicated, not seen as a money-making opportunity.

There are serious practical problems with treating microcredit as an ordinary profit-maximizing business. Instead of creating wholesale funds dedicated to lending money to microfinance institutions, as Bangladesh has done, these commercial organizations raise larger sums in volatile international financial markets, and then transmit financial risks to the poor.

Furthermore, it means commercial microcredit institutions are subject to demands for ever-increasing profits, which can only come in the form of higher interest rates charged to the poor, defeating the very purpose of the loans.

Some advocates of commercialization say it's the only way to attract the money that's needed to expand the availability of microcredit

(*Continued*)

Box 8.6. (*Continued*)

and to "liberate" the system from dependence on foundations and other charitable donors. But it is possible to harness investment in microcredit—and even make a profit—without working through either charities or global financial markets.

Grameen Bank, where I am managing director, has 2,500 branches in Bangladesh. It lends out more than $100 million a month, from loans of less than $10 for beggars in our "Struggling Members" program, to micro-enterprise loans of about $1,000. Most branches are financially self-reliant, dependent only on deposits from ordinary Bangladeshis. When borrowers join the bank, they open a savings account. All borrowers have savings accounts at the bank, many with balances larger than their loans. And every year, the bank's profits are returned to the borrowers—97% of them poor women—in the form of dividends.

More microcredit institutions should adopt this model. The community needs to reaffirm the original definition of microcredit, abandon commercialization and turn back to serving the poor.

Stricter government regulation could help. The maximum interest rate should not exceed the cost of the fund—meaning the cost that is incurred by the bank to procure the money to lend—plus 15% of the fund. That 15% goes to cover operational costs and contribute to profit. In the case of Grameen Bank, the cost of fund is 10%. So, the maximum interest rate could be 25%. However, we charge 20% to the borrowers. The ideal "spread" between the cost of the fund and the lending rate should be close to 10%.

To enforce such a cap, every country where microloans are made needs a microcredit regulatory authority. Bangladesh, which has the most microcredit borrowers per square mile in the world, has had such an authority for several years, and it is devoted to ensuring transparency in lending and prevented excessive interest rates and collection practices. In the future, it may be able to accredit microfinance banks.

(Continued)

Box 8.6. (*Continued*)

India, with its burgeoning microcredit sector, is most in need of a similar agency.

There are always people eager to take advantage of the vulnerable. But credit programs that seek to profit from the suffering of the poor should not be described as "microcredit," and investors who own such programs should not be allowed to benefit from the trust and respect that microcredit banks have rightly earned.

Governments are responsible for preventing such abuse. In 1997, then First Lady Hillary Clinton and Prime Minister Sheikh Hasina of Bangladesh met with other world leaders to commit to providing 100 million poor people with microloans and other financial services by 2005. At the time, it looked like an utterly impossible task, but by 2006 we had achieved it. World leaders should come together again to provide the powerful and visionary leadership to help steer microcredit back on course.

Sources: New York Times. Photo © 2013 University of Salford, cropped; used under Creative Commons 2.0.

Professor Yunus and many others argue along two lines. The first is questioning the ethics of rich investors profiting from the poor. Professor Yunus equates the ethical behavior of today's commercial MFIs with the predatory loan sharks he aimed to displace when founding Grameen. As we noted earlier, he was especially outspoken against the extraordinary wealth created for rich investors by MFI IPOs like Compartamos and SKS.

The second line of concern is mission drift: how commercialization might shift the goals and focus of MFIs from generating returns for society to generating returns for shareholders. By adding shareholders to the equation, a commercial MFI now has two responsibilities: creating profits for its investors as well as providing superior products and services to its clients.

Unfortunately, even though the poorest of the poor may have the most immediate need for financial services, they are rarely the most profitable customers. Thus, an MFI concerned about profitability could move away from the very poorest and serve clients that earn them a higher return. Even though commercialization increases the outreach of MFIs in theory, does it actually mean increasing the client base and loan portfolio by serving higher-income clients, while backing away from poverty alleviation among those most in need?

One indication of potential mission drift is the size of clients' loans. Poorer clients on average take out smaller loans; those with less income have lower ability to pay back larger loans. Critics of commercialization often point to data on average loan size. In Table 8.2 the average loan from for-profit MFIs was $855 compared to $537 for non-profit MFIs. This discrepancy of nearly 60% could be an indication that for-profit MFIs serve higher-income clients, while non-profits generally reach poorer clients.[22] For example, Box 8.7 outlines how the family of for-profit MFIs in the ProCredit Group deliberately underwent a shift like this expressly towards larger loan sizes for relatively higher-income small business clients.

Because larger loans are more cost-efficient to manage, effective interest rates tend to average a bit lower on larger loans. We saw this in Figure 8.7

Box 8.7. In the Field
The ProCredit Group Withdraws from Small Loans

The ProCredit Group is a collection of 16 separately managed commercial MFI banks and one non-bank financial institution across Eastern Europe, Africa and Latin America. The banks are tied together under one umbrella organization called ProCredit Holding, in Germany. The central organization provides the individual MFIs with financing, as well as specialized services such as internal audit support, risk management, marketing, and employee training. This structure allows the various banks to operate independently and to adapt to local environments, while also enabling economies of scale across the larger group and enhancing their ability to attract commercial investments.

(Continued)

Box 8.7. (*Continued*)

Table 8.7. ProCredit Group

Began microfinance operations	1998
Locations	E. Europe, Africa, Latin America
Clients (Dec 2015)	1.2 million depositors; 0.3 million borrowers
Women as % of borrowers	Varies
Self-sufficiency ratio	Varies; overall profitable
Legal status	16 commercial banks and 1 NBFI, all under one holding company

ProCredit began in 1998. A group of development-related consultants created an investment fund to help launch MFIs around the world. That fund later transitioned into a microfinance bank holding company, and the MFIs transformed into commercial banks. By the end of 2009, ProCredit banks had grown to 831 branches and outlets. Collectively, they had more than 920,000 loans and 3.8 million deposit accounts. But since then, as Table 8.4 showed, that customer base has fallen by two-thirds. Why? A shift in strategy away from small accounts.

Consistent with fears about mission drift, ProCredit in 2009 withdrew from issuing any further small loans, those below €10,000, because of increased repayment problems during the Great Recession global economic downturn. ProCredit refocused on financial services for small businesses rather than microfinance for retail customers. The new strategy led to growth in revenues and assets but a marked reduction in the number of clients served. By 2016, only 5% of the loan portfolio remained in loans for €10,000 or less, down from about one-third in 2009.

ProCredit for many years was an outspoken proponent of commercial microfinance, maintaining that MFIs cannot remain sustainable in the long-term if they rely heavily on public subsidies and

(Continued)

Box 8.7. (*Continued*)

charitable donations. They argued that the only way to obtain broad, successful development in the long-term was to become profitable and commercially successful. Indeed, the firm has recorded profits each year. In 2015, ProCredit's return on equity was 10.5%. Even during the global recession in 2009 their return was a profitable 3.8%, lower than their historical norm but still healthy.

With the goal of sustainable profitability in mind, ProCredit now focuses on larger loans and savings services for small and mid-sized enterprises in developing countries. The Group's target customers are sustainable businesses that provide jobs and foster economic growth in the countries in which they operate.

Sources: ProCredit Holding Annual Reports; and ProCredit-Holding.com.

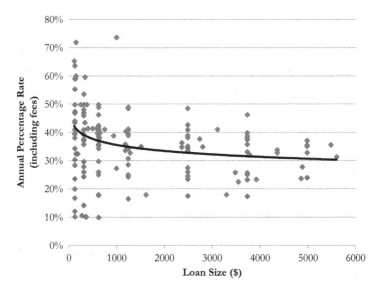

Figure 8.13. APR vs. loan size, Kenyan MFIs

Data Source: Microfinance Transparency, Kenya Country Data, www. MFTransparency.org.

for average rates for different loan sizes in India, and see a similar trend in Figure 8.13 with data on the calculated APR (including fees) on various loan products from 26 MFIs in Kenya. The wide scatter of APRs, from as low as

10% to above 70%, shows that rates vary widely for many reasons, such as loan term and purpose. But, the smallest loans are on average about one-third again costlier than the largest. The pattern of rates falling with loan size is true both in non-profit and for-profit MFIs. This means that the relatively better-off clients with the larger loans tend to face lower microcredit interest rates than the poorest clients.

That said, larger average loan size in and of itself is not necessarily a sign of mission drift. Loan sizes could go higher for at least five different reasons, only one of which is mission drift away from the poorest.[23] Other possible explanations have to do with the maturity of the MFIs. Commercialization is generally reserved for more mature MFIs that can demonstrate a record of profitable operations in order to attract investors.

That maturity has several implications. For instance, more-mature MFIs have a longer-established client base. Thus, a second possible reason for larger average loans has to do with the technique of progressive lending, discussed in Chapter 5, i.e. increasing the size of loans to individuals who demonstrate reliable repayments. Over time, existing clients may expand their capacity and qualify for progressively larger loans, raising the MFI's average. A closely related third possibility that would also help explain higher average loan sizes without mission drift has to do with the evolving structure of an MFI's customer pool even as the MFI continues to serve the poorest. Young MFIs have mostly new clients. For older MFIs, if customers remain loyal, the fraction of clients with experience and who qualify for larger and longer-term loans could grow.

A fourth possibility has to do with learning and reducing information asymmetries discussed in Chapter 3. As an MFI gets more experience, it gains better information on its clients and a better handle on likely risks among target customers more generally. If that learning enables better managing the risks, experienced MFIs may be more willing to offer bigger first loans or accelerate progressive growth for subsequent loans.

Figures 8.14 and 8.15 illustrate the difference between pure mission drift and the other explanations. Figure 8.14 shows pure mission drift, comparing the distributions of income of clients from two hypothetical MFIs. MFI 1, the darker line, serves large numbers of very poor clients with a low average income. For MFI 2, the whole income distribution of its customers has

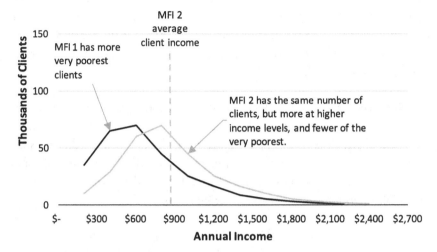

Figure 8.14. Mission drift

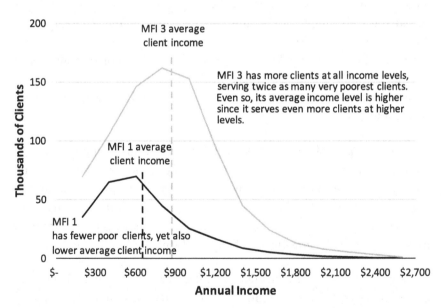

Figure 8.15. Not necessarily mission drift

shifted higher, to the right, leaving many fewer of the poorest clients in the leftmost tail of the income mix.

Figure 8.15 similarly compares two MFIs, but relative to MFI 1, MFI 3 not only has a higher average income clientele, but also has more of the poorest clients. An MFI like MFI 3 might be growing its client base at a range of income levels. It could be adding many new clients with very low incomes, existing clients could be progressing to higher levels, and perhaps new better-off clients are joining the mix as well, helping the MFI gain economies of scale and scope.

Which of these theoretic diagrams more closely represents what is actually happening with real MFIs? The evidence is mixed; both versions appear to be going on. Substantial mission drift is very real for some MFIs. The ProCredit story in Box 8.7 is of a longtime champion of MFI commercialization essentially abandoning all microloans in search of returns for investors. So too, the uncomfortably high interest rates from Compartamos and the "Mexico bump" will continue to fuel critics.

Other evidence points in the opposite direction. For example, Professor of Economics Claudio González-Vega and colleagues at Ohio State University investigated loan size increases at Bolivia's BancoSol, which as noted earlier was the world's first fully commercial MFI. Average loan balances increased from about $125 when the MFI started as non-profit NGO in 1987, to double that by 1992 when BancoSol became a commercial bank, and doubled again to about $500 by 1995. The researchers concluded that the loan size expansion, however, was "consistent with sustained attention to the same market niche," not mission drift away from the poorest clients.[24]

Most of the increase was due to better information about clients, and clients advancing through progressive lending to increasingly larger loans. As Figure 8.16 shows, the median sizes for loans to new clients and to second round borrowers, though slightly higher by 1995 than in 1987, were fairly stable and remained small. Half of new borrowers in 1995 took loans below $107, about 12% of per capita income in Bolivia at the time. Loans for continuing clients became progressively larger in later cycles. Second-round loans averaged 70% larger than loans to brand new clients; third-round loans

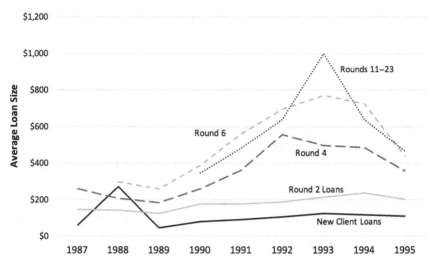

Figure 8.16. Median loan size at BancoSol, by loan cycle, 1987–1995

Data Source: González-Vega et al (1996).

58% larger than second, and so on, with growth slowing through about the sixth round then leveling off. (Some clients by 1995 were on their 20th loan cycle or more.) Some upward drift in later-cycle loan sizes happened around 1992–1993, as the NGO transformed into a commercial bank, but then dropped again as management adjusted lending policies.

A more general noteworthy trend is the average loan size over time in the industry overall. As Richard Rosenberg and colleagues at CGAP found, at non-profit MFIs around the world, average loan size measured as a fraction of per capita income fell slightly to 23% in 2011 from 25% in 2004.[25] Fairly steady targeting of the poor; no mission drift evident there. For-profit loan sizes have remained higher than for non-profits, as we have seen. Yet in for-profit MFIs, the change over time was far larger, dropping from loan sizes averaging 55% of per capita income in 2004 to only 30% in 2011, significantly closing the gap with non-profits. The for-profit MFI sector expanded rapidly during that period, but on the whole grew by moving downward on average, not upwards as mission drift would imply.

Finally, an unfortunate fifth possibility for loan sizes rising, even if the target client base remains the same, is that MFIs might relax their loan discipline, getting overly aggressive and pushing loans bigger than their clients can realistically handle. This can raise the likelihood of clients defaulting and, if too severe, puts MFIs themselves at risk of financial difficulty. Evidence such discipline was deteriorating was a big reason BancoSol's management reined back loan sizes after 1993, as seen in Figure 8.16. More broadly, though thankfully not common on larger scale, systematic risk from weakening of lending discipline has led to occasional industry-wide microfinance market crashes in some countries, including short-term crises in India (see Box 8.8), Bosnia and Herzegovina, Nicaragua, and several other nations.[26]

Box 8.8. In the Field
Crisis and Response in Indian Microfinance, 2010

Commercial microfinance in India plunged into crisis in 2010, amid a volatile mix of industry over reach, questionable high-pressure sales tactics, over-indebted clients getting loans from multiple MFIs, competition with government-sanctioned self-help groups, and politically fueled media hype (still questioned) on suicides among MFI clients. Figure 8.17 shows the result: a substantial loss of customers and market value, reflected in sharp drop in an index of the health of the sector in India. The shock took two years to recover from. Here's a post-crisis take on what happened, from *Mint*, a national business newspaper in India.

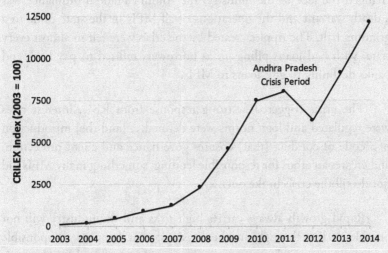

Figure 8.17. Growth of Indian microfinance, 2003–2014

Source: Micro-Credit Ratings International, CRILEX Index of the Indian Microfinance Sector.

(Continued)

Box 8.8. (*Continued*)

Microfinance: To Hell and Back
by Tamal Bandyopadhyay, *Mint*, October 19, 2014.

In a nation where half the population isn't served by formal banking system, [the] microfinance industry acquired a halo.... And then, Andhra Pradesh crisis happened.

A highly successful listing of SKS Microfinance Ltd in July 2010, and strong all-round growth of loan assets created a situation when new funding was on demand in an industry that was then lightly regulated by the Reserve Bank of India (RBI). Then in October 2010, the cookie crumbled, with the Andhra Pradesh government promulgating an ordinance to curb the activities of microfinance companies. The provocation was allegedly the coercive collection policy of [MFIs] that drove many borrowers to commit suicide....

[T]he Indian microfinance sector emerged as one of the largest in the world with Andhra Pradesh—dubbed by *The Economist* as "the state that would reform India"—as its hub. However, the autumn of 2010 changed the face of the industry; the Andhra Pradesh ordinance was a death warrant and the operations of all MFIs in the state came to a grinding halt. The ripples created by the crisis were felt in almost every state, with bad loans piling up as borrowers refused to pay back and banks declining to give loans to MFIs.

The crisis triggered a strong response from RBI...interest rates were regulated and loan norms were defined... [and the] introduction of a code of conduct [that] ensures governance and client protection, and creates an ethos for responsible lending, something many MFIs did not do till the crisis broke out....

Rapid growth always carries high risks and the industry will not be able to live through another crisis, if that happens. Responsible lending has to be the mantra.... The good news for the industry is

(*Continued*)

Box 8.8. (*Continued*)

that the political risks seem to be diminishing, with states including Assam and Kerala accepting RBI as the sole regulator for the industry. Unlike in 2010, microfinance today is a highly regulated industry with the segment of clients, size of loans, purpose and even price being regulated....

Section in Bulletpoint

- Mission drift concerns how commercialization might shift the goals and focus of the institution towards generating returns for shareholders and away from generating returns for society by helping the poor.

- Some critics, including Muhammad Yunus, also question the ethics of rich investors making money from the poor.

- Smaller accounts tend to be costlier and less profitable than larger ones; this creates incentives to drift away from serving the poorest towards relatively better-off clients with larger accounts.

- The cost structure also tends to drive financial service fees relatively higher for the poor than for those who are better-off.

- Average loan size is often used as a measure of mission drift; however, several reasons beyond mission drift might also explain loan size changes.

- Evidence is mixed about the extent of mission drift; clear instances exist, but trends are not universal.

Discussion Questions

1. In order to mobilize savings effectively and increase profitability, some MFIs change focus from the poorest of the poor towards serving small and even medium-sized businesses and higher-income clients. In this sense, do you think commercialization causes MFIs to lose sight of the underlying goals of the microfinance movement?

2. What kinds of evidence would you look for to examine whether or not mission drift is occurring in (a) an individual MFI and (b) the microfinance industry as a whole?

3. Muhammad Yunus says of commercialization: "This is pushing microfinance in the loansharking direction. It's not mission drift. It's endangering the whole mission." Do you agree? Why or why not?

4. As we saw in Box 8.7, the ProCredit Group ceased giving new loans smaller than €10,000. They now prefer to focus on offering loans and savings products for small business enterprises that might create jobs for the poor, rather than on retail micro banking clients. Is this mission drift? In what ways might it be, or not be, a pro-poor move? Argue both sides briefly.

5. Tens of millions of microfinance clients are freely choosing loans from MFIs and willingly paying what many people in developed countries consider very high interest rates. Despite this market demand, should governments restrict the ability to take out loans with such high rates? Why or why not?

6. In your opinion, does charging market-driven interest rates compromise the ability of an MFI like Compartamos to say it is providing social returns?

Chapter Summary

We have seen that commercialized, profit-seeking MFIs charge interest rates that can come down over time as scale and efficiency in competitive markets put downward pressure on prices. Profit-seeking and institutional scaling often lead MFIs to legally transform into regulated institutions, which then face additional shareholder and regulatory pressures to charge less than non-regulated peers. As a result, global microfinance interest rates and fees for client services have fallen steadily as the industry and regulatory systems have matured over the past decades. But not everywhere. Much work remains to fully realize the double bottom line potential of commercial microfinance.

Key Terms

double bottom line
The balancing of the paired objectives of financial stability and social goals in poverty alleviation.

initial public offering (IPO)
Process by which a company receives financing by creating and selling ownership shares of itself, and making them availablefor trading on a public stock market; often referred to as going public.

international financial institutions (IFIs)
Large, publicly funded international banks that are chartered by multiple countries to foster economic and social development in lower-income regions through funding and advice.

microfinance investment vehicles (MIVs)
Behave like Wall Street investment funds, but channel capital into MFIs and related social investments.

mission drift
Reflects concern that MFIs, in seeking scale and financially sustainability, might shift focus to wealthier clients and returns for investors and lose focus on alleviating poverty.

public equity financing
Money provided in exchange for ownership shares of a publicly traded company, where shares trade on a stock market and are available to individual investors.

self-sufficiency
Occurs when an MFI's fees and interest income enable the MFI's own revenues to cover operating costs without relying on donors.

socially responsible investment
An investment strategy which considers both financial return and social good.

transformation
The process where by a non-profit MFI goes through the regulatory steps to become a licensed bank, generally able to take deposits.

yield premium
The rate of interest and fees an MFI gets paid for loans above and beyond the financial costs the MFI paid to acquire the loaned funds; usually adjusted for inflation.

Notes:

[1] Robinson (2001).
[2] Roodman (2012).
[3] Rutherford (2009) p. 191. Quoted in Roodman (2012).
[4] e.g. Christen and Cook (2001).
[5] Robinson (2001).
[6] Soursourian and Dashi (2015).
[7] Reille and Forster (2008).
[8] Malkin (2008).
[9] Data from Mixmarket.org
[10] Microrate (2013).
[11] e.g. von Stauffenberg and Rozas (2011).
[12] Bouuaert (2008).
[13] Symbiotics (2016).
[14] Symbiotics (2016).
[15] Symbiotics (2016).
[16] Symbiotics (2016).
[17] See Hattel and Mongomery (2010).
[18] Rhyne and Guimon (2007).
[19] Symbiotics (2016). See also Reille and Forster (2008).
[20] Rhyne and Reddy (2006).
[21] Reille and Forster (2008).
[22] Microfinance Information Exchange (2009).
[23] See González-Vega et al (1996).
[24] González-Vega et al (1996) p. 21.
[25] Rosenberg et al (2013).
[26] Chen, Rasmussen, and Reille (2010).

Chapter

MEASURING THE IMPACT
OF MICROFINANCE

"Microfinance recognizes that poor people are remarkable reservoirs of energy and knowledge. And while the lack of financial services is a sign of poverty, today it is also understood as an untapped opportunity to create markets, bring people in from the margins and give them the tools with which to help themselves."

— **Kofi Annan, Nobel Peace Prize Winner and Former Secretary General of the U.N.**

Figure 9.1. Sra. Nixon, a microfinance client in Honduras, went from poverty to middle class. A long series of loans, the first for a roadside one-pot stew stand, enabled growing a full scale two-story restaurant in town. But are such happy results typical?

L ook at a typical microfinance institution's website and you will find heartwarming stories about people who managed to dig themselves out of poverty and into prosperity. Often, these narratives, like the one in Box 9.1, suggest people did not do it just for themselves, but also for their children and communities, so that they, too, could have a better future.

Yet, do these select stories fairly represent the true overall impact of microfinance? Or do they paint a biased, too-rosy picture, too good to be true? Single stories are not enough to tell whether or not the poor, on average, benefit from microfinance. Hundreds of millions of people have used microfinance services over the last several decades. Does microfinance help them all? Maybe some microfinance clients or members of their families do not do well with microfinance. Maybe non-participants in some communities lose at the expense of MFI clients who gain. As it turns out, economic researchers have been looking into these sorts of questions deeply over the last couple decades. Using both quantitative and qualitative research methods, researchers are trying to get a better understanding of the impact of microfinance on alleviating poverty, empowering women, promoting education and much more.

This chapter explores microfinance impact assessments and what we have learned from them. Impact assessment studies are widely used by donor agencies, government officials, and investors to evaluate their current strategies and measure their effectiveness—whether they are having enough social or economic impact—and to identify ways to improve.

Impact assessments differ from the financial and social ratings of individual MFIs. Those ratings, provided by companies like Planet Rating and Fitch Rating, for example, focus on how an institution manages its finances and risk, and what type of clients an MFI reaches, and how effectively and transparently it serves them. This type of analysis is crucial for an MFI and its investors, but for development agencies and governments, it does not provide a wide-lens view of the microfinance industry. The impact evaluations discussed in this chapter go beyond the actions of individual institutions to assess whether or not the industry helps alleviate poverty, and often ask if perhaps some problems are exacerbated by the actions of well-meaning, well-rated MFIs. Impact evaluations are primarily a tool for policymakers, foreign development and aid agencies, and investors seeking social impact.

Box 9.1. Faces
Joyce Wafukho's Story from Women's World Banking

Women's World Banking (WWB) is a network organization of 40 MFIs across 29 countries in Asia, Africa and Latin America. Here is an individual success story WWB shared from network member institution Kenya Women Finance Trust (KWFT, more recently transformed into a bank renamed Kenya Women Microfinance Bank).

Joyce Wafukho is a mother of five, who grew up on a farm in western Kenya. As a young woman raised in proximity to the farming business, Joyce noticed that there were no retail hardware stores in her area, and aspired to fill that gap. In 1994, Joyce invested her savings in a small amount of stock, and launched her business in a rented space. However, her plans for a fully-stocked hardware store were hampered by lack of investment capital, and initially she was able to sell only tomatoes and charcoal.

Figure 9.2. Joyce Wafukho used microcredit from KWFT in Kenya to expand her hardware and construction business

(*Continued*)

Box 9.1. (*Continued*)

Joyce contacted numerous banks seeking loans to expand her business, but her loan applications were denied or simply ignored. Finally, after years of rejection by creditors, Joyce's local provincial administration told her about Kenya Women Finance Trust, an affiliate of Women's World Banking. KWFT provides small business loans to nearly 83,000 clients throughout six regions of Kenya, all of them women.

Joining other women in her area, Joyce received training from KWFT in accounting, simple book-keeping, leadership, conflict management and group dynamics. In April 2004, Joyce received her first loan from KWFT for 50,000 Kenya Shillings (Sh): some $680. Since then, Joyce has received, and promptly repaid, five loan installments from KWFT, for a total of Sh 1.2 million ($16,500). The loans have enabled her to increase her inventory, buy machines, expand her business, and diversify into selling lumber and farm inputs, making bricks and culverts, and harvesting sand for construction. In the process, she has also become a contractor, winning tenders to supply materials and construct classrooms and dispensaries.

Joyce currently employs 25 full-time workers, as well as a number of casual labourers at construction sites, generating income for many families in addition to her own. Her business, Lugari Hardware Agencies and Construction Enterprises, also employs her husband, a former policeman, as Director and Debt Collector. Joyce's business has enabled her to build a permanent home for her family and to provide her children and siblings with better nutrition, health care and education. She has also been able to support the college education of her sister, who is pursuing a Master's degree.

Joyce's hardware business has accumulated stock and other fixed assets worth more than Sh 2 millon ($27,500). With access to progressively larger loans from KWFT, she intends to become a direct purchaser of bulk goods from manufacturers. Within the next five years, she plans to open a supermarket.

Source: Glynn (2011), based on original story shared by Women's World Banking.

At one level, if microfinance clients behave rationally and know what is best for themselves, the question about microfinance's impact has a simple answer: the fact that more than 200 million people use microfinance services suggests the industry creates positive value for clients and their communities. Why else would hundreds of millions of rational human beings participate so willingly? Thus, the questions in the impact assessment studies explored in this chapter go beyond "does microfinance work in general?" to deeper and more important questions like: Is microfinance's impact on poverty significant? Are incomes higher? Families' health and education better? Women more empowered? Are some poor people harmed by microfinance, and why?

Moreover, the research evidence helps us and industry practitioners learn about which practices work best and which are ineffective. How might microfinancial services be improved? Indeed, the evolution of the industry we discussed in Chapter 8, particularly the move towards broader bundled "microfinance-plus" packages of financial and non-financial services, has been substantially influenced by the research evidence. We begin this chapter by addressing a number of the challenges researchers face when attempting to measure the effectiveness of microfinance. The chapter then looks into research methodologies commonly used to measure impact, followed by reviewing the broad patterns of what we have learned from the research so far. The short version: while microfinance has not been a magic wand for ending poverty—suggesting that grand transformative potential was over-hyped in the early days of the industry—microcredit does have modest positive impacts on the average client and her family. Concerns about potential widespread harmful effects of microcredit are not substantiated. Hopeful, but so far less robust, evidence is also beginning to emerge that microsavings services may have greater promise than microcredit. Moreover, the industry appears to have large positive impact for a smaller subset of 5–10% of clients, numbering in the tens of millions.

9.1 Challenges to Measuring Impact—Part I

What we would mainly like to know in evaluating microfinance is whether or not people's lives and communities are made better off by participating. It is a simple enough question; but it turns out to be devilishly difficult to answer. Economics is a social science, unlike physics or biology. Real human beings are the test subjects, not bacterial cultures in a test tube. We can scientifically prove, over and again without fail, that an apple will fall from a tree and hit the ground. We can precisely model gravity with mathematical equations. But, when it comes to observing people, the rules are not so clear cut. As Sir Isaac Newton once said, "I can calculate the motion of heavenly bodies, but not the madness of people." In other words, people are complicated and just really hard to study and to understand.

Microfinance researchers face many challenges similar to those faced by other social scientists. Three of the biggest challenges, which this section delves into, are, first, distinguishing correlation from causation, second, what is known as selection bias, and third, the problem of establishing counterfactuals. We start with these issues because dealing with them is central to the microfinance research methodologies laid out in later sections.

Correlation vs. Causation: What's the Difference?

To illustrate the concept of correlation versus causation, suppose a development economist wishes to understand the relationship between access to microcredit and income in villages in rural India. Working in those villages, the researcher and her graduate students gather a large set of data. After running several statistical models on this data, they find a relationship between access to microcredit and income. Specifically, they discover that doubling access to microcredit is correlated with a one-third increase in income. **Correlation** can be defined as the degree of relationship between two variables; variables that move together are correlated. In this example, there exists a positive correlation, since an increase in one variable is associated with an increase in the second variable. A negative correlation, on the other hand, is when one variable increases as the other decreases; moving together but in opposite directions.

Our researchers find an increase in access to microcredit correlates with increase in income. Should we alert the media? Has our economics professor discovered that microfinance works? Not so fast, ma'am. As it turns out, it is generally not enough to simply find correlations.

Correlations exist everywhere in social sciences and are actually fairly easy to find. Many are simply coincidental. Did you know that the annual number of drowning deaths from falling into swimming pools in the U.S. is strongly positively correlated with the number of films Nicolas Cage appeared in that year?[1] It's mathematically true, but clearly a weird, meaningless fluke. What researchers are usually really after is something more elusive: causation. Did our professor find that an increase in access to microcredit causes an increase in income? Maybe, or maybe not. Even in cases where the logic makes more sense than drowning by Nicolas Cage films, causation is still not possible to prove from a mere correlation between two variables. While it may seem intuitive at first to assume that an increase in access to microcredit causes an increase in income, it would be a logical error to do so solely on the basis of correlation.

To illustrate, consider the following simple example. You come back to your apartment after a long day of work (perhaps in the library diligently studying your microfinance textbook?). You are surprised to see six fire engines surrounding your building, which appears to have suffered serious damage. In this case, a high number of fire engines is correlated with high damage. However, it would be a logical error to think that the increase in fire engines caused the damage. Clearly, correlation between these two variables is not at all the same as causation. The causal chain of events that results in the correlation here runs through a different, third variable: the fire causes both the high damage and the high number of fire engines.

Selection Bias Explains Some Correlations

Here is a second common challenge. Another possible explanation for why our economics professor found a correlation between income and access to microcredit, again rather than any causal link between the two variables, might be something known as **selection bias**. When selection into groups being compared is not truly random, results may be biased. For instance, MFIs hoping to improve profitability might locate in areas that are already relatively more affluent, targeting the better-off poor, rather than the poorest poor. Thus, if we simply compare levels of income in places with and without access to microcredit, it should not come as a surprise that those two variables are positively correlated. Microfinance might not be causing the income gap. If MFIs pick higher-income areas to begin with, the causality might actually run the other way.

Likewise, even if MFIs are somehow located randomly, maybe individuals who are more educated and confident in their abilities are also more likely to take the initiative and go get an MFI's services. These sorts of people—more entrepreneurial and educated poor—might also happen to have better incomes in the first place. If people who are already better off are the ones who self-select into using microfinance, whether it was the use of microfinance that caused the higher income would not be clear. In the same way, those who are less entrepreneurial and less educated may choose to avoid microcredit, even if it is available. If true, impact studies could show that obtaining microcredit correlates with higher income, but instead of there being a causal link, the correlation would actually be explained by selection bias.

Selection bias may take yet another form. To evaluate the effectiveness of specific programs, microfinance studies often take place over a period of time. For instance, a study may wish to examine the relationship between business education for MFI clients and profits of microenterprises (Box 9.2 discusses this exact type of study in Peru). Suppose the education program takes two years to complete. An impact study of it might also then last two or more years. However, it is very unlikely that every client of the MFI at the beginning of the study will still be a client at the end of the study. Some people are bound to drop out of the MFI over the course of two or more years. This is can cause problems if there is some non-randomness to those who drop out. This is another form of selection bias known as the **dropout effect**. For example, some less-skilled clients may choose to leave the MFI because they lost faith in their businesses or themselves. If it is mostly lower-performers who drop out, a higher than average proportion of better-performers remain in the data. This would skew any comparisons that only looked at the end, resulting in overestimates of the program's effects. On the other hand, the opposite effect can also occur. Some clients may become so successful during this two-year study that they "graduate" to a regular bank before the study has finished; when these people drop out, there are fewer high-performers in the set of data at the end of the study, skewing the data towards underestimates of the impact.

Box 9.2. Dig Deeper
Business Skills Training—A Study on Its Impacts

Microfinance-plus, a notion we introduced in Chapter 7 to encompass the non-financial services that some microfinance institutions

(Continued)

Box 9.2. (*Continued*)

offer, often includes business skills training for clients. Does such training help the poor improve their businesses and incomes? Two researchers, Dean Karlan of Yale University and Martin Valdivia of Grupo de Análisis para el Desarrollo (Group for the Analysis of Development), set out to tackle this question by examining a program of FINCA Peru.

The program involves training sessions covering general business skills and strategy training, tackling concepts such as the definition of business, competitors, commercial plans and other crucial elements of successfully navigating the business world. The researchers used a randomized control trial that included village banks in Ayacucho and Lima, Peru. In Ayacucho, 55 randomly chosen village banks got mandatory training, 34 were offered voluntary training, and 51 were a control group that received no training. Similarly, in Lima 49 randomly selected village banks got mandatory training, while 50 were assigned to the control group with no training. Data came in three phases. First, at the start of the study, borrowers completed a baseline study. Second, clients also completed a follow up survey at the end of the study. Third, FINCA provided data on clients' banking transactions.

The authors assessed the training's impact in four broad areas: (1) business outcomes; (2) business skills and practices; (3) household outcomes; and (4) results for the MFI.

In terms of impact on business outcomes, there was only weak evidence that training caused any improvement in sales or profit. Changes for clients who received training were small and not statistically significant. On the other hand, even though profits may not have grown, four out of 14 measures of clients' business skills and practices did show significant improvement, including record keeping, reinvestment of profits, and innovation in the clients' businesses. As for household outcomes, neither decision-making empowerment nor child labor showed statistically significant positive impact from training.

(*Continued*)

Box 9.2. (*Continued*)

In the final category, institutional results, the authors did find clients less likely to drop out of an MFI after getting business skills training. Ultimately, note than while most categories showed weak evidence, many moved in the intended direction, albeit only marginally. This could indicate an underlying potential behind business skills training that gets dampened by systematic barriers. This was but one study in one setting, and the central question of the efficacy of training calls for more analysis. Nevertheless, this is a promising early finding in an underexplored subfield.

Source: Karlan and Valdivia (2011).

Establishing the Counterfactual to Determine Causation

The idea that correlation is not the same as causation leads to a natural next question: How, then, does a researcher determine if there is a causal link between two variables? As it turns out, this is one of the most challenging aspects of social sciences. In order to logically determine if one thing causes another—in our case whether using microfinance caused an improvement to the lives of poor families—a researcher must establish what is known as the **counterfactual**, or alternative to reality. How would these poor families' lives have been different if they had *not* had access to microfinance, even though in reality they did?

Let us return to our original example. Our economics professor would have to somehow divine what a client's life would be like without microfinance. Then, she would need to compare the difference between a client's income in the presence of microfinance with the same client's income in the presence of no microfinance, while holding all else equal (i.e. ceteris paribus, in the jargon of economics). This is clearly impossible. A person cannot exist in both circumstances at the same time.

So, what should this professor do? Is the quest hopeless? As you probably guessed, there are methods aimed at approximating the impossible ideal. Generally, such methods start with what are known as **control groups** (sometimes called comparison groups). Social scientists borrow this research technique from clinical research trials. For example, a pharmaceutical company seeking to understand the effectiveness of a new drug in treating illness would undertake an experiment, a clinical trial. Indeed, clinical trials are required by the U.S. Food and Drug Administration for any new drug before the drug can be introduced in the U.S. People who could potentially benefit from the drug are contacted to participate in the experimental study. Some are randomly chosen to receive the treatment (i.e. the new drug), becoming the so-called **treatment group**. Others are randomly chosen to become part of the control group. As long as the groups are reasonably large (often numbering in the hundreds), random sorting into two groups ensures the groups end up similar to each other in terms of the mix of the participants' physical, demographic, educational, and other attributes; except that the control group people do not receive the treatment. Instead, they receive a placebo, a "sham" pill.

Since the groups are otherwise similar, if the treatment group shows noticeable differences from the control group after the experiment is completed, the researchers can deduce whether or not this new drug caused any changes in the participants.

Note, however, one major challenge of finding control groups for microfinance studies. As mentioned earlier, to ensure that the only variable in a study is whether or not a participant receives the microfinance "treatment," the control group would ideally be exactly similar to the treatment group. However, in microfinance it is difficult to find two otherwise similar groups of people, only one of which uses microfinance services. As we noted, selection bias is likely among existing clients because they self-selected into participating in microfinance to begin with. Existing differences in background or locales going in could mean very different outcomes measured after using microfinance, even if microfinance made no difference.

Figure 9.3 illustrates the impact measurement challenge. The two columns on the left represent a potential control group without access to microfinance, first before then after a several year period of time passes. Many factors contribute to personal well-being, as measured perhaps by income, or by other metrics like health, nutrition or social empowerment. Personal attributes, like skills, education, and work habits, will matter, and

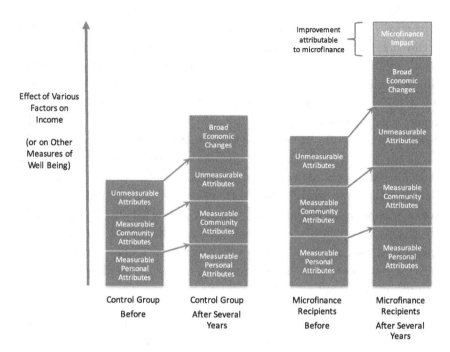

Figure 9.3. Comparing control group with microfinance recipients over time

Source: Modified from Armendáriz and Morduch (2010).

might change with time. So too, characteristics of the community contribute as well; things like population density, and access to clean water, electricity, schools, and so on. A researcher might be able to measure some of these personal and community characteristics directly, like years of education or number of schools for example. Other attributes, such as entrepreneurial mindset or community social cohesion, are harder to measure but may contribute to income nonetheless. More broadly, general economic growth will make a difference over time too. If things improve over time, income would rise from the first column to the second.

The third and fourth columns, on the right, represent the same before-after idea for microfinance clients. Any different initial characteristics compared to a control group might mean microfinance recipients already had a different level of income to begin with. Over time, any advantages microfinance recipients had—say access to better schools and better food—could also mean different changes for the recipients compared to the control group, even (in the counterfactual) without microfinance. The true impact attributable solely to access to microfinance would be only the top slice of the rightmost "After" column. All the rest of the well-being advantage compared to the "After" control group is due, instead, to starting differences between the two groups.

In the next section, we will learn how microfinance researchers overcome this challenge with a method known as randomized control trials.

Section in Bulletpoint

- Two variables might be correlated without necessarily one causing the other.
- In assessing the impact of microfinance, researchers ask the counterfactual question "what would have happened without microfinance?"
- Control groups help social scientists establish counterfactuals to compare to groups that receive some "treatment," such as access to microfinance.
- Research findings comparing treatment and control groups can be biased if selection into the groups is not fully random.

Discussion Questions

1. List several personal characteristics of individuals who might seek to use microfinance services that could differ systematically from those who do not use microfinance. Briefly, how might those differences cause problems for researchers looking to measure the impact of microfinance?

2. Discuss why, as impact assessment researchers try to establish unbiased counterfactuals, it might be problematic that microfinance has already been well established for many years in some countries.

3. Researchers try to get fairly large numbers of individuals in control groups and also in treatment groups. Briefly, what concerns would you have about any "findings" if, instead, only a few individuals were in each of the groups being compared?

9.2 Methodology of Impact Assessments

What does "methodology" really mean? The simple definition of methodology for research is the method used to do the study, how the data is collected and analyzed. However, methodology can imply much more than simply the basic design of an experiment. Methodologies for microfinance impact assessments consist of three fundamental components: (1) the causal model; (2) the level of analysis; and (3) the types of impacts assessed. Although not every impact assessment follows these components exactly, most rely on some aspects of them.

Model of the Causal Impact Chain

The first fundamental part of the framework for an impact assessment is the causal model underlying the study. It outlines what the researchers believe might be the chain of events that causes the impact on clients. The model helps the researchers identify key activities, events, outcomes, and their timing that should be investigated, and dictates when various parts of study, such as data collection, happen.

Figure 9.4 shows an example of a complex causal impact chain for how microfinance might impact clients along several dimensions. Based on a model like this, a researcher might investigate one or more of the proposed pathways, shown with the arrows—such as the links from microsavings to increasing investment for the future in their business or in housing, or reducing the likelihood of losing income due to shocks—to see if there is evidence that microfinance clients differ from non-recipients. As another example, you may recall we saw a different model causal chain back in Chapter 7, Figure 7.6 specifically having to do with the potential benefits for women's empowerment.

Levels of Analysis

The second fundamental part of conceptual frameworks for impact assessment is the level of analysis. For microfinance, Table 9.1 shows a variety of levels of analysis researchers often use, and some key advantages and disadvantages of each level. In practice, studies of impact at the levels of households or business enterprises tend to be the most common. These levels are relatively easy to

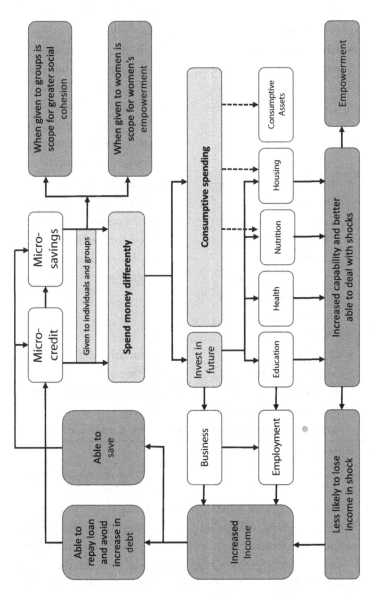

Figure 9.4. Example complex causal chain for microfinance's impact

Source: Stewart et al (2010).

Table 9.1. Levels of assessing impact and advantages and disadvantages

Level	Advantages	Disadvantages
Individual	• Easily defined and identified	• Usually impacts go beyond individual
Enterprise	• Clear metrics (profit, return on investment, etc.)	• Much microfinance used for consumption, not business • In informal sector, often intermingling of enterprise and family funds, and among multiple informal enterprises a family might operate
Household	• Relatively easily defined and identified • Focus is on livelihoods rather than just business outcomes • Permits appreciation of interlinkages across multiple enterprises and consumption	• Sometimes who is "in" a household hard to determine • Not always true that what is good for the household overall is good for every member
Community	• Permits capturing benefits or harms that spill over beyond direct microfinance users (i.e. in jargon, the externalities)	• Quantitative data difficult to gather • Definition of boundaries arbitrary • Can be complex and costly

Source: Modified from Hulme (2000).

define and it tends to be clearer what a researcher might try to measure, e.g. income. Studies of whole villages or communities are useful because social and economic interactions among microfinance clients and non-clients mean impacts—positive or negative—might spill well beyond the clients themselves. However, community studies can be complex and costly, and it is sometimes difficult to delineate the relevant geographic boundaries where impacts might happen. Perhaps counterintuitively, studies of individuals can be the hardest and most complicated to design. It takes considerable time and effort for researchers to study individuals in-depth, and it is difficult to disentangle impacts on the individuals from those in their households or communities more broadly.

Specification of Types of Impact to Assess

Once researchers have determined the overall impact model and what level they are interested in looking into, they then need to specify the type of impact they want to measure. How will they really know if microfinance made an impact on poor people's lives? How will they determine what that impact has been? As you might imagine just by looking at the complex set of possible impact pathways shown in Figure 9.4 previously, researchers can investigate many types of variables. For variables to be of use, they need to be narrowly defined and measurable. Generally, there are two main categories: variables that measure economic impacts, and those that measure social impacts.

Economic impact variables have historically dominated microfinance impact assessments because many related metrics are quantifiable and comparatively straightforward to collect through the use of surveys. Researchers often focus on levels of income, but also look at a variety of other variables such as patterns of expenditure, consumption and assets. As we saw in Chapter 2, income flows for the poor can be irregular and highly variable. By contrast, assets do not fluctuate as much as other variables, so are attractive as an alternative measure of well-being over longer timeframes.

Social impact variables aim to measure well-being and status in broader terms than directly having to do with money. A diverse set of variables such as nutritional levels, educational attainment, access to health services, or contraceptive use can be used to determine if microfinance has made an impact in the quality of clients' lives and social conditions. Other commonly investigated social impact variables include involvement in household and community decision-making, levels of participation in various types of activities, and the nature of social interactions. Such social impact variables can provide more in-depth, multi-dimensional portraits of how microfinance actually changes people's lives beyond just income or asset levels. However, social impact variables can be costly and time-intensive to measure, due to challenges in gathering information on abstract measures such as household decision-making power or on culturally sensitive issues like spousal relations or contraception.

Gathering Information: Qualitative vs. Quantitative Studies

Now that we have discussed the three main parts of conceptual frameworks for microfinance impact assessments, the next question is: How do researchers actually gather information for their studies? For example, let us say researchers are studying the impact of microinsurance on households in India. Some variables for comparison between a treatment group and a control group might be related to household income levels and consumption patterns. Suppose, too, the researchers plan to use social indicators such as children's educational advancement and families' access to health services to see if microinsurance has made an impact on clients' lives. How do researchers actually collect information from these families?

Generally speaking, there are two broad approaches used in collecting and analyzing data in microfinance impact assessments: quantitative and qualitative. **Qualitative research** involves observing, speaking, and sometimes even living with a number of people to understand the complex questions and inter-relationships under study. Moreover, qualitative analysis often involves in-depth interviews or case studies with a defined set of subjects. The information gathered often does not lend itself to specification in numerical form; things like stories, feelings, impressions, or complex social interactions. This kind of research provides a deep, rich understanding of a specific problem in specific settings. However, the complexity and depth of information also makes qualitative research costly and difficult to gather on large numbers of individuals across multiple contexts. Because such studies tend to be narrowly defined, context specific, and involve small numbers of participants, results may be hard to generalize in terms of implications for people in different places or socio-economic situations.

By contrast, **quantitative research** consists of numerical data collected on a set of "observational units" such as communities, families, or people. In microfinance impact assessments, most quantitative data gathering is done through the use of surveys. Households or small enterprises are asked a variety of questions, usually about topics measurable with numbers (e.g. How much did you spend on food last week?) or clearly defined categories (e.g. What material is your roof made of?—a measure of assets). Statistical and mathematical methods are then used to analyze the data collected, explore any general trends and patterns, and make numerical comparison of participants to non-participants. A key benefit of questionnaires is that researchers can survey larger numbers, increasing sample size relative to qualitative research and often improving the generalizability of results. On the other hand, the communication between researchers and participants tends to be more superficial, and compared to in-depth case studies does not yield as rich a set of descriptions of participants lives.

As we explore in more detail later, quantitative studies can be further segmented into whether their research designs are fully **experimental studies** (i.e. any variations controlled by the researcher), non-experimental (the researcher has no real control of variations), or somewhere in between. Those in-between designs are known as quasi-experimental studies, with some experimental elements that the researchers control and some elements not controlled.

In addition to surveys, Table 9.2 outlines key features of a variety of other methods that researchers use to collect data and conduct studies. The next section discusses in more detail the method shown in the last row, the fully experimental randomized control trials.

Randomized Control Trials

As noted earlier, researchers run into multiple problems while trying to determine the effects and degree of success of microfinance programs.[2] The most difficult part lies in crafting a sound, structured experiment that can provide strong and generalizable insights, grounded in clear data, without bias or interfering factors. In particular, disentangling the difference between correlation and causation can be very difficult. There is also the problem of conducting social experiments on real people living their everyday real-world lives. Compared to scientists who can carefully manipulate things in laboratory settings, it can be very hard for social science researchers to conduct experiments in controlled environments. Imagine trying to rigorously control some aspect of people's lives or the communities around them.

Challenges notwithstanding, as we alluded to earlier, one experimental method, known in jargon as a **randomized control trial**, in recent years

Table 9.2. Methods used to collect data in impact assessments

Method	Key features
Sample surveys	Collect quantifiable data through questionnaires. Usually a random sample and a matched control group are used to measure predetermined indicators before and after intervention.
Rapid appraisal	A range of tools and techniques developed originally as rapid rural appraisal (RRA). It involves the use of focus groups, semi-structured interviews with key informants, case studies, participant observation and secondary sources.
Participant observation	Extended residence in a program community by field researchers using qualitative techniques and mini-scale sample surveys.
Case studies	Detailed studies of a specific unit (a group, locality, organization) involving open-ended questioning and the preparation of "histories."
Randomized control trials	Study participants are randomly assigned to one of the treatment groups or to the control group. The control group consists of people very similar to the treatment groups, but only differ in that they do not receive treatment.

Source: Hulme (2000).

has emerged as a leading approach for conducting microfinance impact research. The fundamental idea is for researchers to not just observe reality, but to actually manipulate reality in specific highly controlled ways for the purpose of conducting more useful experiments. The approach has been widely used in medical research for many decades, and has increasingly found applications in the social sciences. The approach does have weaknesses, including comparatively high costs, often short time frames that might miss long-term impacts, and concerns about the validity of information gathered through surveys. The weaknesses leave plenty of need for other approaches such as in-depth qualitative case studies and long-term observational or quasi-experimental work. Yet several strengths of randomized controlled trials are nevertheless compelling.

In randomized control trials similar subjects (people, households, communities) are allocated at random to receive, or not receive, a particular type of treatment. In a microfinance context, this means that a set of similar poor people will be randomly divided. Part of the set will act as the control group. The others will act as the treatment group receiving the microfinance service being studied. Note, in some trials, there may be multiple treatment groups, getting treatments that may differ is some way (say, for a few examples, different loan interest rates, savings requirements, or insurance coverages).

In general, randomized control trials consist of two or more stages of surveys. An initial test, called the baseline survey, is done with participants before the microfinance treatment. Follow up surveys, known as midline and end-line surveys, happen many months or sometimes even a few years after the introduction of the service. The ultimate goal in such studies is to be able to spot key variances over time in the middle or end of the study time period by comparing to the baseline studies. Box 9.2 explores one such multi-stage randomized control trial study about the impact of business skills training for microfinance clients in Peru.

A principal advantage of a randomized control trial is that when the control and the treatment groups are compared at the beginning of the experiment they should be statistically no different. Randomly picking the groups from the same population eliminates selection bias. The control group approximates the counterfactual, an otherwise similar group not receiving microfinance services. Thus, when comparing the control and treatment groups at the end of the experiment, any differences are clean estimates of the impact made by microfinance.

Another method to assessing impact is a **quasi-experimental study**. Like in a fully experimental randomized control trial, researchers establish a control group to compare to those receiving microfinance. However, the main difference is that individuals in the control and treatment groups are not chosen at random. Often individuals in the treatment group have already been using microfinance, and researchers try to identify otherwise similar households or villages without microfinance access to use as controls. Quasi experimental studies allow for something that strictly experimental studies do not: the execution of studies in places where microfinance has already been around for a while or in places or over long-time periods for which randomized control trials are simply not feasible. Researchers try to ensure that the control group is as close to identical to the treatment group as possible, so that the resulting data can logically approximate the counterfactual. A disadvantage, though, lies in the complexity (including mathematical complexity) of creating and designing such studies. And without the advantage of randomization, no matter how careful the researchers are, some risk of unknown sources of selection bias will always remain.

In addition to these two approaches, a third realm of studies are non-experimental. These are not experimental in the sense that there are no control groups. Instead, the participants are exclusively people already using microfinance. The studies are often more qualitative in nature than experimental studies, and may consist of things like client profiles, case studies, detailed field observations, interviews, soliciting stories, or interactive group discussions. Non-experimental methods are sometimes preferred, for example, by anthropologists and sociologists interested in complex social and interpersonal dynamics, or by researchers doing exploratory work trying to uncover unforeseen patterns that present new puzzles for investigation. Detailed non-experimental investigations can offer deeper insights into the experiences of study participants, but lack estimates of the counterfactual. Thus, non-experimental studies cannot generate estimates of the impacts of the provision of services on general clients independent of other changes that may have occurred anyway.

Section in Bulletpoint

- When investigating microfinance's impact, researchers generally start with a model of how they think the impact might happen.
- Researchers then use those impact models to focus on the specific levels and types of variables they are interested in measuring.
- Qualitative research uses techniques like individual case studies and long-term observation to more deeply understand complex social systems that do not lend themselves to quantitative data gathering. However, the complexity can make qualitative research costly.

(Continued)

- In experimental studies, researchers control all the variations in variables of interest, while in non-experimental studies the researcher has no real control of variations.
- Quasi-experimental studies have some experimental elements that the researchers control and some elements not controlled.
- Participants in randomized control studies are randomly assigned either to control groups or treatment groups, so that any measured differences between groups afterwards can be directly attributed to the treatment.

Discussion Questions

1. In both medical and microfinance settings, experimental randomized control trials mean some subsets of participants are not getting "treatment." In what sorts of situations, if ever, do you think withholding treatment from some people is ethical? Why or why not?

2. Pick a microfinance institution you have learned about that you like, and go online to its website. What types of evidence does the MFI make available about the impact of their services? Is it experimental, quasi-experimental, non-experimental, individual stories, some combination? What level is the data? What types of metrics and collection methods did they use? Do you think their conclusions are generalizable to other places or other MFIs? Why or why not?

3. Suppose a researcher is interested in the degree to which a family's race and the economic characteristics of the neighborhood where they live matter in how much a household saves. What level(s) of analysis is this? What types of data and methods of collection might be used? Is a randomized control trial possible? What alternative type(s) of research design might be appropriate?

4. Suppose you are designing a research project to investigate whether easy access to bank ATM machines causes college students to spend more money than if they could not use ATMs. If you could *not* randomly assign participants, what students might you use as a counterfactual comparison group? Why? What concerns would you have about drawing conclusions from your study about the impact of access to ATMs?

9.3 Challenges to Measuring Impact—Part II

Randomized control trials are considered among the strongest research methods, given their advantages in dealing with selection bias and estimating counterfactuals. However, one of their most notable weaknesses is that they are fairly expensive to conduct compared to other quantitative research methods. Considerable resources must be used in order to randomize large groups of people and monitor them over extended periods of time. Furthermore, by relying on random assignment, the method is only useful at the beginning of a particular program's implementation. Any questions about a program that arise after it has already been around for a while will require alternative methodologies to address.

Another weakness of randomized control trials is that they are often limited to relatively short durations of time, perhaps only 18 months or maybe three years. This is because it is often difficult to maintain the integrity of a control group for much longer; eventually, members of the control group will find access to a similar type of treatment on their own, and there is little that a researcher can ethically do about that. Not only are randomized control trials limited to a relatively short duration of time, but they also tend to be limited by geography. That is, researchers constrain studies to specific communities or villages, in order to limit variation that they cannot control. It can be challenging and very costly for researchers to conduct large nationwide or international randomized studies.

Tradeoff between Depth and Breadth

Choosing among methodologies ultimately comes down to a tradeoff between depth and breadth. In a quantitative experimental study, a researcher attempts to gather data from many people (think thousands). By collecting data on so many individuals, the researcher aims for breadth, or representativeness, which allows generalizations about an entire population. However, the researcher sacrifices depth, or quality, in the information. To collect data on so many people, researchers must develop standardized surveys that participants can do in a relatively short period of time.

For instance, imagine going with a clipboard door-to-door in a village, asking dozens of clients each day a series of rather personal questions: How much do you earn? Are you married? Do you have any debt? As you can probably imagine, most people might not be so willing to give up such personal information on the spot. In fact, economists Dean Karlan of Yale University and Jonathan Zinman of Dartmouth College, published a research study they titled "Lying about Borrowing," in which they found that debt carries a particular level of shame. They reported that "half of South Africans who had recently taken a high-interest, short-term loan kept this information from surveyors when asked about it."[3] However, such shallowness in data might not be known or suspected by analysts far from the village, whose only connection to the villagers is data obtained by superficial contact between surveyors and participants.

On the other hand, a researcher who chooses to perform a qualitative study aims to obtain some high-quality data on a particular phenomenon of interest. Such a researcher could get past half-truths survey participants might give in quantitative studies; as a result, constructing a fuller and more human understanding of the participants. In fact, we all perform informal qualitative research on a daily basis in order to navigate the world around us. In microfinance, a researcher may choose to live in a particular village for several months, or even years, in an effort to learn about the lives of people receiving microfinance as well as those who do not receive microfinance. However, the weakness of this sort of research is that it sacrifices breadth in exchange for depth. A researcher may only study a few dozen people, and then will not be able to make generalizations about an entire population. Furthermore, another challenge facing qualitative research is subjectivity. Each of us perceives reality in our own unique way. Two researchers placed in the same village can end up with two different views on how microfinance affects the villagers. Thus, qualitative research is not useful for making generalizations on a population level.

Countless heartwarming and detailed stories, like Box 9.1 earlier, extol how microfinance changed people's lives. In part as a result of compelling storytelling, by the 1990s the microfinance industry became a sensation around the globe—could it be the magic pill to end poverty?! However, in the 2000s, stories also emerged about how microfinance ruined people's lives, leading the media to publish stories sensationalizing the downsides of microfinance. For example, the press in India seized on stories of some clients with micro-loans who committed suicide. As you can probably sense, individual stories—no matter how heartwarming or troubling—do not offer full, representative pictures. They are solely non-experimental.

On the other hand, stories and other non-experimental work can highlight potential questions for further investigation. A detailed story that uncovers a potential link between a suicide and a client's stress over his microfinance debt leads to questions a researcher might now explore using more rigorous methodologies. Occasional suicides among microfinance clients could simply be an unfortunate, yet inevitable coincidence in a nation where tens of millions of people use microfinance. Or something more troubling might actually be happening due to increased debt.

To move beyond storytelling, we would perhaps want to begin exploring by comparing to a quasi-experimental counterfactual control group: are higher rates of suicide found among microfinance users than non-users on the whole? If so, we might then want to dig deeper about why, perhaps with a randomized control trial to see whether stress levels from indebtedness are measurably higher among those with microcredit than those without.

Problems with Mathematical Models

Quantitative studies tend to evoke different reactions from different people. Some place full faith in the rigor, clarity and testability of mathematical models. Other people are skeptical of quantitative studies, perhaps believing them too dependent on fancy math and assumptions detached from reality. In actuality, some quantitative studies are very good; some are not so good. Evaluating the quality of a study requires understanding some of the common weaknesses of the math behind them. Here we will delve into two such weaknesses: the black box problem and the data mining problem.

Quantitative research commonly utilizes statistics and advanced software to analyze large data sets. One of the simpler tools researchers use is a line-of-best-fit on a scatter plot. The resulting line can be informative about the relationship between the two variables in question. For example, imagine a scatter plot that compares the relationship between income and borrowing, where one variable, say borrowing, is represented by the horizontal (X) axis and the other, income, is represented by the vertical (Y) axis. A positive line-of-best-fit would indicate that there exists a positive correlation between income and borrowing.

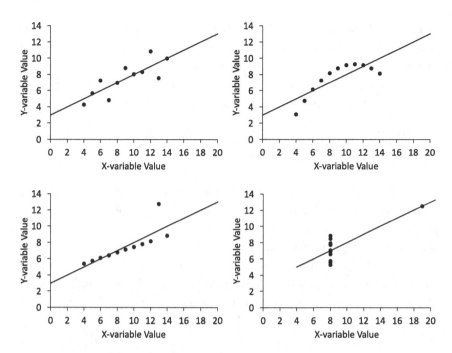

Figure 9.5. Four identical best fit lines, despite very different patterns

Source: Based on Anscombe (1973).

Figure 9.5 illustrates the **black box problem**. Figure 9.5 shows four scatter plots comparing different data sets on income (Y) versus borrowing (X). Each plot consists of 11 data points. If we use basic summary statistics to summarize the data, each of the four scatter plots yields exactly the same average income values, average borrowing values, same variances, and even the exact same best fit lines, as shown on the charts. However, visually they each are clearly very different patterns. A researcher who looks only at the identical numerical results will most certainly not obtain the full picture. To see "inside the black box" behind the summary results, the researcher must look at the graphs. In this case, it is possible to do so; however, with more complicated statistical techniques applied to typically much more complex data patterns found in real social settings, it is much more difficult to check numerical results with a graph, leading to a less than full understanding.

Another challenge faced in quantitative research is the tendency of researchers to consciously, or subconsciously, look for particular conclusions. This is known as **data mining**. To make a simple analogy, a gold miner digging solely for gold may mistakenly miss out on other notable minerals also lying right beneath his feet, such as Benitoite, a gem rarer than diamond that does not look like much to the untrained eye. So too, his eye might gravitate to anything that looks like gold, even if it is not worth much, like pyrite or mica, low value but shiny minerals sometimes called "fool's gold."

Why do researchers succumb to data mining? Aren't researchers interested in seeking the full story, whatever that may be?

Consider an economist who just obtained a data set on several thousand households in Libya. His goal is to examine the impact of microfinance on profits of microenterprises. Any statistical analysis can be run in numerous ways. Run enough model variations and by the laws of random chance, even if there are no real underlying patterns some models are bound to yield significant results—false signals, fool's gold, drowning by Nicolas Cage films. Unfortunately, whether the researcher is aware of it or not, false signals tend to get noticed more than justified by the underlying reality. People doing statistical analysis tend to favor models that indicate statistically significant results. It is an understandably natural tendency to pay more attention to the shiny bit that might be gold.

Indeed, for researchers the data mining incentive is very real. There can be more career reward in reporting results that show something interesting happening, such as microfinance having a statistically evident impact on Libyan microenterprises. This is a key reason why data mining occurs. If two researchers perform essentially similar studies with equally good intentions of seeking empirical truth, the one with a more significant finding is more likely to wind up published in a more prestigious journal compared to a finding that nothing interesting is happening.

The problem is particularly evident these days because computers are so powerful that running lots of different statistical models is straightforward and cheap, enabling researchers to pick and choose those that appear most interesting. Economist Edward Leamer of UCLA, an expert on applied statistical modeling, poetically wrote: "all the concepts of traditional theory utterly lose their meaning by the time an applied researcher pulls from the bramble of computer output the one thorn of a model he likes best, the one he chooses to portray as a rose....This is a sad and decidedly unscientific state of affairs we find ourselves in."[4]

Section in Bulletpoint

- Quantitative experimental methodologies, in seeking representativeness, tend to favor quantity and breadth over the depth of detail and the understanding of complex patterns possible via qualitative methods.

- Individual stories and qualitative studies are not representative or experimental, so it is not possible to draw generalizable conclusions for broad populations.

- However, details uncovered in non-experimental work can highlight potential questions for further investigation.

- Mathematical models can be complex, requiring care avoiding misinterpreting data patterns due to black box issues.

- Data mining and incentives for reporting only more interesting findings remain serious concerns in quantitative research.

Discussion Questions

1. If random assignment into control and treatment groups helps ensure unbiased results, why would microfinance impact assessment researchers ever use any other techniques? Briefly, identify several types of questions that might need alternative, non-randomized research approaches and explain why randomized control might not always be best.

2. Conclusions from individual stories are not generalizable to broad populations. Are individual stories, then, useless for researchers? Discuss both sides, yes and no.

3. Suppose you are working for the World Bank to give grants to researchers to investigate whether micro insurance helps the poor. How might you guard against the data mining problem?

9.4 Evidence of Impact

With background now under our belts of how impact assessments unfold and some big challenges in carrying them out, it is time to turn to the main question: What have we learned from them? Does microfinance work? Throughout this book, we have already seen textboxes on some key studies, illustrating various topics. We will dig into a few more specific studies here too.

Yet many hundreds of studies exist, so it is impossible to look at details of all of them. Thus, our main agenda now is to summarize the overall patterns and general lessons turning up in the research, and to highlight some central puzzles that still remain. Since microcredit has been the longest established feature of microfinance, the bulk of research has focused there. Thus, we will start our review there, then turn to evidence on microsavings and other related services.

Evidence on the Impact of Microcredit

As the most common and widespread service offered by MFIs, microcredit has seen the most scrutiny and analysis of all services as researchers continue to assess its impacts on the poor and their communities. The overarching questions have to do with the effects of microcredit on poverty, well-being, and social empowerment.

The Grameen Foundation has periodically commissioned reviews of the ever-growing body of research in microfinance.[5] The resulting reports are widely well-regarded. The aim has been not only to summarize the state of our collective understanding and to broadly assess microfinance's global impact, but also in part to distill for public consumption what can often be work mathematically impenetrable by all but specialists. The two most recent versions, in 2010 and 2015, were authored by Kathleen Odell, an Associate Professor of Economics at Dominican University's Brennan School of Business in Illinois.

Jumping straight to the spoiler: what conclusions did Dr. Odell draw? What various impacts does microcredit appear to have or not have? Table 9.3 summarizes, dividing the body of research findings into whether the evidence is strong, mixed, or where there is little evidence of a particular type of impact. With regard to microfinance as a whole, she found that the most rigorous studies have uncovered consistently positive, albeit minor, changes in the well-being of most of those on the receiving end of microfinance services. There is good evidence that the credit needs of the poor are now better met so they can borrow more, which in turn increases their business creation and investment, broadens their occupational and consumption options, and tends to focus their spending towards more productive priorities and away from impulse temptation spending on things like cigarettes. Less strong, mixed, evidence in some—but not all—studies is suggestive that microcredit

Table 9.3. Summary of evidence on the impact of microcredit

Strong evidence	Mixed or suggestive evidence	Little or no evidence
• There is good evidence that access to credit leads to increased borrowing, suggesting previously unmet demand for credit. • There is good evidence that access to credit increases business creation, investment, and expansion. • There is good evidence that access to credit leads to increases in occupational choice and consumption choice. • There is good evidence that access to credit reduces impulse consumption of temptation goods (such as cigarettes and tea) in favor of other, often more productive, spending and investment priorities.	• There is evidence in some (but not all) studies that access to credit is empowering for women. • While business profits increase in some studies, the link between business investments and profits is not robust. • There is evidence that access to credit reduces risk and allows households to maintain asset ownership during periods of stress. • There is mixed evidence of the impact of credit on health. A few studies show promising correlations between credit access and children's health. • There is emerging evidence of an important relationship between credit and international migration.	• There is little evidence of large or sustained increases in income or consumption. • There is little evidence of substantial changes in household investment in education. • There is little evidence of harmful effects, even in the case of individual loans and even in environments with some of the industry's highest interest rates.

Source: Odell (2015).

might empower women, reduce household risk and stabilize asset ownership, and improve children's health. On the other hand, there is not convincing evidence for sustained impacts on income, education, or overall household consumption.

Thus, for most clients the impacts of microcredit appear to be fairly modest; helpful but certainly not the magic bullet solution to global poverty. That said, quite substantial benefits have been noted in the lives of about 10% of recipients studied. Furthermore, regarding potential negative consequences, Odell found little statistical evidence pointing to the existence of any broad harmful effects from the provision and receipt of microcredit. Most importantly perhaps, although the impact might be modest or hard to measure, hundreds of millions of people are using microfinance, demonstrating they find value in it. With that, we will now explore some of the specific, highest profile recent studies included in Odell's review.

Experimental Evidence

One important randomized control trial, published in 2015, focused on individual borrowers in Bosnia and Herzegovina who received loans after having been declared too risky by other creditors.[6] The study's nearly 1,000 subjects constituted some of the poorest borrowers in the nation. In the experimental methodology, a randomly selected half of these individuals, the treatment group, were offered loans at a 22% interest rate for a year. The other half, the control group, received no loans. Note the study's relatively short time frame: both groups were surveyed before the loans, and again 14 months later.

Did the availability of microcredit make a difference? Yes, some. After 14 months, those in the treatment group had increased access to liquidity: they were 20 percentage points more likely than those in the control group to have any sort of outstanding loan, and 43 percentage points higher number of loans on average. Likewise, the treatment group were six percentage points more likely (57% to 51%) to have a business, and also had more inventory in their businesses compared to the control group. Among those who intended to use their loans for business, average profits were nearly 1.4 times higher than in the control group ($681 above the control group's average annual profit of $1,772). Microcredit recipients were also less likely to be employed elsewhere for wages, suggesting the loans enabled them to shift the time they spent working to their own self-employment. Similarly, older teenagers (16–19 years old) in recipient households were more likely to work in household businesses.

On the other hand, the study found both consumption and savings actually fell a bit in treatment group households compared to the control group across a range of measures. If microcredit is helpful, this reduction rather than increase in consumption and savings may at first seem curious. While in theory investment and increased profits in a business could improve household consumption and add to savings, this was not the case, at least within the timeframe of 14 months after the loans. In fact, families with microloans actually consumed about 15% less overall.

What might explain this counterintuitive result? The authors attributed this to a substitution by the households of resources away from consumption and into their businesses. In other words, they were investing more than just the loaned amounts into their enterprises. This behavior would be consistent with the loans helping clients overcome inabilities to make usefully large lump sum investments, as we discussed in the saving-up, saving-down discussion back in Chapter 2.

On net, then, the study in Bosnia and Herzegovina identified some benefits for the microcredit clients' businesses, but not any dramatic escape from poverty. Interestingly, the positive difference in average profits was particularly driven by a small fraction of businesses that generated relatively high levels of profit. The lopsided pattern perhaps is a sign that a key pathway for stimulating broad economic growth might be not so much through improving financial access for all the countless run-of-the-mill informal microenterprises, but rather for occasionally unleashing a few relatively big entrepreneurial successes that otherwise would not have emerged.

The study also raised some troubling unanswered questions about potential negative impacts of microcredit. One is whether the reductions in consumption and savings will, over time beyond those 14 months, eventually turn around and become increases, thereby improving household well-being beyond simply business results. A related troubling unknown is whether the move of the families' labor time into self-employment in their own businesses, including the increase in teen employment, might be counterproductively taking time away from potentially more productive options in the long term, such as wage jobs, developing additional skills, or going to school.

Moving now to a second randomized control trial study, Professor Abhijit Banerjee and other economists at MIT and at Northwestern University evaluated the impact of group lending in India. The paper focused on Spandana, among the largest MFIs in the world.[7] Spandana's main product is the basic group loan with joint liability, like those detailed in Chapter 5.

In contrast to the Bosnia and Herzegovina study, the randomization into treatment and control groups was not among individual clients, but among whole neighborhoods. The study team identified 104 poor neighborhoods in the city of Hyderabad where microfinance was not yet available. In half, Spandana opened branches offering joint liability loans to groups of women. The other half of the neighborhoods did not get Spandana branches (although other MFIs did begin to enter some of the control and treatment areas during the study period). In each of the 104 neighborhoods, an average of 65 households were surveyed 15–18 months after Spandana branches opened. The same households were surveyed a second time two years after that.

What happened by the end of those 3½ years? Banerjee and colleagues found an increase in the amounts borrowed by households in the treatment areas compared to control areas. They also found increased likelihood of loans from formal financial institutions rather than informal or family sources, indicating the presence of widespread demand that had previously gone unmet by formal sources. As other MFIs entered the neighborhoods, members in the control group did gain some access to loans too. Nevertheless, because of the lag in time, those in treatment group neighborhoods had had access to capital for longer, and as a result ended up with loans roughly 14% larger than those in control neighborhoods. The researchers concluded that the size of a household's formal credit was related to the amount of time it had had access to MFIs, not simply whether it had access or not.

Again, similar to the pattern in Bosnia and Herzegovina, measured improvements in overall profits were concentrated among the top 5% of businesses. Household consumption and women's empowerment were largely unaffected. However, again like in Bosnia and Herzegovina, the evidence indicated an increase in self-employment for those in the treatment neighborhoods compared to the controls, indicating at least some degree of empowerment in decisions regarding where to work.

Other recent randomized control studies exist as well. In non-technical graphic form, Figure 9.6 summarizes the findings of the two studies we just discussed, together with four other of the most methodologically rigorous randomized control trials, from Ethiopia, Mexico, Mongolia, and Morocco.[8] Geographically, the six studies together cover a diverse swath of the world's major regions for microcredit. For each study, statistically significant evidence for positive

	Bosnia & Herzegovina	Ethiopia	India	Mexico	Mongolia	Morocco
	Men & women, individual loans, $1800, 22% APR	Men & women, group liability, $500, 12% APR	Women only, group liability, $600, 24% APR	Women only, group liability, $450, 110% APR	Women only, individual & group, $700, 27% APR	Men & women, group liability, $1100, 15% APR
Credit access	⬆	⬆	⬆	⬆	⬆	⬆
Business activity	⬆	⬆	⬆	⬆	✖	⬆
Income	✖	✖	✖	✖	✖	✖
Consumption	⬇	⬇	✖	✖	⬆	✖
Social effects	✖	✖	✖	⬆	✖	✖

Legend:
⬆ = (+) significant
✖ = insignificant
⬇ = (-) significant

Figure 9.6. The impact of microcredit: Six randomized control trials

Sources: Graphic based on Sandefur (2015). The six studies are: Bosnia = Augsburg et al (2015); Ethiopia = Tarozzi, Desai, and Johnson (2015); India = Banerjee et al (2015); Mexico = Angelucci, Karlan, and Zinman (2015); Mongolia = Attanasio et al (2015); Morocco = Crépon et al (2015).

impacts are shown in up-arrows; evidence for negative impacts are down-arrows. Areas of impact where statistical evidence is not found, are shown with Xs. The type of loans, target genders, loan sizes and interest rates are also indicated.

As we see from the up-arrows, there is good evidence in all six studies that poor in treatment groups have more access to credit, and microcredit enhances various measures related to business activities in five of the six studies. On the other hand, the evidence on improved income or social effects such as empowerment is not statistically compelling, except for the study in Mexico where women gained (slightly) decision-making power in their households and where there was a small increase in children's attendance at school.[9] Evidence regarding the impact on consumption is decidedly mixed. In Ethiopia, like we saw in Bosnia and Herzegovina, household consumption appears to have fallen with microcredit. Consumption went up significantly only in the Mongolia study.

The Mexico study is notable for the very high loan interest rate (110% APR) charged by the MFI involved, Compartamos. In the previous chapter, we met Compartamos in Box 8.4 and when we looked at the distribution of microcredit interest rates in Figure 8.9. We noted what we called the "Mexico bump," a very high-rate market led by Compartamos. Although the experimental study found weak or no statistical evidence of beneficial effects of access to Compartamos group loans on income and consumption, neither was their evidence detailing negative effects (except for a small reduction in temptation spending), despite the very high rates clients had to pay.[10] Based on the most rigorous evidence so far, fears of potential widespread harm from microcredit appear unfounded, even in the study involving clients paying some of the highest microcredit interest rates in the world.

Evidence from Quasi-Experiments

Let us now move to a study that used a different research design, a quasi-experimental approach. The quasi-experimental methodology made it possible for economist Shahidur Khandker and his colleagues at the World Bank to undertake the longest-term study yet on microcredit.[11] Over a period of 20 years in Bangladesh, about 1,800 randomly selected households were given surveys a total of three times: first in 1990–1991, a second time between 1998–1999 and finally in 2010–2011. However, the study lacks a clean counterfactual control group. If the microcredit clients differed in systematic ways from non-clients, the study may suffer from selection biases, bringing into question the validity of direct comparisons between clients and non-clients. On the other hand, within the treatment group itself, the changes in impact for clients over 20 years are illuminating.

The treatment at hand was the provision of larger loans to households, and the researchers explored the households' subsequent behavior and changes in well-being. The study found positive correlations between microcredit involvement and various measures of household well-being, such as consumption, assets and income. But the authors remain hesitant to draw overarching causal conclusions, given the possibilities of selection bias. Nevertheless, one key takeaway possible by looking within the treatment group itself was that microcredit's impact on households seemed to diminish over the long periods of time between survey rounds.

The authors posit that the shrinking effect could in part be due to the Bangladesh market becoming saturated with microfinance options. The treatment was no longer at all unique. Indeed, initially in 1990–1991, none of the households used multiple microcredit services, but by the end about a third were clients of more than one MFI. This suggests that in a mature, competitive market with lots of options already, such as the one now found in Bangladesh, a single MFI simply providing more loans to more clients does not add much. More beneficial might be additional services such as business training, or other new strategies to ensure continued deepening of impact.

Another quasi-experimental study addressed the effects of credit on the health of children in Indonesia. Stephen DeLoach, a Professor of Economics at Elon University, and his student Erika Lamanna used data from the Indonesian Family Life Survey to explore whether microcredit improves children's health.[12] Healthier children grow more on average, and height is straightforward to measure. Thus, in health-related research height is often used as a key metric. They compared changes in children's heights in geographic areas where microcredit was available to areas where it was not. Children in areas with access to small-scale microcredit services ended up taller than their counterparts in communities whose members did not. DeLoach and Lamanna speculated the effect might come through increased empowerment at home for women, in turn enabling them to steer more household resources towards nutrition for their children, and/or improved social support from women being more engaged in groups and the surrounding community.

However, an alternate explanation is that selection bias in the communities where MFIs chose to operate could be at work. This data was quasi-experimental in the sense that it was from a national survey done for other purposes, not a controlled trial randomly assigning MFI locations. It is possible MFIs picked healthier communities to begin with. Thus, the counterfactual is not necessarily clean.

That said, although fully rigorous experimental randomized trials have not yet been done, the accumulating evidence is hopeful. A number of other quasi-experimental studies have also found similar beneficial potential impacts on health.[13] For one other example in India, children within households in self-help groups—a variation of lending and savings groups that we introduced in Chapter 5—showed better growth rates than older siblings raised when the same households were not in self-help groups.[14] Other positive findings come from elsewhere in South Asia, Africa, and Latin America too. Even if incomes on average are not rising with microcredit, it may be that there are payoffs for improving family health and regular nutrition from things like improved income stability and protection from cash flow shocks or from women's bargaining power relative to their husbands. Researchers will undoubtedly continue to explore this promising avenue.

Box 9.3. Dig Deeper
Evidence and Weaknesses in Early Studies of Wider Impacts

We have focused in this section on recent studies—mostly randomized control trials—and summary conclusions from Grameen Foundatation's 2015 survey of the overall patterns of evidence on microcredit's impact. A decade earlier (2005), the Foundation's first research overview, authored by Nathaniel Goldberg, similarly looked at the evidence available at that time. Here is his take on what we had learned by then about some wider impacts of microcredit beyond income and consumption and some of the weaknesses of early studies. Selection bias was among his key concerns.

Empowerment

Hashemi, Schuler, and Riley, in "Rural Credit Programs and Women's Empowerment in Bangladesh" *(1996), used a measure of the length of program participation among Grameen Bank and BRAC clients to show that each year of membership increased the likelihood of a female client being empowered by 16 percent. Even women who did not participate were more than twice as likely to be empowered simply by virtue of living in Grameen villages. This may suggest that a positive spillover from microfinance is affecting the norms in communities, but it could also imply that Grameen selects relatively empowered communities for program placement.*

Contraceptive Use

"Poverty Alleviation and Empowerment: The Second Impact Assessment Study of BRAC's Rural Development Programme" *(1998), by A. M. Muazzam Husain, reported that members who had been with BRAC the longest had significantly higher rates of contraceptive use.*

(Continued)

Box 9.3. (*Continued*)

[Shahidur Khandker's] "Fighting Poverty with Microcredit" *found credit provided to women reduced contraceptive use among participants. However, as discussed above, the results from Khandker's earlier work may be unreliable.* "The Impact of an Integrated Micro-credit Program on Women's Empowerment and Fertility Behavior in Rural Bangladesh" *(1998), by Steele, Amin, and Naved, estimated that, even after statistically controlling for prior contraceptive use, borrowers were 1.8 times more likely to use contraceptives than the comparison group. Membership in a savings group was not found to have an effect. However, analysis of the actual number of births did not reveal a statistical relationship between either savings or credit and fertility.*

Nutrition

Barbara MkNelly and Christopher Dunford, both of Freedom from Hunger, completed two comprehensive evaluations of Credit with Education programs: "Impact of Credit with Education on Mothers and Their Young Children's Nutrition: Lower Pra Rural Bank Credit with Education Program in Ghana" *(1998), and* "Impact of Credit with Education on Mothers and Their Young Children's Nutrition: CRECER Credit with Education Program in Bolivia" *(1999). In Ghana, participants experienced an increase in monthly nonfarm income of $36, compared to $17 for the comparison group. Participants were more likely to breastfeed their children and more likely to delay the introduction of other foods into their babies' diets until the ideal age, and they were more likely to properly rehydrate children who had diarrhea by giving them oral rehydration solution. These impacts paid off in a significant increase in height-for-age and weight-for-age for children of participants.* "Credit Programs for the Poor and the Health Status of Children in Rural Bangladesh" *(2003) by Pitt, Khandker, Chowdhury, and Millimet, found substantial impact on children's health (as measured by height and arm circumference) from women's borrowing, but not from male borrowing, which had an insignificant or even negative effect.*

Source: Goldberg (2005) p. 8.

Evidence on the Impact of Microsavings

In Chapter 6, we learned about two ways MFIs help poor people save money, namely basic savings accounts and commitment savings accounts. We also noted that, given the potential negative impacts on the poor of high interest payments or spirals into over-indebtedness, some industry observers argue that improving the access and lowering the cost of savings for the poor might be a more beneficial than microcredit. Are they right? What do we know about the impacts of microsavings? Let us look at evidence from several studies, conducted in Chile, Nepal, Kenya, Malawi, and the Philippines.

We start again by jumping right to the spoiler. Turning again to the Grameen Foundation's review of existing research, Table 9.4 summarizes the evidence on the impact of savings.

Table 9.4. Summary of evidence on impact of microsavings

Strong evidence	Suggestive evidence
• When savings accounts become available, they are widely used in a variety of contexts—there seems to be robust demand for a safe and reliable way to save. • Even in the poorest communities, many households are willing and able to save. • Households use savings accounts to buffer short-term shocks and manage uncertainty. • In a number of contexts, extremely poor households with access to savings groups were able to increase savings without reducing household spending.	• Women in Kenya increased business investment when they had access to savings accounts. • There are mixed results on whether commitment accounts lead to better outcomes than basic accounts. • One study in Malawi finds that informal networks and community safety nets are strengthened when households save in a formal account. • Some studies find that savings leads to women's empowerment, as measured in various ways.

Source: Odell (2015).

The Poor Want Formal Ways to Save

As the first bullet point in Table 9.4 noted, the research evidence is clear that there is "robust demand" among the poor for ways to save. This finding is supported by multiple studies. For example, Felipe Kast and Dina Pomeranz, both of Harvard University, worked with an MFI in Chile to study what happens when the poor are offered basic savings accounts.[15] In a randomized control trial, clients received (or not) an offer to open a free savings account. The account had no fees and no minimum balance. Turns out, people wanted it. The authors found that more than half of those offered a savings account actually opened an account and 39% of those offered a savings account actively used one.

Interestingly, this study also found that those who opened savings accounts reduced their use of short-term microcredit by about 20% relative to the control group. A key reason for this reduction is along the lines we introduced in Chapter 2: if savings accounts are not available or are too costly, short-term credit can be a substitute way to manage recurring liquidity needs to cover the ups and downs of uncertain cash flows. The evidence showed that when given a reliable way to save, the poor were better able to smooth consumption as well as to buffer against short-term shocks. The authors concluded that savings and microcredit were alternative forms of self-insurance. Their findings are quite consistent with our discussion of the practical similarities among saving up, saving down and saving through.

A similar study in Nepal by Silvia Prina, a Professor of Economics at Case Western Reserve University, offered free savings accounts to more than 1,000 randomly chosen women who were heads of their household.[16] Of those, nearly 80% actively used them, further supporting that there is an unmet demand for a reliable means to save among the poor, particularly among women. An interesting outcome was that most withdrawals were used for food or lump sum needs like school fees and festivals. The withdrawals were typically not used to fund microenterprises, perhaps suggesting that microcredit is a preferred source of capital for such productive uses. In any case, compared to the control group, those who opened savings accounts also allocated their money differently, spending more on education and nutrition expenses (while spending less on dowries). The families also reported a qualitative sense of better financial well-being overall, with more ability to deal with shocks from unpredictable swings in cash flows.

In Kenya, a randomized control trial by Pascaline Dupas and Jonathan Robinson, Professors of Economics at Stanford and the University of California, Santa Cruz, respectively, also found significant demand for savings accounts.[17] Unlike in the previous two studies, these accounts were not free, but instead charged a withdrawal fee every time a client wished to access their money. Nearly 400 previously unbanked participants were randomly offered (or not) this type of account. Interestingly, despite the fees, clients still strongly demanded savings accounts, albeit at a somewhat lower rate—41% used them, versus the 80% and 53% results from the previous two studies. This suggests that people are still willing to use savings accounts even when there is a cost, since they realize the benefits of saving in a reliable manner. Additionally, compared with those who did not open accounts, those who did also increased their investment in their businesses by a factor of roughly 1.4–1.6 and increased household consumption by 37% on average. This was a relatively large change considering the fairly short time period, four to six months, of the study.

In sum: positive impact indeed. Treatment group members were not only able to save more money, but also to invest more in their businesses, while simultaneously managing to spend more money on household necessities. If further rigorous studies continue to confirm these sorts of benefits, simple microsavings accounts may prove far better than microcredit at living up to its hoped-for potential in poverty alleviation; and without the downside risks. As we will see next, commitment savings may be even better yet.

Commitment Savings vs. Basic Savings Accounts

We met commitment savings accounts in Chapter 6. Clients agree, ahead of time, to save small amounts regularly to achieve a particular savings goal. Often the accounts have rewards or other incentives built in to encourage meeting the goal. We noted that the commitment savings accounts are designed expressly to help the poor overcome the cash flow, social taxation, mental accounting, and self-control barriers to savings that we examined in Chapter 3. If the commitment incentives work, savings rates among the poor should increase. Do they? As Table 9.4 earlier noted, there is growing body of encouragingly suggestive, but somewhat mixed and not yet fully robust, evidence that commitment savings accounts indeed may result in better outcomes than simple savings accounts.

For example, a study in Kenya, again by Professors Dupas and Robinson, collaborated with 113 informal rotating savings and credit associations (ROSCAs) (like those we detailed in Chapter 4) and randomly assigned each ROSCA to one of five types of groups.[18] One group type was given a lockbox, along with the key, which all members could use to deposit their savings, and they were asked to record their deposits and withdrawals; this form of saving is akin to a basic savings account, since the client can deposit and withdraw money at any time without restriction. The second type of group was also given a lockbox; however, they were not given the key until a certain date, by which the members should have saved up target amounts, just like a standard commitment savings account. A third group type was asked to adhere to their normal ROSCA routines, with no lockbox, but to also create a side pot for savings. A fourth group type, again without a box, required that the ROSCA's treasurer manage individual savings accounts for each member. Finally, the fifth type of group was the control group, where members followed the same normal ROSCA structure as before the study.

Consistent with the studies we looked at above using basic savings accounts, demand for savings accounts was high—more than 65% wanted to participate across all groups except the control group. Interestingly, though, not all the types of savings were equal. The incentive structure of the option mattered. The amounts ROSCA members saved depended substantially on the type of savings account used. Those who used lockboxes had higher savings rates. This behavior is consistent with the theoretic idea that commitment savings could help people overcome short-term temptation, social taxation, and other barriers to savings. However, the study did not find significant variation between those who had keys (i.e. basic accounts) and those who had to wait to get the keys (i.e. commitment accounts). Possibly, the need to simply use a key and go to the box and write down their withdrawals was a high enough hurdle to encourage keeping savings in place. These suggestive, but not conclusive, findings will likely stimulate further research to determine whether or not commitment savings accounts are better. Maybe if savings were held with a formal MFI, rather than in lockboxes informally managed by the ROSCAs, there may have been a more noticeable difference in savings amount?

Another set of findings—more strongly supportive of the benefits of commitment accounts—come from a study conducted in rural Malawi by Lasse Brune and colleagues at Yale University.[19] They found substantial evidence that commitment accounts were a more effective savings mechanism than basic savings accounts. Through a partnership with an MFI that provides rural farmers with financial services, the researchers randomly assigned participants to one of the following three groups: offered a basic savings account; offered the option of either a basic or commitment savings account; control group not offered savings services.

The results strongly indicated effectiveness of commitment accounts. In fact, the researchers found that those farmers who chose to receive such an account showed much higher outcomes on nearly every measure. Compared to the control group, the farmers had a 9.8% increase in land under cultivation, a 26.2% increase in agricultural inputs, a 22% increase in crop output, and a 17.4% increase in household consumption. On the other hand, those who only used basic savings accounts showed no measurable changes in any of the metrics. A possible explanation for why this may be the case, according to the research team, is that a strong social safety net exists among farmers in Malawi. Those who were contractually not allowed to withdraw from a savings account until a certain date were better able to avoid the pressures to share money with friends, neighbors, and family members; i.e. relief from social taxation.

One more example before concluding. A study conducted in the Philippines by Nava Ashraf (Harvard), Dean Karlan (Yale), and Wesley Yin (U. Chicago) examined the impact of commitment savings accounts on women's empowerment.[20] A previous study in the Philippines by these researchers found that access to commitment savings increased how much money users saved by 81%, on average.[21] In the second study, to measure the effects of commitment savings on empowerment, they used two metrics: first, decision-making power as reported by the women; and second, presence of "female oriented durables" in the household such as washers, dryers, brooms, sewing machines, ironing boards, and similar items. Results from the study showed significant improvements in both of these metrics. In particular, the most improvement occurred for women who started out with relatively low levels of power in the household. Thus, commitment savings accounts not only improve the ability to save, but can also increase empowerment among women, one of the key metrics for measuring impact of microfinance.

Microfinance industry practitioners have taken notice of the results of the key studies discussed in this chapter and a growing body of similar findings. We have seen the evidence that microcredit alone has proven beneficial, but only to a limited degree, often limited to impacts on informal microenterprises—the original focus and the roots of microcredit—but not more broadly for families and communities. Tantalizing evidence is emerging that microsavings services may have greater promise than credit. In response, many MFIs are expanding savings options for the poor. Time will tell if the impacts overall for microsavings might be as strong as the potential some of these early studies indicate.

We have noted in earlier chapters that other types of microfinancial services beyond credit and savings are growing too; things like insurance products, mobile money and cash transfers, as well as non-financial services like health programs, business training, empowerment efforts, consumer protection, and so on. However, not much rigorous impact research yet exists on the effects of those broader services. (See Box 9.4 for some early evidence on microinsurance.) Even so, as we introduced with microfinance-plus in Chapter 7, a wholesale movement is well underway industry-wide towards a broadly encompassing conception of what best practice financial services for the poor entail. In fact, this shift in focus has shifted the language around microfinance too, which is increasingly referred to as "inclusive finance."

Box 9.4. Dig Deeper
The Impact of Microinsurance

This chapter has not yet addressed the (as yet limited) body of evidence assessing microinsurance. Thankfully, the International Labour Organization (ILO) recently reviewed some of the best microinsurance impact studies. Here are some of the ILO's main takeaways from their review of that literature:

Impact on Use of Health Care Services

Evidence from most cases suggests health microinsurance improved access and use of curative healthcare services by low-income individuals. This increase in what the ILO called "health-seeking behavior" came

(Continued)

Box 9.4. (*Continued*)

"mainly by reducing the cost of care following a health shock." For example, in one study, children in Rwanda covered by health insurance "were between 16–19% more likely to receive treatment at a modern health facility or from trained personnel when being sick.... [and] insured households were more likely to purify water before drinking (8–22%), and to have slept under a mosquito net for protection (3–11%)." Other studies in Nicaragua, India, Cambodia, and Nigeria similarly showed 15–30% increases in visits to formal healthcare providers. However, the research is not uniformly positive, and is particularly mixed on the use of preventative care. A study in Kenya, for instance, found health microinsurance led to no significant increase in access to health services nor improved well-being.

Financial Protection

According to the ILO, microinsurance's "most direct impact is a reduction of the out-of-pocket expenditures for the subscribers.... Most empirical [studies] find a decrease in the health expenditures once insured." A second benefit is helping the poor deal more readily with financial risks, including "a lower need to sell assets in order to cope with unexpected health expenditures.... [D]issaving stops being the only option left to the household." For example, a study in Cambodia, showed microinsurance led to "a 9.2 percentage point lower likelihood of assets sale after a health shock." Other studies found lower levels of loans taken out to cover medical expenses. Similarly, insured Kenyans were less likely to sell livestock to deal with emergencies. In a study in India and another in China, farmers with crop microinsurance were more willing to shift to risker, but higher-yield crop varieties, enabling higher average output. Similarly, insured Colombian farmers needed fewer informal loans to deal with weather hazards.

Health Status

Only a few studies directly measure health outcomes. Those that do show mixed impacts. Infection rates in the Philippines were lower

(*Continued*)

Box 9.4. (*Continued*)

among the insured. Young children in insured households in Vietnam were taller and heavier and adults had higher body mass compared to uninsured households. In another study in next door Cambodia, however, insured children were not measurably different in height or weight than uninsured. By contrast, infant mortality in insured Rwandan households was lower, and young children taller. On the other hand, again next door, health microinsured Kenyans were sick on average the same number of days as the uninsured, suggesting limited impact on prevention. Accident and health microinsurance in Pakistan helped reduce the reliance on child labor for income in poor households. Similarly, in another study in Bangladesh, health microinsurance reduced reliance on child labor among extremely poor families, but only when bundled with microcredit. However, in the same study, families above poverty showed no impact of microfinance. In short, and the evidence on the impact of microinsurance is not uniform. Perhaps not surprisingly, context appears to matter.

Source: De Bock and Ontiveros (2013).

Microfinance's Macroeconomic Effects Remain Unknown

We move, finally but very briefly, to the biggest-picture economic question of all: can microfinance help whole national economies grow? We know that mainstream banking, investment, insurance and other financial services matter a great deal for stimulating healthy economic growth. A large and diverse research literature of macroeconomic evidence suggests a positive, causal, correlation at the national level between a better developed finance sector and better economic growth and improved employment.[22] Unfortunately, the focus has been on traditional high finance. A lack of empirical studies specific to microfinance means that the causal link from microfinance to macroeconomic growth remains, for now, theoretical and speculative.

Certainly, as microfinance expands, financial services in many nations have spread and deepened towards the poor. So, the underlying speculative hope here is that as microfinancial sectors mature and inclusive finance becomes the norm, lower-income economies will grow faster, generate better employment opportunities for the poor, and in turn decrease the widespread income inequalities around the world. But we just do not yet know if that is realistic. There remains plenty of room for focused empirical research regarding the topic.

Meanwhile, inclusive finance practitioners are hard at work seeking to transform that hope into reality. On the whole, we have seen in the evidence that microfinance has not been found to be a magical approach capable of ending all poverty. Rather, it provides previously unavailable services that the poor clearly value and think they need to navigate the financial complexities of their daily lives, helping millions of families worldwide in small ways. Moreover, it benefits a small—but non-trivial—subset very substantially, meaning millions of lives are far better thanks to it. Hopefully, the ratio of high-impact will continue to rise as we learn more about what works and does not, what bundles and combinations are most effective and in what contexts, propelling the next generation of inclusive financial services closer to the poverty-killing potential that microfinance's pioneers envisioned many decades ago.

Section in Bulletpoint

- The most rigorous studies generally find positive, but minor, impact on those receiving microfinance services.
- Evidence of positive impact of the availability of microcredit is strong for microenterprise outcomes, but more mixed and uncertain for income, consumption, social empowerment, and similar measures of household well-being.
- Evidence is clear that microsavings services, when offered, are in high demand among the poor.
- Evidence, though still tentative, is beginning to emerge that microsavings—commitment savings in particular—might be more beneficial for the poor than microcredit in terms of improving consumption, empowerment, and health.
- The emerging evidence on impact has fueled a wholesale movement industry-wide towards "inclusive finance," a much more comprehensive microfinance-plus suite of financial and non-financial services for the poor—well beyond the solely microcredit roots of microfinance.

Discussion Questions

1. Suggestive evidence indicates microsavings services might have more impact on household consumption, empowerment, and health compared to microcredit. Discuss ways in which savings might help the poor more than loans.

2. Reflect on your own current circumstances and financial service needs as a student. Personally, do you think loans or savings or insurance could directly help you more? Why?

3. Given what we have learned about the apparently positive but limited impact of microcredit, do you think funding agencies and policymakers should stop subsidizing microcredit programs and put their scarce resources elsewhere? Write a short opinion piece that would be appropriate for a newspaper editorial page on "Credit Subsidies for the Poor: Why or Why Not?" Pick a side and support your point of view, being sure to acknowledge arguments and evidence on both sides

4. Presumably after this book was written, other more recent experimental research has since been published about microfinance's impact. Search the literature library at Microfinance Gateway (microfinancegateway.org/library) for a new randomized control trial study published in 2016 or later. (To narrow your search, on the library page under "Topic" select "Impact".) Read and summarize the research article in a textbook box (~500 words), that would be appropriate a textbook like this. Explain the main question of the research explored, what the research methodology was, and the main findings. How did the research confirm or change our understanding of microfinance in practice? Many of the articles will use math or statistics you may be unfamiliar with. Do not let that stop you if you are interested in the topic. You just need to be able to understand and communicate the basic approach, methods and results, not the technical details.

5. Imagine you are the professor teaching a course using this book. Write 10 essay questions you think would be fair on a final exam and cover the main landscape the book has addressed.

Key Terms

black box problem
Complex mathematical modeling can sometimes obscure underlying patterns and relationships in the data, creating an effect in which the model over-simplifies reality.

control group
In an experiment, the group that does not receive treatment; used to establish the counterfactual. Sometimes called comparison group.

correlation
The degree of relationship among different variables; variables that tend to move together are correlated.

counterfactual
In research studies, the hypothetical alternative state of the world that would exist if the activity or treatment being studied had not actually happened.

data mining
The mathematical analysis process of looking for patterns in complex data can be useful, but researchers may have incentives to only report favorable, anomalous, or otherwise interesting results, ignoring others.

dropout effect
In research studies, some participants may leave the study before it concludes, due to circumstances or death, which can lead to biased results if those who drop out are systematically different than those who stay.

experimental studies
Studies in which the researchers control all key variations; in the natural sciences more typically done in fully controlled laboratory or clinical settings, but possible in the social sciences with careful design in field settings as well.

qualitative research
Uses techniques like individual case studies and long-term observation to more deeply understand complex social systems that do not lend themselves to quantitative data gathering; often used to generate insights that guide further experimental work.

quantitative research
Research involving collection and analysis of numerical data; in microfinance impact assessments, usually collected by survey of communities, households, or individuals. Commonly utilizes statistics and advanced software to analyze large data sets.

quasi-experimental studies

Studies in which researchers can control only some variations; often used if randomized assignment into control and treatment groups is not possible, such as after some event has already happened.

randomized control trial

Study in which subjects are randomly assigned to either treatment or control groups. The control group does not receive treatment, but if it is otherwise identical to the treatment group, researchers can logically attribute resulting differences in outcomes as being caused by the treatment.

selection bias

When there is not true randomization in selection into groups that are being compared, the groups may differ in systematic ways even before treatment, leading to biases in research results; particularly problematic if one group is used as the counterfactual.

treatment group

In an experiment, the group that receives the treatment under study; outcomes generally compared to an untreated but otherwise similar control group serving as the counterfactual.

Notes:

[1] See http://www.tylervigen.com/spurious-correlations
[2] The discussion in this section and the rest of the chapter draws broadly on Odell (2015).
[3] Karlan and Zinman (2008).
[4] Leamer (1983).
[5] These reports are Goldberg (2005), Odell (2010), and Odell (2015).
[6] Augsburg et al (2015).
[7] Banerjee et al (2015).
[8] The six studies are as follows: Bosnia = Augsburg et al (2015); Ethiopia = Tarozzi, Desai, and Johnson (2015); India = Banerjee et al (2015); Mexico = Angelucci, Karlan, and Zinman (2015); Mongolia = Attanasio et al (2015); Morocco = Crépon et al (2015).
[9] Angelucci, Karlan, and Zinman (2015).
[10] Angelucci, Karlan, and Zinman (2015).
[11] Khandker and Samad (2014).
[12] DeLoach and Lamanna (2011).
[13] See review in Odell (2015), who refers also to reviews by Leatherman et al (2012) and Saha and Annear (2014).
[14] McKelway (2014).
[15] Kast and Pomeranz (2014).
[16] Prina (2015).
[17] Dupas and Robinson (2013a).

[18] Dupas and Robinson (2013b).

[19] Brune et al (2011).

[20] Ashraf, Karlan, and Yin (2010).

[21] Ashraf, Karlan, and Yin (2006).

[22] Odell (2015) refers to the extensive literature reviewed by Pasali (2013).

REFERENCES

Accion International (2015). Network and Partners Monthly Statistics. June 2015.

Accion USA (2006). ACCION USA & Hope Community Credit Union Help Save a Southern Institution. PR Newswire, November 20.

Ahlin, Christian, and Robert M. Townsend (2007). Using Repayment Data to Test across Models of Joint Liability Lending. The Economics Journal 117(517) F11–F51.

Ahlin, Christian, Jocelyn Lin, and Michael Maio (2011). Where Does Microfinance Flourish? Microfinance Institution Performance in Macroeconomic Context. Journal of Development Economics 95(2) 105–120.

Allan, Alice, Maude Massu, and Christine Svarer (2013). Banking on Change: Breaking the Barriers to Financial Inclusion. London: Banking on Change Partnership.

Anderson, C. Leigh, Maya Dietz, Andrew Gordon, and Marieka Klawitter (2004), Discount Rates in Vietnam. Economic Development & Cultural Change 52(4) 873–887.

Anderson, Siwan, and Jean-Marie Baland (2002). Economics of ROSCAs and Intrahousehold Resource Allocation. Quarterly Journal of Economics 117(3) 963–995.

Angelucci, Manuela, Dean Karlan, and Jonathan Zinman (2015). Microcredit Impacts: Evidence from a Randomized Microcredit Program Placement Experiment by Compartamos Banco. American Economic Journal: Applied Economics 7(1) 151–182.

Anscombe, Francis J. (1973) Graphs in Statistical Analysis. The American Statistician 27(1) 17–21.

Armendáriz, Beatriz, and Jonathan Morduch (2010). The Economics of Microfinance, 2nd edition. Cambridge, MA: MIT Press.

Ashraf, Nava, Dean Karlan, and Wesley Yin (2006). Tying Odysseus to the Mast: Evidence from a Commitment Savings Product in the Philippines. Quarterly Journal of Economics 121(2) 635–672.

Ashraf, Nava, Dean Karlan, Wesley Yin. (2010). Female Empowerment: Impact of a Commitment Savings Product in the Philippines. World Development 38(3) 333–344.

Attanasio, Orazio, Britta Augsburg, Ralph De Haas, Emla Fitzsimons, and Heike Harmgart (2015). The Impacts of Microfinance: Evidence from Joint-Liability Lending in Mongolia. American Economic Journal: Applied Economics 7(1) 90–122.

Augsburg, Britta, Ralph De Haas, Heike Harmgart, and Costas Meghir (2015). The Impacts of Microcredit: Evidence from Bosnia and Herzegovina. American Economic Journal: Applied Economics 7(1) 183–203.

Bajaj Alliance (2010). Bajaj Allianz Sarve Shakti Suraksha. Promotional Brochure. Yerwada, Pune, India: Bajaj Allianz Life Insurance Company Limited. September 17.

Banerjee, Abhijit, and Esther Duflo (2007). The Economics Lives of the Poor. Journal of Economic Perspectives 21(1) 141–168.

Banerjee, Abhijit, Esther Duflo, Rachel Glennerster, and Cynthia Kinnan (2015). The Miracle of Microfinance? Evidence from a Randomized Evaluation. American Economic Journal: Applied Economics 7(1) 22–53.

Baydas, Mayada M., Douglas H. Graham, and Liza Valenzuela (1997). Commercial Banks in Microfinance: New Actors in the Microfinance World. USAID Microfinance Best Practices Paper. Bethesda, MD: Development Alternatives Inc. August.

Benavides, Mercedes (2008). Women's World Banking, presentation at Lehigh University, Martindale Center for the Study of Private Enterprise, Microfinance Program, February 27, 2008.

Benzion, Uri, Amnon Rapoport, and Joseph Yagil (1989). Discount Rates Inferred from Decisions: An Experimental Study. Management Science 35, 270–284.

Berman, Peter, Rajeev Ahuja, and Laveesh Bhandari (2010). The Impoverishing Effect of Healthcare Payments in India: New Methodology and Findings. Economic & Political Weekly 45(16) 65–71.

Binswanger, Hans, and Shahidur Khandker (1995). The Impact of Formal Finance on the Rural Economy of India. Journal of Development Studies 32(2) 234–362.

Blau, Francine D., and Lawrence M. Kahn (2006). The US Gender Pay Gap in the 1990s: Slowing Convergence. Industrial and Labor Relations Review 60(1) 45–66.

Blumberg, Rae Lesser (1988). Income under Female versus Male Control Hypotheses from a Theory of Gender Stratification and Data from the Third World. Journal of Family Issues 9(1) 51–84.

Bouman, Frits J.A. (1995). Rotating and Accumulating Savings and Credit Associations: A Development Perspective. World Development 23(3) 371–384.

Bouuaert, Matthijs (2008). A Billion to Gain? A Study on Global Financial Institutions and Microfinance: The Next Phase. Amsterdam: ING Microfinance Support. March.

Bridgers, Elena (2011). Following India's Microfinance Crisis, A Shift to Male Clients. Stanford Social Innovation Review, December 16.

Brune, Lasse, Xavier Giné, Jessica Goldberg, and Dean Yang (2011). Commitments to Save: A Field Experiment in Rural Malawi. World Bank Policy Research Working Paper No. 5748.

Buvinić, Mayra, and Geeta Rao Gupta (1997). Female-Headed Households and Female-Maintained Families: Are They Worth Targeting to Reduce Poverty in Developing Countries? Economic Development and Cultural Change 45(2) 259–280.

CGAP (2009a). Financial Access 2009: Measuring Access to Financial Services around the World. Washington, DC: Consultative Group to Assist the Poor (CGAP).

CGAP (2009b). Government's Role in Microfinance: What is the Optimal Policy Mix? Washington, DC: Consultative Group to Assist the Poor (CGAP). Jan. 26.

Chala, Alberto, Apama Dalal, Tony Goland, Maria Jose Gonzalez, Jonathan Morduch, and Robert Schiff. (2009). Half the World Is Unbanked. Financial Access Initiative, October.

Chen, Greg, Stephen Rasmussen, and Xavier Reille (2010). Growth and Vulnerabilities in Microfinance. Focus Note 61. Washington, DC: Consultative Group to Assist the Poor (CGAP).

Chen, Martha A., and Donald Snodgrass (2001). Managing Resources, Activities, and Risk in Urban India: The Impact of SEWA Bank. Washington, DC: AIMS.

Cheston, Susy, and Lisa Kuhn (2002). Empowering Women through Microfinance. New York: United Nations Development Fund for Women (UNIFEM).

Christen, Bob, and Ignacio Mas (2009). It's Time to Address the Microsavings Challenge, Scalably. Enterprise Development and Microfinance 20(4).

Christen, Robert Peck, and Richard Rosenberg (2000). The Rush to Regulate: Legal Frameworks for Microfinance. Washington, DC: Consultative Group to Assist the Poor (CGAP).

Christen, Robert Peck, and Tamara Cook (2001). Commercialization and Mission Drift: The Transformation of Microfinance in Latin America. Occasional Paper No. 5. Washington, DC: Consultative Group to Assist the Poor (CGAP).

Christen, Robert Peck, Richard Rosenberg, and Veena Jayadeva (2004). Financial Institutions with a "Double Bottom Line": Implications for the Future of Microfinance. Washington, DC: Consultative Group to Assist the Poor (CGAP).

Chua, Peck Gee (2010). Impact of Microfinance on the Schooling of Children. Master of Arts Thesis. University of Minnesota. November.

Churchill, Craig, and Michael J. McCord (2012). Current Trends in Microinsurance. In Craig Churchill, and Michal Matul (eds.) Protecting the Poor: A Microinsurance Compendium Vol. II. Geneva: International Labour Office.

Cohen, Monique, and Jennefer Sebstad (2003). Reducing Vulnerability: The Demand for Microinsurance. Nairobi: MicroSave-Africa. March.

Collins, Daryl, Jonathan Morduch, Stuart Rutherford, and Orlanda Ruthven (2009). Portfolios of the Poor: How the World's Poor Live on $2 a Day. Princeton University Press.

Courtemanche, Charles, Garth Heutel, and Patrick McAlvanah (2012). Impatience, Incentives, and Obesity. Atlanta, GA: Georgia State University, Andrew Young School of Policy Studies Research Paper Series No. 12–20. July.

Crépon, Bruno, Florencia Devoto, Esther Duflo, and William Parienté (2015). Estimating the Impact of Microcredit on Those Who Take It up: Evidence from a Randomized Experiment in Morocco. American Economic Journal: Applied Economics 7(1) 123–150.

Cruz, Marcio, James Foster, Bryce Quillin, and Philip Schellekens (2015). Ending Extreme Poverty and Sharing Prosperity: Progress and Policies. Policy Research Note PRN/15/03.Washington, DC: World Bank Group. October.

D'Espallier, Bert, Isabelle Guerin, and Roy Mersland (2011). Women and Repayment in Microfinance: A Global Analysis. World Development 39(5) 758–772.

D'Espallier, Bert, Isabelle Guerin, and Roy Mersland (2013). Focus on Women in Microfinance Institutions. Journal of Development Studies 49(5) 589–608.

Daily Graphic, Ghana (2013). Non-Bank Financial Institutions to Submit Data to Credit Bureau. Daily Graphic Business News, Sunday, June 2.

De Bock, Ombeline, and Darwin Ugarte Ontiveros (2013). Literature Review on the Impact of Microinsurance. Microinsurance Innovation Facility, Research Paper 35. Geneva: International Labour Office. October.

de Mel, Suresh, David McKenzie, and Christopher Woodruff (2008). Returns to Capital in Microenterprises: Evidence from a Field Experiment. Quarterly Journal of Economics 123(4) 1329–1372.

de Mel, Suresh, David McKenzie, and Christopher Woodruff (2009). Are Women More Credit Constrained? Experimental Evidence on Gender and Microenterprise Returns. American Economic Journal: Applied Economics 1(3) 1–32.

de Soto, Hernando. (2001). The Mystery of Capital: Why Capitalism Triumphs in the West and Fails Everywhere Else. London: Black Swan.

DeLoach, Stephen B., and Erika Lamanna (2011). Measuring the Impact of Microfinance on Child Health Outcomes in Indonesia. World Development 39(10) 1808–1819.

Demirgüç-Kunt, Asli, and Leora Klapper. (2012). Measuring Financial Inclusion: The Global Findex Database. Washington, DC: World Bank.

Deshpande, Rani (2006). Safe and Accessible Bringing Poor Savers into the Formal Financial System. CGAP Focus Note 37. Washington, DC: Consultative Group to Assist the Poor.

Dominicé, Roland, Marina Parashekevova Helmegaard, and Ramkumar Narayanan (2014). Symbiotics Microfinance Index (SMX): 10-Year Track Record Outperforming Mainstream Asset Classes. Geneva: Symbiotics SA. January.

Dupas, Pascaline, and Jonathan Robinson (2013a). Savings Constraints and Microenterprise Development: Evidence from a Field Experiment in Kenya. American Economic Journal: Applied Economics 5(1) 163–192.

Dupas, Pascaline, and Jonathan Robinson (2013b). Why Don't the Poor Save More? Evidence from Health Savings Experiments. The American Economic Review 103(4) 1138–1171.

Fiorillo, Alexandra, Louis Potok, and Josh Wright (2014). Applying Behavioral Economics to Improve Microsavings Outcomes. Washington, DC: Grameen Foundation.

Fischer Klaus, Issa Sissouma, and Ibrahima Hathie (2006). L'Union Technique de la Mutualité Malienne, Mali. CGAP Working Group on Microinsurance Good and Bad Practices. Case Study No. 23. Washington, DC: Consultative Group to Assist the Poorest. August.

Forum for the Future (2007). New Horizons: Creating Value, Enabling Livelihoods. Summary Report. June.

Frank, Christina (2008). Stemming the Tide of Mission Drift: Microfinance Transformations and the Double Bottom Line. WWB Focus Note. New York: Women's World Banking.

Germidis, Dimitri A., Dennnis Kessler, and Rachel Meghir (1991). Financial Systems and Development: What Role for the Formal and Informal Financial Sectors? Paris: Development Centre of the Organisation for Economic Cooperation and Development.

GFDRR (2011). Index-Based Livestock Insurance in Mongolia Protecting Herders from Climate-Related Livestock Mortality. Washington, DC: Global Facility for Disaster Reduction and Recovery. September.

Ghatak, Maitreesh (1999). Group Lending, Local Information, and Peer Selection. Journal of Development Economics 60(1) 27–50.

Giné, X., and Karlan, D.S. (2009). Group versus Individual Liability: Long Term Evidence from Philippine Microcredit Lending Groups. Yale Economics Department Working Paper 61, May 20.

Global Envision (2006). The History of Microfinance. www.globalenvision.org/library/4/1051

Glynn, John (2011). Women's World Banking in Kenya: Microfinance Success Stories. Race4Change. Blog. November 7. http://www.race4change.org/blog/womens-world-banking-in-kenya-microfinance-success-stories

Goetz, Anne Marie, and Rina Sen Gupta (1996). Who Takes the Credit? Gender, Power and Control over Loan Use in Rural Credit Programmes in Bangladesh. World Development 24(1) 45–63.

Goldberg, Nathanael (2005). Measuring the Impact of Microfinance: Taking Stock of What We Know. Grameen Foundation USA Publication Series. Washington, DC: Grameen Foundation.

González-Vega, Claudio, Mark Schreiner, Richard L. Meyer, Jorge Rodriguez, and Sergio Navajas (1996). BANCOSOL: The Challenge of Growth for Microfinance Organizations. Economics and Sociology Occasional Paper No. 2332. Columbus, Ohio: Rural Finance Program, Department of Agricultural Economics, Ohio State University. August.

Grameen Foundation (2012). Savings Volatility Analysis: CARD Bank. Washington, DC: Grameen Foundation.

Grameen Foundation (2013). Solutions for the Poorest: Insights on Savings Behaviors of Clients. Washington, DC: Grameen Foundation. April.

Gullapalli, Srikar (2010). Microfinance in the Field: Interview with a Moneylender. Microfinance Focus. June 16.

Gunter, Frank R. (2009). Microfinance during Conflict: Iraq, 2003–2007, in Todd A. Watkins, and Karen Hicks (eds.) Moving Beyond Storytelling: Emerging Research in Microfinance. Emerald Books.

Guttman, Joel M. (2008) Assortative Matching, Adverse Selection, and Group Lending. Journal of Development Economics 87(1) 51–56.

Halac, Marina, and Sergio L. Schmukler (2004). Distributional Effects of Crises: The Financial Channel. Economia, 1–67.

Hallward-Driemeier, Mary (2013). Enterprising Women: Expanding Economic Opportunities in Africa. Africa Development Forum Series. Washington, DC: World Bank.

Hanke, Steve H., and Alex K. F. Kwok (2009). On the Measurement of Zimbabwe's Hyperinflation. Cato Journal 29, 353.

Harper, Annie (1995). Providing Women in Baltistan with Access to Loans—Potential and Problems. Lahore, Pakistan: Aga Khan Rural Support Programme (AKRSP) Pakistan.

Hatch, John (2004). A Brief Primer on FINCA, unpublished lecture manuscript, University of California Berkeley, July 21. www.haas.berkeley.edu/HaasGlobal/docs/hatch_fincaprimer.doc

Hattel, Kelly, and Megan Montgomery (2010). Promoting Credit Bureaus: The Role of Microfinance Associations. Washington, DC: The SEEP Network.

Hertwig, Ralph, Greg Barron, Elke U. Weber, and IdoErev (2004). Decisions from Experience and the Effect of Rare Events in Risky Choice. Psychological Science 15(8) 534–539.

Hulme, David (2000). Impact Assessment Methodologies for Microfinance: Theory, Experience and Better Practice. World Development 28(1) 79–98.

IBRD (2013). International Bank for Reconstruction and Development/World Bank. Women, Business and the Law 2014: Removing Restrictions to Enhance Gender Equality. London: Bloomsbury Publishing.

IFAD (2003). International Fund for Agricultural Development. Marketing Companies as Sources of Smallholder Credit in Eastern and Southern Africa: Experiences, Insights and Potential Donor Role. December.

ILO (2015). Global Wage Report 2014/15: Wages and Income Inequality. Geneva: International Labour Office.

International Labour Organization (2013). Women and Men in the Informal Economy: A Statistical Picture (Second Edition). Geneva: International Labour Office.

Jacoby, Hanan G., and Emmanuel Skoufias (1997). Risk, Financial Markets, and Human Capital in a Developing Country. Review of Economic Studies 64(3) 311–335.

Jácome, Luis I. (2004). The Late 1990s Financial Crisis in Ecuador: Institutional Weaknesses, Fiscal Rigidities, and Financial Dollarization at Work. IMF Working Paper WP/04/12 Washington, DC: International Monetary Fund. January 2004.

Jan, Stephen, Giulia Ferrari, Charlotte H. Watts, James R. Hargreaves, Julia C. Kim, Godfrey Phetla, Linda A. Morison, John D. Porter, Tony Barnett, and Paul M. Pronyk (2011). Economic Evaluation of a Combined Microfinance and Gender Training Intervention for the Prevention of Intimate Partner Violence in Rural South Africa. Health Policy and Planning 26(5) 366–372.

Kahn, Benjamin, and Tor Jansson (2007) Tough Enough: Microfinance Defies Recession. Web Stories. Inter American Development Bank. December 27, 2007.

Karlan, Dean, and Martin Valdivia (2011). Teaching Entrepreneurship: Impact of Business Training on Microfinance Clients and Institutions. Review of Economics and Statistics 93(2) 510–527.

Karlan, Dean, and Zinman, Jonathan (2008). Lying about Borrowing. Journal of the European Economic Association 6(2–3) 510–521.

Kast, Felipe, and Dina Pomeranz (2014). Saving More to Borrow Less: Experimental Evidence from Access to Formal Savings Accounts in Chile. NBER Working Paper No. 20239. Cambridge, MA: National Bureau of Economic Research. June.

Kedir, Abbi M., and Gamal Ibrahim (2011). ROSCAs in Urban Ethiopia: Are the Characteristics of the Institutions More Important Than That of Members? Journal of Development Studies 47(7) 998–1016.

Kenney, Catherine T. (2008). Father Doesn't Know Best? Parents' Control of Money and Children's Food Insecurity. Journal of Marriage and Family 70(3) 654–669.

Khandker, Shahidur R., and Hussain A. Samad (2014), Dynamic Effects of Microcredit in Bangladesh. World Bank Policy Research Working Paper 6821. Washington, DC: World Bank.

Kim, Julia, Giulia Ferrari, Tanya Abramsky, Charlotte Watts, James Hargreaves, Linda Morison, Godfrey Phetla, John Porter, and Paul Pronyk (2009). Assessing the Incremental Effects of Combining Economic and Health Interventions: The IMAGE Study in South Africa. Bulletin of the World Health Organization 87(11) 824–832.

Kumar, Anjali, Adam Parsons, Eduardo Urdapilleta, and Ajai Nair (2006). Expanding Bank Outreach through Retail Partnerships: Correspondent Banking in Brazil. World Bank Working Paper No. 85. Washington, DC: World Bank.

Ladman, Jerry R., and Gonzalo Afcha(1990). Group Lending: Why It Failed in Bolivia. Savings and Development 14(4) 353–369.

Leamer, Edward E. (1983). Let's Take the Con out of Econometrics. The American Economic Review 73(1) 31–43.

Ledgerwood, Joanna, and Victoria White (2006). Sequencing the Introduction of Public Savings in Regulated MFIs. Transforming Microfinance Institutions: Providing Full Financial Services to the Poor. Washington, DC: World Bank.

Lieberman, Ira W., Anne Anderson, Zach Grafe, Bruce Campbell, and Daniel Kopf (2009). Microfinance and Capital Markets: The Initial Listing/Public Offering of Four Leading Institutions, in Todd A. Watkins, and Karen Hicks (eds.) Moving Beyond Storytelling: Emerging Research in Microfinance. Emerald Books.

Lieberman, Ira, Jenifer Mudd, and Phil Goodeve (2012). US Microfinance at the Crossroads. Scale and Sustainability: Can Lessons from International Experience Help Guide the US Sector. Washington, DC: Center for Financial Inclusion at Accion and Calmeadow.

Lloyds (2010). Insurance in Developing Countries: Exploring Opportunities in Microinsurance, Lloyds 360 Risk Insight.

Mahul, Olivier, Niraj Verma, and Daniel Clarke (2012). Improving Farmers' Access to Agricultural Insurance in India. World Bank Policy Research Working Paper 5987.

Maldonado, Jorge H., and Claudio González-Vega (2008). Impact of Microfinance on Schooling: Evidence from Poor Rural Households in Bolivia. World Development 36(11) 2440–2455.

Malkin, Elisabeth (2008). Microloans, Big Profits. New York Times, April 5. C1.

Martin, Xavier (2013). Inclusive Commitment Savings in Latin America and the Caribbean, Washington, DC: Multilateral Investment Fund, Inter-American Development Bank.

Mayoux, Linda (1999). Questioning Virtuous Spirals: Micro-Finance and Women's Empowerment in Africa. Journal of International Development 11(7) 957–984.

Mayoux, Linda, and Maria Hartl (2009). Gender and Rural Microfinance: Reaching and Empowering Women. Powerguda, India: International Fund for Agricultural Development (IFAD).

McCord, Michael J., Molly Ingram, and Clémence Tatin-Jaleran (2012). The Landscape of Microinsurance in Latin America and the Caribbean. New York: Multilateral Investment Fund (2013).

McCord, Michael J., Roland Steinmann, Clémence Tatin-Jaleran, Molly Ingram, and Mariah Mateo (2013). The Landscape of Microinsurance in Africa 2012. Munich: Munich Re Foundation. March.

McKelway, Madeline (2014). The Impact of Micro-Banking on Health: Evidence from Self-Help Group Involvement and Child Nutrition. Ph.D. Dissertation. Durham, NC: Duke University.

Microcredit Summit Campaign (2014). Resilience: State of the Microcredit Summit Campaign Report, 2014. Washington, DC: Microcredit Summit Campaign.

Microcredit Summit Campaign (2016). Mapping Pathways out of Poverty: State of the Microcredit Summit Campaign Report, 2015. Washington, DC: Microcredit Summit Campaign.

Microfinance Information Exchange (2009). MicroBanking Bulletin 19. December.

Microfinance Information Exchange (2010). 2009 MIX Global 100: Ranking of Microfinance Institutions. January.

Microrate (2013). Microfinance Institution Tier Definitions. Lima, Peru: Microrate. April.

Moebs Services (2014). Checking: The Loss Leader. http://www.moebs.com/PressReleases.aspx

Mukherjee, Premasis, Arman Oza, Lisa Chassin, and Rupalee Ruchismita (2014). The Landscape of Microfinance in Asia and Oceania 2013. Munich: Munich Re Foundation. July.

Mutua, Charles (2010). Health Microinsurance — A Case Study in Kenya. Presentation to the International Congress for Actuaries. Cape Town, South Africa. 7–12 March.

Noble, Gerry, and Michael J. McCord (2007). Health Microinsurance. Microinsurance Note 6. Washington, DC: USAID. June.

Oberdorf, Charles (2006). ProFundInternacional, SA. San Jose, Costa Rica: Omtrix Inc. Available at www.calmeadow.com/pdf/profund.pdf

Odell, Kathleen (2010). Measuring the Impact of Microfinance: Taking Another Look. Washington, DC: Grameen Foundation.

Odell, Kathleen (2015). Measuring the Impact of Microfinance: Looking to the Future. Washington, DC: Grameen Foundation.

Ong, Lynette (2006). The Political Economy of Township Government Debt, Township Enterprises and Rural Financial Institutions in China. The China Quarterly 186, 377–400

Parashar, A. (2008) As Migrants Flock to Delhi and Suburbs, Local Moneylenders Thrive. Express India, April 13.

Pasali, Selahattin Selsah (2013). Where Is the Cheese? Synthesizing a Giant Literature on Causes and Consequences of Financial Sector Development. World Bank Policy Research Working Paper 6655, Washington, DC: World Bank.

Paulson, Anna L., and Robert Townsend (2004). Entrepreneurship and Financial Constraints in Thailand. Journal of Corporate Finance 10, 229–262.

Pistelli, Micol, Anton Simanowitz, and Veronika Thiel (2011). State of Practice in Social Performance Reporting and Management: A Survey of 405 MFIs Reporting to MIX in 2009–2010. MicroBanking Bulletin. July.

Pitt, Mark M., and Shahidur R. Khandker (1998). The Impact of Group-Based Credit on Poor Households in Bangladesh: Does the Gender of Participants Matter? Journal of Political Economy 106(5) 958–996

Pitt, Mark M., Shahidur R. Khandker, and Jennifer Cartwright (2006). Empowering Women with Micro Finance: Evidence from Bangladesh. Economic Development and Cultural Change 54(4) 791–831.

Pitt, Mark M., Shahidur R. Khandker, Omar Haider Chowdhury, and Daniel L. Millimet (2003). Credit Programs for the Poor and the Health Status of Children in Rural Bangladesh. International Economic Review 44(1) 87–118.

Polakow-Suransky, Sasha (2003). Giving the Poor Some Credit: Microloans Are in Vogue. Are They a Sound Idea? The American Prospect 14(5).

Pott, John, and Jeanna Holtz (2013). Value-Added Services in Health Microinsurance. Microinsurance Paper 19. Geneva: International Labour Organization.

Prina, Silvia (2015). Banking the Poor via Savings Accounts: Evidence from a Field Experiment. Journal of Development Economics 115, 16–31.

Qayum, Nayma, MrinmoySamadder, and Rehnuma Rahman (2012). Group Norms and the BRAC Village Organization–Enhancing Social Capital Baseline. Working Paper No. 29. Dhaka, Bangladesh: BRAC Research and Evaluation Division. April.

Rahman, Aminur (1999). Women and Microcredit in Rural Bangladesh: An Anthropological Study of Grameen Bank Lending. Boulder, CO: Westview Press.

Rai, Ashok S., and Tomas Sjöström (2004). Is Grameen Lending Efficient? Repayment Incentives and Insurance in Village Economies. Review of Economic Studies 71(1) 217–234.

Reille, Xavier, and Sarah Forster (2008). Foreign Capital Investment in Microfinance: Balancing Social and Financial Returns. Focus Note 44. Washington, DC: CGAP.

Rhyne, Elisabeth (2009). Microfinance for Bankers and Investors: Understanding the Opportunities and Challenges of the Market at the Bottom of the Pyramid. New York: McGraw Hill.

Rhyne, Elisabeth, and Andres Guimon (2007). The Banco Compartamos Initial Public Offering. InSight Series No. 23. Boston: Accion International. June.

Rhyne, Elisabeth, and Rekha M. Reddy (2006). Who Will Buy Our Paper: Microfinance Cracking the Capital Markets? InSight Series No. 18. Boston: Accion International. April.

Rim, Ji-Yeune, and John Rouse (2002). Group Savings Resource Book. Rome: Food and Agriculture Organization of the United Nations.

Robinson, Marguerite S. (2001). The Microfinance Revolution: Sustainable Finance for the Poor. Washington, DC: World Bank.

Roodman, David (2012). Due Diligence: An Impertinent Look into Microfinance. Washington, DC: Center for Global Development.

Rosenberg, Richard, Adrian Gonzalez, and Sushma Narain (2009). The New Moneylenders: Are the Poor Being Exploited by High Microcredit Interest Rates? In Todd A. Watkins, and Karen Hicks (eds.) Moving Beyond Storytelling: Emerging Research in Microfinance. Emerald Books.

Rosenberg, Richard, Scott Gaul, William Ford, and Olga Tomilova (2013). Microcredit Interest Rates and Their Determinants: 2004–2011. Access to Finance Forum Reports by CGAP and Its Partners, No. 7. Washington, DC: Consultative Group to Assist the Poor. June.

Roth, Jim, and Michael J. McCord (2008). Agricultural Microinsurance: Global Practices and Prospects. Appleton, WI: The Microinsurance Centre.

Roth, Jim, Michael J. McCord, and Dominic Liber (2007). The Landscape of Microinsurance in the World's 100 Poorest Countries. Appleton, WI: The Microinsurance Centre.

Rutherford, Stuart (2000). The Poor and Their Money. New Delhi: Oxford University Press.

Rutherford, Stuart (2009). The Pledge: ASA, Peasant Politics, and Microfinance in the Development of Bangladesh. Oxford: Oxford University Press.

Rutherford, Stuart, M.D. Maniruzzaman, S.K. Sinha, and Acnabin & Co (2004). Grameen II at the End of 2003 — A 'Grounded View' of How Grameen's New Initiative Is Progressing in the Villages. Microfinance Gateway. April.

Sandefur, Justin (2015). The Final Word on Microcredit? Blog Center for Global Development. https://www.cgdev.org/blog/final-word-microcredit. January 22.

Schaner, Simone (2014). The Cost of Convenience? Transaction Costs, Bargaining Power, and Savings Account Use in Kenya. December 16, 2014.

Sengupta, Hindol (2014). Recasting India: How Entrepreneurship Is Revolutionizing the World's Largest Democracy. New York: Macmillan.

Sevron, Lisa J. (2013). RiteCheck 12. Public Books, July 10, 2013. www.publicbooks.org/nonfiction/ritecheck-12

Shefrin, Hersh M., and Richard H. Thaler (1988). The Behavioral Life-Cycle Hypothesis. Economic Inquiry 26(4) 609–643.

Sherwin, Ryan (2007). A Little Goes a Long Way: Microfinance Helping Katrina Victims. Credit Union Strategy and Performance 2Q-07, 54–55.

Shukla, Rajesh (2010). How India Earns, Spends and Saves: Unmasking the Real India. New Delhi, India: National Council of Applied Economic Research, and Sage Publications.

Simtowe, Franklin, Manfred Zeller, and Alexander Phiri (2006). Determinants of Moral Hazard in Microfinance: Empirical Evidence from Joint Liability Lending Programs in Malawi. African Review of Money Finance and Banking, 5–38.

Sinha, Frances (2006). Self Help Groups in India: A Study of the Lights and Shades. Noida and Hyderabad, India: APMAS and EDA Rural Systems.

Soursourian, Matthew, and Edlira Dashi (2015). Current Trends in International Funding for Financial Inclusion. Washington, DC: CGAP. December 15.

Steel, William F., and Ernest Aryeetey (1994). Informal Savings Collectors in Ghana: Can They Intermediate? Finance and Development 31(1) 36–37.

Stewart R., C. van Rooyen, K. Dickson, M. Majoro, and T. de Wet (2010). What Is the Impact of Microfinance on Poor People? A Systematic Review of Evidence from Sub-Saharan Africa. Technical Report. London: EPPI-Centre, Social Science Research Unit, University of London.

Stiglitz, Joseph (1990). Peer Monitoring and Credit Markets, World Bank Economic Review 4(3) 351–366.

Stuart, Guy, Michael Ferguson, and Monique Cohen (2011). Microfinance & Gender: Some Findings from the Financial Diaries in Malawi. Washington, DC: Microfinance Opportunities. May.

Swinnen, Johan F.M., Marc Sadler, and Anneleen Vandeplas (2007). Contracting, Competition, and Rent Distribution in Supply Chains: Theory and Evidence from Central Asia, in Swinnen, Johan F.M. (ed.) Global Supply Chains, Standards and the Poor: How the Globalization of Food Systems and Standards Affects Rural Development and Poverty. London: CAB International.

Symbiotics (2015). 2015 Microfinnce Investment Vehicles Survey: Market Data & Peer Group Analysis. Geneva: Symbiotics. September.

Symbiotics (2016). 2016 Symbiotics MIV Survey: Market Data & Peer Group Analysis, 10th edition. Geneva: Symbiotics. September.

Tanaka, Tomomi, and Quang Nguyen (2009). ROSCA as a Saving Commitment Device for Sophisticated Hyperbolic Discounters: Field Experiment from Vietnam. Working Paper.

Tantia, Piyush, and Tyler Comings (ca. 2011). Commitment Savings Accounts in Malawi: A Product Design Study. Washington, DC: International Finance Corporation,World Bank Group. Undated.

Tarozzi, Alessandro, Jaikishan Desai, and Kristin Johnson (2015). The Impacts of Microcredit: Evidence from Ethiopia. American Economic Journal: Applied Economics 7(1) 54–89.

Thaler, Richard (1981). Some Empirical Evidence on Dynamic Inconsistency. Economics Letters 8, 201–207.

U.S. Federal Reserve (2014). Changes in U.S. Family Finances from 2010 to 2013: Evidence from the Survey of Consumer Finances. Federal Reserve Bulletin. September.

UNDP (1996). Human Development Report 1996: Economic Growth and Human Development. United Nations Development Programme. New York: Oxford University Press.

Urquizo, Jacqueline (2012). The Financial Behavior of Rural Residents: Findings from Five Latin American Countries. New York: ACCION Publications. March.

Vaessen, Jos, Ana Rivas, Maren Duvendack, Richard Palmer-Jones, Frans L. Leeuw, Ger van Gils, Ruslan Lukach, Nathalie Holvoet, Johan Bastiaensen, Jorge Garcia Hombrados, and Hugh Waddington (2014). The Effect of Microcredit on Women's Control over Household Spending in Developing Countries: A Systematic Review. Campbell Systematic Reviews 2014(8).

Valenzuela, Liza (2001). Getting the Recipe Right: The Experiences and Challenges of Commercial Bank Downscalers. USAID Microfinance Best Practices Paper. Bethesda, MD: Development Alternatives Inc. October.

van Tassel, Eric (1999). Group Lending under Asymmetric Information. Journal of Development Economics 60(1) 3–25.

Varghese, Adel (2005). Bank-Moneylender Linkage as an Alternative to Bank Competition in Rural Credit Markets. Oxford Economic Papers 57(2) 315–335.

von Stauffenberg, Damian, and Daniel Rozas (2011). Role Reversal Revisited. Are Public Development Institutions Still Crowding-Out Private Investment in Microfinance? Washington, DC: MicroRate.

Waterfield, Charles, and Ann Duval (1996). CARE Savings and Credit Sourcebook. New York: CARE.

Westley, Glenn D., and Xavier Martín Palomas (2010). Is There a Business Case for Small Savers? Occasional Paper 18. Washington, DC: CGAP. September.

Women's World Banking (2012). Microfund for Women's Caregiver Experience: Lessons from Jordan on Health Microinsurance. New York: Women's World Banking, in partnership with Credit Suisse AG.

World Bank Group (2014). Getting Credit in Ghana. Doing Business: Measuring Business Regulation. June.

World Bank Group (2015). New Insurance Model Protects Mongolian Herders from Losses. World Bank News Feature Story. March 4.

Wright, Graham (1999). The Case for Voluntary Open Access Savings Facilities and Why Bangladesh's Largest MFIs Were Slow to React. Washington, DC: Consultative Group to Assist the Poorest, CGAP Working Group on Savings Mobilization.

Xu, Ke, David B. Evans, Guido Carrin, Ana Mylena Aguilar-Rivera, Philip Musgrove, and Timothy Evans (2007). Protecting Households from Catastrophic Health Spending. Health Affairs 26(4) 972–983.

Yang, Lien-Sheng (1952). Money and Credit in China: A Short History. Cambridge, MA: Harvard University Press.

Yaron, Jacob, Benjamin P. McDonald, Jr., and Gerda L. Piprek (1997). Rural Finance: Issues, Designs, and Best Practices. Environmentally and Socially Sustainable Development Studies and Monographs Series, No. 14. ESSD Environmentally & Socially Sustainable Development Work in Progress. Washington, DC, World Bank.

Yunus, Muhammad (1999). Banker to the Poor: Micro-Lending and the Battle against World Poverty. New York: Public Affairs.

Yunus, Muhammad (2007). Creating a World without Poverty: Social Business and the Future of Capitalism. New York: Public Affairs.

INDEX

Townsend, Robert, 81, 196
transactions costs, 9, 10, 43, 81, 107, 109, 113, 123, 150, 191, 220, 313, 333
transformation, 21, 22, 311–313, 269, 302, 309, 313, 331, 332, 353, 358, 363, 367
treatment group, 375, 382, 385, 415
Triodos Microfinance, 28
Turkmenistan, 76

Uganda, 107, 227, 243
Ujjivan Financial Services Ltd., 339, 342
Ukraine, 256
UniBank, 26
Union Technique de la Mutualite, 254
United Kingdom, 6, 70
United Nations Capital Development Fund (UNCDF), 330
United Nations Development Program (UNDP), 31, 272
United Nations (U.N.), 1, 136
United States (U.S.)
    credit card interest rates in, 324
    financial access in, 77
    gender differences in spending on children in, 282
    gender wage gap in, 273
    income disparities, 70
    informal sector, 86
    microfinance in, 11, 248
    poverty in, 63, 66
    poverty lines, 69
    spurious Nicolas Cage correlation in, 370
United States Agency for International Development (USAID), 31, 254, 309, 340
Universidad de los Andes, 295

University of California, Berkeley, 116
University of California, Los Angeles (UCLA), 102, 224, 392
University of California, San Diego (UCSD), 81, 275
University of California, Santa Cruz, 406
University of Chicago, 81, 196, 408
University of Leicester, 136
University of Leuven, 157
University of Lyon, 132
University of Manitoba, 298
University of Oregon, 101
University of Peradeniya, 81, 275
University of Toronto, 119
U.S. Federal Reserve, 344
U.S. Food and Drug Administration, 375
U.S. Post Office, 47
usury laws, 231, 261

Valdivia, Martin, 373
Valenzuela, Liza, 311
Venezuela, 228
Venmo, 59
venture capital, 310
Vietnam, 102, 132, 240, 411
village banks, 6, 10, 20, 137, 167, 170, 174–176, 178, 183, 192, 209, 266, 274, 280, 285
village savings and loan associations (VLSAs), 168, 177, 209

Wafukho, Joyce, 367
wage gaps, 2, 100—see also gender, wage gap
Wal-Mart, 20, 248
Waswa, Betty, 234
women's empowerment—see empowerment

Printed in the United States
By Bookmasters